A landmark collection on prisoners' citizenship rights in Australia. Partly report-card, partly a plural conversation on options for change, this book should be disturbing reading for citizens concerned about the decency and social justice of our democracy.

Professor John Braithwaite,
Law Program, Australian National University

For decades it was said that the victim was the forgotten party in the criminal justice system. That is no longer true as victims' rights have come to supplant prisoners' rights in the public consciousness. The state of the prisons is now of far less public and political concern than the state of a victim's health. In sentencing, the uneasy balance between the interests of the offender, the state and the victim has shifted from the former to the latter. This important and useful book gives voice to a diverse range of viewpoints, some of which have been suppressed, some ignored and many which have failed to achieve their due recognition because of the significant, but one hopes, not permanent changes in communal priorities. It puts back on the criminological and political agenda the unpopular issues which must be addressed as our prison populations continue to burgeon.

Professor Arie Freiberg,
Department of Criminology, University of Melbourne

Prisoners are often considered the least meritorious of human rights claimants. This book challenges this perception by providing expert historical and contemporary analysis of a range of issues relating to inhabitants of Australian gaols. It includes the voices of prisoners as well as those of academics, politicians, lawyers and bureaucrats. The book provides an important antidote to the general silence about prisoners as citizens.

Professor Hilary Charlesworth, Director, Centre for International and Public Law, Australian National University

At last ... we have a serious look at citizenship from the bottom up! 'Prisoners as citizens' is where any discussion about rights ... in Australia must begin, and this book does it well.

Tim Anderson, former prisoner and civil rights activist

This book has the potential not just to bring back to public attention the issue of imprisonment in Australia; in addition, it also sheds new light on the nature of imprisonment itself, and its pains and deprivations, with contributions from academics, criminal justice policy makers and practitioners and, not least, prisoners themselves.

Dr John Pratt,
Institute of Criminology, Victoria University of Wellington

After a long period in which criminal justice policy in Australia often has amounted to little more than a "law and order auction" played out in the media by the major political parties, we now find-unsurprisingly-that our prison population has exploded. Most worrying is that a very large proportion of prisoners-again, unsurprisingly-are from the most disadvantaged sections of the community, including indigenous people, the mentally ill, and people with an intellectual disability. It is very timely, therefore, for a serious consideration of the state of our prisons and the human rights implications that flow from that. The editors and authors of *Prisoners as Citizens* are to be warmly congratulated on this book, which is at once comprehensive, constructive, scholarly and accessible.

Professor David Weisbrot,
President, Australian Law Reform Commission

Prisoners do have rights and this outstanding collection highlights why it is critical that these rights be recognised by the Australian community. Australians deny the rights of the imprisoned at their own peril, since the behaviour of those incarcerated after their release is largely influenced by their experiences behind the prison walls.

Father Peter Norden SJ, Director, Jesuit Social Services and former Pentridge Prison Chaplain

This book makes a timely and wide-ranging contribution to an overdue debate about our attitudes to imprisonment and detention. Australians who value their freedom are indebted to the co-editors for encouraging such a well-qualified group of contributors to share with us their unique insights.

The Most Reverend Dr Peter F Carnley AO,
Anglican Primate of Australia

A constructive political and public discourse about the role of prisons and prison reform has been sadly lacking in Australia. Instead, fuelled by self-serving political agendas and tabloid journalism penal policy has been punitive, short-sighted and ultimately a failure. Refreshingly, Brown and Wilkie have taken a provocative new approach towards prisons and their inmates arguing that prisoners do and should have rights in any society that professes to be a democracy.

Professor Paul Wilson, Chair of Criminology, Bond University

This is a timely and important publication. The controversial issues surrounding penal policy and specifically, the perception of, and treatment of, prisoners and their role in their community are regularly misunderstood and misrepresented in public discourse. This well-researched and thoughtful series of accounts by a diverse range of authors usefully presents eclectic perspectives. Many of the themes explored could have been fruitfully extended to additional areas including juveniles in detention, the international transfer of prisoners and the detention of asylum seekers. Nevertheless, the book represents a significant contribution to an understanding of the status, role and rights of prisoners and their capacity to participate in their community as full citizens.

George Zdenkowski, NSW Children's Court Magistrate

As the language of rights is manipulated to serve questionable ends and as rights become exclusive, often only available to those who are visible and able to voice their concerns, *Prisoners as Citizens* offers a comprehensive and challenging consideration of the diverse rights and interests of an ever-increasing but invisible population group within our society.

Andrea Durbach, Director, Public Interest Advocacy Centre

Prisoners as Citizens

Human Rights in Australian Prisons

Prisoners as Citizens

Human Rights in Australian Prisons

editors

David Brown & Meredith Wilkie

THE FEDERATION PRESS
2002

Published in Sydney by:
       The Federation Press
       PO Box 45, Annandale, NSW, 2038
       71 John St, Leichhardt, NSW, 2040
       Ph (02) 9552 2200 Fax (02) 9552 1681
       E-mail: info@federationpress.com.au
       Website: http://www.federationpress.com.au

National Library of Australia
Cataloguing-in-Publication entry

       Includes index.
       ISBN 1 86287 424 7

       1. Prisoners – Legal status, laws, etc. – Australia.
       2. Civil rights – Australia. I. Brown, David (David
       Bentley). II. Wilkie Meredith.

365.6400994

Typeset by The Federation Press, Leichhardt, NSW.
       Printed by Southwood Press Pty Ltd, Marrickville, NSW.

Foreword

The prison is a machine that silences as well as segregates. It deprives inmates of their voices along with their liberty. By hiding prisoners behind the scenes of social life, prison walls serve as a means of political as well as physical exclusion. The lawbreaker is incapacitated but also excommunicated.

If democracy lives through dialogue and public discourse, then the prison and its captives are outside of democracy. And where imprisonment is used on a massive scale, as it now is in certain democratic nations, this contradiction becomes increasingly salient – for those who care about prisoners and the conditions in which they live, and for those who care about democracy and the conditions in which it can flourish.

This book addresses these issues directly and forcefully, and with a collective voice that deserves to be heard. In its pages we read how Australia's leading academics, activists and prison experts would have us view prisoners as *citizens* – as members of the polity who have violated its laws, and must endure its penalties, but for whom the deprivation of liberty need not mean the cancellation of citizenship. This vision, which seems altogether in keeping with contemporary ideas of human rights and democratic citizenship, turns out to entail profound challenges to our current ways of thinking, our laws, and our institutional routines. These challenges are taken up here in an informed, accessible and practical manner. The authors understand the ideals of democratic debate and try to extend that debate in a manner that is at once principled and constructive.

But there is another sense in which this book exemplifies the ideals that motivate it. In a modern, democratic polity, citizens are represented by elected officials but they must also be allowed the maximum of space in which to represent themselves. Citizens have the right to speak, to disagree, to debate the issues that affect them, and to have a voice in the institutions through which they are governed. The most striking feature of *Prisoners as Citizens*, and its most powerfully eloquent one, is its inclusion of the voices of prisoners, speaking directly of their experience. These statements remind us that the strength of a modern democracy depends on its inclusiveness and the diversity of the voices that are allowed to be heard. They stand as testimony to the principle that any well-governed, democratic institution must find a place in its discourse for the voices of those most affected by its power.

David Garland
Professor of Law and Professor of Sociology, New York University
Foundation editor-in-chief , *Punishment and Society*,
The International Journal of Penology

Table of Contents

Acknowledgements

This project was initiated as a partnership between the Human Rights and Equal Opportunity Commission and the Australian Human Rights Centre at the University of NSW. However, the views expressed in this volume cannot be attributed either to the Commission or to the Centre. The editors wish to acknowledge the contribution of the former Human Rights Commissioner Chris Sidoti and the former Director of the Human Rights Centre Melinda Jones to the direction and substance of the project as a whole including this book and also a workshop convened in Sydney in November 2000. Their early commitment has ensured a successful conclusion.

Also advising us were Brett Collins and Michael Strutt from Justice Action in Sydney, Liz Curran from the Catholic Commission for Justice, Development and Peace in Melbourne, John Delaney from the NSW Aboriginal Prisoners' and Family Support Service, and Associate Professor Sandra Egger, Dr John Pace and Anne McNaughton of the Faculty of Law at UNSW.

An Academic Advisory Board was established to referee chapter submissions and we thank all members for their advice and assistance:

- Associate Professor Christine Alder, Department of Criminology, University of Melbourne
- Dr Eileen Baldry, School of Social Work, University of NSW
- Dr Harry Blagg, Crime Research Centre, University of WA
- Associate Professor Chris Cunneen, Faculty of Law, Sydney University
- Associate Professor Mark Findlay, Faculty of Law, Sydney University
- Professor Richard Fox, Faculty of Law, Monash University
- Professor Richard Harding, WA Inspector of Custodial Services
- Professor Garth Nettheim, Faculty of Law, University of NSW
- Dr John Pratt, Institute of Criminology, Victoria University of Wellington
- Dr Matthew Storey, Northern Territory Anti-Discrimination Commission
- Associate Professor Julie Stubbs, Faculty of Law, Sydney University
- Professor Alice Tay, President, Human Rights and Equal Opportunity Commission

Janis Constable from the Human Rights and Equal Opportunity Commission organised the November 2000 workshop and assisted the project in other ways during its initial stages. Also from HREOC, Jane Thomson, Bassina Farbenblum and Susanna Iuliano assisted the editorial process by checking bibliographical references and commenting on chapters, Chris Holt, Clare Moss and Margaret Farmer at The Federation Press displayed their customary efficiency and commitment in the production process.

Finally, we gratefully acknowledge the contributions of prisoners who, with the exception of Noel Han, one of whose poems is printed here, must remain anonymous. The Human Rights and Equal Opportunity Commission received written submissions from 51 prisoners in all Australian jurisdictions with the exception of the Northern Territory. Twenty-six submissions are quoted in this book: nine from Victoria, seven from Queensland, three each from WA, SA and NSW and one from Tasmania.

David Brown & Meredith Wilkie
May 2002

About the Authors

Greta Bird is Associate Professor, Director of the National Centre for Cross Cultural Studies in Law and Director of Research at Southern Cross University. She has worked for a number of years teaching and writing in the area of law and cultural diversity.

David Brown is a Professor of Law at the University of NSW teaching criminal law and criminal justice. He has been active in criminal justice movements, issues and debates for nearly three decades and is a regular media commentator. He has published widely in the field with over 100 articles and chapters in books and conference proceedings. He has co-authored or co-edited *The Prison Struggle* (1982), *The Judgments of Lionel Murphy* (1986), *Death in the Hands of the State* (1988), *Criminal Laws* (in three editions: 1990, 1996, 2001) and (with Russell Hogg) *Rethinking Law and Order* (1998).

John Dawes has been a probation officer, prison manager, director of correctional services in Victoria and head of the South Australian Department of Correctional Services (1982-93). In 1997 Flinders University awarded him a PhD for his study of prisoner deaths in SA. From 1993 to 1998 he was SA's first Public Advocate. In 1999 he was elected to membership of the International Work Group on Death, Dying and Bereavement and currently holds adjunct appointments at Charles Sturt University (NSW) and in the Law School at the Flinders University in Adelaide.

Jenny Green is an academic at the University of Technology Sydney. She is the Director of the postgraduate Community Management Program which focuses on non-profit, non-government organisations. Over the past 20 years Jenny has worked with disability issues in education, employment and accommodation services in both government and non-government sectors. She has been a keen advocate for progress and change operating at all levels from government advisory committees to community-based management committees.

Mark Finnane is Professor of History at Griffith University and currently Dean of Postgraduate Education. He has published four books and numerous refereed and chapter articles dealing with a wide range of topics in criminal justice history, the history of social regulation, labour history and covering his main research fields in Australian as well as Irish history. His most recent books are *Police and*

Government: Histories of Policing in Australia (Oxford University Press, 1994) and *Punishment in Australian Society* (Oxford University Press, 1997). He was a consultant to the Royal Commission into Aboriginal Deaths in Custody and was the first Chair of the Management Committee of the Prisoners Legal Service Queensland.

Sam Garkawe is a Senior Lecturer at the School of Law and Justice of Southern Cross University, where he teaches courses on Victimology, Human Rights, International Criminal Justice and International Law. Sam holds a Masters of Law from London University and has been admitted to practice law in both Victoria and California. He has published articles in the areas of victimology, human rights, legal education, international criminal justice and multiculturalism and the law. Between 1998 and the end of 2000 Sam was the Law School's representative on the Board of the Centre for Professional Development Corrective Services, an industry partnership between Southern Cross University and the NSW Department of Corrective Services. He has been on the editorial Board of the Australian Journal of Human Rights since its establishment in 1994 and was appointed to the executive of the Australasian Society of Victimology in May 2000.

Camille Giffard is a member of the Human Rights Centre at the University of Essex and a PhD candidate in the Faculty of Law, University of Bristol. Since completing an LLM in International Human Rights Law at the University of Essex in 1996, she has worked as a researcher for the International Committee of the Red Cross in a major study on customary humanitarian law, as an assistant to the United Nations Special Rapporteur on Torture, as a case-manager for a series of applications being brought under the European Convention on Human Rights and as a lecturer in a number of human rights related subjects. She is the author of the *Torture Reporting Handbook*, a guide to documenting and reporting allegations of torture and ill-treatment in the context of international human rights mechanisms, funded by the UK Foreign and Commonwealth Office.

Russell Hogg currently teaches courses on criminology and punishment in the School of Sociology and Justice Studies at the University of Western Sydney. He was formerly a senior lecturer in law at Macquarie University. He is co-author (with David Brown) of *Rethinking Law and Order* (1998) and has otherwise published widely in the areas of criminology and criminal justice studies.

Loretta Kelly (BA, LLB (UNSW)) is an Indigenous woman from the Gumbaynggirr and Dhangatti language groups on the mid-north coast of NSW. Loretta is a lecturer in the School of Law and Justice, Southern Cross University. She also teaches at the College of Indigenous Australian Peoples at Southern Cross University and specialises in the field of alternative dispute resolution in Indigenous communities.

As an Indigenous person who was raised amongst the poverty and discrimination of the Aboriginal experience in Australia, Loretta feels that she has inherited, in Mick Dodson's words "a lifetime of on-the-job experience studying human rights". Loretta is involved in the executive management of several Aboriginal organisations including the NSW Aboriginal Prisoners and Family Support Service which monitors Aboriginal deaths in custody. She is committed to ensuring that the human rights of Indigenous Australians are protected.

Debbie Kilroy is the Director of Sisters Inside. Debbie has over 20 years extensive experience both personally and professionally in the criminal justice system. She has a Bachelor of Social Work and is presently studying law.

Michael Levy (Associate Professor, MB (Hons) (UNSW); MPH (Sydney), Fellow of the Australian Faculty of Public Health Medicine) holds a conjoint appointment between the New South Wales Corrections Health Service (CHS) and the University of Sydney. As Director of Population Health, he is responsible for public health activities of CHS and for research activities within the service. Previously he has worked with the World Health Organisation and staff of the International Committee of the Red Cross to develop tuberculosis control guidelines for prisons. He was the convenor of the 1998 Public Health Association of Australia Conference on prisoners' health, 'Minimising the Harm'.

Catharine Lumby is Associate Professor of Media Studies and Director of the Media and Communications Program at the University of Sydney. She is a journalist who has been widely published in the *Sydney Morning Herald, The Age* and *The Australian.* Catharine currently writes a regular column for *The Bulletin.* Her most recent book is *Gotcha: Life in a Tabloid World* (Allen and Unwin, 1999). Her research interests include news and current affairs journalism, popular culture and human rights.

Craig Minogue has survived in Victoria's prison system for the past 15 years. He is an off-campus undergraduate student who has attained high distinctions in his tertiary studies. Craig's academic achievements place him in the top 5% at his University and he is currently planning a post-graduate career. In addition to his academic work, Craig has met a need for advocacy services assisting his fellow inmates with issues associated with access to the courts and information about the law and education programs. He has litigated in the Federal and High Courts of Australia in an attempt to establish whether State prisoners have enforceable protection from human rights violations. As a writer and anti-prison activist, Craig continues to utilise the legal processes to resolve prison issues.

Ronnit Redman is a Lecturer in Law at the University of NSW. She has been a Senior Legal Officer at the Human Rights and Equal Opportunity Commission and has worked in private legal practice specialising in employment and discrimination law, as well as in a variety of policy roles in the public service. The views she expresses in this volume are her own and cannot be attributed to HREOC.

Melinda Ridley-Smith was admitted as a solicitor in 1993. She worked as a Senior Legal Officer with the Human Rights and Equal Opportunity Commission from May 1999 until November 2000. Prior to this time, she was a senior solicitor in commercial litigation with a large national law firm. The views she expresses in this volume are her own and cannot be attributed to HREOC.

David Robinson is a Senior Policy Officer at the Human Rights and Equal Opportunity Commission. He is a lawyer by training although the main focus of his career has been in the area of public policy. Since commencing employment at the Commission in 1992 he has worked on a number of domestic and international projects. In recent years his policy work has had a particular emphasis on children's rights. The views he expresses in this volume are his own and cannot be attributed to HREOC.

John Rynne is a Research Fellow at the Crime Research Centre, University of Western Australia. For the past three years, together with Emeritus Professor Richard Harding, he has been studying the impact of private prisons on various public correctional systems in Australia and overseas. Prior to this he worked for ten years in corrections in Queensland, primarily in community corrections and in psychological assessment of sex offenders. He has a Master of

Philosophy in personality assessment and is currently completing his PhD on changes in organisational cultures in Australian custodial corrections centres.

Vivien Stern CBE is Senior Research Fellow at the International Centre for Prison Studies at King's College, London. She is also Honorary Secretary General of Penal Reform International (PRI), a non-governmental organisation promoting penal reform throughout the world. From 1977 to 1996 Vivien was Director of the National Association for the Care and Resettlement of Offenders (NACRO) UK. She is the author of *A Sin Against the Future: Imprisonment in the world* (1998), *Imprisoned by Our Prisons* (1989), *Bricks of Shame: Britain's Prisons* (updated second edition 1993), *Alternatives to Prison in Developing Countries* (1999) and editor of *Sentenced to die? The Problem of TB in prisons in Eastern Europe and Central Asia* (1999).

Anne Warner is the President of Sisters Inside with extensive experience in social change processes. She was the Minister of Family Services and Minister of Aboriginal Affairs in Queensland for 6 years. She is also a social change consultant for government and non-government sectors including the international arena.

Meredith Wilkie is Director of the Race Discrimination Unit at the Australian Human Rights and Equal Opportunity Commission. During the preparation of this book she was Director of the Human Rights Unit there. She has taught law, including criminology and human rights law, at the University of WA and at Murdoch University. She was a Research Fellow at the Crime Research Centre at UWA from 1990 until mid-1993. The views she expresses in this volume are her own and cannot be attributed to HREOC.

Tony Woodyatt is a legal and social policy researcher currently working in crime prevention. He has worked mainly in criminal justice – for community legal centres, the Queensland parliament, government reviews and agencies, and as a consultant. He was the first solicitor/coordinator of the Prisoners Legal Service in Brisbane.

Introduction

David Brown & Meredith Wilkie

If a justification is needed for a book of this sort at this time, it is that prisoners have faded somewhat from sight as political subjects since the mid-1980s. Prisons and prisoners went through a period of upheaval and reform in Australia and elsewhere in the 1960s and 1970s. The prison became a far more visible site of political struggle and prisoners gained a voice. This increased visibility owed much to the upsurge of prison disturbances and prisoner militancy. Significant riots occurred in the Bathurst prison (NSW) in 1970 and 1974, the latter largely razing the prison. Between 1974 and 1976, there were other major disturbances at Maitland, Parramatta and Goulburn gaols in New South Wales, Boggo Road in Queensland, Pentridge in Victoria and Yatala in South Australia. Prison action groups espousing radical reforms and programs emerged. Prisoners became part of the wider discovery of new subjectivities, along with second-wave feminists, Aborigines, psychiatric patients, environmentalists and many others.

In 1972, the Whitlam Labor Government was elected federally. Its election slogan – 'It's Time' – gave expression to the desire for change forged in a climate of mass opposition to the Vietnam War, the end of the White Australia immigration policy and an isolationist foreign policy. Riots and reprisal bashings created the focus for governmental inquiries into the penal system, such as the Nagle Royal Commission in 1978 (see Nagle 1978; Zdenkowski & Brown 1982; Findlay 1982; Vinson 1982; Grant 1992; Brown 1998). Such inquiries did much to verify what prisoners were saying and a period of reform in penal and sentencing politics occurred.

However, a very different response emerged in the mid-1980s, led by populist politicians and espoused by large sections of the public. The backlash against the reform period was lead by Michael Yabsley in New South Wales and like politicians in other States who sought to exploit law and order issues electorally. Declaring his desire to be remembered as 'someone who has put the value back in punishment' (O'Neill 1990: 20; Brown 1990; Brown 1991), Yabsley led a savage attack on prison conditions, aiming quite literally to intensify the punitive force of the experience of imprisonment. This attack coincided with the rise in popularity of retributivism as a sentencing aim, as the initially liberal 'just deserts' model was transmuted into populist slogans such as 'truth in sentencing' and a rhetoric of punitiveness. While outcomes varied across States, common policies involved the abolition of remissions, lengthening the time actually served in prison, restricting parole, cutting welfare, educational and rehabilitation programs and, in New South Wales, confiscating prisoners property. The excesses of Yabsley's policies led to widespread rioting and with a New South Wales prison system in turmoil; he was removed from office and the more extreme policies were modified. But, as a broad generalisation, from the mid-1980s through the 1990s, a new retributivism was played out in penal and sentencing policies across Australia as part of a more general 'uncivil politics of law and order' (Hogg & Brown 1998: 1–17). Racially inflected mandatory sentencing policies in Western Australia and the Northern Territory were a further manifestation of this trend (Johnson & Zdenkowski 1999), a trend widely evident across western democracies (Garland 1996).

Among the effects of this stifling of penal reform since the mid-1980s has been the muting of the voices of prisoners and a lack of political interest in prisoners and prison conditions other than as manifestations of a convenient 'other' against which to vent a range of anxieties and insecurities and as a site of tabloid fantasies of 'motel conditions' and taxpayer funded 'luxury'. In a period of widespread social anxiety over rapid social, technological and economic restructuring and change, prisoners have dropped to the bottom of the league table of deserving causes. Far more popular concern is not surprisingly directed to the victims of crime, albeit very selectively and often to little practical effect save for longer sentences and reduced rights for offenders. While reform efforts have not been wholly abandoned, they are approached with caution for fear of political backlash from the media and populist politicians. Significant improvements in some areas have occurred but largely 'on the quiet', a consequence of which is that such achievements lack a democratic grounding. The political imperative for corrections ministers in Australia in the 1990s through to the present has been to: 'Keep the lid on, keep prisons quiet, take them off the front page. Engage in reforms if you like, but do so on the quiet. No news is good news'. The overriding assumption is that of public and media punitiveness that must be both slaked and appeased at all cost.

A major problem generated through operating within such a political imperative is that neither the discourse nor the constituencies of public support for penal reform are built up. To take one example, as soon as a prisoner escapes from a useful and socially responsible work release program, the political quick fix demand is to 'close the program down'. Because the benefits of such programs have not been openly argued and politically justified, few oppose their closure or restriction and those who do have little established public currency of support and argument to build on. Even where the arguments are spelled out clearly in a rational, democratic and well-researched way, they will not necessarily find favour with major political parties. Nowhere was this more apparent than in New South Wales after the release of the New South Wales Legislative Council's Select Committee on the Increase in Prisoner Population report, *Interim Report: Issues Relating to Women* (2000). The Committee comprised three government (Labor) members, two members of the Coalition (Liberal/National Party) opposition, a Democrat and a Green. It recommended that plans for building a new women's prison should be suspended pending the implementation of a range of specific diversionary measures, followed by the monitoring of both the cost and effectiveness of those measures in comparison with the costs of building a new prison. Despite the fact that the report was carefully and cogently argued along a 'let's see what works and what is the most responsible and effective use of resources' line, it was immediately repudiated by both the government and the opposition in a bipartisan response which showed clearly the very real political limits to claims of 'non-ideological', 'evidence-led' policy formation in the law and order area.

Stimulating prisoners' voices

The aim of this collection then is to take a small step in trying to open up debate around the need for a more open, informed and responsible penal politics. Such an endeavour involves trying to stimulate the recognition and development of a variety of constituencies intimately engaged in and knowledgeable about a range of penal issues, so that issues of penal reform and prisoners' rights are put back on the political agenda. It involves trying to open up channels of communication so that prisoners' voices and those of their support organisations are heard and their identities and concerns recognised in all their diversity.

Consistent with this aim, the collection includes numerous short extracts comprising comments from prisoners made in response to an invitation from the Human Rights and Equal Opportunity Commission (HREOC) for submissions from prisoners on topics of concern to them and on health care, segregation and voting rights in particular. Chapter 12, 'An Insider's View: Human Rights and Excursions from the Flat Lands', is written by Craig Minogue, a long-serving Victorian prisoner and activist. He gives an insight into his and others' efforts both to employ international human rights provisions through complaints to HREOC and to address human rights abuses experienced in prison through various court actions.

In the prisoners' submissions to HREOC, health issues in particular attracted much comment, an indication of their central importance to many prisoners. In Chapter 14, 'Prisoners' Right to Health and Safety', Michael Levy of the New South Wales Corrections Health Service describes and evaluates provision of health care services to prisoners against four international minimum requirements: access to health care; equivalence of care to that available in the community; respect for prisoners' confidentiality and informed consent; and adequate illness and injury prevention programs.

The expression and communication of prisoners' voices in their diversity depends in great measure on their access to various forms of media, electronic and print, and to family and various support groups and services, governmental and non-governmental. However, one familiar aspect of tabloid print media and commercial television 'current affairs' treatment of prisoners and prison issues is a tendency to sensationalise and exploit the crimes and personas of particular notorious prisoners, constituting them as 'monsters' with a high fascination/repulsion quotient and appeal to audiences. In Chapter 7, 'Televising the Invisible: Prisoners, Prison Reform and the Media', Catharine Lumby reflects on one such campaign around paedophilia, using it to question the common demand for more 'sympathetic' or 'realistic' portrayals of life in prison from the mainstream media. Lumby stresses rather the development of new media such as the internet and advocates policies and programs which 'facilitate and encourage prisoners to use the media themselves to discuss, publicise and most importantly personalise and humanise issues' (p 112).

So that while there is always the risk of exploitative treatment of stories, especially those organised around particular prisoners and allegedly 'luxurious' prison conditions, these can be countered to some extent by stories that give expression to prisoners' voices and pers-pectives. For this to occur, prisoners' access to media is a vital element in publicising abuses and stimulating public debate over prison conditions. A rudimentary scan of print media over a few months in 2001 indicates that much press treatment of prison issues is not simply sensationalist but has a critical edge and serves to draw public attention to quite a diverse range of issues. Published stories include the increase in prison population and overcrowding (Thornhill 2001), the criminalisation of those with mental illnesses and intellectual disabilities (Jacobsen 2001a; 2001b), the strip-searching of visitors including young children (Paine 2001), the building of a high security 'supermax' prison at Goulburn prison in New South Wales (Doherty 2001), deaths in custody (Andersen 2001), the forcible taking of DNA samples from prisoners (Jackson 2001; Paxinos 2001; Monk 2001), legislation to protect DNA samples taken unlawfully from prisoners (Rollins 2001), and the failure to use DNA testing until well after the conviction and jailing of a man in Queensland whose conviction was quashed after a test (Balogh 2001). Such stories highlight the important role media can play in giving voice to prisoners' concerns and informing public and policy responses.

Much media treatment of prisoners tends to postulate the interests of prisoners as antithetical to those of victims. In Chapter 15, 'Crime Victims and Prisoners' Rights', Sam Garkawe describes how the role of crime victims in criminal justice processes has increased, with part-icular focus on the decision when to release from prison and on what conditions. Garkawe proposes an approach to balancing prisoners' rights with the interests of victims.

Difficulties and limitations in access by prisoners to media and media workers to prisoners were thrown into stark relief in Queens-land in July 2000 when police charged north Queensland journalist John Andersen for interviewing prisoners without the authority of the Corrective Services Department. This followed a story that appeared in the *Townsville Bulletin* on 21 July 2000, quoting Townsville Correc-tional Centre inmates (Johnston 2000; Murray 2000). A *Courier-Mail* editorial commented:

> this particular provision of the Corrective Services Act goes too far if it can be used to prevent prisoners who are victimised within the prison system from revealing their problems, and to prevent problems in prison administration from being aired ('Freedom of speech lost in prisons', 10 July 2000).

In one of the short extracts between chapters, former Queensland ALP Senator Margaret Reynolds describes the difficulties involved in and suspicions attached to her attempts to visit Queensland prisons during the 1980s. In Chapter 8, 'Institutional Perspectives and Constraints', John Dawes, a former head of Corrective Services in South Australia, examines other institutional blockages to the promotion of prisoners' rights.

The contemporary environment

The contemporary environment in relation to prisons is marked by a number of key features. One of these is an escalating prison population, both in numbers and as a rate per unit of population. Over the decade 1990 to 2000, the number of Australian prisoners on census day 30 June increased from 14,305 to 21,714. The rate of imprisonment per 100,000 adult population has increased from 111.6 to 147.7, an increase of 32.3% over the same period (Australian Bureau of Statistics 2001b: 28-9). The increase is not uniform across all Australian jurisdictions that have, in any event, had a history of considerable diversity in imprisonment rates.

Nor are the increases as great as those in the United States, where 2001 imprisonment rates were five times what they were in 1972 (Garland 2001: 5) and commentators now talk of 'mass imprisonment'. Mass imprisonment is defined as 'a rate of imprisonment and a size of prison population that is markedly above the historical and comparative norm for societies of this type' and where imprisonment 'ceases to be the incarceration of individual offenders and becomes the systematic imprisonment of whole groups of the population' (Garland 2001: 5-6). With one in three African-American males in the United States aged 20-29 in prison or under penal supervision, young African-American men in urban centres have become a group for whom imprisonment is a 'normal' expectation and experience. Australian imprisonment rates are, with the exception of those in the Northern Territory, much lower than those in the United States and have not increased as rapidly. But the highly disproportionate imprisonment of Indigenous people is a striking feature of Australian imprisonment, not unlike the situation of African-Americans in the United States. In Chapter 1, 'Prisoners and the Penal Estate in Australia', Russell Hogg sets out a general introduction to the contours of contemporary imprisonment in Australia, including the increasing imprisonment rate, the over-representation of Indigenous people, prison conditions and overcrowding, health and violence in prisons and levels of recidivism.

The over-representation of Indigenous people in prison — in June 2001, the ratio of Indigenous to non-Indigenous rates of imprisonment was 15:1 (Australian Bureau of Statistics 2001a: 5) — illustrates the centrality of race to the history of penality in Australia (Broadhurst 1997; Finnane & McGuire 2001; Hogg 2001). It also illustrates the particularity of prison issues and voices; prisoners are not a homogeneous and unified group with unitary interests. In October 1987, a Royal Commission was established in response to growing concern over the number and causes of Indigenous deaths in police and prison custody. The Royal Commission into Aboriginal Deaths in Custody issued a number of reports from 1988 and a National Report in 1991. In Chapter 2, 'The Rights of Indigenous Prisoners', Loretta Kelly uses the Royal Commission's recommendations and international minimum standards as reference points to evaluate changes in the treatment of Indigenous prisoners since 1991, with particular emphasis on health care, family visits and recognition of Indigenous cultures in prison.

The emphasis on particularity and difference is continued in the following three chapters. In Chapter 3, 'Deprivation of Liberty — Deprivation of Rights', Debbie Kilroy and Anne Warner of Sisters Inside in Queensland, a prisoners' support organisation of ex-prisoners and others, discuss some of the key concerns of women prisoners, in particular medical treatment, access to children and drug issues. In Chapter 4, 'Experiences of Inmates with an Intellectual Disability', Jenny Green looks at the way in which imprisonment is experienced by six New South Wales prisoners with intellectual disabilities while in Chapter 5, 'Prisoners of Difference', Greta Bird examines the concerns of non-English speaking background prisoners in Victoria, including religious freedom and practice, contact with family, attitudes of prison officers and communication within the prison.

Sometimes particularity and difference is generated not so much out of a specific subjectivity and identity but out of some specific context or place in which prisoners are held. For example, new issues have arisen in relation to Australia's relatively high take-up of private prisons (Moyle 1994, 2000; Harding 1997). Private prisons are operating in Queensland, Victoria, New South Wales and Western Australia, with approximately 20% of prisoners nationally and 50% in Victoria in private facilities. In 1999, the newly elected ALP government in Victoria stated that it would take private prisons back into public ownership and subsequently did so in relation to Deer Park, a private women's prison, in late 2000 (George 2000; Correctional

Services Commissioner (Vic) 2000; Private Prisons Investigation Panel (Vic) 2000). This led to suggestions that privatisation has 'peaked' (*Current Issues in Criminal Justice* 1999).

Late in 2000, one of the leading private prison companies operating in Australia, Australasian Correctional Management, a consortium of Wackenhut Corporation (US) with Thiess Contractors and ADT Security, came under sustained criticism for its operation of six immigration detention centres, especially the centre at Woomera, leading to increased scrutiny of its private prison operations (eg Lagan 2000). In Chapter 9, 'Protection of Prisoners' Rights in Australian Private Prisons', John Rynne describes and evaluates the monitoring and complaint handling mechanisms which can be utilised by prisoners in private prisons to assert and protect their rights in the context of government arrangements for the oversight of private prison contracts.

Similarly, prisoners held in segregation conditions experience very specific problems. As Professor Richard Harding, Inspector of Custodial Services in Western Australia, notes in the *Report of an Unannounced Inspection of the Induction and Orientation Unit and the Special Handling Unit at Casuarina Prison* (2001):

> the treatment of prisoners who are segregated from mainstream accommodation and services is a vital indicator of the health of a prison. From the prisoner perspective, if the experience of being taken 'down the back' is seen as little more than the arbitrary and oppressive exercise of authority by line management, great tensions may build up over time. For example, one of the immediate triggers for the riots of 25 December 1998 at Casuarina itself was the decision of officers to take a prisoner to the Special Handling Unit (Western Australian Inspector of Custodial Services 2001: 4; see also Smith, Indermaur & Boddis 1999; Carter 2001).

In Chapter 13, 'Segregation', David Robinson from HREOC evaluates the use of segregation for prison disciplinary offences against three minimum requirements: the need for legal authority to impose segregation, minimum conditions and the opportunity to have the 'sentence' reviewed.

Rights and citizenship

Much of the discourse around prisons and prisoners is conducted in terms of prisoners' rights: their assertion, denial and limitation. The notion of rights has a long and complex history and, by and large, most of the contributors to this book approach rights not from a philosophical perspective but from a more concrete concern with rights as claims to certain minimum standards of treatment and with respect to the various incidents and guarantees of citizenship. Many of the contributors are concerned with the specific content of prisoners' rights and, even more particularly, with their ability to assert and enforce them. For while rights can exist in the abstract as high-sounding statements of principle, it is in the ability to enforce certain standards and actually exercise the trappings of citizenship that real content and meaning is breathed into the claim of rights.

The legal status and legal enforcement of rights claims is a key element in many of the chapters, as is the increasing importance of international law in relation to both sources of rights and their potential enforcement through domestic and international law. One source, although lacking the force of law, is the *Standard Guidelines for Corrections in Australia* (1996), the domestic version of the UN *Standard Minimum Rules for the Treatment of Prisoners*. In Chapter 11, 'International Human Rights Law Applicable to Prisoners', Camille Giffard from the Human Rights Centre at Essex University takes up the international dimension. The chapter reviews the international minimum standards applicable to imprisonment, prisoners' conditions and treatment and their interpretation as well as summarising prisoners' access to international complaint handling mechanisms.

The practical application of international standards in a variety of European jurisdictions is the subject of Chapter 10, 'Prisoners as Citizens: A View from Europe', in which Vivien Stern of the International Centre for Prison Studies at King's College, London, offers a comparative survey of monitoring and respect for prisoners' rights with particular emphasis on the activities and findings of the European Committee for the Prevention of Torture.

Mark Finnane and Tony Woodyatt, who were both involved in the establishment of the Prisoners Legal Service in Queensland, trace the history of the assertion of prisoners' rights in Chapter 6, '"Not the King's enemies": Prisoners and their Rights in Australian History'. Their discussion ranges from the convict period — in which vigorous assertions of rights abounded — to the 'high age' of the prison — where rights were largely replaced with administrative regulation in an era of 'welfare penality' — through to the more recent revival of rights advocacy and mechanisms of protection.

In Chapter 16, 'Prisoners and the Right to Vote', HREOC legal officers Melinda Ridley-Smith and Ronnit Redman provide a detailed examination of the voting rights of prisoners and evaluate them against international human rights law. which prohibits discrimination in the enjoyment of human rights and unreasonable restrictions on the voting rights of citizens. In the concluding chapter, Chapter 17, 'Prisoners as Citizens', David Brown uses the historical issues of voting rights, rights to sit on juries and rights to sue at common law as a legal subject to examine the continued pertinence of notions of 'civil death', 'convict taint' and 'forfeit' to the constitution and treatment of contemporary prisoners. He explores the limitations on the citizenship experienced by prisoners, their construction as typically 'partial' or 'conditional' citizens, 'neither enjoying full citizenship nor entirely outside it' (p 321).

We hope this book will be read as a contribution to the task of turning that 'partial' or 'conditional' citizenship of prisoners into something fuller and more complete. The difficulties facing such a project are considerable and the benefits to be gained from assertions of prisoners' rights in the abstract are limited. The standards and principles expressed in both domestic and international human rights sources must be operationalised and made enforceable, for the existence of rights is most manifest in their exercise. The chapters in this collection explore various ways of doing this, often in the context of specific issues of great concern to prisoners such as health care, segregation and family contact. The contributors do not share a single standpoint or perspective and include prisoners, academics, prison administrators and workers in prisoner support services as well as in government. Ultimately, we hope they have all contributed to an exercise in which prisoners, their families, supporters and the wider and diverse constituencies and networks of interest and connection around penal issues can be seen to have taken part in an act of discursive, democratic citizenship, in which multiple voices are circulated, debate is stimulated and subjectivities and humanities are acknowledged.

PART ONE

Prisons and Prisoners

CHAPTER 1

Prisoners and the Penal Estate in Australia

Russell Hogg

A profile of adult imprisonment in Australia[1]

The principal constitutional responsibility for the administration of the criminal law and thus also of prisons in Australia lies with State and Territory governments. All jurisdictions have their own prison systems, although the Australia Capital Territory (ACT) has only one remand centre and one periodic detention centre. Offenders sentenced to prison in the ACT are detained in New South Wales (NSW) prisons under contractual arrangements between the two governments. Offenders convicted and sentenced to prison for crimes against Commonwealth law are also detained in State prisons (Constitution s 120).[2]

In 1999, there were 97 prisons and 12 periodic detention centres throughout Australia.[3] The trend in recent years in the biggest States — NSW, Queensland and Victoria — has been towards fewer, bigger prisons. These States, along with South Australia, also have privately operated prisons.[4] The scale of the private prison system, as measured by the average daily prison population, has doubled in the four years between 1994-95 and 1998-99 (Steering Committee 2000: 741), making Australia one of the world leaders in the development of private prisons (Stern 1998: ch 13). Victoria and Queensland have shown the most enthusiasm for private prisons (Moyle 2000; Harding 1997).

In 1998-99, the average daily prison population in Australia was 19,850 persons, of whom 16% were held in private prisons (Steering Committee 2000: 774). By the national prison census on 30 June 2000, the total Australian prison population was 21,714, a rate of 147.7 per 100,000 adult population (Australian Bureau of Statistics 2001b: 29). This conceals a quite massive disparity in State and Territory imprisonment rates. The Northern Territory (458 per 100,000 adult population) exceeded the national average by three times and Western Australia (218:100,000) by about one and a half times. NSW (172:100,000) and Queensland (165:100,000) also exceeded the national average. South Australia (111:100,000), Tasmania (109:100,000) and Victoria (85:100,000) were all below it (Australian Bureau of Statistics 2001b: 10).

An expanding prison system

The data in Table 1.1 indicate the quite striking increases in prison populations and rates in Australia from the early 1980s to the late 1990s, involving an increase in the national rate of almost two-thirds in 18 years. Imprisonment rates have increased in all jurisdictions, although these increases have been significantly higher for some than for others. The Queensland and NSW prison populations have been the fastest growing in relative terms, with dramatic increases in the former coming after 1993, while the prison population of the latter has been progressively expanding over a longer period. The Northern Territory and Western Australia have for a long time had disproportionately high rates of imprisonment. Coming off higher base rates and numbers, recent increases in the absolute numbers in these jurisdictions do not therefore translate into sizeable rate increases. However, no State or Territory is unaffected by the upward trend which does not look like abating in the immediate future. As a consequence of these trends over the last two decades, present imprisonment rates in Australia are higher than they have been at any time since the beginning of the 20th century.

The prison as an instrument of public policy may be in the process of returning to the prominence it once had but progressively lost over the course of the 20th century. The trend moreover is a global one. The prison is now a universal institution and few, if any, countries of 'the West' have failed to experience dramatic rises in their prison populations and rates over the last 20 years (Stern 1998: 277-80). The United States stands out in this regard. Not only has it got the highest imprisonment rate in the world, barring Russia, but it has been by far the most rapidly growing one, even in the face of recent declines in serious crime rates. Between 1980 and 2000, the US prison population grew from around 500,000 to over 2 million, a rate of more than 650 prisoners per 100,000 population.

There may be a salutary lesson here for those enamoured of the US economic and social model. Such trends obviously have implications for government policy generally, but they particularly underline questions concerning the treatment and citizenship rights of the growing number of persons immediately affected by the expansion of incarceration, namely prisoners themselves and also their families and communities. The wider community has an obvious stake in these questions as well, for all but a very small number of those incarcerated re-enter society at some time.

Table 1.1. Prisons and the prison population in Australia, 1999-2000

	NSW	Vic	Qld	WA	SA	Tas	ACT	NT	Total
Total number of prisons[1]	26 (1)	13 (3)	24 (10)	15 (-)	8 (1)	5 (-)	1 (-)	4 (-)	97 (15)
% prison population in private prisons[1]	8.6	45.7	23.3	--	7.4	--	--	--	16.0
Prison population in June 2000[2]	8,547	3,153	4,482	3,124	1,299	390	84	635	21,714
% increase in prison population between 1982 & 2000[3]	129.8	79.8	173.6	131.4	60.0	64.5	NA	103.5	121.0
Imprisonment rate 2000 (per 100,000 adult population)[2]	172.0	85.4	165.5	218.4	111.5	109.1	NA	458.1	147.7
% increase in rate between 1982 & 2000[3]	78.6	40.4	78.5	53.5	34.2	40.4	NA	24.0	64.5

1   Steering Committee 2000: 775. Data for the year 1998-99. The non-bracketed number is the total number of prisons. Appearing in brackets is the number privately operated. The total does not include periodic detention centres in NSW and the ACT.
2   Australian Bureau of Statistics 2001b: 10 (National Prison Census, 30 June 2000).
3   Carcach & Grant 1999: 3; Australian Bureau of Statistics 2001b: 10 (National Prison Census, 30 June 2000).

Moreover, the expanding prison system 'devours' resources that might otherwise be spent on social investment in education, health, housing, family support and other community services, all of which contribute to the long-term prevention of crime. In the four year period from 1994-95 to 1998-99, national expenditures on justice (police, courts and corrections) increased by 23%. Most of this expansion was in corrective services, expenditure for which increased by almost 33% or an average annual increase of more than 7%. In the same period, education expenditure increased by less than 12% (Steering Committee 2000: 506).

Conditions in prison

The modern penitentiary prison, dating in its conception from the late 18th century, was a purpose-designed and built institution in which the minutiae of personal existence — habitation, dress, diet, daily routine, interpersonal communication, activity — was to be subjected to rigid formal supervision and discipline through an exhaustive regime of social, spatial and temporal ordering within a world enclosed and separate from the wider society (Foucault 1977: 235-6). The prison was to be a thoroughly programmed space, an unembellished temple of utilitarian control. Prisons, in the words of Erving Goffman, are 'total institutions' (Goffman 1961: xiii).

Contemporary prisons of course vary quite considerably among themselves and do not necessarily contain every feature projected by the founders of the penitentiary or in the ideal-typical depiction in works of sociological inquiry. Having said that, the typical modern maximum security prison bears an unmistakable resemblance to this model of the penitentiary and prisons mostly continue to embody many of their elements.

There were always going to be serious difficulties reconciling such a conception of the prison and its role with the idea that prisoners retain their status as citizens along with such rights as are not explicitly or by necessary implication abrogated by incarceration. The tension is in no way lessened by the irony that many of the high priests of 19th-century liberalism, like Jeremy Bentham, were among the chief protagonists (and in Bentham's case, literal architects) of the modern penitentiary. In the event, Anglo-Australian jurisprudence largely opted for the view that life within prisons was a judicial 'no go' area and that courts should, in the time-honoured phrase, defer to executive authority in 'the management of the good order and discipline of the prison'.[5] In the annals of Australian prison jurisprudence, the point was made succinctly by Justice Dixon in the High Court decision in *Flynn's* case (1949).

It is pointed out in the case of *Horwitz v Connor* that if prisoners could resort to legal remedies to enforce gaol regulations responsibility for the discipline and control of prisoners in gaol would be in some measure transferred to the courts administering justice. For if statutes dealing with this subject matter were construed as intending to confer fixed legal rights upon prisoners it would result in applications to the courts by prisoners for legal remedies addressed either to the Crown or to the gaolers in whose custody they remain. Such a construction of the regulation-making power was plainly never intended by the legislature and should be avoided. An interpretation of the power to make prison regulations and of the regulations made thereunder as directed to discipline and administration and not to the legal rights of prisoners is in my opinion supported by the decision of this court in *Horwitz's* case. (*Flynn v The King* (1949) 79 CLR 1 per Dixon J at 8)

More is said in other chapters of a detailed and specific nature concerning the varying conditions under which prisoners in Australian prisons are held, the quality of life behind bars and the scope of prisoners' rights. This chapter confines itself to a broad brush approach, highlighting what can be gleaned from the available statistical data about the systematic conditions of incarceration in the different Australian prison systems. This is presented for some important indicators in Table 1.2 below.

Prison capacity, cellular confinement and overcrowding

Prisons in Australia, with some exceptions, are organised around the cellular confinement of inmates. Most, but not all, cells are designed to house a single prisoner. Prisons are carefully designed therefore to hold a designated maximum or optimum number of inmates. Prison use rate is a measure of the relationship between the actual number of prisoners and the designated capacity of the prison system. As such, it affords a general guide to levels of prison overcrowding (as well as perhaps the efficient use of public resources).

The optimum use rate should always be somewhat less than 100% in order to accommodate short-term fluctuations in the prison population, transfers, different levels of security and the special needs of some prisoners (Steering Committee 2000: 757). Viewed in this way, it is clear that most Australian prison systems were operating above optimal capacity in 1998-99 and some of them, like those in Western Australia, South Australia and Queensland, appear to have had a serious overcrowding problem at that time. This means that a not insignificant number of prisoners were 'doubled up', that is, detained two (or more) to a cell designed for one person. Growing prison populations mean that overcrowding and its attendant problems are an endemic feature of contemporary prison systems in Australia and elsewhere.

Cell sizes, as well as other attributes of the physical plant, vary quite considerably throughout the Australian prison system. This is in part because the buildings themselves vary greatly in age, some of them having been built in the last decade, others dating from the second half of the 19th or early 20th centuries. Parramatta is the oldest operational prison in Australia. Its standard cell size is 8' x 7'. Bathurst and Long Bay penitentiaries (built 1884 and 1907 respectively) followed the Pentonville standard of 13' x 7'. The first new generation prison in NSW, built at Parklea in north-western Sydney in 1979, provided for maximum security cells of 14' x 7' (Kerr 1988: 153). That is to say, most prisoners are confined in cells that in some cases are slightly bigger and others slightly smaller than the average-sized contemporary Australian bathroom, a function which they also satisfy as part of the *complete* living space they are designed to afford a prisoner, and sometimes more than one prisoner.

This highlights the fact that imprisonment involves much more than separation from the outside world and loss of freedom of movement and association. It also typically involves a severe deprivation of autonomy and privacy *within* the confines of the prison and forced association with persons not of the individual prisoner's choosing.

'Secure' and 'open' prisons

His or her cell is where an Australian prisoner will, depending upon classification and jurisdiction, be confined for between about seven and about 16 hours every day. The norm lies much nearer the upper than the lower limit, as the data in Table 1.2 indicate. Most of the prison capacity in Australian prison systems is 'secure' rather than 'open'. The distribution of prison capacity between low or open classification and secure classification influences the quality of life in prison in significant ways. Aside from the longer out-of-cell hours each day that are apparent from Table 1.2, those prisoners classified as low security and held in open facilities can generally expect much more freedom of movement within the prison, more access to programs denied maximum-security prisoners (like work release), significantly greater access to visits and other outside communication and a generally much more relaxed and safe environment.

Aside from NSW with an open capacity of 43.3%, in no other jurisdiction does this reach a third of total capacity. (The greater open capacity within the NSW system is offset slightly by the fact that out-of-cell time in open conditions is less generous in NSW than in other jurisdictions.) The predominance of secure capacity means that the majority of Australian prisoners spend more than half of each day (and sometimes significantly more) confined to cells. Overcrowding or 'doubling up' may exacerbate the physical and psychological deprivations intrinsic to incarceration under these conditions.

Violence in prisons

Social isolation, substantial erosion of personal autonomy and forced association in a single-sex environment are conditions liable to foster tension and conflict (even putting to one side that many prisoners already have criminal records, in many cases involving violent behaviour). Consequently, many prisons are violent places in which aggression and a reputation for toughness are regarded as important resources for survival.

Strictly speaking, incarceration does not, or should not, cast prisoners out of the ethical and legal community in which the bodily integrity of the individual commands respect and protection. The reality, however, is quite different.

Table 1.2. Prison conditions in Australia, 1998-99

	Prison use rate[1]	Open prison capacity[2]	Secure prison capacity[2]	Out-of-cell hours per day in open prisons[3]	Out-of-cell hours per day in secure prisons[3]	Prisoner-on-prisoner assaults (%)[4]
NSW	95.9	3,105 (43.3%)	4,071 (56.7%)	13.6	9.2	14.1
Victoria	99.3	371 (12.9%)	2,504 (87.1%)	14.8	11.5	10.6
Queensland	101.4	1,184 (23.8%)	3,791 (76.2%)	16.9	11.2	10.0
Western Australia	113.2	727 (30.7%)	1,644 (69.3%)	15.7	11.2	1.4
South Australia	105.3	201 (15.3%)	1,113 (84.7%)	16.1	9.7	9.4
Tasmania	75.1	113 (25.6%)	329 (74.4%)	13.8	9.9	8.1
Northern Territory	82.1	140 (18.4%)	620 (81.6%)	16.3	10.2	12.0
ACT	100.1	–	42 (100%)	–	10.4	NA
Total	99.5			–	–	10.4

1   This refers to the average daily rate of utilisation of total prison capacity (ie both open and secure institutions): Steering Committee 2000: 785, Table 9A.16.
2   Steering Committee 2000: 785, Table 9A.16.
3   Steering Committee 2000: 784, Table 9A.13.
4   Reported number of prisoner-on-prisoner assaults per 100 prisoners: Steering Committee 2000: 784, Table 9A.12.

The data on prisoner-to-prisoner assaults presented in Table 1.2 need to be treated with enormous care, as they make no allowance for variations in severity and result from variable systems for recording and handling prisoner complaints in different Australian jurisdictions.[6] Violence and intimidation in the prison environment (even of a serious nature) is likely to be generally under-reported to a much greater extent than in the general community. The 1998 Crime and Safety Survey found the total rate of assault (both reported *and* unreported to police) in the general Australian community to be about 4.3 per 1000 persons aged 15 years and over (Australian Bureau of Statistics 1998: 7). The national rate of *recorded* prisoner on prisoner assaults is about two-and-a-half times the rate (both recorded and unrecorded) of assault in the general community. If the ratio of unreported to reported assaults in the prison system were the same as that in the general community (about 4 to 1), the differential between prisoner assaults and the assaults in the community would be about ten times. Admittedly, these are extremely rubbery statistics but they still leave little doubt as to the heightened risks of violence that exist within prisons.[7]

The risk and threat of interpersonal violence and its corrosive effects on the personal sense of security of many prisoners has also to be considered in relation to the limited control that prisoners exercise over their immediate situation and over the possibility of avoiding or negotiating the friction and conflict that are endemic to many prison environments.

A social profile of the Australian prison population

Beginning in 1982, a national prison census has been conducted each year in Australia on 30 June. The census was administered by the Australian Institute of Criminology until 1993 and thereafter by the Australian Bureau of Statistics (ABS). It provides a very useful snapshot of the prison population frozen in time. It cannot, however, convey a sense of flux and flow within the prison population. In any given year, a large number of individuals spend short periods in prison, having been remanded in custody, convicted of less serious offences or imprisoned for fine default. This significant and perhaps in other respects distinctive sub-group within the prison population is necessarily under-represented in the census in favour of long-term prisoners convicted of more serious offences. The ABS also publishes quarterly data provided by correctional authorities based on average daily prison populations, but this is limited to a few characteristics of the prisoner population. The discussion below is based on the annual prison census unless otherwise stated.

Legal status, offence and recidivism

On census night 30 June 2000, 83% of prisoners were under sentence and 17% were on remand, awaiting trial or sentence or held pending deportation. The average time spent by remandees in custody at the time of the census was four months. As a consequence of tougher bail laws and court delays, the remand prison population has been steadily growing in recent times. It is a distinctive population in many respects: often unversed in the ways of the prison, making the forced transition from civilian to prison life with all the disruptions to family, employment and social life that that entails, often incarcerated for a limited though uncertain duration, and understandably anxious and distracted by pending court proceedings. Remand sections and remand prisons are consequently often the most tense and unsettled sections of the prison system (Anderson 1989: 7-16) and otherwise give rise to special problems in program delivery in areas like work and education. Although in law these prisoners remain innocent of any crime with the consequence, technically speaking, that their incarceration is non-punitive in nature and justification, the conditions and deprivations in remand prisons are often worse than in the mainstream.

For those under sentence, the average aggregate sentence was 4.8 years and the average expected time in custody was 3.1 years. 4% were serving an indeterminate sentence (life, governor's pleasure, etc) and less than 0.5% were imprisoned for fine default.

At the 2000 census, 49% of sentenced prisoners had been convicted of an offence[8] involving violence or threat of violence, including homicide (9%), sexual offences (12%), robbery (13%) and assault (12%). 24% of sentenced prisoners had been convicted of a property offence, including break and enter (13%), fraud and misappropriation (4%) and receiving stolen property (1%). 8% of prisoners were serving a sentence for a drug offence. As has been indicated already, the census provides a rather misleading portrait of the offences of many prisoners passing through the system as it undercounts those who in any year are imprisoned for short terms for less serious offences, for fine default and so on.

On prison census night 2000, 56% of prisoners were known to have served a prison sentence on a previous occasion. Such data are not a true measure of recidivism, for they do not indicate what proportion of total persons who pass through the prison system never return. What they do suggest, though, is that, at least for a significant (though uncertain) number of people, incarceration is anything but an isolated experience. For some it is more like a revolving door in which progressively longer periods of institutionalisation are interspersed with shorter spells of freedom in the community, although the age structure of the prison population suggests that this pattern of repeat imprisonment begins to taper off for many in middle age. Of course, imprisonment by its very nature tends to fracture family and social networks in the community and undermine employment prospects, while often replacing them with alternative (criminal) networks and opportunity structures.

Prisons typically do not do a very good job of preparing inmates for a return to the community and a resumption of their status as ordinary citizens, although as the above data indicate, the vast majority of prisoners return to the community after serving sentences of at most a few years and only a handful of prisoners are not released into the community at some time. Penal policies have not always reflected very well the fact that incarceration, while severely disruptive of the lives of the incarcerated (as in some sense it is intended to be) and thus of relationships likely to inhibit crime, is also temporary. Many leave prison with few resources, few community supports, few marketable skills and few prospects. That prison is a revolving door for many should not therefore come as a surprise. On the other hand, it suggests imprisonment is an extremely costly endeavour in more ways than one. The economic cost of incarceration is substantial. It costs on average about $50,000 a year to detain a person in prison. This is an enormous outlay of public resources on a system that may add to the crime problems which many believe it is designed to alleviate.

The social characteristics of the prison population

The profile of the Australian prison population reflected in the census has remained, in core respects, unchanged over the years. The prison population is massively disproportionately male and young. The 20-24 years age group is the one most over-represented in the census and 60% of all prisoners are males aged between 20 and 35.

Prisons are also perhaps one of the last redoubts in which gender segregation remains unquestioned in most jurisdictions. Although in recent times a growing number of women are seen staffing male prisons and men have always staffed female prisons, the segregation of male and female prisoners is treated as an unquestionable principle of incarceration in Australia. There appear to be some obvious reasons for this. Sexual deprivation is an essential part of the punishment sought by incarceration (if not exactly achieved, since it assumes heterosexual behaviour). Secondly, there is also the legitimate concern that women prisoners would be at considerable risk in a mixed penal setting. Thirdly, there is evidence that men and women prisoners constitute quite different groups with different needs and for whom different programs are appropriate.

At the 2000 census, only 6% of the Australian prison population were women. The female prison population has been increasing at a significantly higher rate than the male population in recent times, but because the gender disproportion was so great to begin with, this has yielded only a minor proportionate increase in female to male imprisonment (see Select Committee on the Increase in the Prisoner Population 2000). The female prison population tends to be distinctive in some other respects. Female prisoners tend to be imprisoned for less serious offences and for shorter periods than men (Edwards 1995). They also suffer disproportionately from drug dependency and histories of abuse (Butler 1997: 86-7). The family responsibilities of women prisoners are often said to raise particular issues for them and for correctional authorities.

On the other hand, the small size of the female prison population makes it difficult to cater properly within separate institutions for the diverse needs of sub-groups *within* that population, some of whom may share particular problems confronted by sub-groups within the male prison population. An example would be non-English speaking prisoners. It is not clear therefore that rigid gender segregation is always conducive to addressing diversity of need and condition within the female (or male) prison population. Nor is it clear that it is either necessary (or in itself sufficient) to address issues of personal security for female prisoners. If we dared question the principle, it might be possible to imagine some alternative prison regimes that better served the interests of male and female prisoners and the general community. After all, the family responsibilities of men (to take but one factor often referred to in connection with women) should not be regarded as having terminated at the gates of the prison. The gendered assumptions of the prison system are highlighted by the particular difficulties that arise in relation to transgender prisoners, in respect of whom some jurisdictions such as NSW have at times developed specific policies (Perkins 1991).

Although there is a widely shared view that prisoners are over-whelmingly drawn from a very distinct, low socio-economic stratum of society, the evidence for this tends to be mostly impressionistic, anecdotal and partial in nature. There has not been an abundance of published social research carried out for the Australian prison 'system' as a whole and we do not have a detailed socio-demographic profile of the national prison population. The data available, however, do confirm the common sense view. It confirms the general picture of prisoners, whether in Australia or overseas, as disproportionately drawn from multiply disadvantaged backgrounds (NSW Bureau of Crime Statistics and Research 1974; Stern 1998: 115).

In 1973, the NSW Bureau of Crime Statistics conducted one of the few such systematic Australian studies comparing the prison population with the general population (1974). It took the form of a survey of 1,000 male prisoners who were serving a sentence of 12 months or more in the NSW prison system (or 40% of the prison pop-ulation undergoing a sentence of this duration). Although now dated, it is worth listing some of its findings and comparing them to more recent research. The survey found:

- Only 4% had completed the Higher School Certificate, compared to over 20% of the general male population aged 15 years or more.

- More than two-thirds belonged to the lowest occupational strata ('unskilled'), compared to just over one-fifth of the general adult population; a further 30% belonged to the second lowest strata ('clerical, trades skilled') and under 2% were from professional or middle management backgrounds compared to almost one-quarter of the general adult population.

- More than one-third said that they had been institutionalised in a children's home of some kind, including juvenile detention centres, at some time between the ages of 6 and 18.

- More than two out of five had not had a visit from their main social contact outside the prison system, a finding that reflects the array of practical and psychological difficulties that surround the maintenance of family and social networks and which are attested to by prisoners themselves in an array of studies.

- One-third said they had received professional help or treatment for a nervous, emotional or mental problem.

In 1996, the NSW Corrections Health Service conducted an Inmate Health Survey that also affords a much fuller picture of the social char-acteristics of the NSW prison population (Butler 1997).[9] The survey was of a randomly selected sample of 789 prisoners (approximately 12% of the total prison population) from all NSW prisons. Like the 1973 study, it depicts a population which by comparison with the general NSW (or Australian) population is severely disadvantaged: ill-educated, with poor employment histories, long-standing entanglement with the criminal justice system and poor physical and mental health. To highlight just a few salient issues, it found:

- 50% of male prisoners and more than 75% of females had not been employed in the six months prior to their imprisonment.

- More than 50% of males and almost 50% of females had not completed secondary schooling to school certificate level and fewer than 10% of each had experienced any post-secondary education, a finding that suggests a serious deterioration in the educational levels of prisoners compared with 1973, despite dramatic increases in school retention rates for the general population over the same period.

- One-third of males and almost one-quarter of females had been confined in a juvenile institution at some time.

- 48% of female prisoners and 16% of male prisoners reported having been involved by an adult in some form of sexual activity before the age of 16.

- More than 30% of men and almost 80% of female prisoners reported having been in at least one violent relationship and almost half of the latter female group had been in two or more violent relationships.

- About one-third of male prisoners and approximately two-thirds of females tested positive for Hepatitis C.

- Almost 30% of females and 20% of males had heart problems.

- Almost 40% of females and 30% of males said they had a long-term illness or disability.

- One-fifth of men and almost one-quarter of women reported having used heroin in prison.

The findings in respect of the health status of prisoners need also to be considered in light of the fact that the prison population is disproportionately young by comparison with the general population.

Indigenous prisoners

It is of course no secret that Indigenous people in Australia are incarcerated at massively disproportionate rates compared to the general population. This aspect of the prison system has been one of the most widely studied in recent times involving a national Royal Commission into Aboriginal Deaths in Custody (1991) conducted over three and a half years (from 1987 to 1991), which itself prompted further studies and a substantial, on-going monitoring program in relation to issues raised by and implementation of recommendations of the Commission (see, for example, Dalton & Carcach 1997; Broadhurst 1997; Cunneen & McDonald 1997).

As at the 2000 prison census, there were 4095 Indigenous prisoners in Australian prisons, constituting 19% of the prison population. The national rate of Indigenous imprisonment was 1727 per 100,000 adult Indigenous population. This was almost 15 times the non-Indigenous imprisonment rate. The Indigenous imprisonment rate varied between jurisdictions from a high of 2908 per 100,000 adult Indigenous population in Western Australia to a low of 417 in Tasmania. The national Indigenous female imprisonment rate was 250 per 100,000 adult Indigenous females compared to a male Indigenous rate of 3318 per 100,000 adult Indigenous males. Interestingly, this means that Indigenous women in Australia are incarcerated at a similar rate to the general male population, or almost 15 times the general female population.

Between 1988 and 1999, the number of Indigenous prisoners steadily grew both in absolute terms (from about 1800 to about 4300) and as a proportion of the increasing general prison population (from 14.7% to 20%). Some care has to be exercised with this data because the statistics are likely to be in part an artefact of changing levels of Indigenous identification. However, this could account for only part of the increase. In 2000, the number of Indigenous prisoners dropped slightly for the first time.

The current position with respect to Indigenous incarceration in Australia is, however, a deeply worrying one, not only on account of its scale and consequences but also because it has occurred during a period in which unprecedented public and policy attention has been accorded the issue.

Conclusion: Penal policy, citizenship and political regimes

There is of course a long history of incarceration being used as the instrument of authoritarian political regimes (Millett 1995). The Enlightenment philosopher Montesquieu drew attention to the link between penal severity and political despotism in the 18th century

(Garland 1990: 10-11). Democratic societies of course like to think of their systems of incarceration as non-political, that punishment is essentially a function of the type and incidence of crime in the community and is underpinned by a moral consensus among ordinary citizens. However, this hardly accounts for the great variation in the form and scale of punishment, including imprisonment, between different jurisdictions that otherwise share a commitment to democratic political institutions. Suggesting a somewhat more complex relationship between political and penal institutions than is reflected in Montesquieu's remarks, Alexis de Tocqueville was moved to comment on the American prison system in the 19th century that 'while society in the United States gives the example of the most extended liberty, the prisons of the same country offer the spectacle of the most complete despotism' (quoted in Garland 1990: 11). The observation carries even more weight as we enter the 21st century, as the earlier data on rapidly growing US imprisonment rates and its comparative international record suggest.

The scale and nature of incarceration is 'political' in the broadest sense of that term. Political leaders from Winston Churchill to Nelson Mandela have made the point and, in a slightly more academic vein, the American sociologist James Jacobs elaborated it.

> A comparison of the residuum of legal rights left to the prisoner with those rights held by society's members-in-good-standing illuminates the meaning of both citizenship and criminality. The extent to which prevailing humanitarian norms and values apply to prisoners, the most peripheral members of society, indicates a great deal about the overall moral order. (Jacobs 1983: 17)

The citizenship status of prisoners is also likely to strongly influence the scale of crime and the general quality of citizenship beyond the walls. An essential component of citizenship is the right to personal security. This is one of the justifications for punishing and restraining those who infringe this right. On the other hand, the manner in which the penal task is undertaken can contribute to or mitigate crime problems. It is prisoners themselves who have most graphically described the 'outlaw culture' that may be fostered in prison systems where rights are blatantly abrogated and arbitrary authority rules (Anderson 1989; Boyle 1985). They have astutely noted how brutal treatment can ironically serve to 'free' individuals from the unwritten codes of civility and reciprocity upon which a civil society is ultimately founded. The consequences of this are likely to be visited on society when such prisoners are released. From this standpoint, respecting the rights of prisoners is not a luxury or indulgence extended to the unworthy; it is (as it has always generally been in democratic political cultures) an important means of schooling individuals in the qualities and requirements of citizenship.

This is not to say that this is a matter of simple policy choices or the instrumental will of governments. Rather, it depends on the complex array of social factors that shape moral sentiments and cultural sensibilities within the body of society as well as the attitudes and policies of legislative, bureaucratic and judicial agencies (Freiberg & Ross 1999). In this respect, there does appear to be some general correlation between political culture and imprisonment rates within the western democratic world. The United States is, of course, in a league of its own. Way behind the United States but with imprisonment rates noticeably higher than most western European countries, we find the cluster of other Anglophone countries (Britain, Canada, New Zealand and Australia). The greater weight accorded social solidarity within the political culture of the European social democracies may explain their lesser reliance on penal discipline as a mechanism of public policy. Generally, the more pronounced this commitment, the lower their imprisonment rates, so that the Scandinavian countries and the Netherlands have enjoyed significantly lower imprisonment rates even than their western European neighbours (Stern 1998: 31). The winds of global economic and social change are, however, currently blowing through Europe no less than elsewhere and eroding parts of the fabric of the 'social state'. This has seen steep rises in European imprisonment rates in recent years, but they nevertheless remain significantly lower than those of the Anglo countries.

Whatever the precise forces driving rising imprisonment rates and harsher penal policies at the present time, the trend is already having to contend with another global force. In the face of the new international human rights dispensation and the growing activism of global NGOs around the domestic penal policies of nation states, it will no longer suffice for governments to invoke their democratic credentials in order to pre-empt criticism, as the recent controversy surrounding mandatory sentencing in the Northern Territory and Western Australia attests. International human rights standards and discourse are set to play an increasingly important role in judging the administration of punishment, as they do official conduct in so many other domains of institutional life.

Notes

1　The *Report on Government Services 2000* (Steering Committee for the Review of Commonwealth/State Service Provision 2000) is an invaluable and up-to-date source of information on Australian prison systems. This section of the chapter draws heavily upon it. Most of the data relates to the 1998-99 period. Other useful sources include the annual national census of prisoners, compiled and published by the Australian Bureau of Statistics, and the Australian Institute of Criminology website on 'Corrections in Australia'.

2　The discussion in this chapter is confined to prisoners convicted of crimes against civil law. It does not include persons detained under immigration laws or military law. Detention of these groups is administered by the Commonwealth.

3　All of the latter were in NSW or the ACT, these being the only jurisdictions where the sentence of periodic detention is available.

4　Western Australia is set to join other States in the move towards privatisation. It has announced the establishment of a new 750-bed medium security facility, Acacia, to be privately operated. This will be the largest prison in Western Australia and the government sees it as an important step in the creation of a mixed public/private prison system with common operating standards. Victoria, on the other hand, has recently taken over the daily operation of the maximum security Metropolitan Women's Correctional Centre at Deer Park from Corrections Corporation of Australia because of a failure by the private operator to comply with security and drug prevention obligations.

5　Courts in the United States have generally taken a much more interventionist approach to conditions in prisons.

6　In particular, the Western Australian rate appears to be suspiciously low by comparison with other Australian jurisdictions, especially given the apparent levels of overcrowding in that State. It is hard to believe that this is not an artefact of the recording arrangements employed there.

7　On the issue of sexual violence in prisons, see Heilpern 1998.

8　This refers to the most serious offence for which the prisoner was sentenced.

9　I am grateful to Michael Levy for providing a copy of the preliminary findings of the survey, which I draw on here.

Impacts of Overcrowding

I began my sentence by being placed in the Brisbane City Watchhouse for a period of 20 days. I shared a one man cell with another inmate and was only released from that cell, to a cell double that size, for exercise, twice in the 20 days. Prior to my conviction I was under heavy medication from my family doctor for a number of ailments including severe clinical depression. This medication would have been valued at possibly $100, for which I was never compensated. All medication was taken off me and thrown out by the Watchhouse staff and I was allowed no medication or even referral to a doctor for at least one month.

Queensland male prisoner

When you are taken from the court to a police lockup, which is usually close by, they are not designed for anyone locked up to keep up with their own personal hygiene. My scenario was exactly 13 days with no shower, no change socks, jocks, no teeth cleaning, no change of clothes. When I finally got prison greens my own clothes had to be thrown away. Many people here have gone through the same scenario.

Victorian male prisoner

CHAPTER 2

The Rights of Indigenous Prisoners

Loretta Kelly

I wish that I, the politicians, the bureaucrats, the social workers, the lawyers, the psychologists, the prison officers and all others who work with the prisoners could stand inside their shoes for just one time. We may then be able to understand the problems prisoners experience, and work towards improvement which would result in improvement for society in the long term. (Trezise 1994)

Introduction

Aboriginal incarceration rates have actually increased rather than decreased since the publication in 1991 of the final report of the Royal Commission into Aboriginal Deaths in Custody (RCIADIC). Despite the RCIADIC's numerous recommendations in relation to the prison experience and custodial health and safety, the prison system continues its long tradition of ruthlessly processing and degrading Indigenous people. By its actions (or omissions), the system seems to view Indigenous people as less worthy than other citizens of this land.

This chapter explores the rights of Indigenous prisoners in light of the recommendations of the RCIADIC. It argues for legislative backing for those recommendations relating to prisoners' rights and custodial health and safety measures.

Further, the chapter discusses citizenship rights from an Indigenous perspective. It explores the notion of basic health care being a citizen's right and the failure of correctional centres to uphold this right in relation to Indigenous prisoners. It concludes with a discussion of international human rights in relation to the continued high rate of Indigenous deaths in custody resulting from the high incarceration rate of Indigenous people.

Citizenship rights

> [A]spects of Australian citizenship have been deeply flawed, and certain of its practices – particularly in relation to the Indigenous people of this country – have been morally repulsive. (Chesterman & Galligan 1999: 2)

Substantive citizenship in Australia should guarantee the vote, free speech, freedom of religion, freedom to move, equal protection of the law, free basic health care, a minimum wage, social security and education. However, according to Chesterman and Galligan, there is no clear understanding about the meaning of citizenship in Australia (1999: 1). Mick Dodson, former Aboriginal and Torres Strait Islander Social Justice Commissioner, has argued that citizenship as a concept is 'ill-defined, poorly understood, confused and confusing' (quoted in Chesterman & Galligan 1999: 1).

Citizenship may be understood as full membership in any society. Yet for most of Australia's post-invasion history, the great majority of Indigenous people were denied full membership of Australian society and consequently the rights of equal treatment that other Australians take for granted (Peterson & Sanders 1998: 1). The *Nationality and Citizenship Act* 1948 (Cth) created the formal legal category of Australian citizen. Chesterman and Galligan argue that Aborigines, along with other Australians, automatically became citizens under this legislation. However, Aborigines were 'systemically excluded from the key rights and privileges of citizenship while having its formal shell' (Chesterman & Galligan 1998: 2-3).

It has been noted that:

> [t]he fact that, after a long hard struggle, [I]ndigenous people finally secured full formal equal rights within the encapsulating settler society in the 1960s, gaining access to the same set of citizenship rights as non-indigenous Australians, was a vital step. (Peterson & Sanders 1998: 1)

Just over 30 years ago, in 1967, a national referendum overwhelmingly supported Indigenous representation in census data collection on Australian citizenship. Chesterman and Galligan argue that there is a myth that surrounds the 1967 referendum – the myth that the referendum granted Aborigines citizenship (Chesterman & Galligan 1998: 9). As they point out, the referendum merely altered the Commonwealth Constitution's two references to Aborigines (Chesterman & Galligan 1998: 9) and furthermore:

> [f]rom the 1960s the formal Commonwealth and State restrictions that denied Aborigines any meaningful status as citizens were slowly

being abandoned. These legislative changes at both levels coincided roughly with the timing of the 1967 referendum, a fact that probably explains why the referendum is accorded the status of citizenship maker. (Chesterman & Galligan 1998: 193)

Regardless, the referendum was symbolically very significant to Aboriginal people and to those who voted overwhelming for the change (Chesterman & Galligan 1998: 9). Aboriginal people interpreted the successful referendum as an improvement of our human rights. The fact that 91% of Australian voters voted in favour of the amendments encouraged Indigenous Australians to feel that we had achieved a stronger sense of 'citizenship' (Lui & Blanchard 2001: 16).

However, many Indigenous Australians would argue that our access to citizenship rights is simply a theoretical construct. The reality is that Indigenous Australians are denied basic citizenship rights. Mick Dodson refers to '20,000 Aboriginal people without adequate water, the 5,000 homeless Indigenous families, the 14,000 Aboriginal people in Western Australian remote communities who live without proper sewerage systems, power sources, or other essential services' (Dodson 1998: 29). These facts illustrate the point that citizenship does not live up to its reputation of incorporating the principle of equality when it comes to Indigenous Australians.

Substantive equality as the basis for citizenship is eloquently pleaded by Aboriginal poet Oodgeroo Noonuccal (Kath Walker) in 'Aboriginal Charter of Rights'.

> Make us neighbours, not fringe-dwellers;
> make us mates, not poor relations,
> citizens, not serfs on stations.
>
> (Walker 1970: 37)

According to Lui and Blanchard, '[c]itizenship implies rights and responsibilities. It is the right of individuals – including the most vulnerable – to expect dignity, respect and non-violence from others' (Lui & Blanchard 2001: 16). Aboriginal inmates are amongst the most vulnerable and the prison system's duty to uphold their rights of citizenship is therefore more onerous.

An elaboration of the ideals of citizenship can also be found in the 1948 *Universal Declaration of Human Rights* and the preamble to the 1966 *International Covenant on Economic, Social and Cultural Rights*. The latter states:

> ... the ideal of free human beings enjoying freedom from fear and want can only be achieved if conditions are created whereby everyone may enjoy his economic, social and cultural rights, as well as his civil and political rights ... States under the Charter of the United Nations

[have an obligation] to promote universal respect for, and observance of, human rights and freedoms ...

I asked an Aboriginal man who had been gaoled for 20 years for attempted murder what citizenship meant to him. He replied, 'We're second class citizens – on the inside and on the outside'.

The Royal Commission into Aboriginal Deaths in Custody

> Through the files, Commissioners could trace the familiar pattern of State intervention into and control of Aboriginal lives. The files start from birth; perhaps recording a child adopted out, perhaps its birth merely noted as a costly additional burden; through childhood, perhaps forcibly removed from parents after having been categorised as having mixed racial origin and therefore being denied a loving upbringing by parents and family; through encounters at school, probably to be described as truant, intractable and unteachable; to juvenile courts, magistrates courts, possibly Supreme Court; through the dismissive entries in medical records ('drunk again'), and in the standard entries in the note books of police investigating death in a cell ('no suspicious circumstances'). (RCIADC 1991: 5)

The Committee to Defend Black Rights was established in Sydney following the acquittal of five Western Australian police officers of the murder of John Pat, a 16-year-old Aboriginal youth. The Committee monitored Aboriginal deaths in custody and lobbied for the establishment of a Royal Commission.

In October 1987, the Royal Commission into Aboriginal Deaths in Custody was established. The RCIADIC investigated 99 Indigenous deaths in custody (either in police lock-ups or correctional centres) between 1 January 1980 and 31 May 1989 (RCIADC 1991: 1).

The RCIADIC also examined official actions following the deaths, such as coronial and police enquiries. It took more than three years to complete its investigations. The RCIADIC made 339 recommendations designed to prevent Aboriginal deaths in custody.

Historical factors were considered relevant to the investigation of these deaths. The RCIADIC commented on the 'deliberate and systematic disempowerment of Aboriginal people starting with dispossession from their land and proceeding to almost every aspect of their life ...' (RCIADIC 1991: 8). It was argued that the 'damage to Aboriginal society was devastating. In some places, it totally destroyed population. In others, dependency, despair, alcohol, total loss of heart wrought decimation of culture ...' (RCIADC 1991: 9).

The RCIADIC concluded that the:

> consequence of this history is the partial destruction of Aboriginal culture and a large part of the Aboriginal population and also disadvantage and inequality of Aboriginal people in all the areas of social life where comparison is possible between Aboriginal and non-Aboriginal people. (RCIADIC 1991: 11)

The RCIADIC documents poignantly depict the denial, over and over again, of the citizenship rights of Aboriginal people, both in and out of custody. They paint a clear picture of Indigenous inequality before the law.

Findings of the RCIADIC

One of the crucial findings of the RCIADIC is that Aboriginal people in custody do not face a greater risk of death than non-Aboriginal people. Rather, Aboriginal people are at greater risk of dying in custody because they are much more likely to *be* in custody (RCIADC 1991: 6).

The RCIADIC found that Aboriginal people constituted 29% of the persons held in custody, but were only 1.1% of the Australian population aged 15 years and above. Furthermore, it noted that Aboriginal people are at least ten times more likely than non-Aboriginal people to be in prison.

The Commission published a report for each of the 99 deaths it investigated. It also published its analysis of the underlying issues that contributed to the high rates of deaths in custody and to over-representation. These underlying issues included a lack of education, unemployment and poverty, lack of economic opportunity, poor housing and infrastructure, lack of land and dispossession and poor health (including the harmful use of alcohol and other drugs).

Recommendations of the RCIADIC

The recommendations cover various aspects of criminal justice reform necessary to reduce the number of Aboriginal people dying in custody. The RCIADIC made broad policy recommendations and particular program proposals to improve the prospects of Aboriginal youth and to encourage strategies for dealing with Aboriginal health (including excessive alcohol consumption and drug dependence), educational opportunities and the state of housing and infrastructure in Aboriginal communities.

The RCIADIC also made a significant number of recommendations concerning prisoner welfare in terms of health and safety, meeting cultural needs and appropriate treatment by authorities and officers.

Implementation of the RCIADIC recommendations

> Government bodies and government agencies such as police are not implementing the recommendations. They say they are but they aren't in practice. It is Aboriginal people and Aboriginal organisations that are making all the effort to implement the recommendations. (Author's telephone interview in 2000 with Neville Brown, Chairperson, NSW Aboriginal Prisoners' and Family Support Service)

The failure to implement the recommendations has led to widespread criticism by Aboriginal people and human rights activists, the most vocal activist being former Aboriginal and Torres Strait Islander Social Justice Commissioner, Mick Dodson.

Aboriginal people continue to be over-represented in the criminal justice system despite all of the recommendations of the RCIADIC. Aboriginal people continue to die in custody at an alarming rate. In 1996, Indigenous people represented 21% of all deaths in custody while constituting approximately 2% of the general population. This figure remains largely unchanged, with Indigenous people constituting 22% of all prison deaths in 1999 (Dalton 2000: 6). The number of deaths of Indigenous persons in prisons increased from 39 in the period 1980-89 to 93 in 1990-99 (Williams 2001: 2).

It is not surprising that Aboriginal people, researchers and activists have argued that the recommendations have not been fully implemented. Back in 1992, Behrendt and Behrendt warned us that the recommendations were not being implemented.

> The hundreds of recommendations delivered by the Commission have gone largely unheeded. As a result the national rate of Aboriginal custodial deaths has not decreased, and many of those who have died have done so because key areas of reform highlighted by the Commission have not taken place. (Behrendt & Behrendt 1992: 4)

Federal and State Governments issue various implementation reports annually, arguing that they are in fact implementing recommendations. Yet the reality is that the recommendations are not being implemented.

Behrendt and Cunneen stated in 1994:

> It is our view that many of those who have died have done so because key areas of reform highlighted by the RCIADIC have not taken place. Clearly despite the fact that all governments have publicly supported the vast majority of the RCIADIC recommendations, and with many governments claiming to have already implemented recommendations, the question remains as to whether these recommendations have been implemented to any meaningful degree. (Behrendt & Cuneen 1994: 4)

They argued that recommendation 152 (on the need for corrective services to examine the provision of health services to Aboriginal people in custody) had been frequently breached despite all governments having acknowledged their support for this recommendation (Behrendt & Cuneen 1994: 6). Another recommendation frequently breached, which is also unanimously supported by all governments, is recommendation 126. This recommendation states that in every case of a person being taken into custody, a screening form and risk assessment should be completed (Behrendt & Cuneen 1994: 6).

The 1996 report *Indigenous Deaths in Custody 1989 to 1996* described in detail numerous incidents of breaches of the recommendations (Human Rights and Equal Opportunity Commission (HREOC) 1996b). In relation to custodial conditions, the report found the following.

> The profiles indicate a growing awareness by custodial and medical staff of issues concerning the proper treatment of both Indigenous and non-Indigenous prisoners. However, implementation of the recommendations is uneven. Some recommendations have not been implemented in any jurisdiction. (para 8.1)

> In nine of the 61 investigated cases concerning deaths in institutional settings there was evidence that police, prison officers and medical staff were unaware of their duty of care to detainees. There was also a noted absence of internal disciplinary proceedings to deal with breaches of instructions relating to the care of people in custody. (para 8.2)

> De-briefing procedures have not been properly utilised to prevent future deaths in the same circumstances. Avoidable deaths occurred in almost identical circumstances in a number of cases. (para 8.3)

Recommendations as rights

> That word 'rights' it's a funny thing. We have no rights as black
> people. This is even more the case on the inside. I was on the inside for
> many years and I had no rights. I still don't think that Aboriginal
> inmates have many rights today. (Author's telephone interview in 2000
> with Neville Brown, Chairperson, NSW Aboriginal Prisoners' and
> Family Support Service)

Chesterman and Galligan argue that, over the last 25 years, changes
have occurred that have challenged the view that it is enough for
Aboriginal people to be given formal equality with non-Aboriginal
Australians (Chesterman & Galligan 1998: 193-4). Furthermore, they
state that only recently has legal recognition been given to the view
that Aboriginal people have certain Indigenous rights over and above
their rights as Australian citizens (Chesterman & Galligan 1998: 194).

Our over-representation in custody, as documented in the findings
of the RCIADIC, illustrates that it is not enough to accord Aboriginal
inmates the same 'rights' as non-Aboriginal inmates. If we are to
achieve substantive equality rather than the superficiality of formal
equality, additional rights must be accorded to Indigenous people
and, in this context, this means rights additional to those acknowledged for all inmates.

The recommendations of the RCIADIC are arguably a source of
rights for Indigenous prisoners. Although the recommendations
have no legislative basis, they can have legal implications under
common law.

> The recommendations are not mere suggestions. They can have legal
> implications under the common law relating to negligence,
> misfeasance in a public office and, potentially, other actions. If a
> custodial authority breaches recommendations, and that contributes to
> a death in custody, the custodial authority may be liable in damages.
> (HREOC 1996b: para 12.2)

Rosa argues that, prior to the RCIADIC, there was little recognition by
the Department of Corrective Services and the Corrections Health
Service of the issues facing Indigenous prisoners and their special
needs in the custodial system (Rosa 2000: 197). She describes how the
implementation of some of the recommendations has strengthened
the 'rights' of Indigenous prisoners. However, in practice, these rights
are not being observed. An Indigenous person working with
Indigenous prisoners commented: 'There are cases where their rights
have been observed but too many cases when they're breached'.[1]

The following section describes some of the 'rights' as contained in the recommendations of the RCIADIC and how these rights have been violated.

A right to basic health care

RCIADIC recommendation 126 states:

> [i]n every case of a person being taken into custody, and immediately before that person is placed in a cell, a screening form should be completed and a risk assessment made by a police officer or other such person, not being a police officer, who is trained and designated as the person responsible for the completion of such forms and the assessment of prisoners. (RCIADIC 1991: rec 126)

The author was informed by another Indigenous person working with Indigenous prisoners in New South Wales that, in relation to risk assessments: 'There have been numerous incidents when this [a risk assessment] hasn't been done, or hasn't been done properly. They say they're doing it, but Aboriginal inmates tell us that it wasn't done for them'.

The *Indigenous Deaths in Custody 1989 to 1996* report found that in one-third of the cases investigated, 'at-risk' information concerning the Aboriginal inmate was not passed between medical and prison staff, or from police to prisons (HREOC 1996b: para 8.7c).

Recommendation 150 states that the health care available to people in correctional centres should be of an equivalent standard to that available to the general public and that a 24-hour service should be available. The author was told about numerous incidents where the health needs of Indigenous inmates have not been adequately met.

> In a Sydney centre there was a woman in chronic pain and all she was given was Panadol. They are supposed to have 24-hour access to a doctor but this Aboriginal woman was denied this.

> There was an incident recently when the health needs of an Aboriginal inmate were neglected. One fella was given Panadol for a severe headache, and after persisting with medical staff, tests revealed that he had a brain tumour.
>
> (interviews with author)

A recent Aboriginal death in custody concerned an inmate who had recently been transferred from a juvenile correctional facility to an adult correctional centre. His record as a juvenile showed that he suffered from schizophrenia and had previous self-harm incidents. His juvenile record was apparently not transferred to adult corrections, so he was not identified as being a person at risk of self-injury. It is widely known that juvenile inmates being transferred to adult prisons suffer from anxiety and fear of their new institution. How much more anxiety would this young man have been subjected to at the time of his suicide? It is no wonder that the *Indigenous Deaths in Custody 1989 to 1996* report found that the 'provision of psychiatric services is a continuing problem in all jurisdictions' (HREOC 1996b: para 8.7b).

The report also stated that the circumstances of deaths in prisons indicated that 'health services in some prisons were well below community standards' (HREOC 1996b: para 8.7a). Hence, it is a fair conclusion to say that the right to basic health care enjoyed by most Australian citizens is certainly questionable when it comes to Indigenous prisoners.

The RCIADIC noted the obvious vulnerability of Aboriginal people who died in custody due to their poor health (RCIADIC 1991: ch 23). Given the poor health of Indigenous inmates, basic health care is insufficient. The well-known principle in the law of negligence, the 'egg-shell skull' rule, must be emphasised to those working in corrections. The application of this rule means that greater than average diligence amongst corrections workers is required when dealing with Indigenous inmates. Health care provision at a standard *above* that currently provided for the general prison population is required if Indigenous deaths in custody are to be prevented. Additional Indigenous rights to custodial health care, above that of the supposed 'basic' right to health care, must be acknowledged as a requirement to reducing Indigenous deaths in custody.

A right to visits

Indigenous people are the most socio-economically disadvantaged group in Australia. When Indigenous prisoners are placed in gaols far from family, and family members have difficulty accessing financial assistance to travel to visit inmates, family members are often prevented from visiting their loved ones.

RCIADIC recommendation 168 provides:

> That Corrective Services effect the placement and transfer of Aboriginal prisoners according to the principle that, where possible, an Aboriginal prisoner should be placed in an institution as close as possible to the place of residence of his or her family. (RCIADIC 1991: rec 168)

Recommendation 169 states that, where it is impossible for the prisoner to be placed close to the family, financial assistance should be given to the family to allow them to visit the inmate (RCIADIC 1991).

The author's research conducted for this paper indicates that, as far as Indigenous prisoners, their families and Aboriginal organisations working in this field are concerned, recommendations 168 and 169 are the most frequently breached recommendations.

> [T]hese recommendations are rarely implemented. Aboriginal inmates being so far away from their family, community and traditional lands causes them enormous stress and it's one of the triggers for them being at risk. Corrective services sometimes have an excuse for this such as their classification preventing them from being at the centre closest to home. But other times there's just no logic to why an Aboriginal inmate has gone to one centre instead of the one near their community. Then when we try to get them transferred there's just no sympathetic consideration at all.
>
> (interview with author)

Access to accommodation and financial assistance for travel for the families of Indigenous prisoners is of real concern.

> We don't even know how much funding is actually allocated to this need in the corrective services budget. They haven't advised us of how much money is available to [the families of inmates]. We can't even tell [the families] what the deal is. Yet all we're told is 'sorry there's no funding available'. A lot of the applications of Aboriginal families have not been granted due to a lack of funding.
>
> (interview with author)

Corrective Services in NSW requires that applications for accommodation and financial assistance must be made 21 days prior to the journey for consideration by a senior welfare officer (Rosa 2000: 200). Yet the author was informed by an Indigenous worker: 'This is really problematic with people at risk. There needs to be a shortened time frame requirement for when the inmate is at risk because they desperately need contact with family at that time' (interview with author).

Furthermore, Corrective Services should give recognition to the kinship and family obligations of Aboriginal prisoners. Corrective Services should acknowledge that family obligations extend beyond immediate family and that they should give favourable consideration to requests by inmates to attend occasions of special significance; in particular, funeral services (RCIADIC 1991: rec 171).

Trezise argues that despite suggestions by correctional departments that all is well with enabling prisoners to attend funerals, problems still arise (Trezise 1994: 7). Trezise is correct in stating that '[t]here is probably nothing which gives rise to more distress than the refusal by the Department for a relative to attend a funeral' (Trezise 1994: 7). She states that there are huge problems in persuading the South Australian Department of Corrective Services to allow prisoners to attend funerals at far distant places (Trezise 1994: 8). Another concern is refusal based on insufficient notice to the Department, yet prisoners are often unable to give sufficient notice because they themselves receive little notice (Trezise 1994: 8). Obviously, in the case of an unexpected family death, little more than a few days notice of a funeral can be given.

These concerns are not specific to South Australia. The author was informed by Indigenous people working with Indigenous prisoners in NSW that the approval process and the grounds for considering compassionate leave for prisoners are unclear. Corrective Services decisions have been ad hoc and inconsistent.

> A welfare officer or the Governor will say yes then the regional commander will deny the application. This causes enormous stress for the inmate.

> Some do get [compassionate] leave. But there's more that don't get it than those that do.

> (interviews with author)

A right to be treated fairly and with dignity

Deprivation of liberty as a form of punishment should never deprive prisoners of their dignity. The power a prison officer has over a prisoner is total and this day-to-day power over the lives of prisoners has been a constant source of complaint (Trezise 1994: 1).

RCIADIC recommendation 179 refers to procedures for requests by prisoners to prison officers. It states that procedures should be made as simple as possible and that necessary arrangements should be made as quickly as possible (RCIADIC 1991). Trezise argues that, in reality, requests are very much dependent on the whim of the officers and that requirements that such requests be made in writing simply cannot be met by inmates with poor literacy (Trezise 1994: 8).

What should be a straightforward process can in reality be dehumanising and subsequently prevents Indigenous prisoners from asserting their rights. 'There is a tendency for some prison officers to be very sarcastic about requests made by prisoners which inhibits some prisoners making requests' (Trezise 1994: 9).

It is often argued that cross-cultural training of staff is one of the best ways to ensure that the actions of correctional staff are just and humane. Recommendation 177 states:

> [t]hat appropriate screening procedures should be implemented to ensure that potential officers who will have contact with Aboriginal people in their duties are not recruited or retained by police and prison departments whilst holding racist views which cannot be eliminated by training or re-training programs. In addition Corrective Services authorities should ensure that all correctional officers receive cross-cultural education and an understanding of Aboriginal – non-Aboriginal relations in the past and the present. Where possible, that aspect of training should be conducted by Aboriginal people (including Aboriginal ex-prisoners). Such training should be aimed at enhancing the correctional officers' skills in cross-cultural communication with and relating to Aboriginal prisoners. (RCIADIC 1991: rec 177)

The theory is that such training programs will re-educate those holding racist views, the aim being to eliminate racist or racially abusive comments from Corrective Services staff. This would ensure compliance with recommendation 182, which states that instructions should require correctional officers to interact with prisoners in a manner which is both humane and courteous and that Corrective Services authorities should regard it as a serious breach of discipline for an officer to speak to a prisoner in a deliberately hurtful or provocative manner (RCIADIC 1991).

Trezise has raised concerns about the effectiveness of cultural awareness training.

Cultural awareness courses are of value if they assist prison officers in understanding the reasons that bring Aboriginal people into custody and the needs of Aboriginal people in custody. This understanding needs to be put into action and become part of the prison officers' response to Aboriginal prisoners. If such understanding and implementation is not a consequence of attending cultural awareness courses then the cultural awareness course has failed.

> Thus there needs to be an evaluation of cultural awareness courses, not so much the content, but as to the long term effect on the interaction between prison officers and Aboriginal people and to the understanding of prison officers of Aboriginal prisoners and their positions (Trezise 1994: 3).

All too often, cross-cultural training courses are tokenistic; there is a 'tick the box' attitude, whereby attendance is usually the measure of success rather than the evaluation of learning outcomes. Furthermore, even the best training can have limited impact on certain officers. Trezise recalls overhearing a conversation between prison officers at Yatala Labour Prison where Aboriginal inmates were referred to as 'loony Abos' as they discussed which inmate was the 'most loony' (Trezise 1994: 4).

International human rights

> Another obvious area where the human rights of Indigenous Australians are being abused is in the criminal justice system. And here I include not only deaths in custody, but our appalling over-representation in the prison population, and prison conditions. (Dodson 1998: 24)

Mick Dodson, former Aboriginal and Torres Strait Islander Social Justice Commissioner, states that despite all of its many imperfections, international law is the most highly developed body of human rights law that exists (Dodson 1998: 21). He argues that those 'better moments' in Australian law were grounded in, if not derived from, international law. He states that Indigenous Australians must use every tool available to 'get our young adults out of detention centres and our men and women out of lock-ups and prison' (Dodson 1998: 24).

Elizabeth Evatt, former member of the UN Human Rights Committee, argues:

> [s]o far as indigenous rights are concerned, the paradox is that, while international standards can be, and have been, drawn upon to advance indigenous rights in Australia [principally through the *Racial Discrimination Act* 1975], the fact remains that many of our most glaring failures to meet international standards concern indigenous people (Evatt 2001: 181).

The *International Covenant on Civil and Political Rights* (ICCPR) protects many well-recognised rights and freedoms, including:

> [t]he right to life, the right not to be tortured or subjected to cruel, inhuman or degrading treatment, the right not to held in slavery or servitude, the right to liberty and security, the right not to be subjected to arbitrary detention ... equality before the law and protection against discrimination on any ground and protection of the rights of members of minorities (Evatt 2001: 183)

Evatt argues that art 6 of ICCPR, which protects the right to life, requires positive action to prevent arbitrary killing by police and security forces and to protect life in situations of recognised threat. She argues that 'the right to life of [I]ndigenous people in Australia is seriously prejudiced by their high rates of incarceration, which contribute to the many Aboriginal deaths in custody' (Evatt 2001: 200).

According to Evatt, if it could be substantiated that a particular death was caused or contributed to by failure to respect the ICCPR, the possibility of an individual complaint could be considered (Evatt 2001: 200). Mick Dodson believes that the conditions in which Indigenous Australians are incarcerated are inconsistent with ICCPR art 6. 'Placing a human being in conditions which are likely to induce suicide, and the flagrant disregard for this eventuality may well breach Article 6' (Dodson 1998: 24-5).

In 1994, the UN Committee on the Elimination of Racial Discrimination (CERD) was concerned at the high rate of Aboriginal deaths in custody (Evatt 2001: 200). In March 2000, CERD was gravely concerned at the disproportionate rate of incarceration of Indigenous people (Evatt 2001: 200). In the same year, the UN Committee Against Torture recommended that Australia continue its efforts to address the socio-economic disadvantage that leads Indigenous Australians to come disproportionately into contact with the criminal justice system (Evatt 2001: 200).

Mick Dodson argues that the 'obscene number of Indigenous people in prisons are no strangers to solitary confinement, forcible separation from family, community and country, with no opportunity for communication, squalid conditions, refusal of medical care, and humiliating treatment' may be grounds for a complaint to the UN Human Rights Committee under ICCPR arts 7 and 10 (Dodson 1998: 25). Article 7 prohibits cruel or inhuman treatment and art 10 requires that persons deprived of their liberty must be treated with humanity and with respect for the inherent dignity of the human person. Mick Dodson stated: 'I hardly think that having prison officers dangle pairs of socks in front of you with suggestions that you could become the next death in custody qualifies as treatment with dignity and humanity' (Dodson 1998: 25).

Hearing stories like this, it comes as no surprise that Mick Dodson should question whether the UN *Standard Minimum Rules for the Treatment of Prisoners* are being applied to Indigenous prisoners serving time in lock-ups in remote communities in Australia.

Is the watch-house in Mornington Island a healthy, well-ventilated and well-lit cell with adequate space as in Rule 10? Is the kid in Murray

Bridge who was locked up and refused his asthma medication receiving adequate medical care as in Rule 24? Is shoving a suicidal prisoner in a cell and poking him every two hours the local version of specialist psychiatric service as in Rule 22? (Dodson 1998: 25)

Evatt notes that in November 2000 a particular concern of the Committee Against Torture was the need to keep under constant review the use of instruments of restraint that may cause unnecessary pain and humiliation and to ensure that their use is appropriately recorded (Evatt 2001: 200).

Concluding remarks

The painful Indigenous experience of incarceration continues to subvert official announcements of the implementation of RCIADIC recommendations.

According to the report by the Human Rights and Equal Opportunity Commission (HREOC):

> [t]he reporting process [for implementation of the RCIADIC recommendations] was flawed from the outset, and has not resulted in accurate evaluations of progress in implementing recommendations at either Commonwealth or State and Territory level. This is a fundamental question of public accountability. (HREOC 1996b: para 11.1)

The recommendations of the RCIADIC are not being implemented. Studies 'support the view that the mere commonsense and moral authority of the recommendations have not led to full implementation' (HREOC 1996b: 272).

There are many suggestions for achieving more effective implementation of the recommendations. These include enshrining the recommendations in legislation, the use of various legal remedies at both domestic and international levels, as well as the establishment of new structures, institutions or dialogues to secure the goals sought in the recommendations (HREOC 1996b: 272).

It is the author's view that where RCIADIC recommendations are able to be effectively implemented by legislation, this should be done. However, I do acknowledge that it would be impractical to implement some recommendations through legislation.

Legislative backing for those recommendations relating to prisoners' rights and legally enforceable custodial health and safety measures is essential. It is also essential that Indigenous people become more aware of the potential use of the courts under the present law to provide remedies and to use existing structures such as the Ombudsman and anti-discrimination bodies. International human rights law offers some hope for the pursuit of prisoners' rights. That Indigenous prisoners might have to go to international bodies to ensure that our rights as citizens of this country are protected is disheartening to say the least.

Notes

1   The author spoke at length with several Indigenous workers who work in correctional centres with Indigenous inmates. These workers wished to remain anonymous for fear that their prison clearances and 'privileges' would be jeopardised.

Prisoners at Risk

Under the auspices of placing me under strict protection I was held in isolation in Darcy 3 for a period of four days without my medication. The cell had a shower, toilet and bed, a bedside shelf below a glass window. I had no other amenities during this period. I was let out for one hour in every 24 hour period but not necessarily at the same time as the preceding day. On the fourth day without my medication I suffered what had been to this date my worst attack of angina ever.

Despite repeated requests to the officers on duty during the one hour let out, I did not receive my medication. I was told that it was at my previous location, and that I would receive it in due course. I made it known that I was on heart and diabetic medication, but the officers on duty didn't want to know, displaying their disinterest by telling me to stop whinging.

NSW male prisoner

I have since coming to prison a history of self harm thoughts which led me to being put in the D.U. (Detention Unit – Solitary) numerous times, the longest period being over 1 week. I think it was under section 70 [Qld]. I was monitored by a camera in the cell and saw the nurse three times a day with my medication for my Diabetes and asked how I was going on odd occasions. I saw the White Coats (Shrinks) every second day when they would come and assess me to see if I was getting better so to speak.

Over the various times I have been allowed a book only on one or two occasions but no TV or radio. I was given two hours exercise each day in the small exercise yard. I was allowed visits by my friends and family in the normal visits area. The cell was small with a mattress, a suicide blanket and pillow (sometimes). A toilet and water basin all stainless steel plus heavy grilled window for ventilation.

Queensland male prisoner

I have usually only been locked away at times when I have been judged as unwell, or seen as suicidal, but not much longer than a couple of days. Medical help was always available, visits not stopped but most of these times I had no radio or television. On a few occasions cigarettes were rationed, though under category 'A' suicide watch the inmate is not allowed to smoke. This compares with 'N' Division, the main gaol's solitary section where smoking is also not allowed. There is a point I'd like to make about this. Inmates in 'N' Division on the methadone program are not refused their methadone, so shouldn't smokers be allowed their cigarettes, considering that nicotine is very addictive also.

Tasmanian male prisoner

In WA if a prisoner becomes depressed, they are slammed into a medical observation cell with canvas clothes that do not fit, canvas blankets, a plastic mattress, a cement bed and nothing else but their thoughts. Instead of being afforded any caring chance to address their problems, it is a matter of literally 'lock them away and forget them'.

WA male prisoner

CHAPTER 3

Deprivation of Liberty –
Deprivation of Rights

Debbie Kilroy & Anne Warner

Introduction

We were asked to contribute this chapter because we are part of an organisation called Sisters Inside (SIS). SIS is an organisation that advocates for female prisoners in Queensland and is founded on the principle of participation from the women in prison. Indeed, more than half of the organisation's Steering Committee is comprised of women currently in prison. The information and argument provided in this chapter has largely emerged as a result of SIS's experience of women prisoners and their stories.

There is a fundamental philosophical contradiction within our criminal justice system: it aims both to punish and to reform. Society attempts to fulfil both these contradictory aims within the context of custodial care. However, this contradiction means that the system fails to do either very successfully.

This chapter takes the position that the whole system of incarceration is not necessarily the best social response to crime. It describes some examples of how human rights are denied within our women's prison system. Women should be able to expect that their basic physical, emotional and medical needs are respected and protected while they are in prison. The examples in this chapter show that the prison system is, by its very nature, abusive and far from correctional. It further demonstrates that a stringent understanding and application of human rights to women prisoners would create an environment in which women are better able to address their offending behaviour and therefore reduce recidivism.

Overall, this chapter shows how the treatment of women in prison can be seen to constitute an abuse of their rights in several ways. We particularly wish to highlight how issues of isolation, drug use, motherhood and health care in the context of the prison system contribute to a deprivation of rights.

Rehabilitation

Our prison system is called 'Corrective Services'. There is, however, little evidence to suggest that incarceration reforms offending behaviour. In fact, the evidence seems to point in the opposite direction. Once women go into the prison system, they become more likely to re-offend. In Queensland, there is a 57.47% recidivism rate for women (Department of Corrective Services Qld 2000: 5). The reality for most women in prison is that they are there for minor offences: 84% are serving under two-year sentences, with an average serving only 2.1 months. Corrective Services offer 'Core Programs' to address offending behaviour. These programs have a poor record and poor reputation in regard to assisting women to address their offending behaviour. Furthermore, Corrective Services takes absolutely no responsibility for reintegrating women into society. The moment a woman walks out the gate, she no assistance to meet her immediate needs such as shelter and food, let alone the re-establishment of family ties or employment. It is little wonder that 19 women have died within three months of leaving prison in the last two years or that 57.47% are recidivists (Department of Corrective Services, Queensland 2000: 5).

Isolation

Isolation for women in prison has three dimensions:

1. The isolation from the broader community, family and friends
2. The experience of individual isolation within the prison system
3. The physical isolation that women are subjected to when they are further punished for 'breaches' and placed in detention units or when they are removed from the communal section of the prison because of suicidal or self-harming behaviour

Ironically, within this context of isolation, the authorities' stated aim is to re-socialise women so that they may become productive members of civil society.

The separation that women experience from family, friends and the broader community is perceived as a powerful signal to the women that they have been rejected by ordinary society and are forced because of their 'badness' to live apart from civil society. It has been the experience of SIS that women have powerful emotional responses to their separation from society and quite often turn their anger in on themselves, becoming suicidal, self harming or, alternatively, using chemical substances to deaden their emotional pain. From this position, they are most unlikely to learn the necessary skills to reintegrate into society on release.

Incarceration is, in and of itself, an isolating experience. Our experience indicates that isolation from society is compounded by further isolation within prison because of the 'informal' norms of prison culture and because of disciplinary procedures in prison.

Women are locked up in a community of women but their capacity to interact with other women is constrained by the norms of prison life. The culture that exists within prison determines, for example, who may speak to whom. Long-term prisoners ('long termers') maintain a separateness from short-term prisoners ('short termers') for a number of complex reasons. Long termers find short termers' complaints about the deprivations of prison life threatening to personal strategies that they have developed in order to survive in prison. Long termers cannot afford to dwell on what they consider minor irritations. This view of short termers' complaints is reinforced by 'screws' (prison officers), whose interests are maintained by characterising any short termers' complaints as trivial. Thus a situation develops where those who know most about the system do not share this knowledge with inexperienced and frightened short termers. Short termers' experience of isolation is exacerbated by their exclusion from the close-knit long-term society. Short termers find it difficult to interact with each other because of the transient nature of their stay (Kilroy 1999: 7).

Ironically, when women react to their initial rejection and isolation by becoming emotionally distraught, suicidal or self-harming, they experience further rejection when they are placed in isolation for the purposes of observation. It is remarkable that prison authorities should think it appropriate to respond to women's cry for help by compounding the cause of the problem with further isolation.

Usual forms of internal prison discipline are to 'breach' women and place them in total isolation in a detention unit (DU). Cameras observe the DU on a 24-hour basis. Women are denied any privacy for using the toilet or showering. No books, TV, radios or any form of interaction with the outside is allowed. The women are aware that male prison officers may be observing them, which increases the trauma of the whole experience. This punishment may be meted out for offences including assault, drug use, insubordination towards prison authorities, hanging towels on cell doors, smoking in cells, obscene language, walking on the grass and, alarmingly, in some cases, women are punished for self-harming behaviour.

In September 1999, a woman on remand was driven to suicide by hanging herself with plaited wool the night after her release from the DU. SIS was informed that she had been placed in the DU for two days because she was in possession of prohibited articles (incense sticks that were sent to her through the prison mail system and a towel with a hole in it). She was released and then returned to the DU for a further 24 hours for swearing at a senior officer. After the alarm was first raised, prison officers were reluctant to open the door because they thought she was in the corner and about to attack them. One-and-half hours later, they finally entered and found her dead. It was reported to us that a senior member of staff was heard to repeatedly lament, 'My new jail! How could she do this to me?'. This whole incident indicates that prison authorities were totally lacking any consideration or empathy for the disastrous impact of severe isolation.

Women who are considered unmanageable within the mainstream prison system experience a further level of isolation. They are sent to the Crisis Support Unit (CSU), which is located in a male prison. The staff are predominantly male and women have reported that 'they were asked by a male officer monitoring the cells to perform sexual acts for the entertainment of male officers' (Koch 2000). In another incident in Townsville, three women reported that they were placed in straightjackets, denied water for long periods of time, given no access to toilet facilities and forced to drink their own urine (Andersen 2000). These incidents may not be the norm for the CSU but if any such incidents occur, it is a clear and undeniable violation of the human rights of prisoners and is indicative of the sort of abuses that inevitably occur within isolated institutions. The greater the isolation, the greater the propensity for abuse.

The war on drugs

Within the Queensland prison system, a number of practices have been introduced as part of the ineffective 'war on drugs' strategy, including strip-searching, routine urine testing, searching of cells and the increasing prevalence of surveillance cameras. The overall effect is dehumanising, objectifying, degrading and, furthermore, seemingly useless in preventing significant levels of drug abuse in prison.

Routine strip-searching is a common practice within the prison. In the first 12 months of the new Brisbane Women's Correctional Centre, opened in 1999, 12,136 body pat searches, including 5,346 strip-searches, were carried out, including the strip-search of a baby, with not one piece of contraband being found (documents supplied in respones to a freedom of information application by SIS in 2001). However, the availability of drugs in prison remains at an all-time high. A recent survey has demonstrated that 51% of women in prison are using drugs (Kilroy 2000: 14).

Recent research estimates that 89% of women in prison have experienced sexual violence (Kilroy 2000: 14). Given this, the practice of routine strip-searching is experienced by the women as further abuse. Furthermore, the practice may reinforce and trigger the emotional pain that has lead to their offending behaviour in the first place. Research indicates that the emotional pain of abuse leads women to use drugs as a form of self-medication (Kilroy 2000: 14). Thus the various practices of the prison that are aimed at controlling drug use are in fact contributing to the cycle of abuse and drug use.

The 'war against drugs' has been so ineffective that there is higher availability of drugs in prison than in the community (Kilroy 2000: 14). Intravenous drug taking in prison is a hazardous activity because of the obvious risks involved in the sharing of syringes ('picks'). Many women contract Hepatitis C while in prison through this practice. They further risk contracting HIV. Prison authorities persist with their ineffective, punitive measures to combat drug use while neglecting education and prevention strategies that could be hardly less successful. Such strategies might also address some of the underlying issues of offending behaviour. Overall, the draconian anti-drug strategies of the prison system contribute to violations of the human rights of prisoners while strategies that would provide support for prisoners without violating human rights are ignored.

Women as mothers

Women's role as mothers, daughters and family members are shown scant respect by the prison system. Often women have their children taken into care because of imprisonment rather than for any evidence of poor parenting (Kilroy 2000: 13). While this may be necessary for the period of incarceration, women experience significant difficulties in persuading authorities to return the children into their care on release.

The prison system makes virtually no provision to maintain or encourage women's role as mothers. Indeed, women prisoners are routinely referred to as 'girls', indicating no recognition of their status as adult women. SIS's work with children of mothers in prison has shown that this absence of the maternal role from policy is dehumanising for women, removing from them a vital aspect of their identity. The effect on the children is emotionally catastrophic. Sentencing policies rarely take into account the long-term consequences on the women and children of imposing custodial sentences on women, often for the most trivial offences. SIS has observed that women are regularly imprisoned for failure to pay fines including parking, dog licences, library books and failing to vote. Aboriginal women are often imprisoned for the 'trifecta': drunk and disorderly, resisting arrest and obscene language. The extreme reaction of imprisoning women for such trivial offences could be considered cruel and unusual, particularly given that these punitive measures punish not only the woman but also her children.

Medical care

It has been the experience of SIS that medical facilities in Queensland prisons are of poor quality, badly organised, lacking in sensitivity and sometimes overtly neglectful. Almost every day, horror stories emerge about the inappropriateness of medical attention. A recent example of medical neglect in prison was the case of a pregnant woman who repeatedly requested medical attention over a period of 12 hours. She subsequently miscarried in the toilet block. Her baby died. She was then taken to a hospital in shackles (Coffey 1999). It has been reported to SIS that women who require medical attention in hospitals are always escorted in shackles. On one occasion, a woman was kept in shackles while giving birth.

A number of women have reported to SIS that their requests for medical attention are most frequently met with the response 'take two Panadol', usually without any further inquiry. SIS is also aware of a woman who complained of abdominal pain. She was effectively ignored until her condition deteriorated and she died. It was subsequently discovered that she had a twisted bowel which may have responded to treatment had proper medical attention been provided.

A common and recurrent practice is to over-prescribe antidepressant drugs for women in prison. This, of course, has an added bonus because the drugs keep women quiet and compliant (George 2000: 51).

Conclusion

Women who are in prison for minor offences and then subjected to the rigours of prison life are often criminalised by this experience and become persistent and more serious offenders. Women who are incarcerated for more serious offences find that prison does not address their offending behaviour. Given that a large number of women are incarcerated for minor offences and that incarceration increases recidivism, there is a strong argument to suggest that all minor offenders should be sentenced to non-custodial alternatives. Further, given the difficulties of ensuring that human rights are not abused behind closed doors, there is a further argument that custodial sentences are an abuse of human rights. Because custodial sentences can constitute a breach of human rights and because they do not work to reform, there is a strong argument that they should not be used at all.

There are those in society who believe that crime should be punished and that harsh punishment will, somehow, reduce the incidence of crime. Our rates of imprisonment are increasing dramatically and the crime rate either remains the same or increases (Criminal Justice Commission 2000a: 7). There is definitely no reduction in the crime rate while levels of incarceration have increased.

There are those who believe that punishment is a necessary moral response to crime and who reject reform and rehabilitation. This group will never be satisfied by any model of criminal justice and remain impervious to any argument other than their own.

There is a dominant view that prisons are necessary to protect the community from wrongdoers. While the cost of imprisonment escalates on an annual basis, reducing the available funds for roads, schools and hospitals, it is our belief that prisons act neither as a deterrent nor a correction; further, they represent a significant threat to human rights.

Our experience with the prison system and with women in prison has demonstrated to us that the risk of a descent into abuse is ever-present and that, with the best will in the world, it is going to be impossible to avoid all abuses in a closed system such as a prison. Therefore, we believe that alternatives to custodial sentences must be sought. However, while the current system of custodial correction is in place, Sisters Inside will continue to be ever-vigilant to advocate on behalf of women's rights and to attempt to minimise harsh treatment for women.

Family

Telstra has special rates on week nights, like 40¢ phone calls after 7pm for STD. As we are only allowed $50 per month for STD phone calls, I don't see why these rates are not permitted to the prisoners as we try to stay in contact with our families as much as possible. Even a local call is cheaper than 40¢ these days and with the phone here being the main contact, why aren't we getting cheaper rates?

Victorian male prisoner

Since 1994 [third sentence], I was kept in a single cell in solitary confinement for 5 years, 23 hours a day. I had a TV and was given 1 hour exercise in a yard. I never had any visits. (Dad, my only relative, had Alzheimer's disease). I had not seen him since 1993 when I visited the UK. A special visit was arranged for me to visit Dad in the nursing home but on the day, I was told Pentridge did not have the staff. I never got to visit my father. I was his only relative in Australia. We had lived together since 1958 in Australia. Dad died aged 90 in '98. I chose not to attend his funeral, as Barwon could not guarantee to have me at Springvale crematorium by 10am on the day and informed me I would be taken there in handcuffs with two armed guards. I felt if I had gone, the funeral would have been disrupted as I was sure there would have been several hours delay before getting there and such cremations can't be held up as others are booked the same day and there was a possibility of not being taken at all.

Victorian male prisoner

I have felt very isolated many times in gaol, mainly because of the distance from home and visits are very spasmodic due to distance and finances.

Victorian male prisoner

Both these men, whose stories I will detail, are housed in the Port Augusta Prison, which is 300kms north of Adelaide, their family's residential base.

Ties with family and friends depends on expensive STD phone calls and 6-hour round trips for visits. Both these men have had visits terminated and visitors banned for periods of up to a year on the pretence that their visitors were suspected of involvement in the transport of illegal drugs.

The first had his girlfriend (the mother of his only child) banned for a year. Then recently his friend was banned for a year too. The second has had 15 visits prematurely terminated and visitors banned in every instance. These are regularly followed up with periods of segregated lock-up in punishment cells. Two weeks last time.

The guise under which prison authorities administer these injustices is that they say they 'suspect' some sort of illegal activity – ie exchange of drugs. Where is the proof? None of the instances I have recounted have resulted in the seizure of any drugs – or even evidence of any improper behaviour.

South Australian male prisoner

CHAPTER 4

Experiences of Inmates
with an Intellectual Disability

Jenny Green

Introduction

In 2000, Meredith Martin, Jim Simpson and I completed 11 case studies of people with intellectual disabilities who were in contact with the criminal or juvenile justice system. The case studies were part of the investigative stage of the Framework Project and were developed to illustrate the diversity in the target group. Six of the participants who were interviewed were either serving sentences or had recently served sentences in adult correctional facilities. This chapter relates their stories. Together, they paint a powerful picture of prison experience. However, it was the bigger picture of their lives that emerged during the interviews and the prospect of their lives in the community *after* prison that raised most issues.[1]

The Framework Project

The Framework Project was managed by the New South Wales (NSW) Council for Intellectual Disability (CID) and the Intellectual Disability Rights Service (IDRS). They received funding from the Ageing and Disability Department (now Department of Ageing, Disability and Home Care) and the Law and Justice Foundation of NSW to develop a framework for the provision of appropriate community services for people with intellectual disabilities who are in contact, or at risk of contact, with the criminal or juvenile justice system. Jim Simpson, Meredith Martin and I were engaged as consultants to carry out the project.

Prevalence

The 1996 Law Reform Commission report, *People with an Intellectual Disability and the Criminal Justice System,* was a critical piece of work that contributed to the inception of the Framework Project (NSW Law Reform Commission 1996a). The Commission surveyed a number of studies completed in Australia and overseas that sought to determine the proportion of people with an intellectual disability in different parts of the criminal justice system. There are some similarities between overseas and Australian research. Gudjonsson et al found that 9% of suspects interviewed at two London police stations had significant 'intellectual impairments' compared to the expected 2% to 3% in the general population (Gudjonsson et al 1993). Lyall, Holland and Collins studied the incidence of persons with 'learning disabilities' detained in police custody at the city police station in Cambridge, UK. The results showed that 15.2% of people in police custody had learning disabilities, comprised of 4.4% attending schools for those with moderate learning difficulties, 0.4% attending schools for those with severe learning difficulties and 10.4% attending schools for those with emotional or behavioural difficulties or a learning support unit within a mainstream school (Lyall, Holland & Collins 1995).

Hayes and McIlwain (1988) and Hayes (1997) are the studies generally referred to in New South Wales (NSW). Hayes and McIlwain cited 12.9% of the NSW prison population as having an intellectual disability: 2.4% with a mild or greater disability and 10.5% borderline (Hayes & McIlwain 1988: 25). In 1992 and 1995, Hayes carried out research at six local courts, four in the country and two in the city. From this study, she concluded that 23.6% of people before the courts in NSW had an IQ of less than 70, which placed them in at least the mildly intellectually disabled category. In addition, there were 14.1% who functioned within the borderline range (Hayes 1997). The Law Reform Commission concluded that people with intellectual disabilities were over represented in the criminal justice system (NSW Law Reform Commission 1996a: para 11.4), a conclusion that was recently reiterated by the Standing Committee on Law and Justice of the NSW Legislative Council (1999: para 8.4).

Case studies

The case study participants were Chuan, Roland, Peter, John, Tony and Joanne.[2] Their interviews were loosely structured and open-ended. They were asked about the life experiences that led to their convictions, their views on their circumstances and their ideas for support and assistance in their lives. There has been no attempt to establish 'fact' or 'truth' in the accounts of their experiences. The purpose of the interviews was to gain an understanding of the thoughts and opinions of the participants. It is acknowledged that just a single interview is not an adequate means to establish anything for certain including thoughts and opinions. Nonetheless, it is a record that gives an impression of their experiences.

It was clear in the conversations with John, Chuan, Roland and Peter that their experiences in prison were in the forefront of their minds. They identified four main areas of concern. The first and most common was threatened and actual physical and sexual violence. The second area of concern related to meeting financial obligations and demands when incarcerated. The third was access to advocacy and the fourth was in regard to lost property. Four of the six participants strongly expressed their fear and confusion in relation to the prison system and decisions that were made about their location. These concerns are explored in each of their stories.

It is easy to understand that the participants' desire to talk about their current or recent situations tended to dominate the conversations. Their fears and concerns revealed experiences that disregarded and, in some cases, violated their rights. Their intellectual disability and their inability to protect and look out for themselves in the hostile prison environment exacerbated this. Nonetheless, the stories of childhood, adolescence and adult life that all six participants told describe a much bigger picture of concern that suggests a dearth of community support and services that left these individuals vulnerable and at risk, resulting in their crimes and incarceration.

Chuan

Chuan is in his late twenties and has a mild intellectual disability. In his files, he is described as 'not simply hampered by his extremely low level of ability but also by his very faulty and bleak socialisation'. He was born in China. His family immigrated to Australia in the early 1980s, whereupon his parents commenced a restaurant business in Sydney. They worked long hours, which took their toll and a few years later they separated. Chuan has had no contact with his father since that time. Chuan's mother had no knowledge of the social security benefits available to her and worked six days and nights a week as a live-in housekeeper for a Chinese family. Chuan was left to cope alone; he was

13 years old. Chuan attended the local public school. The school did not realise that Chuan had an intellectual disability and assumed that his poor performance was instead a conduct disorder. He had great difficulty learning English. He was bullied and bashed by other boys and his behaviour deteriorated. He left school before his School Certificate under suspension for fighting. Curiously, his school reports implied that he was a normal and adequate student. He never saw a school counsellor or a specialist staff member. Chuan is functionally illiterate.

It appears that Chuan did not receive any moral guidance from his parents. Nor did he receive any relationship or sex education that he understood. In 1993, at the age of 20, he was convicted of the sexual assault of a seven-year-old girl and sentenced to a term of three years' imprisonment. In prison, Chuan was naively forthcoming about his conviction when asked. He did not understand the differing social perceptions of crimes. While on remand in the mainstream prison, he was assaulted and nearly strangled to death by other inmates. He was later placed in the Developmental Disability Unit (DD Unit). He received a modest victim's compensation settlement.[3] Nonetheless, the effects on Chuan were severe. He became depressed and extremely anxious. He was prescribed Melleril. However, after taking Melleril, he experienced hallucinations at night, which scared him and inhibited his sleep. Chuan believed that prison officers were deliberately persecuting him and deliberately inhibiting his access to 'buy ups'. He attempted suicide on a number of occasions. While in prison, Chuan was diagnosed as suffering post-traumatic stress disorder. Moreover, after his release he suffered serious epileptic seizures and was hospitalised. The seizures were attributed to the injuries he received during the prison attack.

A few years after his release from prison, Chuan was convicted of the sexual assault of an intellectually disabled woman. It was at the beginning of this prison sentence that he was interviewed. Chuan had difficulty expressing himself in the interview. He was highly anxious and jittery. Notwithstanding the stress Chuan appeared to experience in the interview, he was very keen to relate his experiences and convey his fears and anxieties. He clearly felt at constant risk and he was confused and uncertain about his future in the DD Unit, fearing that at any time he may be taken to another prison. Chuan's focus on his physical safety made it difficult to explore any other issues. It appeared that no other issues featured next to his fear of life-threatening violence from which, he believed, staff chose not to protect him.

Roland

Roland is in his early twenties. In his files, he is described as having a mild intellectual disability with an attention deficit hyperactivity disorder (ADHD) and an oppositional and defiant disorder. He has had a history of setting fires since the age of two. Roland lives at home with his family. His parents both work, his father has a day job and his mother works night shift. They appear to have been actively involved with him all his life. Roland attended a regular primary school and at eight years of age, he went to a special school. He said that he hated school and used to truant a lot, finally refusing to attend at all. Roland said that he couldn't read or write but that he is good at maths. When he was 15, his sister left home and he missed her company. Roland said that he did not have any friends and his sister was not at home anymore so he started to run away for up to four days at a time. He said that he lived on the streets and travelled on public transport over long distances. At this time, Roland had his first contacts with the criminal justice system.

At the time of interview, Roland was incarcerated for arson and malicious damage. He said he had been in juvenile justice facilities seven times and in adult correctional facilities four times. Roland said that he had been the victim of bashings at a detention centre. More recently he said that he was the victim of sexual assaults in prison. He said that he was forced to participate in oral and anal sex. He said that he participated because he was physically threatened with bashings. When we interviewed the staff in the DD Unit in which Roland was located, they expressed the view that Roland was homosexual and sought sexual contact with other prisoners as favours for 'smokes and things'.

Roland said that he made some friends in the detention centres and that he and his mates would get together when he was released. Roland saw that his mates were not a good influence on him but he did not know what else to do because he did not have any other friends.

Peter

Peter is Aboriginal and in his early twenties. In his files, Peter is described as 'an uneducated man with limited insight, blunted affect, poor communication skills and a low level of intellectual functioning'. Peter was born in western NSW but moved with his mother to Sydney when he was about five years old when she remarried and started another family. He did not get along with his stepfather. Both his mother and stepfather had alcohol problems. Peter was sexually abused when he was ten. At this time, he was attending a 'special school' where he was teased for being Aboriginal. He also had his first contact with the criminal justice system for theft. Peter started smoking marijuana and sniffing solvents to cope.

Peter's schooling was disrupted with three school changes and truancy. Eventually, he left school in year 8 at the age of 13. Peter was illiterate. He spent his time 'hanging around with [his] mates' and he stole to get money and clothes. Peter had constantly felt unwelcome at home and was eventually 'kicked out'. He has spent some time living on the streets and sometime living with his grandmother. At 18, Peter was incarcerated for break and entry. At 20, he began to use heroin and cocaine daily.

Peter is currently serving concurrent sentences for breaking and entering, stealing and assaulting a police officer. He is located with other Aboriginal prisoners and not in the DD Unit. During the interview, Peter had two main concerns. The first concern related to outstanding warrants for train ticket fines. He believed that the fines were increasing at a rate of $50 a week while he was in prison. Furthermore, he believed that the moment he was released he would be incarcerated again for the outstanding fines which he would be unable to pay. He said that he had not received any assistance in solving this problem while he was in prison. He was afraid that debt recovery officers would take items of value to settle his debts without his knowledge or consent. He expressed the view that it was a hopeless situation and that it would be difficult to get out of the cycle of trouble and prison.

The second concern was about managing himself post-release. Previously, when Peter was released from prison, he went to live with his aunt whose house is close to his grandmother's. Peter stated that one of the problems of living with his aunt was that she lives in an area where there are many people who 'get him into trouble with drugs and the law'. He thinks he will return to his aunt when he leaves prison this time because it appears to him to be his only option. Peter expressed a desire to learn to read and write, play football again and get a job but he had no idea how to make these things happen. He did say, however, that he would like the assistance of an Aboriginal pre- and post-release program to help and support him to meet any parole conditions. Clearly. Peter felt that establishing a law-abiding life outside prison was quite daunting and risky.

John

John is in his mid-thirties and the eldest of the participants. He also had the most to say. In his files, John is described as having a mild intellectual disability and mild cerebral palsy with left hemiplegia. John grew up with his family. During his childhood, he had a number of hospital admissions. He went to a special school. When he was 16, his rebellious reaction to his father led to his placement in a large residential facility for people with intellectual disability. He stayed there until he was 20, during which time he commenced working at the local sheltered workshop.

In 1985, John was referred to a psychiatric hospital from the residential facility because he was wandering and displaying aggressive behaviour. He stayed at the hospital for quite a while and was finally discharged to a boarding house. Over the next five years, John developed a history of admissions to psychiatric units and hospitals in NSW and interstate. The admissions followed self-injurious gestures and threats. However, he was never identified as having a psychiatric disability.

John has been in prison more often than the other participants. Since 1989, John has had approximately 54 court appearances in NSW alone. He also mentioned a number of interstate appearances. The following list provides an example of the range of charges.

- false alarms
- malicious damage
- offensive conduct
- public mischief and nuisance
- improper use of a telecommunications service
- entering enclosed lands
- assault
- lighting fire in a prohibited time zone
- impersonating a police officer
- breaching an apprehended violence order
- false representation resulting in police investigation
- maliciously destroying and damaging property
- use of offensive language in a public place
- stalking/intimidation
- attempted armed robbery (using a toy gun)

John has spent periods of time in different prisons. Since 1990, he has lived a somewhat itinerant lifestyle around NSW and interstate. At times, John has received the support of accommodation services;

however, his history with services and assistance is marked by disputes. Consequently, he has often been homeless and he has spent more time in prison than he might have otherwise because there were no satisfactory community alternatives available to him. John developed an interest in criminal law and spent considerable time observing proceedings in the courts. He was active in conducting his own defences against all his criminal charges.

John was keen to discuss his experiences. He talked extensively about his disputes, his encounters with the law and his times in prison. He was quite clear and articulate in expressing his views on the rights' violations that he experienced during his prison terms. There is some evidence suggesting that John received victim's compensation for an assault in prison, although it is not clear when this occurred.[4] He expressed considerable fear of the violence prevalent in prison and this was his overriding concern.

> I was on remand in 1997, for 16 days I was at the Reception Induction Centre at Long Bay Prison where I was stood over by inmates [who] made fun of me. I reported the matter to [the] clinical nursing staff 10 days later. [The] reason for this was I did not want to complain in front of inmates then risk getting bashed up, so I waited till Corrective Services got an appointment to see someone [and] I was transferred to the DD Unit[5] located in the SPC [Special Purpose Centre] at Long Bay.

> [Another time I was] in Tamworth [and] I was kept on protection [but] some inmates got into where I was and stuffed a drug cigarette in my cell. I pressed the emergency buzzer and officers came. I was checked by the clinical staff and the officers were requested to keep the protection gate locked at all times. After Court I was returned to Long Bay Prison DD Unit.

> In November '98 I was sentenced to two months prison for alleged assault on a legal aid officer which I defended. Following an appeal, which was dismissed, I was taken to Silverwater Prison where I was placed in a cell with someone else despite a recommendation that I be kept 'one out' which means [in] a cell on my own. I was stood [over] for my prison rations so I had to hand over my rations or be bashed. So I gave my cellmate my rations which were milk, coffee and sugar. Later I was taken to the DD Unit at Goulburn.

> It is easy for a judge or magistrate to send a person with a disability to prison but the Court does not realise that people with disabilities are vulnerable to attacks.

The second area of concern that John raised was about lost property. John was released from custody after an appearance in Wollongong

Court. He immediately returned to Silverwater Prison to claim his possessions. John was informed that his possessions had been sent to Goulburn Gaol. However, they were unable to be located there. The staff at Goulburn assumed that John's possessions had been mistakenly sent to Cessnock Prison. Prison officers at Cessnock were unable to locate John's possessions and he finally gave up trying to retrieve them. As a man of limited means and few possessions, this concerned John greatly. Finally, John's church followed up on his possessions and after some time located them at Long Bay's holding facility where they were stored with unclaimed items. On their return, John discovered a bundle of letters from the church sent to him during his imprisonment that he was told had been 'put in the wrong people's letter boxes'. John said that the church warned the Department of Corrective Services that if there had been a breach of confidentiality, appropriate action would follow. They also arranged for John to get legal advice.

The final concern that John raised was in relation to access to advocates in prison. He has had an advocate for some time and regularly relies on this person for support, particularly when he is 'in trouble with the law'.

There is another point. How would a person with an intellectual disability access an advocate or communicate with their advocate in custody? How would an advocate be able to visit a person with an intellectual disability in gaol under the harsh visiting rules that [say] visits can only be done on weekends? People with intellectual disabilities should have access to an advocacy service. Advocates should be entitled to have unrestricted access to visits to people with disabilities 24 hours every day including phone calls.

The circumstances, stories and concerns of John, Chuan, Roland and Peter describe a picture of prison that is frightening, confusing, unpredictable and often negligent. Notwithstanding these impressions, it is clear that, with the exception of Peter, they all felt safer in the DD Units. By contrast, Tony has a different story that gives a picture of staff in the system trying their best, within constraints, to meet the particular needs of prisoners with intellectual disability. Tony also had the benefit of an advocate who liaised with staff in Corrective Services on his behalf.

Tony

Tony is in his early twenties. He is described as having a borderline/ mild intellectual disability with moderate deficits in adaptive behaviour.

He lived with his mother until he was about 13. After some arguments with his mother, Tony set fire to the home. He was made a state ward and lived in an institution for a while. After Tony left the institution, he stayed with a friend's family on and off, lived in youth refuges and led an itinerant lifestyle. He was convicted of many minor offences such as fare evasion, stealing, offensive behaviour and assault. He did a number of short periods in prison. A couple of years ago, Tony was convicted of maliciously wounding a man who teased him. Tony was sent to prison for a year. Initially, he was placed in a mainstream prison, where he expressed a wish to stay. The staff of the Disability Services Unit, which is the professional unit that supports prisoners with an intellectual disability, and Tony's advocate were concerned for his welfare but respected his choice and watched his progress closely. When Tony was victimised and 'stood over' by other prisoners, he was quickly moved to the DD Unit. Tony was quite satisfied with his circumstances in the DD Unit. He was able to contact his advocate on a regular basis. Moreover, the prison staff accommodated meetings between Tony and his advocate whenever needed. Tony enjoyed the activities in gaol. He had a job in the prison kitchen and did it well. Tony speculated about his future and said that he would like to do a TAFE course in farming to continue the education that he was getting in prison.

All the participants so far would have preferred sentences other than prison. For Joanne, however, prison has met a number of her needs that went unmet in the community.

Joanne

Joanne is in her mid-thirties. She is described as having a 'mild to moderate intellectual disability, complicated by alcohol dependence and escalating behaviour problems in latter years'. There was considerable alcohol abuse in Joanne's family home. Her father was an alcoholic and her sister and her sister's de facto were also heavy drinkers. The only abstainers were Joanne and her mother. Under the influence of alcohol, her father physically and sexually abused Joanne. She finally moved out of home at the age of 30 to become independent. She was provided with a Department of Housing bedsit. This proved to be an unsatisfactory situation for Joanne. She felt unable to cook, clean and budget for herself even with the support of services and agencies. Moreover, she had 'no real friends' and she said that she started drinking because she was lonely. Under the influence of alcohol, Joanne committed a number of minor offences involving damage to property, petty theft and breaches of orders and recognisance. Finally, she was given a prison sentence. Since then, Joanne has been in prison 17 times. Typically, upon release from prison Joanne re-offends within a week. In prison, Joanne received counselling and participated in the education programs. However, she was heavily influenced by her peers and learnt new maladaptations from other inmates. The most serious of these was self-harm or 'slashing up'. Prison staff thought that Joanne enjoyed the attention that she attracted when she engaged in 'slashing up' and suggested that she received secondary gains from imprisonment. It appeared that Joanne agreed with their assumption in part.

[at] first [I] liked [prison], now I don't. Now [I'm] sick of being here.

Joanne has expressed a desire to live with others in the community but she is uncertain about how this could happen.

[I] want help with drinking. People won't let [me] live at Mum's place [because of the] alcohol. There's nowhere to live.

In terms of drug and alcohol treatment, Joanne does have a problem because most treatment programs are either unwilling or unable to accommodate people with an intellectual disability (Simpson, Martin & Green 2001: 56-7).

The bigger picture

The participants told stories of real need and inadequacy. Their prison experience and recidivism only made sense in the broader context of their lives past and present. Interestingly, their issues are not just common to one another but common to other participants in similar studies (Benda 1991; Denoff & Pilkonis 1987; Farrington & West 1990; Levine 1984; Lyall, Holland & Collins 1995; Robertson 1981; Winter, Holland & Collins 1997).

Informal support networks were a problem for all the participants. There was either a common complaint of no friends or the 'wrong friends' who encouraged criminal behaviour. It is well documented that social support networks are important in reducing recidivism in deviance and that informal support declines with greater social and emotional impairment (Benda 1991; Denoff & Pilkonis 1987; Levine 1984). Benda found that a common characteristic of homelessness is the lack of informal support networks (Benda 1991: 58-9). Roland, Peter, John and Tony had all experienced extended periods of homelessness. Winter, Holland and Collins (1997) conducted a study of the factors contributing to suspected offending behaviour by adults with learning disabilities taken into custody at the city police station in Cambridge, UK. The results suggested that the study group was significantly more likely to experience migration events and that this was likely to reflect high levels of homelessness (Winter, Holland & Collins 1997: 606).

Prolonged, recurring periods of unemployment were common to all the participants, which is another well-documented characteristic of convicted men (Farrington & West 1990). In the same study, Farrington and West also found high levels of drug use (Farrington & West 1990). All the participants with the exception of John admitted to the use of alcohol and illicit drugs, primarily marijuana, at some time. For Peter and Joanne, drug and alcohol use was a serious problem. In their study, Winter, Holland and Collins found a high level of drug use in their alleged offending group. Their results also suggested that the presence of childhood behavioural problems, truancy, police contact, family separation and other social disruption were potentially the most important factors in trying to understand why their study group engaged in criminal behaviour (Winter, Holland & Collins 1997: 603-6). These findings are consistent with the experiences of the participants. Chuan, Roland, John and Tony reported childhood and adolescent behavioural problems and truancy. Roland, Peter and Tony had their first contact with the police in their teens. Chuan, Peter, John, Tony and Joanne reported family dysfunction which, for Peter and Joanne, included sexual abuse.

Supports

Prison is a very threatening experience as the case studies testify. The most successful and supportive specialist service appears to be the one received in prison from the Disability Services Unit. The particular support provided by the Disability Services Unit in the prison system gave the participants, with the exception of Peter, a 'life-raft' in a very turbulent and squalling environment. Moreover, it is concerned with the welfare of prisoners beyond the prison experience. It has an emphasis on post-release planning so that prisoners move into the community with support networks in place.

Community support networks are important for people with an intellectual disability at any time but they are particularly important after the prison experience. This is because of the post-traumatic stress that may result from the violence and abuse experienced in prison and because of the adjustment difficulties experienced in moving from a highly structured and restrictive life in gaol to the freedom of the outside world. The Disability Services Unit liaises with the Department of Community Services, the Department of Ageing, Disability and Home Care, families and advocates to assist in establishing supports for prisoners on release from custody. The explicit intention of this is to manage their vulnerability at the time of transition and to reduce the risks of recidivism long term.

Notwithstanding the obvious post-release needs of prisoners with an intellectually disability and the good intentions of the Disability Services Unit, the success of their efforts is heavily constrained by the lack of supports and services in the community. Indeed, whilst it is not possible to draw any hard and fast conclusions from the case studies, if there is a theme to be found in the participants' stories, it is perhaps one of a lifetime of services absent, or present but unco-ordinated resulting in little effect. It is not a new theme for people with an intellectual disability at risk of contact with the criminal justice system. The literature is full of recommendations for vocational, residential, social and therapeutic programs, all of which have merit. The challenge has always been government commitment, funding and implementation. Articulating this challenge and strategising a process is the purpose of the Framework Report (Simpson, Martin & Green 2001).

The themes of the Framework Report

As previously mentioned, the case studies are six of the 11 from *The Framework Project*. In addition to the 11 case studies, the investigative stage of the project examined the existing service system in NSW, consulted extensively with stakeholders, reviewed Australian and international literature and explored the implications of the case studies with a clinical issues group. As a result of these inputs, the project made 117 recommendations that articulated actions for the following *seven key themes*.

1. **The provision of support and services to the target group is a cross-agency problem** It is neither feasible nor appropriate for specialist disability services alone to seek to address the needs of the target group. A wide range of government and community agencies needs to be accessible to the target group and provide them with an equitable share of services.

2. **Equity of access to disability services** At present, specialist disability services usually do not provide services to the target

group. This needs to change. The risk to an individual flowing from his or her offending behaviour should be recognised as an important component in assessing relative need for disability services under the *Disability Services Act* 1993 (NSW) standards.

3. **A specialist capacity** A specialist capacity is needed with expertise in assessment, interventions to address offending behaviour, support coordination and related tasks. The specialist capacity would do some direct work with the target group and foster a better response from existing generic and disability services. The recommended option includes a specialist capacity in disability services comprising:

- *A forensic clinical team* This team would do assessments and design and implement behaviour intervention and support programs for some individuals. It would be a training and consultancy resource to other professionals. It would be multidisciplinary in line with the wide-ranging needs of the target group.
- *A statewide network of forensic support coordinators and forensic support workers* The support coordinators would foster the roles of local services and communities including by being a consultancy and training resource. The support workers would provide a hands-on support and case management role with some members of the target group.
- *Some accommodation* focused on the target group.
- These systems would be linked to existing or proposed specialist capacities in other agencies.

4. **Links with the justice system** Service provision needs to occur in close liaison with the justice system. This would allow the justice system to make well-informed decisions about issues like bail and parole. The report proposes links including:

- Justice plans developed in cooperation between justice system and disability service personnel. These plans would link services that will reduce the likelihood of offending to bonds and parole conditions.
- A specialist capacity in probation and parole and juvenile justice community based services.

5. **Cross-agency cooperation** Given the range of agencies that have roles if the needs of the target group are to be met, cross-agency cooperation is essential. This needs to cover both systemic issues and coordinated responses where an individual has complex cross agency needs.

6. **Prevention and early action** Wherever possible, preventative and early action should occur before offending behaviour becomes entrenched. The roles of schools and child and family services are particularly important here.

7. **Additional budget allocations** There is some scope to improve the situation of the target group through existing services and budget allocations. However, there need to be additional budget allocations if major improvements are to occur.

Last word

In this chapter, the participants' views have been related as closely as possible to the way they were expressed. The concerns raised represent those concerns that were in the forefront of their minds at the time of the interview. It is possible that there were other experiences that would have been relevant that they did not think to mention at the time. As a last word, we return to John and his explanation for the over-representation of people with intellectual disability in the prison system.

> I have heard it all before through CID [Council for Intellectual Disability] and PWD [People With Disabilities] that people with disabilities are being sent to prison on remand or sentences because there are no services available through the Department of Community Services. It is not fair that people with intellectual disability should be sent to prison because services are not available. The courts and the Attorney General's Department should be doing more to ensure that people do get the services. Gaol should be seen as the last resort.

Notes

1   The case studies were developed using information gained fom interviews and files. The files used for Chuan, Roland, Peter and Joanne were from the Department of Corrective Services. John's files were from the Intellectual Disability Rights Service (IDRS) and Tony's file belonged to his advocate.

2   Pseudonyms are used to protect the identity of the participants.

3   The attack for which Chuan received his victim's compensation took place in 1993, prior to the amendment of victims' compensation legislation in NSW (*Victims Support and Rehabilitation Act* 1996) which prevented most claims arising from criminal injuries sustained by prisoners in prison.

4   Evidence suggests that John received his victim's compensation prior to the amendment of victims' compensation legislation in NSW (*Victims Support and Rehabilitation Act* 1996), see note 3 above.

5   The DD Units have recently undergone a name change to 'Additional Support Units'.

Staying Healthy in Prison

The things that are of concern to me in here are the poor quality food, lack of proper medication and medical support, unsafe work practices, discrimination if complaints are made, not providing a smoke-free environment and the sub-standard condition of the cells. I am forced to live in a cell with two smokers who continually smoke whilst we are locked up. I have complained to the senior prison officer and the prisoners concerned have been spoken to but they still continue and it seems that the officer cannot stop this practice. If I take the matter further, then I fear retribution from those in charge as well as the offending prisoners.

Victorian male prisoner

In the hospital, we have no complaints about the cold as it is air conditioned, but having been in the main gaol, I know how cold it gets up there. Tasmania is cold, the yards are fairly open to the elements, and the heaters in the cells are in no way adequate. I don't think anyone should have to put up with being cold.

Tasmanian male prisoner

Sharing cells causes inhumane problems for 95% of prisoners (5% tolerate sharing because of boredom at night). Ararat prison is not suitable for long-term prisoners and should be demolished like Pentridge ASAP. We have a large amount of elderly people in their 70-80s. Most are ex-servicemen. The conditions here would not be tolerated in an elderly citizens home or hostel, or for that matter, in a zoo or RSPCA pound. We have chronically deaf and blind prisoners. Some have limbs missing. Elderly prisoners are mixed up in cells with younger prisoners who often make their lives miserable. Citizens over 60 should not be placed in prisons (like what some European centres practice). ...There are no words in English to describe the conditions elderly people suffer in Victorian prisons and C.O.R.E. cannot care less.

Victorian male prisoner

Re health: the system as it stands is totally inadequate. My health is progressively deteriorating; as requested by myself and other persons (doctors), health issues are not being addressed. I have recently moved from Loddon to Beechworth apparently for medical reasons and under the same (medical) contractor am receiving inadequate treatment. I should not enter this system with my health being 8 points out of 10 with the real possibility of leaving with a permanent deformity through inferior medical treatment which ultimately the Office of Corrections is controlling, not the doctor. I have been advised civil action is a positive action with an 80% chance of a win but this is no compensation if I am a cripple.

Victorian male prisoner

CHAPTER 5

Prisoners of Difference

Greta Bird[1]

There shall be no discrimination on the grounds of race, colour, sex, language, religion, political or other opinion, national or social origin, property, birth or other status.

(Principle 2, *Basic Principles for the Treatment of Prisoners*)

Prisoners' rights

In Australia, the term 'rights' is used in a number of senses. It may refer to rights arising from the common law, the Constitution, federal or State legislation or more broadly from government policies, such as multiculturalism or international instruments to which Australia is a signatory. Rights discourse is also a way of conceptualising a 'multi-cultural law' (Tie 1999: 228-32). If we look specifically at *prisoners'* rights, these derive from international documents, State legislation and the Operations Procedures Manuals of the various Departments of Corrective Services.

Article 10 of the *International Covenant on Civil and Political Rights* states: 'All persons deprived of their liberty shall be treated with humanity and respect for the inherent dignity of the human person'.

This can be regarded as a starting point for an overall principle of prisoners' rights. However, words such as 'humanity' and 'dignity' are capable of many interpretations. International instruments are the product of negotiation in a culturally diverse setting and are couched in broad language that is difficult to incorporate in domestic policies, laws and practices. In response to principles of humanity and dignity, we can develop rights for Australian prisoners and detainees in line with commitments to foundational Australian values of 'fair play', the recognition of the rights of Indigenous peoples and respect for cultural diversity.[2] Our aim should be to attain the highest possible standards.

As Solange Rosa argues, '... prison is a prime place for dehumanisation, thanks to such rituals as strip searches, prison 'greens', being a number, limited personal belongings and the dependence on staff and welfare services for everything' (Rosa 2000: 4).

Background to imprisonment

Michael Ignatieff asserts that 'prisons raise the issue of the morality of state power in its starkest form' (Ignatieff 1978: xii). In much liberal legal theory, there is a social contract between citizens and the state whereby citizens give up some liberty and in return the state maintains public order and ensures the well being of those within its borders (Pateman 1989: 33). This aim is jeopardised by outbreaks of violence and other anti-social acts, such as corporate fraud, and prisons are deemed necessary as a place to warehouse or reform citizens whose status or behaviour is believed to threaten the state. In this theoretical model, all citizens are 'equal before the law'. However, the Australian nation was built on the substantial dispossession of the original inhabitants and policies of racially based exclusion.[3] In reality, issues of race, ethnicity, gender, class and sexuality affect the operation of the criminal justice system today via such mechanisms as the policing and sentencing of 'deviant' bodies. In this chapter, I am looking at the prison experience of non-Anglo citizens and, in order to understand that experience, I want first to explore the context of their imprisonment. This I would argue is, in part, connected to the stereotypes surrounding groups deemed 'other' in Australian society.

A moment's reflection allows these stereotypes to spring to mind. They involve beliefs that members of certain racial or ethnic groups are 'deviant' and constitute a threat to 'Australian' values. 'Moral panics' circulate around the bodies of Indigenous, Indo-Chinese and Muslim Australians and create fears that these 'others' will disturb what Henry Parkes first named the 'crimson thread of kinship' (Bird & McDonell 1997: 122). The response is to call for 'law and order' and a surveillance of 'ethnic gangs' and other sites of ethnic disruption (Cunneen 1995: 111-2).

Australia has a strong commitment to international human rights instruments. However, the basic institutions of politics, law and the economy favour members of the dominant group (Bird 1993: 1). These are the white men, preferably of Anglo-Celtic ethnicity, who are still predominant in terms of numbers and in terms of wealth and political power. These men have been referred to as 'the benchmark'; the further a person falls from their attributes, the more likely she is to suffer personal and systemic discrimination (Thornton 1990: 1). Structural factors provide a background to the over-representation of certain groups in Australian prisons and to the often unconscious ethnocentrism of the treatment prisoners receive.

Reports and articles on the involvement of non-English speaking background (NESB) people with the criminal justice system document the activities of police, lawyers and magistrates. However, they mostly neglect to investigate gaols. They do not, in most cases, even refer to the selection, training and practices of correctional officers,[4] nor do they critically analyse the policies underpinning correctional facilities and the impact of incarceration on this group of prisoners. There are now mechanisms in place to ensure that police officers are cross-culturally trained and legislation has been passed in most jurisdictions to ensure that properly qualified interpreters are used during police interviews and court proceedings. However, research establishes that the same attention has not been given to policies and practices in the correctional system.

As policies such as 'truth in sentencing', 'three strikes' and 'mandatory sentencing' take effect, we see evidence of bias in the criminal justice system. In class terms, we know that 70% of prisoners are unemployed at the time they are incarcerated. Underlying the statistics are elements of racism that infect all Australia's institutions (Bird 1993: 2), including the criminal justice system. Indigenous Australians and Australians from some ethnic backgrounds, for example those born in Vietnam, are over-represented in prison for a range of reasons including the exercise of racially inflected policing, prosecutorial and sentencing discretions and practices. The independent investigation into Victoria's adult private prisons (the Kirby Report) found that 25% of prisoners were born overseas. Indo-Chinese Australians were over-represented, being 4.3% of male prisoners and 6.6% of female prisoners (Private Prisons Investigation Panel 2000: 11).

A similar picture emerges from the juvenile justice system. Chris Cunneen states:

> To the extent that information is available from juvenile justice agencies themselves, it would appear that particular groups of young people are especially vulnerable including young people of Pacific Island, Indo-Chinese and Lebanese background. It is these groups, particularly Indo-Chinese young people, who are significantly over-represented in detention centres (Cunneen 1995: 119-20).[5]

There is, as Adrian Howe points out, a 'lack of theorisation of penality' in relation to women and imprisonment (Howe 1994: 165). A shift in theory from a punitive to a therapeutic regime has had little impact on the day-to-day running of gaols. Non-English speaking background inmates in Australian gaols suffer much of the humiliation and privation of Anglo inmates. However, there are also perceptions that they are treated less favourably because of the racism in the prison sector (Easteal 1992; Bird & McDonell: 1997). The *Report of the National Inquiry into Racist Violence* documented cases of racist violence by staff at the Brisbane Correctional Centre and Bathurst Gaol, particularly in connection with strip searches (Human Rights and Equal Opportunity Commission 1991).[6] However, research studies conducted in prison and focused solely on racism are not available.[7]

More focused research

My proposal in 1995 to undertake research, together with Dr Patricia Easteal, into the experiences of male and female NESB inmates in New South Wales (NSW) gaols was rejected by the Department of Corrective Services. We were advised that permission to undertake the study was denied on grounds connected to the project methodology and the claim by the Department that such research would impact on 'the privacy of prisoners'.[8] Dr Easteal's earlier interviews with non-English speaking background prisoners are published in *The Forgotten Few: Overseas Born Women in Australian Prisons* (1992). Details revealed there establish that many inmates suffered harassment from other prisoners connected to their perceived difference. Bird and McDonell's case study of Muslim women held in Grafton Gaol also pointed to the institutional racism that made incarceration difficult for prisoners of non-English speaking background (Bird & McDonell 1997).

The books and research studies on incarceration refer to the position of NESB prisoners in only a few pages, paragraphs or sentences. While there has been a study into racist violence in the Australian community, the inquiry did not explore the prison system. The Royal Commission into Aboriginal Deaths in Custody found instances of a breach of a duty of care by correctional officers towards Aboriginal and Torres Strait Islander inmates (Royal Commission into Aboriginal Deaths in Custody 1991). However, there has not been a major inquiry into the deaths in custody or general experiences of NESB inmates.

To flesh out the information from published research and to obtain current data, I therefore conducted a series of semi-structured interviews with workers at agencies in Victoria, primarily the Federation of Community Legal Centres, Flat-Out (an agency that assists released prisoners obtain accommodation) and the Prisoners' Advocacy Service. A small number of interviews were also conducted with a prison activist and with recently released Indo-Chinese women.[9]

The focus of the fieldwork for this chapter is Victoria and the majority of Victorian prisoners in 2001, unlike those in other States, are in the private sector, although the Bracks Labor government is now reversing that phenomenon (Astudillo 2000). There is not the space here to canvass the arguments for and against private prisons. However, I note Richard Harding's conclusion in his study: 'The evidence is clear that private prisons could act as a catalyst for improvement across the whole prison system, but only if they are effectively regulated and properly accountable' (Harding 1997: 165).

The women's gaols focused on in this chapter are Deer Park (a large, assessment and high security facility, recently returned to public control) and Tarrengower (a low security rural facility).

In Victoria, policies are in place to allow prisoners human rights such as religious freedom, freedom of association and cultural expression and access to education.[10] However, on a day-to-day level, it is clear from published research and fieldwork conducted for this chapter that the policies themselves are deficient and the practices flowing from the policies require change.

Religious freedom

The UN minimum human rights standards for prisoners include the right to religious freedom and this right is included in Victorian legislation. The *Corrections Act* 1986 (Vic) guarantees prisoners the right to practice the religion of their choice.[11] The recent independent investigation into private prisons in Victoria includes a section detailing the implementation of the right to religious freedom. However, there is little reference in either the Act or the investigation's report to the multicultural nature of Australian society.

The policy operating in prisons appears to guarantee rights to religious freedom yet, in practice, it privileges the Christian religions. The relevant statutes should include a reference to the major religions, including Christianity, Islam, Judaism, Buddhism and Indigenous spirituality. In the Kirby Report, the independent investigation into private prisons concluded:

> [a]ll prison providers fund chaplaincy programs within their prison. CORE [Public Correctional Enterprise] directly funds a number of chaplains from a range of denominations to provide services within the public prison system. Each private provider funds a position of Coordinator then negotiates to ensure the prisoners' religious needs are met. (Private Prisons Investigation Panel 2000: 75)

However, evidence was given to the inquiry that current arrangements in the private prisons were 'unsatisfactory ... because the contracts between the government and the private prison operators are very vague on the issue of religious practice' (Private Prisons Investigation Panel 2000: 75).

The over-imprisonment of groups such as Indigenous and Indo-Chinese Australians suggests that spiritual leaders appropriate to these groups should be available to prisoners. 'In [one Victorian prison] Catholic and Baptist chaplains visited and a Catholic nun' (former inmate).

There were no religious figures appointed from other denominations. The Indo-Chinese women requested a Buddhist religious adviser and a Chinese-speaking Buddhist monk was contacted and attended the prison. The problem with this arrangement was that none of the women could speak a Chinese language. Finally, a Vietnamese-speaking Buddhist nun came to minister to Buddhist inmates. The Indo-Chinese informants noted that this person was not able to move about the prison as freely as the Catholic nun was. In these subtle ways, inmates perceived that the Christian religion is taken as the 'norm' against which the non-Christian is seen as 'other'.

> One Muslim woman had to fight for permission to wear the hijab. It was argued that she could hide stuff in the scarf. This issue was portrayed as a security problem. The religious principle was not regarded as a priority. (agency worker)

Incidents such as these demonstrate that religious freedom is naturalised for Christians but is a site of contention for those of non-mainstream faiths.

The prison authorities set aside a space for religious observance. This is designed to be non-denominational. However, the presence of the Christian cross designates it as a place sacred to Christian worship. It is perceived by some non-Christians as an alienating place. In Australia, 1996 census data show that significant religious affiliations include Jews, Muslims, Buddhists and Hindus.[12] The religious services that take place in this particular prison space are Christian. As an agency worker reported: 'The [chapel] space is a very Christian one being dominated by a representation of the crucified Christ'.

One informant, a recently released Indo-Chinese woman, was interviewed in her living room at home. A Buddhist shrine dominated this space. Teng (a pseudonym) told me that she could not have her religious icons with her in the gaol.

This investigation received a submission asserting that:

> [c]haplains from faiths other than Christianity face additional problems in negotiating on behalf of their members for access to appropriate facilities for the practice of their faith because their requirements are not well understood by prison staff.[13]

The Report concluded that religious freedom was difficult to achieve in the prison sector.

> The particular problems of Muslim prisoners in gaining access to chaplaincy services, to halal meals and fasting during Ramadan were highlighted in submissions to the Investigation Panel. The panel endorses the concerns expressed in the submissions regarding the necessity to facilitate access by prisoners of faiths other than Christianity to chaplaincy and faith appropriate services (Private Prisons Investigation Panel 2000: 76).

In Grafton Gaol, Bird and McDonell found that a chaplain from a Christian denomination is provided who is sensitive to the spiritual needs of prisoners. The chaplain will try to meet spiritual requests. However, the request must come from the inmate and where people cannot speak English, 'communicating their religious needs is problematic' (Bird & McDonell 1997: 128-9).

Communication

One of the rights commonly thought to belong to Australians is the right to 'free speech' or communication. However, this 'right' is neither legislated for nor part of the common law. Speech is hemmed in with restrictions arising from laws such as those dealing with blasphemy and defamation. The High Court has implied in the Constitution some rights to speech but these are connected to political speech (*Nationwide News Pty Ltd v Wills* (1992) 177 CLR 1; *Australian*

Capital Television Pty Ltd v Commonwealth (1992) 177 CLR 106). Only speech unregulated by law is free. However, communicating with others by speech and writing are activities closely associated with being human.

The right to communicate with family members, friends and legal and other advisers is severely curtailed for all prisoners. Further, NESB Australians are often unable to exercise even those limited rights accorded to the incarcerated. 'There is racism in the system and a refusal to use interpreters largely in the 'Asian' community' (former inmate).

Recently released prisoners referred to a failure to provide interpreters for Indo-Chinese speakers. An Indo-Chinese Victorian prisoner with some fluency in the English language was called often into the gaol office and asked to interpret for other Indo-Chinese prisoners. This practice is prevalent too in NSW gaols, although departmental policy is to use inmates to translate only in emergencies.

Staff have traditionally relied on other prisoners from the same or similar backgrounds to translate directions. However, many prisoners have expressed resentment at being required to translate for others, arguing that they sacrifice work bonuses or education hours to explain procedures to fellow prisoners. As well, it is often difficult for prisoners to rely on other prisoners to translate for them, with the threat of inaccurate translation, sudden transfers, and issues of trust to be negotiated. (Rosa 2000: 207)

As an agency worker expressed it, 'there are misinterpretations and the practice breaches privacy'. Even legal aid workers and private solicitors, who often speak what an agency worker described as the 'mumbo jumbo of legal language', rarely arrange for interpreters to be present at interviews.

Prisoners can only make calls to approved numbers and approval can take weeks. The phone numbers are then attached to the prisoner's swipe card. No 1800 numbers can be included. The interpreter services' 1800 numbers cannot be accessed and other numbers for interpreter services must be paid for at STD rates, which are prohibitive for prisoners. This situation makes it difficult for non-English speaking prisoners to communicate with the world outside the prison (Prisoners' Advocacy Service interview). Problems also arise because of authorities' failure to provide or facilitate access to qualified interpreters and because of the high cost of telephone calls and the complexities of Telstra's Arunta[14] phone system.

As Bird and McDonell wrote about Muslim women incarcerated in Grafton Gaol:

Hanifa and Fatima feel 'absolutely isolated' in Grafton. No one else speaks their language, Hanifa's child has been taken away, and there are no provisions for their special diet, or for ritual washing. There is no access to an interpreter during their eight days in gaol and their closeness to the male prisoners is culturally inappropriate.

Although they are allowed to make any number of calls this freedom is constrained by reality. They can purchase a phone card, if they have the money. They can make calls, but they can only do so in their one hour a day out of the cell, and then only if the phone is free. This freedom to make contact with the outside world is rendered further illusory given their inability to speak English. (Bird & McDonell 1997: 128)

Rights of privacy

It's worse than having a baby or a medical, that's the honest truth, because you've got no dignity when you're behind bars. (Hampton 1993: 42)

Many women — particularly those who have suffered past sexual abuse — find it so shocking that they prefer not to relive the degradation by talking about it. (Devlin 1998: 36)

A basic human right is the right to privacy. Prisoners have these rights severely curtailed because part of their punishment is a reduction in personal autonomy. There is, however, provision for phone calls and prison visits and those in low security may be granted day release for family contact.

For NESB Australians, there may be impediments in the exercise of these rights above those for Anglo prisoners. Everybody dislikes strip-searches. However, for Muslim women, religious beliefs make this practice particularly abhorrent. The requirement that visitors and prisoners must be strip-searched before and after visits and inmates before and after day release can lead to a refusal by these women to take advantage of the right to associate with family and friends. As Craig Minogue writes in Chapter 12 describing his 'day out': 'This is no day out, prefaced and concluded as it is by the borderline sexual assault of the strip search ...'.

As Blanche Hampton writes, recording the voice of an inmate, '[y]ou've got men who are having the power and the authority to strip search you'.

According to the Bulletin, strip searching of female inmates by males is permitted in an emergency or when staff shortages require it, despite departmental protestations that it never occurs. (Hampton 1993: 144)[15]

Correctional officers

How can people with limited skills themselves be expected to deal appropriately with culturally sensitive issues. (agency worker)

Correctional officers in Victoria undergo a six-week training program. Informants stated that all correctional officers were 'Skips', or Aussies; that is, they are born in Australia or an English-speaking country and are of an Anglo-European background. Correctional officers are not well educated. One officer admitted to an inquiry into the deaths of three women in Deer Park that he was not able to read the facility's policy on self-harm.

The Kirby Report stated:

At present [October 2000] there is no formally established recruitment standard across Victorian corrections ... [I]nterviews with management, correctional staff and prisoners highlighted the seemingly universal lack of confidence and credibility among key stakeholders regarding the adequacy of current training provided to custodial officers (Private Prisons Investigation Panel 2000: 48).

Given the multi-cultural nature of Australian society and the complex cultural issues that arise for negotiation in the prison system, it is disheartening that the staff selection processes and training programs appear overwhelmingly biased toward Anglo-Australian culture. In such a climate, stereotypical beliefs and mono-cultural practices unconsciously become embedded in correctional institutions.

Education

All prisoners shall have the right to take part in cultural activities and education aimed at the full development of the human personality. (Principle 6, *Basic Principles for the Treatment of Prisoners*)

Victorian gaols have a range of cultural and educational activities aimed at the development of prisoners. However, these are difficult to access for those who do not have an adequate grasp of English. Informants asked such questions as 'How can you learn to use a computer if you don't speak English and the instructions are given only in English?'.

English language classes are offered on a very limited basis, which does not allow English language skills to be quickly acquired. The classes are limited because too few resources are allocated for this purpose. For example, at Tarrengower, there were few Indo-Chinese women; no English language classes were provided, just a workbook and advice to 'do your homework yourself'. None of the teachers there could speak an Indo-Chinese language. At Deer Park, with a larger number of Indo-Chinese women, there are English language classes two days per week.

> In the women's prison there are [NESB] women who want to learn literacy and English. They are provided with about 2 hours per week in a group setting. They are then told to take their books back to their rooms and 'learn the language'. This is no way to learn a language. (agency worker)

Conclusion

> These special arrangements ... will generally be worse than the normal arrangements, because difference is presumed to be an aberration or deviation. (Hudson 2000: 178)

As Adrian Howe has argued, 'some women, notably black and other minority women, suffer from the coercion and oppression of institutionalised racism within Western criminal justice systems' (Howe 1994: 164). This study has demonstrated that there is little published research on the conditions for NESB Australians in gaol. Inmates or ex-inmates, agency workers and prison activists provide the best evidence available of what is happening 'inside'.

There is an urgent need for an inquiry into the position of female and male NESB inmates in Australian gaols. There is evidence that certain racial and ethnic groups are over-represented in the criminal justice system and that this is, in part, connected to racist practices. There is a perception of ethnocentrism operating in gaols; however it has not been clearly documented. Often the racism is unconscious and is denied by members of the dominant group. In this study, informants told of stereotypes held by correctional services staff about 'Asian' women which led to their being treated less favourably in terms of release visits, work rosters and educational opportunities. As Sue Zelinka points out, those who experience racism often perceive it as more of a problem than those who have never experienced it (Zelinka 1995: 213). If Australia is to live up to the highest standards in terms of treating prisoners with humanity and dignity, it must pay special attention to the recruitment and training of correctional officers. As Blanche Hampton has argued, 'Racism and sexism are ... areas where effective screening should take place' (Hampton 1993: 126).

Nearly ten years have passed since Patricia Easteal's book on NESB women in prison, a group she called 'forgotten', was published. Little has changed since her research and the suggestions she offered for improvement are still valid today. I conclude with a quote from Barbara Hudson.

> Once the subject of justice is given back her [or his] social context and flesh-and-blood reality it becomes clear that difference is the standard case ... the task of justice is to find ways of hearing non-commensurate perspectives and balancing competing or conflicting rights. (Hudson 2000: 178)

Notes

1   I would like to thank Charandev Singh for reading an early draft of this chapter and making valuable comments and Jo Bird for assisting with internet searches. Other sources are acknowledged in the section on field research.

2   Australians have not yet repatriated their Constitution and have not created a document setting out foundational values. The values mentioned here have been widely accepted by the population, however, and have been subject to bipartisan government policies. They are encapsulated in documents such as the *National Agenda for a Multicultural Australia* (Department of the Prime Minister and Cabinet, Office of Multicultural Affairs, (1989) *National Agenda for a Multicultural Australia*, AGPS, Canberra (since replaced by *A New Agenda for Multicultural Australia*; www.immi.gov.au/multicultural/agenda.htm#agenda)). These values are contested by a minority of citizens who perceive cultural diversity as a threat to 'Australian values' (that is, the British heritage). I have not included 'mateship' as a shared value because of its connotations of fraternity.

3   The Constitution, even when amended at the referendum in 1967 (Coper 1987: 371; Patapan 2000: 142), was premised on the now discredited doctrine of terra nullius and the legal system did not allow for full citizenship for Indigenous people until the *Mabo* case in 1992 (if indeed full Indigenous citizenship has been achieved) (*Mabo v Queensland (No 2)* (1992) 175 CLR 1). The first piece of policy legislation on this issue from the Commonwealth Parliament was the *Immigration Restriction Act* 1901 (Cth), designed to prevent the entry of non-British immigrants.

4   See, for example, Australian Law Reform Commission 1992.

5   Regarding Indo-Chinese youth, see also Doan 1995.

6   On the issue of strip searches in gaol, see also Rosa 2000 and Devlin 1998.

7   Books such as Angela Devlin's *Invisible Women* (1998) and Blanche Hampton's *Prisons and Women* (1993) make some mention of the specific needs and concerns of non-English speaking women, but this is in the context of dealing with women's imprisonment in general.

8   Dr Easteal's earlier interviews with NESB prisoners are published in Easteal 1992.

9   I would like to acknowledge and thank Renata Alexander (Feminist Lawyers), Amanda George (Federation of Community Legal Services), Catherine Gow (Prisoners' Advocacy Service) and Kay Thompson (Flat-Out) for their assistance as well as those newly released Indo-Chinese women who shared their stories with me and whom I shall not name to protect their privacy.

10   Eg see the *Corrections Act* 1986 (Vic) s 47; the UN *Basic Principles for the Treatment of Prisoners*; and the *Declaration on the Rights of People Belonging to National or Ethnic, Religious or Linguistic Minorities* (1993) art 2(1).

11   See s 47(1)(i). For a discussion of the NSW situation, see Rosa 2000.

12   Australian Bureau of Statistics, *2002 Year Book Australia*, No 84, ABS Catalogue No 1301.0, Canberra, Table 5.57 Religious Affiliation, p 108.

13   Submission from the Chaplains Advisory Committee to the Criminal Justice Sector in Victoria to the Independent Investigation into the Management and Operation of Victoria's Private Prisons: Private Prisons Investigation Panel 2000: 76.

14   The Arunta system supplied by Telstra allows each prisoner to nominate up to six telephone numbers which are linked to a phone card and PIN. Prisoners need special permission to telephone other numbers. Outside calls are no longer forwarded to prisoners on their wings.

15   See also *Correctional Centres (General) Regulation* 1995 (NSW) reg 24.

Catering for Prisoners Speaking English as a Second Language

In 1998, I was sentenced to three years in prison, with the sentencing judge recommending that I be eligible for parole after 12 months. In 1999, this parole was denied to me, with the Parole Board stating that I remained a high risk to re-offend if released. This view was obviously not shared by the sentencing judge; otherwise, he would not have recommended a short parole eligibility period.

The Parole Board prefaced its remarks by stating:

> You need one of the sex offender programs and a cognitive skills program to enable you to address your offending behaviour. Despite the fact that you have participated and made positive progress in the Literacy Program, your English comprehension skills are not sufficient to enable you to participate in the cognitively behaviourally based programs. Even with the use of an interpreter, the Board is advised you would face difficulties achieving successful completion of these programs.

In 1998, I commenced the Cognitive Skills program as required by the Department, but was removed from it after completing two sessions, with the report reading:

> R has considerable difficulty completing much of the written work required in the program. He also demonstrated difficulty understanding and translating a number of basic concepts in the English Language.

I would like to point out that I completed a College Education in [country of origin] before I came to Australia, so I am not lacking in mental skills.

In 2000 one-third remission was also denied. The Corrective Services system in Queensland allows that an inmate be granted one-third remission of his sentence if he has been of good conduct and industry ...

The situation is that the Department requires me to do courses which I am perfectly happy to do, then tells me I cannot do them because of my English language deficiency, and then tells me it will not grant me the normal entitlement to remission because I cannot do the program they will not let me do.

Queensland male prisoner

PART TWO

Regulating Prisons and Prisoners' Rights

CHAPTER 6

'Not the King's enemies': Prisoners and their Rights in Australian History

Mark Finnane & Tony Woodyatt

> Those who break the law – whether it be contained in the Crimes Act or the Liquor Act – are punishable by the King's Courts, but they do not become the King's enemies.
>
> (*Gibbons v Duffell* (1932) 47 CLR 520 at 535 per Evatt J)

Introduction

As a society founded in the first place as a penal settlement, modern Australia has had a complex history in its treatment of prisoners' rights. This chapter examines the transitions from the convict period when prisoners were active advocates of their own rights to the high age of the prison when the language of rights was largely suppressed. The legal and administrative impediments to prisoner retention of civil and political rights during what has been characterised as the era of 'welfare' penality will be examined. The historical sources of a contemporary revival of rights advocacy, by prisoners and by penal reform groups, will be reviewed. The chapter draws on the authors' historical research on the history of punishment and imprisonment as well as their role in the establishment of Australia's first independent prisoners' legal service.

Regarding their proposed collaboration on a book about criminal law in Australia, John Barry advised George Paton in 1944 of the problems he faced in dealing with the conditions of prisons: 'What happens to the prisoner after he is convicted is a dark mystery which most practitioners do not trouble to resolve' (Barry Papers MS 29 April 1944). The silence and ignorance about what happened after sentencing signified a historical moment. The 'dark mystery' was a product of an era in which a prisoner's life was most likely to be subjected to a regime of supervision free of judicial oversight or even of effective political accountability. To study the history of prisoners' rights is to approach a process of assertion, deconstruction and reconstruction of rights. We might capture graphically the history of prisoners' rights in Australia since the late 18th century as a 'reverse J-curve': rights asserted by those under sentence were gradually whittled away by the growth of administrative regulation, defining more precisely what it meant to be a citizen, and what imprisonment thus took away. Only in the last three decades have we seen some move back towards an affirmation of prisoners' rights and some enhancement of the mechanisms for protecting them.

It will be evident that the approach to the history of prisoners' rights taken here will be historical, not philosophical. We do not wish to approach the topic with a preconceived statement of what prisoners' rights are or might be. Rather, the intention is to provide an account of the relation between changing forms of imprisonment and the assertion of rights (very often implied rather than positively articulated) by prisoners and others concerned with their experiences. In summary, the argument is as follows.

At the outset of European settlement in Australia, the dominant form of punishment under the imported criminal law was that of transportation. The conditions of settlement allowed unusual freedoms to many who were still serving sentences – and assertion of rights through common law litigation was common. In the course of the 19th century, the consolidation of the penitentiary as the preferred mode of punishment proceeded alongside a construction of citizen rights that implicitly, and sometimes explicitly, excluded prisoners, or categories of them. Judicial reluctance to intervene in administrative processes was balanced in part by a readiness of political representatives to entertain appeals by prisoners themselves against the more egregious institutional abuses. At the same time, penal and administrative reform that focused on the rehabilitation of prisoners rendered them into objects of a tutelary state that further diminished their status. Not only were prisoners deprived of citizen rights by virtue of their incarceration, but they also became objects of positive intervention aimed at changing their behaviour and disposition. In the last third of the 20th century, however, there was some reversal of these historical processes as a just-deserts framework in sentencing was asserted alongside affirmations by prisoners and support groups of their rights, entitlements and the need to protect them institutionally. While more recent changes have diminished the influence of just-deserts principles, a range of institutional supports and processes has in the last 20 years enabled a more confident assertion of prisoners' rights. In translating into reality the judicial observation which forms the epigraph to this chapter, enunciated by Justice HV Evatt of the High Court in 1932, the joint affirmation and protection of prisoners' rights may be said to have played a vital role in turning around the writing down of a prisoner's status during the high age of the penitentiary.

The convicts assert their rights

In establishing a penal colony in New South Wales (NSW), the British government sought to reinstate a form of punishment that had been threatened with extinction by the outbreak of the American War of Independence. Scarcely had Botany Bay begun than Jeremy Bentham was embarked on a philosopher's crusade against it, urging the advantages of the 'Panopticon' penitentiary. The convict colonies, however had a long life and were the means by which many attained a new status in a new land.

At least some among the convicts possessed an assertive sense of their own rights. The language of rights, in particular its moral appeal to those which were said to be the birthright of free-born Englishmen, flowed over into convict sensibilities and the claiming of rights was facilitated by the conditions of convict settlement. We can summarise briefly the ways in which this became evident.

In the first place, although convicted felons were burdened at home by civil disabilities, such as the loss of a right to sue, the early colonial courts ignored, perhaps even connived at ignoring, such restrictions. In his study, *The Rule of Law in a Penal Colony*, Neal has highlighted the extraordinary facts concerning the first civil action in the colony, brought by the convicts Henry and Susannah Kable, who successfully sued a ship's captain for the loss of a parcel containing their possessions.

> [T]he first sitting of a civil court in Australia and the first civil case to be heard, occurred at the behest of two convicts under sentence .... It vindicated the property rights of two convicts and publicly demonstrated the ability even of convicts to invoke the legal process in the new colony. (Neal 1991: 6)

As the convict colony developed, a local system of pardons saw to it that 'ticket of leave' convicts had extraordinary freedoms. In the words of Kercher, 'ticket holders lived as if Australia were a vast debtors' prison, confined by the walls and some regulations, but otherwise free to live as they could afford' (Kercher 1995: 32). Of course, this did not mean that convicts prior to obtaining their ticket of leave were not subject to the rigours of punishment that was seen to fit their status. And so, a second instance of assertion and recognition of convict rights was evident in the phenomenon of convict actions against the masters to whom they had been assigned. Convict protest against conditions of labour imposed by pastoralists and others they worked for in the 1820s and 1830s has been described by Atkinson (1979). Among the weapons used were those of industrial protest, including arson and go-slows, but there was also a resort to the law. Hence, convicts in the early decades of the colony could and did act against their masters in civil suits. As Kercher has shown, even after the formal re-institution in 1820 of the common law of attaint, which prevented convicts holding property and suing or giving evidence in the courts, colonial conditions could still justify convict freedoms unknown to English law. And in the argument of John Hirst, English law itself, especially the Masters and Servants Acts, provided access to the courts for aggrieved convicts on assignment to masters (Kercher 1995: ch 2; J Hirst 1983: 108-13). Only as the winds of change in the convict system brought to the colonies all the elements of the penitentiary were convicts effectively shut out of the liberties they had unusually enjoyed in the NSW penal experiment.

The fluidity of early colonial social and political relations thus allowed some assertion of rights in spite of the status of being a sentenced prisoner. At the same time, the status of being sentenced placed convicts under systems of exceptional cruelty and the arbitrary rule of overseers and governors. Popular historical accounts of the brutal convict system like those of Robert Hughes rest on layers of historical memory recoiling from such a system but also on the archival evidence of the realities of this system (Hughes 1988).[1] The development of the places of secondary punishment, the prisons within the prison of NSW and Van Dieman's Land, is the other side of the convict story in Australia and overlaps the most important institutional development shaping the subsequent lack of prisoners' rights, that of the penitentiary.

Prisons and the penitentiary regime

Prior to the 19th century, the prison was either a place for holding those undergoing trial or a place of detention for the purpose of correction through labour. The relation between the latter and those monuments of the new system of punishment in the 19th century has been a matter of historical dispute (Spierenburg 1991). With respect to our focus on prisoners' rights, however, there were a number of aspects of the penitentiary development that, in the longer term, shaped the restriction of these rights.

In the first place, the very rationale of the penitentiary was the subjection of the prisoner to a uniformity in regime; an eradication of individual differences and an elimination of communication between prisoners were the centrepieces of this program of reform of the convicted prisoner. While Australian prisons tended to become hybrids of succeeding fashions in institutional design (Kerr 1988), their dominant regimes were those of the Victorian penitentiary in its various demeanours, using separation, silence and labour in various combinations to assert authority over prisoners who were incarcerated as punishment for their crimes.

Secondly, the design of the penitentiary regime was reinforced by statute and regulation. In place of the chaos of the 18th century prison, with its porous boundaries, and its privatised regimes of supply, the public penitentiary of the 19th century was an institution whose order was the object of close definition. Prisoners had a status in Acts and regulations – but as objects of detention, not subjects of limited rights. Regimes of punishment, of diet, of daily scheduling of prison labour, reflection and sleep ordered prisoners' lives. We can see this in the Acts and regulations defining prison life in the 19th century, changes which also signified a tightening of the administrative bonds around the prison, with a consequent diminution of prisoner options.

The 1840 *Prisons Regulation Act* in NSW, and its successor consolidated *Prisons Act* of 1899, may stand as an instance. The 1840 Act empowered the Governor to proclaim prisons and gaols and made the Sheriff responsible for their 'charge care and direction' (s 3). The gaols and prisons were to be governed by rules and regulations which in turn established, in often minute detail, the everyday life of the prisoner. Prisoners of the 7th class, for example, were instructed as follows on their exercise of one hour each day.

> At the order 'Prepare for exercise' the prisoner shall, as soon as the door is opened, move out of the cell to the exercise circle, and take up

the position assigned to him by the officer: at the word "One" he shall stoop down and take hold of the rope handle attached to the marching-chain; at the word "Two" he shall at once assume an erect position, retaining hold of the marching-chain, and so remain at attention until the officer calls "Walk round". (*Regulations for the Management of Gaols* 1901, reg 35.10)

The 1840 Act focused especially on the maintenance of order in the prison, prescribing the mode of dealing with disciplinary offences through the office of Visiting Justice. Under s 12, the Visiting Justice had the power to hear complaints against prisoners for a wide range of offences, including the blanket provision of 'disobedience of the rules of the prison'. But some measure of external appeal was still allowed the prisoner since any conviction by the Visiting Justice could be appealed to the Quarter Sessions (*Prison Regulations Act* 1840 (NSW) s 20). Whatever the use made of this appeal right, it had disappeared by the end of the 19th century, while the disciplinary hearings and punishment powers of the Visiting Justice remained (*Prisons Act* 1899 (NSW) ss 14-19). Such writing down of the rights of convicted prisoners was consistent with the changes that wrought the late 19th century prison an institution for the rehabilitation of immoral or defective subjects more than a place for the punishment of offenders. We examine later the implications of this change.

So the foundation of prison discipline was the system of rules and regulations established under the authority of the various prisons Acts. While these set out in detail what kinds of treatment a prisoner might expect, at no stage could these be regarded as rights. Their rationale was the good order of the institution and the punishment of prisoners for the duration of their sentence. When the High Court was called on to express its opinion on the matter in two cases in the first half of the 20th century, its judgment made clear the inseparable relation between prison regulations and prison discipline. In the words of Justice Dixon in *Flynn v The King* (1949) 79 CLR 1 (at 8), previous cases in Australia and Britain had established '[a]n interpretation of the power to make prison regulations and of the regulations made thereunder as directed to discipline and administration and not the legal rights of prisoners'. By extension, the long-standing colonial innovation of the marks system, in the form of Western Australia's remissions system (a prison regime for encouragement of good conduct, rewarding such by early release), did not 'confer on prisoners a legal right to be set at liberty, but is concerned only with the management and discipline of the gaols' (*Flynn v The King* (1949) 79 CLR 1 at 7 per Dixon J).

The 19th century thus laid the foundation for a system that for much of the subsequent century was also a world almost unknown to the law. The twin pillars of external inspection, intended to monitor conditions and gaol governance, could be found in the offices of the Visiting Justice, an English inheritance from an age in which gaols had been local institutions subject to local governing elites, and the Inspector-General or Comptroller-General as the office was known in NSW. While these offices had statutory functions, the confusion of responsibilities entailed in gaol managers also being from time to time gaol judges is well illustrated in the intimate accounts by prison governor JB Castieau of life inside Melbourne's prisons from the 1850s.

Castieau was a humane and generally principled governor, so his observations on his own prison might be taken as representing the softer end of the punishment system, seen from a prisoner's perspective. Part of his duties required his overseeing visits to the prison by any officials or judicial officers, including the Visiting Justice. His records of these visits suggest the way in which they might become routinised but also the extent to which the Visiting Justice was already a vital part of the prison's authority relations.

[*Tuesday 20 February 1855*] The Visiting Justice called and put his name in the Book.

[*Friday 4 May 1855*] Nothing of particular consequence occurred during business hours. The Visiting Justice and Mr Price the Inspector of Penal Estabts visited and inspected.

[*Thursday 12 July 1855*] The Visiting Justice sentenced a prisoner to four months labour in irons for striking one of the Turnkeys. This was a secondary punishment for the turnkey returned the blow with compound interest

[*Saturday 21 July 1855*] Visiting Justice called there were no complaints for him.

[*Monday 6 August 1855*] Mr Wintle & the Visiting Justice were here this morning, as we were mustering the prisoners for the Visiting Magistrate's inspection, one of them a notorious vagrant of the name of Thomas Jones came forward and struck me a blow, as may be supposed I immediately returned the compliment & partly from my blow and partly from what was, I believe an intentional slip my antagonist fell to the ground.

Dr Youl [the Visiting Justice] immediately tried him for the Assault to which he pleaded guilty & put forward as his only excuse that when previously he had asked me for a pair of shoes I had told him to wear what he had got on. He was sentenced to six months labor in Irons. If I did not know this customer so well I should regret his receiving so heavy a punishment on my account, but he has since I have been connected with the Gaols been a continual nuisance to the authorities, on receiving his last sentence at the Police Court, he was told by the Magistrate that he would be sent to break stones for three months. It is very few stones I'll break was his impudent rejoinder.

(Castieau diaries, Mss 2218)

Castieau's candid account makes clear how discipline and control were constructed both by informal (indeed violent) and formal responses. The end always was the maintenance of authority within the prison but the readiness with which physical blows would be traded between prisoner and keeper suggests the brutal nature of this authority. In this world, the Visiting Justice was an indispensable aid to the governor when exemplary punishment was sought.

[*Tuesday 10 June 1856*] I brought a poor devil before the Visiting Justice for Insubordination & got him four days additional sentence. I am not anxious or even desirous to punish those under my charge, but am occasionally compelled to do so in defence of discipline & the preservation of something approaching decency & order.

(Castieau diaries, Mss 2218)

A year later, Castieau had transferred to the Beechworth Gaol, where we see that there was at least some pretence to justice standards in the adjudication of a case in which a prisoner was seen to have been provoked.

[*Tuesday 30 June 1857*] The Visiting Justice was at the [Beechworth] Gaol in the morning and tried the prisoner that I spoke about on Sunday for misconduct. The fellow escaped in consequence of the irritation he professed to have received at my hands, and because the Senior Turnkey in giving his evidence made use of a threat stating that had this prisoner kicked him as he tried to do, He the Senior Turnkey would have knocked his teeth down his throat. I was very much annoyed at this as the Magistrate would probably leave the Gaol under an impression that the prisoners were improperly treated and that they were subject to be bullied or knocked about. I told the Magistrate that if he had any such idea I must request him to make a full inquiry into the whole system [within] ... the Gaol.

(Castieau diaries, Mss 2218)

If we are to believe Castieau, the prisoners were ready enough to conduct their own persistent campaigns of complaint. The following case centred on the aggravation caused to the women by their transfer into the cramped conditions of Melbourne Gaol rather than being housed in the new facilities at Pentridge.

[*Saturday 25 March 1871*] Mr Sturt the Visiting Justice came to the Gaol a little after twelve o'clock & heard several Charges against the women. He then went up to the Female Wing where there were several termagants most anxious to make complaints about their food & the treatment they received from the officers. I was very firm & would not yield an inch but told the Visiting Justice the women were not speaking the truth. As usual odious comparisons were drawn between the comforts of Pentridge & the Hulks & the discomforts of Melbourne Gaol. Indirectly also allusions were made to the difference between the Visiting Justices. The one at Pentridge & the Hulk was a thorough gentleman & so by the bye were the Superintendents I was told a few days ago. Miss Davidson again convinced the Visiting Justice by her tongue & manner that she was a most unsuitable prison officer & he made a memo. respecting her in his book.

(Castieau diaries, Mss 2218)

The minimal standards of justice maintained through gaps and discretions allowed in the legislation and regulations was demonstrated equally by the silent understandings between prison governor and other monitoring authorities, only occasionally tested by the latter's reticence or irritation. Again Castieau is a voluble witness.

[*Tuesday 9 October 1855*] Mr Wintle [the Sheriff, then with oversight of the gaols] called & showed off a little by enquiring in the Yards if any of the prisoners had complaints to make to him. I can afford to laugh however at what I consider on his part harmless recreation.

[*Monday 2 December 1872*] In the afternoon Mr Sturt put in an appearance. I attended upon him. The old gentleman was rather queer, seemed to have been primed by someone for he began to make objections to what he had always previously appeared to have been favorable to viz, the asking the prisoners in the different Yards if they wished to make any complaints. This system I have always found a wise one though it is contrary to the Regulations now in force. Mr Sturt also found fault with the office thinking it was not solemn enough for a Court. By Jove if he would only be a little less believing & punish prisoners according to the evidence against them & not according to their own statements, he might try in a barn as effectively as in a Court House with Bench, Dock & other &c's of Justice. He is a good old fellow however & I hope while I am Governor he will continue to be V.J.

(Castieau diaries, Mss 2218)

The systems of inspection, whether by the Visiting Justice or Sheriff or Inspector-General, for the most part rendered prisoners administrative objects, to be managed and disciplined for the duration of their sentence. But as these examples of the everyday work of the Visiting Justice show, there were gaps, and perhaps opportunities, which articulate and more assertive or even rebellious prisoners might seek to exploit. *Horwitz v Connor* (1908) 6 CLR 38 and then *Flynn v The King* in 1949 might be legal authority mandating a century of *judicial* indifference to what went on within gaols but that is not to say that there were never any avenues for complaint and demands for inquiry when abuses multiplied.

Prisoner complaints and their political reception in the late 19th century

In spite of the appearance of closure, the 19th century prison proved more permeable than later generations might imagine. By the 1870s, the oversight of prisons was given to Inspectors or Comptroller-Generals. Their role was to administer institutions according to the statutes and regulations; the evidence from Castieau's diary above also suggests the ways in which a prison governor might be made conscious of the need to attend to abusive behaviour by the warders. In the Australian colonies as in Britain and elsewhere, the press also had an informal function of inspection. No less than today, the press fluctuated between salacious interest in the scandals and abuses of prison life and an advocacy of the need for improved conditions. Occasionally, a muckraking journalist would take it on himself to expose the worst of abuses or simply the random and everyday humiliations of prison life. But prisons were also a place where moral tales about the fate that awaited wrong-doers could be found and there were journalists around ready to expound the moral. Such a person was Julian Thomas, 'The Vagabond', who got himself admitted to a number of Victorian institutions in the 1870s and then wrote of what he found in a series of newspaper articles that were eventually turned into popular volumes (James 1969). Popular journalism was not a trustworthy friend of the prisoner but was nevertheless an important means of affirming some accountability on the part of government for what went on in institutions. But if institutions failed or abused their trust, this was a matter to be addressed through institutional and political reform rather than through an assertion of the individual prisoner's rights, unknown as these were.

The fact that most prisoners served only limited terms assisted the exposure of some abuses. And the more astute prisoners served their own cause by directing complaints to parliamentarians or others. Such complaints might be taken up in parliament or the enthusiastic colonial press, in some cases prompting extensive official inquiry. The colonial liberal politician Henry Parkes chaired a parliamentary inquiry into Sydney's prisons in 1861, prompting evidence from 136 prisoners, including some who were delegated by prisoners at Cockatoo Island to petition on a range of issues such as remissions, alleged illegal treatment and prolonged detention, physical coercion and a lack of complaints mechanisms (Finnane 1997: 144).

Later inquiries similarly appeared, open to the evidence of prisoners while always cautious about their credibility. Located south-west of Sydney, the Berrima Gaol was a so-named 'model prison' but poorly constructed with very small normal cells and especially tiny refractory cells devoid of light. Its regime was strict, in line with its designation as a gaol following the 'separate treatment' system. Throughout the late 1860s and the 1870s, the conditions at Berrima were a subject of critical press comment which focused on excessive punishments, including use of devices such as the 'gag' (a wooden mouth-piece used to silence prisoners who were verbally abusive) (Ramsland 1996: 92-8). With pressure building from both the Sydney press and political critics, the parliament established a select comm-ittee of inquiry before the government relented by appointing a Royal Commission in 1878.

What distinguished this inquiry was the large number of prisoners prepared to come forward to give an account of the abuses that could arise in the closed world of the penitentiary and the difficulty they predictably faced in establishing credibility. The public exposure of the world inside the prison was nevertheless an important achieve-ment of political agitation by prisoners or by those concerned about their plight. Other parliamentary inquiries would give space to prisoner allegations and sometimes acknowledge their credibility; in Western Australia, inquiries into Aboriginal imprisonment at Rottnest Island in 1886 and into conditions at Fremantle Prison in 1898 were important instances (Western Australia Parliament 1884; 1899). In such a world, a legal discourse of rights was yet to be established but it is important nevertheless to acknowledge the kinds of constraints within which institutions were expected to operate. The formal elimination of torture in criminal law was a context for official estimates of what was permissible within the prison. And comple-menting the official benchmark, it is also clear that prisoners' own sense of what was legitimate punishment in effect constituted a popular discourse of rights before their time, protection against violence, harsh treatment and arbitrary punishment being the focus of prisoner complaint. What was absent from the equation was any capacity or potential of the courts to oversee or adjudicate contests over the treatment meted out in prison.

Consequently, protection against abuses within prison for a century and more after 1850 remained limited to the capacity of prisoners to protest their treatment in the press and through parliament. The latter offered some interesting possibilities, given the potential of political oppositions to embarrass a government. Some politicians went beyond this more obvious reason for attention to prison conditions to articulate claims to liberty and rights that were in clear defiance of the rationale of imprisonment. Most startling perhaps was the sympathy of colonial politicians in the 1890s for the notion that escape from prison was something that displayed a virtue on the part of the prisoner. As it was put by a Queensland politician opposing harsh corporal punishment of escapees, it was 'the first instinct of a man to regain his liberty' (Finnane 1997: 94). But another discourse was already in play – familiar to more recent generations – one in which prisons were depicted not as places of punishment but imagined as colonies of luxury in which prisoners lived better than the honest poor outside. In 1903, the Victorian Parliament would be told that the members of the working class were deliberately committing crimes in order to enjoy the comforts of prison life (Victoria Parliament 1903: 2059-64). In 1923, advocates for the closure of the prison on the picturesque island of St Helena in Brisbane's Moreton Bay were describing it as equivalent to the 'finest resort' (Queensland Parliament 1923: 1856-8). The attempt of authorities to provide a wider range of more open institutions left them frequently open to ridicule, with Queensland's Palen Creek prison farm being regarded by another parliamentarian in 1942 as a 'holiday home' (Queensland Parliament 1942: 1110-5). In Victoria in the same year, the responsible minister responded to a question about poor cond-itions at the Castlemaine reformatory that he did not want to make the inmates 'more comfortable' (Victoria Parliament 1942: 2451-2). In such a climate, it is scarcely surprising that frequently only a prison riot would arouse attention in the parliamentary forums which alone, in the absence of judicial intervention, might provide some redress of prison abuses.

Reclamation through incarceration

A dominant motif of penal discourse from the 1890s was the imperative of citizenship. Prisoners were those who had forfeited, most only temporarily, their rights to participation in the full range of society's activities. So their political rights were limited; the 1893 *Elections Act* in NSW excluded from the now universal male franchise a wide group of convicted prisoners. Inside prison, the convicted might be put out to work but were remunerated at nominal rates. Their seclusion ensured that their access to the outside world was equally nominal – and prison rules and regulations were intended to control that access. The rationale of imprisonment shifted from the prison as punishment to its function as a mechanism of reform and rehabilitation. In consequence, the first half of the 20th century saw in Australia the development of a variety of penal institutions styled to address better the expectation that one day a prisoner would return to the social world and take up those rights and freedoms and respon-sibilities that had earlier been forfeited.

If anything, this era implied a further writing down of any rights that prisoners might once have had as those simply sentenced to a punishment for a specific period of time. The not-quite-fulfilled aspiration of progressive penal reformers was the adoption of indeter-minate sentencing. Prison was to be the 'cure from crime', argued freethinker Thomas Walker in a Perth lecture in 1898 (Finnane 1997: 71 referring to a report in the *Sunday Times*, 4 December 1898). Prisons were moral hospitals, said progressive penal reformers, like the most famous of them in Australia, the NSW Comptroller-General, Frederick William Neitenstein, but 'criminal therapeutics have special diffic-ulties to encounter'. In particular, unlike mental hospitals which detained patients until they were sane, the prison moral hospital had to discharge the inmate after a pre-determined amount of time (Neitenstein 1897: 44). One answer was the indeterminate sentence. Most fervently taken up in Victoria, its object was to ensure that discharged prisoners were fit to re-enter society. While the 1907 Victorian legislation (*Indeterminate Sentences Act*) was intended to address the repeat offending of three-times convicted offenders, it was also applied to first offenders on multiple charges. When Western Australia followed up with such legislation a decade later, the deeming of ordinary prisoners as potential subjects for specialised reformatory treatment became possible (Finnane 1997: 79-80).

The interest in penal reform extended from the process of sentencing, enacted through new options enshrined in legislation, to institutional design and internal management. All of these innovations can be seen to have profound implications for the status of prisoners. The establishment of reformatories and prison farms was intended to allow a finer grading of the prisoner population according to its social characteristics. Women's prisons were founded in some states from the 1890s; they were the result of progressive social reform in responding to a demand for recognition of the distinctive needs of women. But their establishment also entailed a mandate for regimes that diminished the adult status of the inmate; a limited range of work opportunities and a daily schedule that treated the women inmates as children were among the early criticisms (Finnane 1997: 84-92; compare *Report of the New South Wales Task Force on Women in Prison* 1985).

A multiplication of types of institution in the larger jurisdictions meant that by the 1950s, there were no less than 14 separate penal establishments in NSW, ranging from penitentiary to prison farm and afforestation camp. The adoption of systems of classification of prisoners had a reformative rationale but also was a means of management of rebellious prisoners, the objective of the maximum security facility at Grafton from 1943. In the postwar period, Australia began to feel the effects of the criminological and penological enthusiasm for rehabilitation through the development of prisoner programs and the probation and parole systems. The objective was the production of useful citizens – but containment remained fundamental. Speaking in 1952 to the first major revision of the prisons statutes since 1899, the Attorney-General affirmed the priorities.

> The statutory obligation of the prisons administration is to keep secure the person committed to its charge by the courts and to maintain its institutions in clean, wholesome and orderly fashion. Concurrently with this statutory obligation, the administration ... endeavours to reclaim as useful members of the community as many prisoners as possible. (NSW Parliamentay Debates, 18 March 1952, vol 198: 5376)

Consequently, the new statute (*Prisons Act* 1952 (NSW)) retained many features of the older statute (*Prisons Act* 1899 (NSW)) while introducing some matters that had previously been mentioned only in regulations, such as the general standard of diet, clothing and medical treatment. None of these matters of course created entitlements which could be litigated.

The longevity of prisons legislation and regulations was not confined to NSW. Indeed, into the 1970s and 1980s, the Victorian penitentiary heritage was deeply embedded in the rules and administration of institutions. Queensland's prison legislation, finally replaced by the *Corrective Services Act* of 1988, went back to 1890, with only minor changes in a 1957 statute. The system mandated by such legislation is evident in the ways prison discipline was constructed within Queensland prisons as *the* priority of the system.

Discipline regimes

The Queensland *Prisons Regulations* 1959 provided that:

> Prison Officers shall, at all times, bear in mind that discipline is the purpose of a Prison and of their employment therein. They shall endeavour to enforce and observe discipline. Any breach of discipline shall be an offence under the Act and these regulations. (reg 8)

The regulations attempted to reinforce an almost monastic regimen in Queensland prisons to isolate and subdue the inmates, an inheritance of the penitentiary's 'separate and silent' systems. Such regulations required for example:

- whilst in cells [prisoners] shall observe strict silence [requiring silence to be observed between 9.30 p.m. or earlier, to 6.30 a.m. daily]

- [prisoners] shall be decorous and orderly in their conduct. Unnecessary conversation, singing, shouting, or undue noises will not be permitted

- Personal and family matters only and matters concerning a prisoner's case may be discussed [at visits]. No discussion shall be permitted on matters affecting the Prison or its administration, general news of the day or other prisoners. (regs 227, 238, 289)

Regulations controlled all prisoners' property. They were not permitted to decorate their cells and were permitted only limited possessions They could only wear prison clothing, except their own underclothes, footwear, socks or pyjamas. They were permitted to carry handkerchiefs. Prisoners were allowed five photographs; possession of any more could lead to charges. They were limited to three novels and/or magazines at any one time.

Informally, however, prisoners were permitted at times to decorate their cells. Some prisoners put up posters or photographs on their walls. Some at times obtained possessions from their private property not normally allowed. These minor privileges might be and were removed on the caprice of a different officer or under a different security climate. Posters could be approved one week and disallowed the next. This was a regular and arbitrary feature of prison life.

For instance, at Woodford Prison in 1986, the degree of administrative surveillance of daily life can be seen in the classification of prisoners entitled to wear particular types of apparel (viewed by one of the authors in the course of providing legal assistance to prisoners).

> Prisoners approved soft footwear at all times
> Prisoners approved soft footwear at work only
> Prisoners approved to wear sunglasses at all times

Prisoners approved to wear sunglasses at times approved by the Superintendent

Prisoners approved to wear sunglasses at sport only

The controls extended to communication. Drawing on a long history of penitentiary control over communications, Queensland's *Prisons Regulations* 1959 (reg 262) provided that '[t]hey [ie the prisoners] shall not be permitted to write any letter or other document unless authorised, nor shall they have any unauthorised writing whatever in their possession'.

In cases documented by the Prisoners Legal Service in the 1980s, this regulation resulted in notes of complaints for a solicitor being confiscated, while possession of notes on issued foolscap and on an old departmental form led to a disciplinary charge and lock-up. One prisoner who wrote a complaint about medical treatment was forced to tear it up by a prison officer. A prisoner who witnessed an assault of another prisoner by a prison officer wrote a statement but was caught handing it to the prisoner who was assaulted and was locked up for three days on a charge of making a frivolous complaint. And another prisoner who was found to have written a statement about prison conditions was charged and convicted of having illegal writing.

The stated purpose of rules on property and written documents was to prevent the crowding of a prisoner's cell with possessions, making searching for contraband difficult and in other ways impeding the maintenance of order. Such rules were backed up by the random searches authorised in Queensland by Regulation 210 which provided that '[s]earch of a prisoner shall be conducted with due regard for decency and self-respect and in as seemly a manner as is consistent with the thorough searching of any concealed article'. Such formal norms of decency and respect were disregarded in practice. The Nagle Report acknowledged that in some NSW prisons, searches 'were used as a means of punishing prisoners and settling scores' (Nagle 1978: 224). Searches were used to harass and intimidate, disturbing property and breaking possessions without an effective search being performed. Mail, already censored, was read, court documents perused, property removed and important documents confiscated. Searches were carried out often, at any hour, even though nothing was found or suspected. These 'ramps', as they are called by prisoners, target a sensitive point – the only point of real privacy in the prison – and they usually result in a severe reaction from prisoners, especially when the consequence is a charge of 'illegal writing'. Protests against such practices became a feature of prisoner protest over prison abuses by the 1970s. Complaints by Queensland prisoners relating to the loss of property in riots or on transfer, especially the hurried forced transfer where prisoners are given no time to organise their property, or through ramps, were easily frustrated. Claims for compensation were immediately rejected, walls were erected, the prisoner was blamed and long delays ensued.

Prison justice

Avenues for justice in this system were limited and the problems of obstruction and collusion between prisons administration and the Visiting Justice, noted in our earlier observations on this system in the mid-19th century, were just as evident more than a century later. In NSW, Justice Nagle condemned the prison justice system in 1978, noting that '[b]y far the most damning criticism is the accusation that the Visiting Justice is not seen by prisoners to be an independent adjudicator. To them it is said, he is "the Department's man"' (Nagle 1978: 289). The operation of the system was one that a prisoner challenged at peril. Again, Nagle captured the prisoner's dilemma.

> If a prisoner makes a complaint against, say, a prison warder, the prisoner is charged with making a false complaint. In every case known to me of a prisoner foolish enough to complain to the magistrate and a charge of making a false statement being laid, the prisoner is always punished with cells and extra gaol. So, in practice, the prisoner is deterred from laying a complaint. (Nagle 1978: 300)

Nagle added that from his investigation of prison files, Visiting Justices 'have overlooked the requirement that the statement be not only false but false to the knowledge of the prisoner' (Nagle 1978: 300). The Prisoners Legal Service had received similar complaints about the Queensland Visiting Justice system.

As Zdenkowski and Brown noted, these characteristics of the prison justice system were inherent in the structural position of the Visiting Justice who was required by the prison rules to reinforce the authority of the officers (Zdenkowski & Brown 1982: 100-1). This conflict of interest between justice and authority existed in other states, including Queensland where the Visiting Justice had morning tea with prison officers, invariably accepted the word of prison officers without question and also performed the dual function of hearing complaints by prisoners and disciplinary charges against them.

While prisoners were entitled to be heard and to cross-examine any witness, they were not entitled to call witnesses. There was no effective adversarial system or adoption of the formal rules of evidence and it was apparent from many cases that prisoners were in effect called upon to establish their innocence. Natural justice did not have to be observed, yet conviction could lead to extra time. Inherent in the structure of the prison, guarded by such disciplinary rules and regulations, was the control over prisoner access to information about their status. Access to justice within the prison was foreclosed by the perceived disciplinary requirements of the institution and access of outsiders to what went on within the prison was equally limited. Occasional complaints by lawyers, for example about difficulty of access to their clients inside the prison, point to the long-term effects of the closure that characterised the penitentiary from the middle of the 19th century (Victoria Parliamentary Debates, 4 July 1939: 44).

Prisoners' rights in a changing climate

Against the background of statutory prescription of prison discipline and judicial indifference to the standing of prisoners, the most substantial development after the mid-20th century was the growth of a prisoners' rights movement, within and outside the prison. The importance of this movement in sustaining attention to prison conditions and the rights of prisoners is evident if we compare the aftermath of two serious prison riots at Bathurst NSW, separated by 50 years.

In 1924, a sequence of prisoner protests, prompted by an alleged bashing of a prisoner by warders, resulted eventually in widespread refusals to work and destruction of cell amenities. Baton bashings were used on a number of occasions and eventually the prison authorities ordered warders to be armed with loaded rifles with fixed bayonets. Together with police reinforcements, the warders charged a crowd of prisoners in a yard, wounding a large number. The events were widely covered by the press and calls were made for an official inquiry. The matter came to nothing, with the Labour government able to withstand the criticism (Ramsland 1996: 202-04). This was perhaps the most serious of the interwar prison disturbances but it was far from an isolated instance in the 1920s and 1930s. While attracting press comment and even criticism, no sustained campaign of prison reform developed in a political context in which there was substantially a consensus about what prisons were for and what kind of programs should be conducted in them (Finnane 1997: ch 5).

In 1974, in well-known events, prisoners at Bathurst destroyed the prison and were subject in the aftermath to brutal beatings (see

Zdenkowski & Brown 1982). This time, the attempts by government to control the impact were less successful. The difference was the nature of political discourse and organisation around the prison by this time. As we have argued earlier, those promoting penal reform and decent conditions in prisons in the 19th and early 20th centuries were concerned primarily with making punishment more effective. If prisons were to be criticised, it was not because they offended standards of justice in their treatment of individual prisoners but because they did not do what they were supposed to do: produce reformed convicts or effectively deter would-be criminals. Within this discourse, prison abuses would be criticised but primarily because they signified a weakness in administrative controls, in the effective governance of the prison which relied on a rigid regime of rules and regulations. This is not to ignore the substantial contributions to prison reform which were made by social reformers but to note the almost inevitable condition of reform projects, that they are part of the conditions of their time. Hence, a prominent feminist like Rose Scott, engaged in radical reform on many issues including the status of women in prison, was nevertheless very much part of her age in her attachment to indeterminate sentences and the role of the reformatory, which should work towards 'the development of self-respect and the awakening of a sense of duty to others' (Rose Scott Papers: item 2/15).[2]

In the 1970s, by contrast, prison reform had turned another corner. Not reform but abolition was the cry from some on the radical left of the prisoners' rights movement. Moreover, the political distance between prisoners protesting their conditions from inside the prison and their sympathisers working in a variety of groups outside was diminished. Pushing from the outside against a system which was weakened from within by the collapse of older certainties about the functions of the prison and punishment, advocates of prisoners' rights succeeded slowly in turning the violent circumstances of Bathurst into an inquest, official and unofficial, on the whole approach of prisons administration. Fundamental breaches of rights such as systematic beatings at Grafton Gaol would be exposed during the Nagle Inquiry and become a focus for criticism of the system which had produced such a phenomenon.[3]

The number of prisoner and civilian lobby groups concerned with prison conditions by the 1980s was impressive. So also was the breadth of objectives, the range of targets of action and reform. Abolition of the prison itself represented one end of a spectrum that still included the older penal reform bodies such as the Howard League. Unique to the era, however, was the capacity of prisoners in a number of states to organise and publicise their resistance to prison conditions and their demands for change. As we have noted, even during the high age of the penitentiary prisoners' voices were to be heard, though usually only after release or in the context of an official inquiry already prompted by significant disturbances. In a climate of sustained support for the political organisation of minorities, prisoners too could now be found among those agitating for prison reform.

In consequence, there were occasional achievements in institutional recognition of prisoners' rights and the obligations of prison administrations. A unique legislative statement of 'Prisoners rights' emerged in the 1986 Victorian *Corrections Act* which set out rights including access to open air, maintenance of health and access to medical treatment, rights of complaint and communication (*Corrections Act* 1986 (Vic) s 47).[4]

The establishment of the Office of Ombudsman in the various jurisdictions has provided a new avenue of review for prisoners. But already in the 1970s, Nagle had been critical of the NSW Ombudsman's practice of requesting the Prisons Department to investigate complaints received by the Ombudsman (Nagle 1978: 301). The effectiveness of the Ombudsman in responding to complaints by prisoners is limited by a number of inherent functions. The Ombudsman is confined to the investigation of *administrative* matters, so many prison issues, such as allegations of assault, fall outside this jurisdiction. The Ombudsman's Office is empowered to investigate but usually lacks powers to enforce its recommendations, relying instead on its power to report to Parliament to seek compliance through disclosure, without guarantee of success.

Other developments in recent decades might have been expected to increase prisoner protections. In 1982, the English decision of *Raymond v Honey* ([1982] 1 All ER 756; [1983] 1 AC 1) established the principle that a prisoner retains all civil rights which are not removed expressly or as a necessary consequence of imprisonment. This principle is yet to be adopted by Australian courts. In Australia therefore, the position seems to be that prisoners are not accorded rights but privileges which can be taken away at the will of the prison authorities. These privileges can be protected in only limited ways by the courts that are generally loath to interfere in prison administration. This is in spite of concurrent developments in international law.

Prisoners' rights have been incorporated into international law by the *International Covenant on Civil and Political Rights* (ICCPR). However, adoption of the ICCPR by Australia in 1980 and adoption of the First Optional Protocol in 1991, which permits prisoners to complain to the UN Human Rights Committee, have afforded little opportunity for Australian prisoners to enforce the rights provided by the ICCPR. Rights under the ICCPR include the right not to be subjected to torture or to cruel, inhuman or degrading treatment and the right not to be subjected to arbitrary or unlawful interference with privacy and family contact. In any event, many of the rights in the ICCPR are subject to overriding State and Territory legislation. Even with the Optional Protocol, all Australian domestic remedies must be exhausted before the Human Rights Committee jurisdiction is invoked.

International norms were also the reference point for the Australian Institute of Criminology's 1978 *Minimum Standard Guidelines for Australian Prisons* (now the *Standard Guidelines for Corrections in Australia* (1996)) for the guidance of prison administrators. Yet to this day these remain just guidelines, providing no enforceable protection of the basic prison conditions of prisoner comfort, security and dignity, and therefore guarantee no rights.

In contrast to the mid-Victorian faith in the possibility that the penitentiary would reform through punishment, by the 1980s the dominant mood was one of conflict over the ends of punishment and division over its means. There was even emerging an important policy shift in the very management of imprisonment, as privatisation developed as an option on both sides of politics in Australia, an option entailing significant delegations of the right to punish with potentially important consequences for the rights of prisoners (see especially Moyle 2000: chs 6, 8). In such a climate, there has developed a more assertive discourse of the rights of prisoners as citizens whose loss of rights should be only such as serve the limited purpose of their incarceration for a limited period of time.

Notes

1   For an account of the uses of violence and repression at Moreton Bay, see Evans & Thorpe 1992.

2   See J Allen 1994: 153-9 for Scott's work in prison reform.

3   See Zdenkowski & Brown 1982 on the merits and shortcomings of the Nagle Commission as well as a detailed account of its political context.

4   The Act has been amended a number of times during the 1990s and s 47 was most recently amended in 2001. It is set out in full as Appendix B to Chapter 12 in this volume.

Law and Order

Noel Han

The politicians vote winning ticket. Law and order. We will make sure that they're convicted.

Gee it's a bathroom with a bed and shower. Every day is repetitive by the hour.

The sun comes up and goes down. The door swings open when the screws come around.

Inmates are housed, clothed and fed, but are still being found dead.

Screws don't care. One more from out of their hair.

Just another vacant space in this kind of place.

Put him in a body bag, take him away before the space starts smelling of decay.

Tough Law and Order on crime. Out of sight, out of mind. Inmates lost in time.

Public demands, lock them up, throw away the keys. The politicians sniggering to themselves 'Lucky it's not me, for being a flee'.

CHAPTER 7

Televising the Invisible: Prisoners, Prison Reform and the Media

Catharine Lumby

It was a stainless spring morning the day I drove out to Long Bay, a maximum security prison located in Sydney's southern suburbs. I had no idea what to expect. Prison wasn't a place I'd thought much about. As a law student who went through Sydney University when lecturers took a black-letter approach to criminal law, I'd never once been asked to think about what actually happened to people convicted of crimes. Sentencing was the end of the judicial process. The rest was a matter for police, wardens and psychiatrists. As a journalist, I'd avoided writing about crime, afraid someone might ask me to do a death knock or attend an autopsy. Prison was an abstract concept, an unimaginable place.

When I returned to my car some three hours later after an extensive tour of the jail, that had changed. Indeed, the world itself seemed to have changed. Seeing the inside of a prison, even on a visit, is like having a friend die suddenly. Normal, everyday life suddenly appears bizarre. For a time, you can't understand how people can go about their lives as if they're not going to die. They seem so oblivious. Sealed off. Their concerns seem surreally trivial. And then, gradually, you re-enter the flow of everyday existence. Death recedes. The world seems normal again.

The experience got me pondering the roots of the phrase 'ghosts of the civil dead'. Enormous quantities of ink and videotape have been spilled examining the plight of disadvantaged groups in our society. The media is awash with stories on single mothers, welfare recipients, Indigenous people, people with drug dependencies, the homeless and refugees. Not all of the coverage is positive or even fair-minded. But at least the issues and the people who go with them are visible.

Prisoners, in comparison, barely register on the daily media radar screen. Sure, they rate the odd mention in the tabloids or on talkback if there's any suspicion they might be getting 'treats' like free art classes or internet access. And the oppressive aspects of prison life have also been the focus of the occasional mainstream film or documentary: Frank Darabont's 1994 film *The Shawshank Redemption* or David Goldie's 1997 film *The Big House*, for instance.

But in everyday, popular media terms, prison life remains a hidden, uncharted world. A world which begins where police dramas and court reports end. When prisoners are mentioned in the media at all, it's usually only as a set of statistics, as 'a surge' in rates of incarceration or inmate suicide. Indeed, it's often only when inmates come up for parole that the presses and the videotape really start to roll. Inside prison, prisoners live outside the media's unblinking eye. And, because the media has become the foundation of our social memory, that is to say they live largely outside the social itself.

This chapter explores the nature and consequences of that exclusion. It looks at the deeper political significance of media visibility and invisibility. And it argues, following the work of Michel Foucault, that the invisibility of prisoners in the media is the flip side of the intensive surveillance they experience on the inside. In Australia, the bulk of work on the media coverage of prisons and crime has been written by criminologists and has focused on inaccuracies, misrepresentations and the dominance of populist perspectives, perspectives Russell Hogg and David Brown dub 'law and order commonsense' (Hogg & Brown 1998: 21). This chapter deliberately sits at a tangent to such work and brings a media studies perspective to bear on the field. Rather than arguing that prisoners' rights would be advanced if the media adopted a more sober, careful and abstract approach to issues, I suggest that what's required in the first instance is a far higher level of visibility of prisoners in the popular media generally, regardless of whether that coverage is positive or negative.

The latter claim will doubtless seem counter-intuitive to many readers. The popular media, it is frequently argued by thinkers on the left, trivialises, personalises and distorts key social issues and serves up entertainment in place of information. The popular media, in short, is portrayed as the enemy of democracy and informed citizenship. It's a perspective, however, which has been increasingly critiqued by media studies scholars, a number of whom now argue that, in a mass media era, the public sphere must be understood as a zone in which there are many different ways of communicating and making sense. Analysing today's public sphere, however, John Hartley finds a reversal of many of the hierarchies our intellectual and political traditions have held dear. In the postmodern world, he argues, the image has triumphed over the word and the vox pop has triumphed over the opinion of experts. Far from arguing that this shift spells the end of meaningful public communication, Hartley suggests that it's in the interaction between popular media products and their audiences that political, social and cultural debate is produced (Hartley 1996). In these terms, the focus is less on whether a given media report or program accurately or even positively 'represents' the prison system but on whether prisoners are able to achieve a high enough level of visibility to establish their membership of an increasingly mediated public sphere.

It is this threshold issue of visibility that I intend to focus on in the chapter which follows. In particular, I want to argue that the moral panics that so often attend the sentencing and release of prisoners charged with socially abhorrent crimes are a reflection of the deafening silence that begins when the prisoner enters the prison system. Finally, this chapter argues that advocates of prisoners' rights need to focus on the potential of new media for delivering new opportunities for prisoners to speak out on their own behalf.

Seen and not heard

Women are used to men watching them. And popular mythology has it that men in prison are men who are starved of the sight of women. A woman visiting a prison might reasonably expect to be stared at. The man who showed me around Long Bay confirmed these expectations by insisting I put his jacket on over my knee-length dress and warning me not to make eye contact with the prisoners. It came as a shock, then, to discover that prison is a place where the gaze is almost entirely reversed. Most of the men we encountered averted their eyes or looked right through us. At one point, a large group of prisoners filed into a room waiting to be locked into their cells. Some of them began stripping down to their underpants. All of them seemed oblivious of the presence of strangers. The psychiatrist who was briefing me on the mental health problems many prisoners faced continued to speak loudly enough for the inmates to hear.

It was an experience which is entirely familiar to anyone who has spent time working or living in the prison system. As one of the readers of this chapter noted, it speaks of two things: the internalisation of prison discipline and the fear of having their status as prisoners confirmed in the gaze of outsiders.

The author of *Discipline and Punish: The Birth of the Prison*, Michel Foucault, argues that it is this threat of constant surveillance which defines punishment in the modern era. In his analysis of the evolution of modern prisons, Foucault is concerned not just to trace the development of particular kinds of modern punishment, but to ask us what prisons can tell us about the society outside the prison walls (Foucault 1977). As one of Foucault's most insightful interpreters, Paul Patton, puts it:

> [t]he political weight of Foucault's book is borne less by the question of the origins of the prison, than by the question of its persistence for more than 150 years, in spite of its obvious failure to reduce crime … The prison itself, Foucault suggests, needs to be located within a broader complex of institutions whose function is the normalisation of individuals (Patton 1979: 114).

Foucault famously focuses on the British philosopher Jeremy Bentham's plan for the Panopticon, an architectural scheme for the surveillance of prisoners devised in 1791. It consisted of a large courtyard with a tower in the centre that looked over a series of buildings arranged around it, divided into cells with windows facing the tower. The cells, Foucault writes, are small theatres in which each actor is alone, perfectly individualised and constantly visible (Foucault 1977: 200). The whole idea of the Panopticon is that the inmate can't see whether he is being watched or not, so he must always behave as if he is. Inmates effectively internalise this surveillance; they literally become their own guards.

As Hubert Dreyfus and Paul Rabinow, two commentators on Foucault's work, write of the Panopticon, it 'operates through a reversal of visibility'. Whereas in former regimes, it was the King or others who held power who had the greatest visibility, in modern times 'it is those who are disciplined, observed, and understood who are made the most visible' (Dreyfus & Rabinow 1982: 191). Foucault contrasts this system of surveillance with earlier, pre-Enlightenment regimes of punishment which relied heavily on whipping, torture and execution often carried out in public (Foucault 1977: 43).

These ritual public punishments, Foucault argues, were profoundly political. They were public spectacles designed to display the power of the King or head of state in an era in which holding on to power demanded an open display of superior physical force. The ceremony of punishment was a demonstration to the King's subjects of his superior force. The emergence of the modern Western prison saw, with some exceptions, the removal of intentional physical harm from the process of punishment. Correction became an internal matter; control passed from the body to the soul (Foucault 1977: 11). For Foucault, the Panopticon wasn't simply a device that perfectly illustrated the disciplinary technology at the heart of the modern prison. Rather, it was a symbol of the general way power operates in modern society. It's a society Foucault characterises, at least in this part of his work, as a society of surveillance. As Paul Patton writes:

> Bentham's plan, it seems, encapsulates a number of the general characteristics of power in modern society; its continuity and anonymity, for instance. The one-way relation of visibility it sets up between the individual cells and the central tower places the prisoner in a position of feeling himself to be constantly under observation.... Further, since this power may be applied equally to the hierarchy of surveillants, it becomes deindividualised. (Patton 1979: 131)

Foucault subsequently refined his analysis of the way power operates or flows in modern societies (Foucault 1977). But it's interesting to note that his concept of the society of surveillance is one which has some similarities with the way many politically progressive groups came to see the role the media plays in our society. By surveilling, reproducing and (crucially) selecting the world, it's often argued, the media cause the people who live in it to behave as if they are themselves under constant surveillance; normality becomes mediated, it is always measured against images of normality. The Peter Weir film *The Truman Show*, in which an all-seeing media producer governed and screened the life of the oblivious Truman 24 hours a day, took this theme to its sublime and ridiculous conclusion. The moral message of the film was simple: it's only by literally breaking free of his mediated world, by finding an exit in the vast television studio in which he unknowingly lives, that Truman finds truth and freedom.

The Truman Show presents a familiar story about life in a media-saturated world. But its portrayal of power and the implicit opposition in the story between power and truth or knowledge is not something Foucault would have endorsed. What's missing from this account of how power works, in Foucault's terms, is the recognition that power is not predictable and uniform in its effects (Foucault 1977: Pt 4.3). There are always avenues of resistance, competing discourses or versions of the truth and competing groups in society who are able to contest normative models of behaviour. A simple example of the latter is the way feminist critiques of the media's portrayal of women have become a standard part of media commentary. Quite often the same magazines which run diet supplements and feature images of thin models will also run stories about celebrity eating disorders and question whether the media encourages anorexia.

Similarly, if we look at the realities of our prison system today, it becomes clear that, despite living with constant surveillance, prisoners resist the system in a multitude of ways. Drug use is high, a result of a collaboration between visitors, prisoners and some of their guardians. At a deeper level, the prison system can work to make recidivist prisoners more efficient at crime. In this sense, some prisoners are able to take the negative stereotypes applied to them and fashion that identity into a career. As the authors of *Understanding Foucault* argue:

> Prisoners are brought together where they can exchange ideas, experiences, techniques, contacts, strategies — in other words where they can learn to be effective and efficient criminals. This is reinforced because the prison system treats them like criminals. (Danaher, Schirato & Webb 2000: 80).

Their point is not that prisoners are destined to be criminals but rather that the prison system itself is set up in many ways to stigmatise and label inmates in ways which don't often take account of the reasons they fell foul of the law or of their other potentials as citizens, parents, friends and members of a community. One way of resisting this subordination, then, is to turn the negative labels into a badge of honour, to literally fashion a career out of being an outsider.

And in a similar vein, the proliferation of the media has also provided many marginalised social movements with a public platform: feminists, advocates of Indigenous rights, environmentalists, advocates of gay and lesbian rights, to name a few. The media does not treat these groups and their concerns in a uniformly positive way but it's equally true that media coverage has been instrumental in politicising and mobilising a broader public in support of these causes.

Indeed, one of the great problems faced by those who'd like to see prisons transformed, prisoners' rights respected and prison populations significantly reduced is the lack of media coverage on this subject. As a senior editor put it to me when I asked to write a major series on our prison system: 'Mate, nobody out there wants to know'. In many ways, I think he was right. Few of us know people in prison and most of us don't want to bear witness to the brutal and dehumanising regime that guarantees our social order and comfort.

The latter proposition was graphically illustrated when American talk show host Phil Donahue suggested that executions should be televised. He thought Americans ought see the results of their justice system. He was, somewhat ironically, howled down by those who thought it inhumane to televise another human's death. It's a response which points up a paradox: it's apparently far easier to get people exercised about televisual depictions of violence than it is to get them angry about the state putting a fellow citizen to death.

Watching them, watching us

John Lewthwaite first came to public attention in 1974 when he murdered a five-year-old girl, Nicole Hanns, in her bedroom. He'd broken into her parents' house with the intention of kidnapping and sexually assaulting her nine-year-old brother Anthony. But Nicole spoiled his plans when she woke up. Lewthwaite stabbed the little girl 13 times and fled the scene. The next morning, he surrendered himself to the police and made a full confession. The case was, not surprisingly, the focus of enormous public outrage at the time. Lewthwaite, who was still a teenager at the time of his trial, received a mandatory life sentence. In 1992, Lewthwaite's sentence was reviewed by the same judge who imposed the original sentence, Justice Slattery of the NSW Supreme Court. After reviewing all the expert psychiatric reports on Lewthwaite and considering his conduct while in custody, Slattery modified his original view that there was 'no future' for Lewthwaite in society and fixed his minimum sentence at 20 years, a term which meant that Lewthwaite became eligible for parole in 1994. It was 1999 before the Parole Board decided to release the prisoner, by which time he'd spent 25 years in gaol.

The response of politicians, sections of the community and the media was immediate. The NSW State Government sought urgent advice from the Solicitor-General on grounds to appeal against the decision to release the prisoner and the Corrective Services Minister was quick to distance the Government from the Parole Board. 'The State of NSW argued in the strongest possible terms against parole,' he told reporters, and he was personally 'gravely disappointed' by their decision. Opposition leader Kerry Chikarovski was even more strident in her attacks on the decision to release Lewthwaite, telling the media that she was 'horrified' and adding hyperbolically, 'I cannot imagine how the Hanns family must be feeling at the moment — to have to struggle on with the knowledge that the killer is back on the streets is beyond comprehension' (Baird 1999: 2). Illustrating the ignorance about the case that drove much of the political comment, she went on to argue that the Parole Board should have listened to the advice of the original sentencing judge who said that Lewthwaite had no future in the community (Baird 1999: 2). Chikarovski was apparently unaware that it was the very same judge who later recommended that Lewthwaite become eligible for parole.

Despite the tough talk, Lewthwaite was released under strict parole conditions the following week. He was to be taken to his mother's house, the location the Parole Board concluded was the place which gave Lewthwaite the best start in his bid to rejoin society, but the move was aborted when sections of the local community objected after learning about its location in the media. Instead, Lewthwaite was released into the care of another sponsor who lived in the inner-city Sydney suburb of Waterloo, one of the city's poorest areas. Within 24 hours, media revelations of Lewthwaite's whereabouts had given rise to a local vigilante campaign against the former prisoner. An aggressive mob gathered outside the house he was staying in, threw eggs and rocks and put a hose in through the letterbox. The media joined the siege. After only two days, Lewthwaite was forced to move on. He offered the media a brief statement as he left. It read in part:

> If I had any doubt about re-offending in any way, I would not have taken on this responsibility of hopefully being allowed a chance to go back into society … although I could never truly understand the grief my crime has caused the family of my victim and I could never ask their forgiveness, I ask that maybe a little understanding can come my way from you. ('PM' 23 June 1999, ABC Radio National: <www.abc. net.au/pm/s30971.htm>)

Reporting Lewthwaite's move *The Daily Telegraph* epitomised the hysteria-provoking tone that coloured so much of the media reporting on the case. The subheading on its front page story read: 'Lewthwaite quits Waterloo for a suburb near you'. The ex-prisoner was referred to as a 'child killer' and his residence dubbed a 'bolthole' (Trute & Morris 1999: 1).

The reaction of politicians, the media and sections of the NSW public to Lewthwaite's release is a classic instance of what has come to be popularly known as a moral panic: a frenzied and accelerated cycle of public concern which is grounded in the 'othering' of a person or group. The frequency of moral panics over criminals going in or out of the justice system has caused many on the side of prisoners' rights and prison reform to view the media as a hostile entity and journalists with great suspicion. In contrast, I want to argue that what's required to quell these moral panics is not *less* but *more* media.

One of the key reasons that politicians, social conservatives and current affairs producers are so able to fan the fires of moral panic about crime and punishment is that so little is known about what actually happens in prison. John Lewthwaite's life and crime were raked over before he entered detention and once again on his re-entry into society. No one in the media concerned themselves with what really happened in the 25 years in between.

As a man who murdered a child who got in the way of his desire to sexually assault another child, Lewthwaite embodies the inhuman in the social imaginary. In the late 20th century, paedophiles are regarded as subhuman. They are portrayed as monsters who live beyond the boundaries of civilised society. They're the prisoners that 'ordinary' violent criminals despise. And the popular claim that they can't change — a claim not supported by many of the psychiatrists and others who work with offenders — encapsulates their demonic status. Theirs is an evil that is supposedly rooted in the soul.

But there's another way of looking at the current horror of paedophiles. Paedophiles, if Lewthwaite can be taken as an instance of the monster the public fears, are simply individuals onto whom it's safe to project deeper-rooted anxieties about child abuse. They are strangers who prey on children, rather than the family members, priests, teachers and other carers that commit the great bulk of sexual crimes against children. Paedophiles are child abusers who don't fit into ordinary family or community life in the first place and, therefore, the convenient logic goes, paedophilia is something inhuman and outside us.

Until child sexual abuse is widely understood to be something that is a profoundly regrettable part of everyday life, then children and the adult predators who are at risk of abuse and abusing are less likely to disclose these crimes or their propensity to commit them. Child abusers get away with their crimes because adults have the power to frighten children into silence. But it's a conspiracy of silence that is only fuelled by the notion that paedophiles are monsters who can only be found outside the boundaries of regular life.

In a similar way, prisoners are dehumanised in the popular consciousness. They are rarely presented as individuals and when they are, it's only their crimes and their scarred backgrounds which are brought to light. Prisons are places that delimit the social; they are places beyond community, places few of us wish to even imagine.

Throughout his life, Foucault was active on behalf of prisoners' rights and helped set up the Groupe d'Information sur les Prisons in 1971. As Paul Patton recounts the aims of the group:

> [the idea was] not to denounce the prison system in the name of universal values, not, therefore, to claim to speak for the prisoners or on their behalf, but rather to create conditions such that the prisoners could speak for themselves, and be heard. (Patton 1979: 109-10)

He goes on to comment:

> To the extent that the secrecy which surrounds the penal apparatus is an essential element of its normal functioning, breaking down that secrecy and creating the possibility for other kinds of discourse on prisons was seen to be a method of upsetting that normal functioning. (Patton 1979: 110)

If we follow Foucault's logic, then we need to stop asking how we can encourage the mainstream media to be more sympathetic or even simply realistic about life in the prison system. Rather, we need to advocate policies and education programs which facilitate and encourage prisoners to use the media themselves to discuss, publicise and most importantly personalise and humanise issues. As a medium which offers media consumers the chance to become media producers, the internet is already playing a critical role in breaking down the dominance of the traditional media in setting the agenda for public discussion.

Queensland prisons:
1980s and 1990s

Margaret Reynolds, former Queensland Senator (ALP)

In the early 1980s it was not easy for me to access visiting rights. As a left wing Labor politician questioning the National Party State Government, it could have been anticipated that I may have been denied entry to a state-controlled institution. Yet finally approval was granted from the Brisbane hierarchy and I made arrangements for the local visit. The approach to the 19th-century style building with its high walls, perimeter fencing and guard towers does not adequately prepare the visitor for the personal experience of hearing the vast steel gates slam shut. The forbidding atmosphere was enhanced by the rigidity of routine and uniformed escorts. It was unusual for a woman to be 'inside' and there were sniggers, cat-calls and furtive glances as I made my way to the interview room. On the way childish voices called a greeting and, as I looked their way, I saw several former students – Aboriginal boys I had failed to adequately prepare for life in a still violent and racist environment. Their offences were petty, but their future was predictable – detention would lead to a revolving door experience for many while others would become brutalised by prison life and sadly two known to me became tragic statistics for the Royal Commission into Aboriginal Deaths in Custody.

My interview was overseen by prison officers initially hostile to this 'interfering bloody sheila' but when I reported the approach I was adopting to the prison transfer there seemed some acceptance of my intrusion if indeed I was able to assist the young prisoner concerned. Within weeks of that first visit my office began receiving letters from prisoners and phone calls from families. My presence within the Stuart Prison had generated enormous interest and high expectations. I had started something I could not now ignore and so for the sixteen years of my parliamentary career I found myself acting on behalf of prisoners and speaking for greater recognition of prison officers' conditions. Perhaps the most surprising aspect of this association was the fact that on occasions staff actually contacted me to request I visit a particular prisoner.

At this time still in the 1980s, staffing numbers were low and there were no educational or counselling staff. The entire prison community relied on visiting clergy and a medical officer to deal with the spiritual and health needs of inmates. The involvement of a local politician at first seen to be somewhat suspicious became accepted – even welcomed. My staff and I actually provided much needed resources to assist in resolving individual and family crises. While some officers were no doubt dismissive of our efforts, others saw that we took on issues that needed to be raised whether they were personal or political.

Corrective Services Commissioner Keith Hamburger brought a more enlightened view to prison administration in Queensland. Yet some of his own officers, parliamentarians and community representatives were sceptical – even hostile – to the reforming advocacy of this senior bureaucrat who actually considered the social conditions which led to imprisonment. His annual report to Parliament in 1995 drew vocal criticism when he said:

jail would never be a deterrent to criminals, especially those from abused families which showed a lack of understanding of the sub-culture from whence these children have come.

He went on to explain:

Eight out of ten prisoners serving sentences in excess of five years come from a background of ineffective, neglectful and abusive parenting.

Therefore, he said:

there was nothing the state could do to these children in terms of punishment that would in any way match the horror already inflicted on them.

This rational plea for a new approach to punishment and rehabilitation was lost in a tirade of verbal abuse. Opposition Prison Spokesman, Russell Cooper responded irately.

People are sick of this soft, weak system that gives them no hope. For Mr Hamburger to say these criminals should be forgiven because they came from molesting families is utter nonsense.

But it is not only senior prison administrators who are criticised for addressing humanitarianism in corrective services policy. Glen Milliner, a Labor Minister in the Goss Government, was demoted because the then Premier wanted to see 'stronger ministerial control over corrective services'. My own experience of individual prisoner advocacy suggested that Mr Milliner was both a competent and caring minister who tried to administer a difficult portfolio on a limited budget and with little support in Cabinet. When breakouts and riots occurred in the early 1990s, the Minister was held responsible but there was little reflection on the causes of frustrated anger leading to this turmoil.

CHAPTER 8

Institutional Perspectives and Constraints

John Dawes

Introduction

In this chapter, I will discuss some of the factors impinging upon the development of and ongoing commitment to prisoners' rights within correctional institutions (ie prisons). I will describe and analyse some in-prison issues that are important in the way they impact upon and limit a full expression of prisoners' rights. But before dealing with the in-prison issues, it is important to recognise that, while prisons remain essentially closed and secret administrations, community influences are increasingly important. My position is that the work of prisons is not only critical for the well being of the community but correctional philosophy and the way it is administered also reflects the way the community sees itself, its values, its compassion and the sense of community we have.

Punitiveness

The first factor, and perhaps the most important at the present time, is the new *punitiveness* manifest in a number of policy changes in the criminal justice system. This can be argued on the basis of the increasing use of imprisonment in Australia as reflected in the imprisonment rates,[1] the over-representation of Indigenous people in the prison system,[2] the increasing use of mandatory sentencing,[3] longer sentences and 'truth in sentencing'.[4] In the last few years of the 20th century, the general community has profoundly influenced criminal justice and correctional policy. While some of these influences have been benign, others have seen benefits for victims won at the expense of offenders.[5] Ryan characterised a similar movement in the United Kingdom as 'populist' compared with the previous 'elitist' period 'when policy making was dominated by a small, male, metropolitan elite' (Ryan 1999: 1).

Prison authorities must organise the prison systems to cope with 'accusations of indulgence and repression made with equal vigour' (Grant 1992: 20) because there is not a predominant view about how prisoners should be cared for or managed. Today it might be more accurate to suggest that there is pressure within the community for more repressive approaches to be taken in the management of serious offenders. We need to be watchful about a narrowing of agency missions and a concentration on security and outcomes at the expense of processes. Processes are vital in human services.

Another measure of this shift is that Australia's commitment to the United Nations and its obligations to UN treaties and conventions has wavered under attacks from the One Nation Party and some other politicians. Although it is the Commonwealth that is the signatory to these documents, many are relevant to the criminal justice administrations of the States and Territories. The Commonwealth's flawed administration of its detention centres for unauthorised arrivals and less than forthright intervention in the Northern Territory in regard to mandatory sentencing weakens the Commonwealth's moral authority and leadership in regard to Australia's treaty obligations.

The context of prisoners' rights

A discussion of what constitutes prisoners' rights is beyond the scope of this chapter although various factors and forces leading to fluidity in those rights will be identified. This is shown in Figure 8.1. Figure 8.1 shows prisoners in the centre located within a prison that is, in turn, located within the community. The arrows pointing outwards represent efforts by prisoners directed at both the prison authorities and the community to maintain and extend their rights. This effort can take many forms, such as lobbying prison authorities and Ministers and seeking support from community members and groups sympathetic to their views. The arrows pointing inwards represent efforts by the community and prison authorities to qualify and restrict prisoners' rights. That is, prisoners' rights expand and contract as governments and courts respond to changing community views about prisoners.

Figure 8.1. The context of prisoners' rights

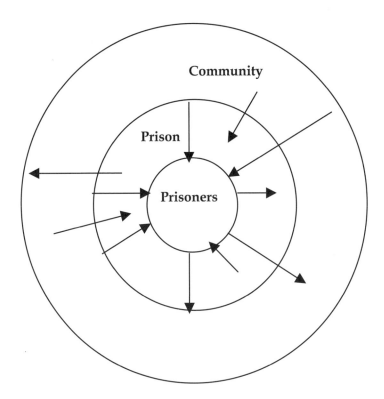

The emergence of prisoners' rights

The 1970s have been described as the period in modern Australia when governments advanced prisoners' rights (Zdenkowski 2000: 172; Lynn & Armstrong 1996: 156-74). The enhanced status of prisoners was not always a result of government altruism but developed in response to lobbying by prisoners and their supporters, direct action by prisoners and recommendations by Royal Commissions and Boards of Inquiry.[6] The 1970s was also a period of great upheaval in Australian prisons as prisoners, following the lead of others overseas, took spectacular direct action to improve their conditions and bring to public attention their grievances and lack of response to their needs by the various prison systems.[7] The enhancement of prisoners' rights was achieved from a minimal starting point and many prisoners lived in deplorable conditions and were treated harshly. The 1980s can be thought of as a period of consolidation of new programs and policies following the upheaval of the 1970s and the beginning of managerialism as the first efforts by governments were made to contain costs. The 1990s can be regarded as the decade of the new punitiveness. As stated above, there is neither a common view about the purposes of imprisonment nor is legislation always instructive. This lack of clarity and agreement about the purposes of imprisonment will now be discussed.

Jurisprudential justifications of imprisonment

Operationalising the justifications or purposes of punishment into objectives and aims of imprisonment is difficult from the point of view of managing prisons. How do the jurisprudential justifications of imprisonment create a 'technology of salvation' (John Howard, cited in Ignatieff 1978: 57)? The jurisprudential justifications for punishment are regarded as retribution, deterrence (individual and general), reformation or rehabilitation and incapacitation. More recently, denunciation has been advanced as a reason for punishment. This dilemma has often been characterised tritely as the offender is sent to prison *as* punishment, not *for* punishment.

It is instructive to return to the *Report of the Royal Commission into New South Wales Prisons* (Nagle 1978: 36-41) and read Royal Commissioner Nagle's chapter on the objectives and aims of the New South Wales (NSW) Department of Corrective Services and his examination of Mr Walter McGeechan, then Corrective Services Commissioner. While Nagle's questioning may appear harsh, it is equally true that the Department did not acquit itself well. Nagle was 'unable to discern any clear or consistent penal philosophy to which the Department has adhered' (Nagle 1978: 36). Nor did the expert witnesses advance the discussion much further. Later, Nagle asserted that 'there are many in the community who nevertheless believe that the loss of liberty is not sufficient punishment' (Nagle 1978: 40) and this remains a critical issue in contemporary Australia. Nagle rejected this view and summarised what the Commission believed to be a modern statement of objectives for imprisonment: 'the inmate should lose only his [sic] liberty and such rights as expressly and by necessary implication result from that loss of liberty' (Nagle 1978: 40). Imprisonment should be used sparingly and sentences should be as short as possible and 'those who are in prison should be housed in the lowest appropriate security'. Nagle did not address the issue of rehabilitation or reformation in this chapter but expressed the view that, if prisoners were treated humanely and with dignity, 'then it is to be hoped that the prisoners will leave prison no worse than when they entered it' (Nagle 1978: 40). The lack of clear justifications for imprisonment leads to problems in gaining widespread agreement to the purposes of imprisonment. This lack of agreement, even in prison agencies that have attempted to state their objectives clearly, results in ambivalence and staff working at cross-purposes. These difficulties are compounded in our liberal western democratic tradition of common law and legislative statements and commitment to international treaties and conventions; each of these traditions carries different weight and is not capable of being set out in a charter that can be regarded as binding. 'Rights' in legislation are not secure. For example, efforts are being made by certain actors in the federal arena to remove prisoners' right to vote (already a restricted franchise) (see ch 16, this volume). During the 1990s, governments removed remissions from prisoners in order to achieve 'truth-in-sentencing'. Ironically, these actions were described as 'reforms', as was the introduction of remission programs in the 1970s and 1980s. The removal of remissions as an incentive for prisoners to work productively and behave appropriately, that is, prosocially, is inconsistent with wider community approaches to socialisation. The lack of agreement about the purposes of imprisonment and how prisons should operate has major implications for prisoners' rights, especially in the handling of and accountability for incidents.

Incidents in prison

In the *Report on Government Services 2001*, assaults are discussed as a measure of the effectiveness of containment (Steering Committee for the Review of Commonwealth/State Service Provision 2001: 458). While the figures are qualified with a reminder that small differences may be reflected in larger trends, I want to discuss the assaults in terms of their meaning within the discourse of rights. In 1999-2000, Western Australia (WA) reported the lowest rate of assaults by prisoners on other prisoners (1.1 assaults per 100 prisoners, based on the daily average for the year) and NSW reported the highest (17.4 per 100). What do these differences mean? Is the NSW prison system that much more unsafe than WA's? Can different counting rules explain the difference? The rate in South Australia (SA) is 13 incidents per 100. The SA figure suggests that different counting rules may be used to provide the statistics or, more significantly, the threshold test for what might constitute an in-prison assault may vary from one jurisdiction to another. Perhaps there is greater tolerance of in-prison assaults in WA? Another meaning might be that NSW is being more open about this aspect of effectiveness. When we turn to assaults by prisoners on officers, the rate ranged from 1.1 per 100 prisoners in both WA and Queensland to 5.3 in SA. Assaults by officers upon prisoners are not reported. My view is that assaults, prisoner on prisoner, prisoner on staff and staff on prisoner, represent serious offending behaviour and need to be treated diligently, that is, investigated and perpetrators charged and punished if at all possible. A high level of assaults suggests that there are problems in the correctional agency. At the local prison level, assaults may occur as a result of poor supervision, staff who do not care about their work and/or are not engaged with the prisoners. It may also suggest that staff do not identify with or support broader departmental policy and the need for prisons to be safe and lawful.

And if assaults occur, as they do from time to time even in the best-managed prison, how do the local authorities respond? For it is here that a powerful message can be sent to prisoners, eg 'this prison does not tolerate assaults and every effort will be made to investigate the incident thoroughly and action taken to try and prevent occurrences'. The management task is to do this without over-reacting and applying group punishments that diminish the rights of all prisoners in the unit. Staff also have a right to a safe workplace and may also put pressure on management leading to an over-reaction. This is difficult work and investigating assaults in prison is often an almost impossible task because of the code of silence observed by prisoners (and also by correctional officers). Additionally, in the case of assaults by correctional officers upon prisoners, there is the difficulty for the prosecution of gaining proof beyond reasonable doubt when presenting a case that relies on the word of a prisoner against an officer.[8] The stereotype suggests all prisoners are dishonest although this is not the reality. At the other end of the scale is a prison where staff walk away, turning their backs on the incident, effectively saying 'we do not care'.

At the agency or departmental level, assaults in prison may represent one of the costs of operating crowded prisons, which over-stretch the agency's capacity to deliver good classification and reduce pressures in prisons which have recently experienced prisoner unrest. The prison system itself may simply not have enough separate living units to ensure that different groups of prisoners, especially those with protection needs, can be kept apart from potential assailants. In overcrowded prison systems, it is not unknown for a prisoner expressing a need to be kept apart and safe to be placed in some form of administrative segregation, thereby sending a message to the rest of the prisoner population that asking for assistance may lead to action which is perceived as punishment. Conditions in segregation are inevitably more spartan and there is often confusion among staff as to whether the prisoner is being punished or simply kept apart from others. More will be said about this below.

Bullying is another manifestation of assaults in prison and can be a factor in the growth of despair and perhaps even suicide. Mr B died on 17 January 1980 at Yatala Labour Prison in Adelaide. This young man was being sexually harassed in the locker shop and this was happening 'all the time' (Clarkson 1981: 16). The Royal Commissioner on this inquiry, Mr Gresley Clarkson QC, stated:

> 'B ... was driven to take his own life by the treatment he received from fellow prisoners. He would have received no comfort by the apparent lack of concern on the part of the prison authorities. Those authorities failed to take proper care of B ...' (Clarkson 1981: 17)

These are damning words and Clarkson's criticisms of the SA prison system bring together the behaviour of other prisoners associated with B and the neglect by prison staff (Dawes 1997: 12). This tragic incident breached most of Commissioner Nagle's criteria for a modern prison system (Nagle 1978). It is unlikely that the authorities in SA paid much attention to the NSW Royal Commission or used its recommendations as a litmus test of the modernity and humanity of its own administration. Incidents in prison are a test of staff competence and integrity as well as a test of management's capacity to manage effectively and efficiently.

Prison staff

Professor Richard Harding, who has written extensively about prison privatisation, stated that public service prison agencies 'run on an input-based management strategy' (Harding 1997: 19). Prison staffing remains the most contentious issue for modern prison managers. Harding's point is that prisons are costly enterprises to operate and the largest single recurrent cost is that for staff.[9]

Traditionally, prisons have operated on an inflexible regime of 'fixed posts'. This practice continues to bedevil prisons in England and Wales and became a part of Australian systems, along with paramilitary structure and uniforms. In simple terms, a prison cannot operate effectively and safely, from the point of view of prison officers, if all the 'fixed posts' are not filled according to an agreed formula. If an officer who was rostered for position X called in sick, another officer would have to be called in from days off or leave to fill the post to enable the prison to operate. The cost of the replacement officer is at an overtime level. If the vacancy occurs on a weekend or public holiday, then the agency pays a premium for the replacement staff because of the additional penalty rates that have to be paid. The 'fixed posts' formula is inflexible and is the key element in the 'input-based' management strategy referred to by Harding. Staff would use the additional monies earned through overtime to boost their annual salaries.

Staff pay an enormous personal cost in loss of recreation time, contact with their families and negative impact upon their health. Some of the 'fixed posts' need to be filled for short periods of time but for large portions of the day can be left unfilled without compromising security. Prison officers rostered as guards on towers overlooking prison walls are frequently the epitome of wasted resources. Prison staff can effectively hold governments to ransom and frequently did, often at Christmas and Easter in SA, when such action was calculated to do the most damage and gain government attention. Lockdowns, work to rules and strikes were quite common in some Australian prison systems during the 1970s and 1980s (Lynn & Armstrong 1996: 157; Grant 1992: 88-89). During these events prisoners were often locked in their cells, denied an opportunity for recreation, showers, medical appointments and, in some cases, court appearances. When specialist medical appointments were cancelled, prisoners frequently lost their places in the queue.

Not only does industrial action impact upon prisoners' rights, it also increases relatives' anxiety and distress. Angry relatives would then complain to the Minister, thereby bringing further pressure to bear.

In unsewered prisons, without showers in cells, such as parts of Pentridge Prison and Adelaide Goal, prisoners are subjected to 'cruel and unusual punishment' over and above loss of liberty during lock-downs. In response, the NSW, Victorian and SA authorities provide some compensation to prisoners by way of additional remissions. In SA, prisoners are given extra remission (four days for every day served) when their lives were disrupted and they did not have access to their usual programs and amenities. The extra remission is subject to prisoners maintaining law and order.

Perhaps the two most extreme examples of unions forcing on governments rigid staffing formulae occurred in NSW and SA. The 'sight and sound' rule in NSW required that an officer was not to work out of sight or hearing of a colleague. This was to protect the officer from allegations of assault by prisoners. The rule also keeps staff numbers high and impacts upon effective prison operations if, in the view of staff, there are insufficient staff available. The 'apostolic rule' in SA requires all prisoners located in a high-security prison to be escorted by two staff, both within the prison and on escorts in the community. This inflexible and very costly rule is applied even when a prisoner from an open prison was returned to Adelaide, for example, for treatment of injuries received while playing football for the local community team. Occasionally prisoners at Cadell Training Centre in the Riverland might require hospitalisation. In selected cases when this happened, prisoners were not guarded while in the local hospital but visited intermittently by staff. If their conditions required a return to Adelaide for hospitalisation, two guards were required, three shifts per day, representing an unnecessary increase in costs.

A common response by staff to incidents such as the one described above at Yatala, was to argue that there was insufficient staff. Simultaneously, staff resisted the idea of a pool of casual officers who could be called upon to assist during shortages within prisons. And so the emphasis upon the input-based structure would start again. This rigidity in prison staffing arrangements was and remains in some prisons an ingredient in the construction of prison regimes which diminishes prisoners' rights.

Government responses

One key result of the action of prison officers and their unions was that during the late 1970s and through the 1980s, prison officers, along with some other members of the public sector, came to be regarded by governments with pathological antipathy (Harding 1997: 19). A climate for privatisation was created through a desire by governments to rid themselves of the responsibility of being the employer of such difficult employees and to give that responsibility to the private sector, thereby reducing the recurrent expenditure on wages for prison staff. The first private prisons in Australia were State-owned assets operated by a private contractor. As the cost of borrowing money by State governments increased, as it did during the 1980s and early 1990s, especially when some governments had their credit ratings down-graded as a result of poor financial management, then 'DCFM' prisons became possible. Here a contractor would Design, Construct, Finance and Manage a prison on behalf of the State government. Victoria pursued this approach (see Private Prisons Investigation Panel (Vic) 2000: 8). Within State-run prisons, governments responded with increased emphasis on and commitment to the ideas of unit management.

Another government response was to see enterprise bargaining as a way of dealing with prison officers. Pay increases and improved conditions could only be financed from savings or where clear benefits through efficiencies could be demonstrated. Enterprise bargaining was a slow and painful process although some increased flexibility in the deployment of staff was achieved. Privatisation has had mixed benefits for prisoners' rights and these will now be discussed.[10]

Privatisation

Privatisation refers to the provision of correctional services by non-government trading companies supervised by the Australian Securities and Investments Commission. Since 1990, with the opening of Borallon Prison in Queensland, privatisation has meant the private operation of a state-owned correctional facility. It is beyond the scope of this chapter to argue the philosophical and legal merits of private corrections. Rather, for the purposes of my argument, I regard the provision of correctional services by private companies as just another aspect of the external provision of corrective services. Such services have been provided by churches, not-for-profit incorporated bodies, statutory bodies including government departments and individuals since soon after the establishment of NSW as a penal colony on 26 January 1788. Indeed, a compelling case can be made for the provision of many services to prisoners by contracting to other agencies.

I will consider this matter by way a brief case study. A prisoner died in Adelaide Gaol on 4 January 1983. The Royal Commission into Aboriginal Deaths in Custody (RCIADIC 1989) report relating to his death contains very little comment that can be construed as critical of departmental officers, prison procedures or the medical services provided to the prisoner at the time of his death. The RCIADIC indicated that there is a need for formal procedures to ensure correctional officers *know* about prisoners with medical conditions, such as diabetes and epilepsy, so that appropriate action can be taken if health problems arise (RCIADIC 1989: 50). It is worthwhile to note this recommendation in conjunction with the recommendation contained in the RCIADIC Interim Report, suggesting that prison health services should be completely independent from correctional authorities (RCIADIC 1988: 54-55). This was and remains the situation in SA.

The RCIADIC also highlighted the need for prison medical authorities to attempt to introduce a system to ensure that a prisoner's medical history at other hospitals and medical centres is obtained and placed on the prisoner's medical records and recognised that the consent of the prisoner would be required to enable such information to be obtained (RCIADIC 1989: 15). It is pertinent in regard to this, and the previous issue, to note the RCIADIC comment that 'a balance must be kept between systems designed to ensure proper medical care of prisoners and the introduction of systems which create further inroads into a prisoner's privacy and self-reliance' (RCIADIC 1989: 19). This is a difficult outcome to achieve.

The brief summary of the discussion in the 1989 RCIADIC report raises extremely complex human rights issues which are still to be resolved. If the prison health service is independent of the correctional agency, how does that service advise the correctional authorities about medical conditions such as diabetes, tuberculosis, epilepsy, HIV/AIDS and Hepatitis C, for example, while ensuring the confidentiality of the prisoner's health status? A prisoner might be prepared to advise about their diabetes or asthma but be much more reluctant to advise about HIV/AIDS or Hepatitis C status. The cost of the latter conditions becoming general knowledge in a prison may have enormous consequences, as the same information may have in the workplace or local community. One approach to overcoming this difficulty with an independent health service or contract general practitioner is for the medical service to advise the custodial author-ities in general terms about an appropriate regime for the prisoner. The law regards the prisoner as a competent individual who, in regard to her or his health status, has the same rights as any other citizen. The correctional authority has responsibilities (duty of care) to its staff and other prisoners. Where medical services are operated by the correctional authority, as in some Australian jurisdictions, it is much easier, even if not intended, for medical information to be regarded as the property of the correctional agency and generally accessible to staff.

If the prisoner is not competent, who should make decisions about medical and dental treatment? Legally, a surrogate decision-maker should be sought and the laws of the Australian States and Territories provide for a *responsible person* (usually a nominated relative) or an appointed guardian to make such decisions (eg *Guardianship and Administration Act* 1993 (SA); *Guardianship and Administration Act* 1990 (WA)).[11] I suspect, in practice, this is often overlooked, as it continues to be not infrequently in the community. The rights of a mentally incapacitated prisoner can easily be set aside and the appointment of a surrogate decision-maker is one way the power of the state can be checked, just a little.

Perhaps it is the *scope* of private prison operations rather than privatisation or profit-making as such that causes concern about the development of private correctional programs in Australia. Private contractors, such as medical practitioners, psychiatrists and psychologists, have been providing private services to offenders for a long time and making their living from their professional activities. Another important benefit of privatisation has been to achieve a greater degree of staffing flexibility, not only in privatised prisons but, as a result of cross-fertilisation, also within public prisons. However, increased flexibility in staffing is not without its problems and the private operators in Victoria make such extensive use of casual staff and rosters are so structured (12-hour shifts and shortened weeks) that permanent staff can be absent for quite long periods of time (Private Prisons Investigation Panel (Vic) 2000: 54). This in turn has an impact on prisoners' rights, as staff without an investment in the unit's operation can change regimes or be unaware of a prisoner's particular needs or vulnerability.

Administrative separation

Considerable controversy during the last 25 years has accompanied the use and development of special areas within prisons to house those prisoners regarded as constituting major threats to the security of the prison and, in some cases, the community. It is here that the rights of certain prisoners may be set aside in the interests of the good order of the remainder of the prison. Examples of such units are the underground cells at Boggo Road Prison in Brisbane, Grafton Gaol and Katingal, S & D Divisions at Yatala Labour Prison (SA) and H Division and Jika Jika High Security Unit (K Division) at Pentridge. All of these facilities with the exception of Grafton Gaol are now closed. The operations of Katingal Special Security Unit and Grafton Gaol have been thoroughly described in the Report of the Royal Commission into NSW Prisons (Nagle 1978). It is sufficient to state that Katingal was in some ways the successor to Grafton. Both places were centres of brutality (physical and psychological) by staff against prisoners and their official aims were poorly understood and enunciated. In the case of Katingal, the Royal Commission recommended it be closed (Nagle 1978: 134).

In considering the operation of special security units, the underlying debate has been about dispersal (that is, placing difficult-to-manage prisoners throughout the prison system) and congregation (that is, placing such prisoners in a central facility). This philosophy has been expressed dichotomously — either you congregate or disperse. But another approach is to use both dispersal and congregation. Whatever approach is taken, care needs to be exercised and while, on occasions, prisoners will be administratively segregated, this should occur for the shortest time possible. Classification and placement of prisoners in special security units cannot be arbitrary and capricious (see, for example, *Bromley v Dawes* (1983) 10 A Crim R 98; *Bromley v Dawes* (1983) 34 SASR 73; *Bromley v Dawes (No 2)* (1983) 10 A Crim R 115). As well, the decisions need regular and independent review. Those responsible for making the decisions to segregate should be required to record their reasons in detail; those records should be available to an external review body and the staff should be available for interview. Special units should be regularly inspected by senior personnel from the correctional agency as well as by independent review and accountability bodies.

Prison management can often be understood as an act of balance — dealing with a difficult prisoner while recognising that the remainder are living in an environment where there is an already diminished recognition of individual rights because prisons, as institutions, need rules and a regular known regime in order to operate. This was described eloquently by Goffman as prisoners 'together lead an enclosed, formally administered round of life' (Goffman 1961: xiii).

Community contact

Most prison administrators recognise the importance of contact with the outside world. Such contact is achieved through visits by family and friends of prisoners, sending and receiving mail, making telephone calls to family members and having unrestricted access to newspapers, radio and television. Other important ways in which prisoners maintain contact with the outside world is through official visitors, visits by sports teams and sports personalities, other visiting officials and concerts within prisons. Nearly all of these avenues to enhanced contact with the outside world carry a risk. Without doubt, improved personal visiting arrangements for prisoners (contact and private visits rather than cubicle or box visits) have provided a conduit for drugs to be brought into prisons. Without reference to clear guiding principles and understanding of the value of maintaining family contact, it would be tempting for prison administrators trying to contain costs and the flow of drugs into prisons to abandon contact and private visits and so diminish the rights of the majority.

Conclusion

This chapter has provided a brief exposition of the institutional context of prisoners' rights and some of the challenges and issues that have led to those rights being quite fluid and the need for vigilance in ensuring those rights are not further eroded in the current punitive climate.

Many other examples of the fragility of prisoners' rights could be discussed. For example, developing and maintaining useful work for prisoners is difficult in every jurisdiction. Care has to be taken that in providing work for prisoners, free citizens do not have their work opportunities diminished. The impact of crowding on prison operations and on prisoners' rights is another contemporary issue.

There are no simple formulas for ensuring that prisoners' rights are appropriately observed. Prisons are complex organisations not easily managed by the application of rigid rules. While it might be argued that the privatisation of corrections (especially the custodial operations of prisons) may lead to less scrutiny of those facilities, staff decisions and their impact on prisoners' lives, it is equally true that a major trend in Australia during the last decade has been to strengthen government and legislative control over prisons. For example, recently the Queensland Corrective Services Commission was abolished and replaced by a ministerial department. Re-affirmation of government control should be regarded as a positive development. Clear government control means that Ministers can be held accountable for abuses of human rights, that they can be questioned in Parliament and that the full array of administrative and other methods of scrutiny can be applied. This means that Ministers will not just receive political credit for the good news stories about prisons but be forced to grapple with the complex and challenging issues that arise within and that affect all associated with prisons — prisoners, staff and citizens. A cost is that prison issues are more likely to be caught up in the 'law and order' politics so characteristic of Australia today with less bureaucratic buffering from capricious change. Given Australia's increasing imprisonment rate, more people will be affected by imprisonment and thus more people are likely to be affected by prisoners' rights issues. The danger, however, is that these will be overwhelmed by budgetary considerations with the result that prisoners will be warehoused. This would be a return to our national origins.

Notes

1   There are 97 prisons in Australia housing more than 21,500 prisoners each day. In 1976-77, the daily average prisoner population was 8743 prisoners, equalling an imprisonment rate of 90.7: 100,000 population of imprisonable age. In 1988-89, the daily average was 12,004, a rate of 96: 100,000 (J Walker 1994: 24, 25). For the June quarter 2001, the daily average was 21,487, equalling an imprisonment rate of 146.5: 100,000 (Australian Bureau of Statistics 2001a: 10, 13).

2   On 1 June 2001, there were 4,273 Indigenous prisoners in Australia or 20% of the Australian prison population (Australian Bureau of Statistics 2001a: 19) although Indigenous people constitute approximately 2.1% of the Australian population (Australian Bureau of Statistics 1999: 5).

3   Mandatory sentencing 'refers to the practice of parliament setting a strict penalty for the commission of a criminal offence' (Roche 1999: 1).

4   'Truth in sentencing' means that the prisoner serves the full term of imprisonment as determined by the court. There is no scope for administrative shortening of the sentence through executive actions such as remissions, temporary leave and early release.

5   The 'victims movement' is perhaps the most spectacular and successful: see Daly & Immarigeon 1998.

6   See for example any of the following reports: Board of Inquiry into Allegations of Brutality and Ill-Treatment at HM Prison Pentridge 1973 (Victoria); Nagle 1978 (New South Wales (NSW)); Clarkson 1981 (South Australia); Royal Commission into Aboriginal Deaths in Custody 1991 (national).

7   The riot at the New Mexico State Prison (Sante Fe) on Saturday 2 February 1980 and the riot at the New York State Prison (Attica) in 1971 were widely publicised in Australia: see Dinitz 1981: 3-19.

8   The *Annual Report of the Department of Correctional Services 1988-1989* (Government of SA, 1989) for SA highlights that the Adelaide Remand Centre (ARC) (opened on the 26 August 1986) was the focus of many complaints by prisoners about staff on prisoner assaults, especially in Unit 7 (p 4). The Ombudsman commented upon the behaviour and attitudes of certain staff employed at the ARC (p 4). I shared this concern and requested a Government Investigations Officer (from the Attorney-General's Department) to investigate a series of complaints made since April 1988. Given the preliminary findings of this officer and the prima facie criminal nature of the allegations, the Commissioner of Police was approached to establish a Task Force to undertake further inquiries into the allegations (p 4). At the end of the investigation, one officer was charged on summons but was acquitted at the Holden Hill Magistrates Court. As a result, the police decided not

to proceed with any further cases. Altogether, 21 employees of the Department allegedly engaged in conduct that caused concern, in this incident and others, and led to disciplinary charges being laid. The investigations caused concern to staff and their union and much media attention: Rice 1988e; 1988c; 1988d; 1988a; 1988b.

9   Nationally, system-wide recurrent expenditure on corrective services (net of revenue derived from own sources) totalled $2345 million in 1999-2000: $1174 million (87%) for prisons, $137 million (10%) for community corrections and $35 million (3%) for transport and escort services. Recurrent expenditure per capita ranged from $43 in Victoria to $179 in the Northern Territory. Nationally, recurrent expenditure was $71 per person (Steering Committee for the Review of Commonwealth/State Service Provision 2001: 449).

10   The *Report of the Independent Investigation into the Management and Operation of Victoria's Private Prisons* indicates that the standard of prisoner accommodation has improved by the opening of three DCFM private prisons, with a result that less than 10% of prisoners are now accommodated in prisons built more than 100 years ago (Private Prisons Investigation Panel (Vic) 2000: 4).

11   All States and Territories have similar legislation.

CHAPTER 9

Protection of Prisoners' Rights in Australian Private Prisons

John Rynne

Introduction

Since Australia's first privately managed prison opened in January 1990 at Borallon, Queensland, the popularity of private sector involvement in custodial corrections has increased. Currently, seven privately run custodial centres accommodate approximately 15% of the secure prisoner population in Australia (Steering Committee for the Review of Commonwealth/State Service Provision 2001).[1] These prisoners are held in prisons either owned and operated or managed by private providers (see Table 9.1). The purpose of this review is to detail prisoners' rights in private prisons by identifying the various options prisoners have to ensure their basic rights are protected. Prisoners' rights in this discussion include those rights and freedoms which are inherent; that is, they are enjoyed as a consequence of being a human being, they are inalienable, cannot be removed or abandoned, are universal and apply to all regardless of race, religion and gender (*Universal Declaration of Human Rights*, arts 1 and 2). These rights are agreed by the community of nations and set out in a range of international conventions, standards and other instruments including the *International Covenant on Civil and Political Rights*, the *Standard Minimum Rules for the Treatment of Prisoners* and the *Basic Principles for the Treatment of Prisoners*.

The non-government sector has long been involved in the delivery of components of Australian criminal justice systems. Church groups, nonprofit organisations and various community groups have for some time participated in the provision of community-based corrections facilities, such as juvenile institutions, halfway houses and drug rehabilitation units. The involvement of these non-government, not-for-profit organisations has been referred to as being at the 'soft-end' of corrections (Palley 1992: para 20). The discussion here, however, includes only those for-profit companies that successfully tendered for the delivery of custodial correctional services.

Australia is party to various international treaties and concurs in many standards and rules concerning human rights and imprisonment. Despite this, and because the international system has no enforcement mechanism, in place of rights, prisoners 'enjoy' privileges or entitlements as dictated by relevant State authorities. Notwithstanding this lack of rights, governments have a responsibility to ensure that lawful punishment is the period of imprisonment and that, while imprisoned, further punishment is not administered through inhumane treatment or exploitation. Regardless of the style of correctional centre management, that is, whether public or private, there are three main mechanisms that can be called on to advance the protection of prisoners' rights:

1. constitutional and parliamentary
2. legislative and judicial
3. inquisitorial and administrative (Harding 1997: 52).

Notes for Table 9.1 (opposite page)

1   ACM = Australasian Correctional Management
    AIMS = Australian Integrated Management Services Corporation
    CCA = Corrections Corporation of Australia
    MTC = Management and Training Corporation

2   Prison populations are based on built approved capacity. Total prison population was that reported in Steering Committee for the Review of Commonwealth/State Service Provision 2000: 773-838 (Corrective Services Attachments). The Acacia figure is the author's prediction, based on 1998-99 total State prison population.

3   While MTC was awarded the management and operation contract for Borallon on 1 October 2000, CCA agreed to continue managing the centre under a separate arrangement until the effective contract date of 1 January 2001.

4   On 3 October 2000, the Victorian Commissioner of Correctional Services relieved CCA of its management and operational responsibilities at the Metropolitan Women's Correctional Centre (Deer Park). The Corrections Minister Andre Haermeyer intervened following a report from the Correctional Services Commissioner Penny Armytage stating, 'The operator was given repeated opportunities to fix the problems and meet its contractual obligations, but failed to adequately respond to verbal and written warnings and three default notices' (Mickelburough & Anderson 2000: 3).

5   The original agreement for the DCFM (Design, Construct, Finance, Manage) of Acacia was signed between the Western Australian Ministry of Justice and CCA on 21 December 1999. Since then, ownership of the centre was transferred to AIMS Corp.

Table 9.1. Private correctional facilities in Australia, 2000

State	Centre	Start/ change of contract	Current owner/operator[1]	Contractual arrangements	Capacity & % of total State prison population[2]		Classification (male except where noted)
Qld	Borallon	Jan 1990–Oct 2000[3]	CCA	Manage & operate	492	9.75%	Sentenced, Medium security
	Arthur Gorrie	January 2001	MTC				
		April 1992	ACM	Manage & operate	710	14.08%	Remand & Reception, High security
NSW	Junee	April 1993	ACM	Design, Construct, Manage (DCM)	600	8.72%	Sentenced, 500 medium, 100 minimum
SA	Mt Gambier	Nov 1995	Group 4	Operate	110	7.95%	Sentenced, Medium and low
Vic	Met. Women's Corr. Centre	Aug 1996 3 Oct 2000	CCA[4] CORE	Build, Own, Operate, Transfer (BOOT)	125	4.38%	Female, Remand & Reception
	Fulham	April 1997	ACM	BOOT	590	20.65%	Sentenced, Medium and low
	Port Phillip	Sept 1997	Group 4	BOOT	600	21.00%	Remand & Reception, High
WA	Acacia	April 2001	CCA/AIMS[5]	Design, Build, Finance, Operate & Maintain	750	27.93%	Sentenced, Medium

133

Constitutional and parliamentary mechanisms

Unlike the United States, where rights are enshrined in the federal constitution, the Australian Constitution generally provides only the barest outline for rights protection and not any definitive statement of entitlements. Express constitutional rights include a right to vote (s 41), religious freedom (s 116) and a right to a jury trial (s 80). Implied rights include freedom of speech in political discussion, the right to a fair trial and the right to have one's legal rights determined by a court, at least at the federal level. However, whether express or implied, Constitutional rights in Australia are ill defined. Where US prisoners have asserted their rights in constitutional litigation, Australian prisoners in both private and public facilities have limited recourse at this level for successful litigation should they feel their rights have been compromised.

As a method of monitoring private correctional services, parliamentary debate initially focused on the legitimacy of privatisation and enabling legislation (Harding 1997: 53). While initially limited, debate has since increased and become a positive factor in contributing to improved monitoring of prisoners' rights in private prisons. For example, in South Australia there was extensive debate regarding access and continuation of the Ombudsman's powers to investigate complaints against private providers and, similarly, access to freedom of information. In Victoria, parliamentary debate of private prison performance has been particularly active. Driven by the initial, and in some instances ongoing, poor performance of some private providers with regard to prisoner safety and high death/self-harm rates (Biles & Dalton 1999; Victoria. Legislative Assembly. 2000: 1891; 1999: 1141), parliamentary debate and continued public exposure of deficient performance provides a monitoring role for prisoners' rights.

In Queensland, notes accompanying the recent redrafting of corrective services legislation discussed the inclusion of specific prisoners' rights beyond recognition of basic human entitlements (Corrective Services Bill 2000 (Qld)). However, on the basis that specific prisoners' rights would create legal difficulties, it was concluded that the Bill should ensure basic human entitlements only, such as access to adequate accommodation, health and medical care, fair treatment and the necessities of life.

Legislative and judicial mechanisms

The most fundamental and legally enforceable impact on prisoners' rights is derived from legislation and the consequential prison rules. While referred to as 'rights', privileges are authorised and implemented by the relevant prison system and can be revoked, without question, under that same authority. Only in Victoria, under s 47 of the *Corrections Act* 1986, do prisoners have specific legislated rights that in many instances represent minimum standards, although they are not enforceable by civil action. As privileges encompass rights, it is critical that the various systems established to award and remove privileges are closely monitored. In private prisons, this is particularly important as failure of the State to monitor the system of privileges transfers responsibility for the administration of punishment to a corporate entity.

The most obvious means of protecting prisoners' rights is through the contract. In States with private prisons, apart from South Australia,[2] relevant legislation has been amended to provide for the contracting out of correctional services. While there is interstate variance in legislation and contract specifications, the contract between the State and private provider is the conduit for ensuring prisoners' well being. While referring to relevant legislation as the basis for service delivery, the contract details only those factors concerned with service delivery and performance expectations. However, as the prisoner is not a party to the contract, the contract does not create individual prisoners' rights. Contracts cannot include specific prisoners' rights nor deny any existing entitlements under legislation. Accordingly, prisoners' rights in private prisons are identical to those in public prisons (Harding 1997: 54).

While the system of prison rules, procedures, instructions or standards varies between States,[3] prison rules represent the most immediate and dynamic influence on prisoners' rights and entitlements. Notwithstanding the interstate variation, there is considerable consistency among prison rules in Australia. For example, usual categories include safety and security, reception, health care and administrative arrangements for prisoners with grievances, such as access to Official Visitors and the Ombudsman. As private providers are contractually bound to abide by the same legislation, they must develop specific centre rules and procedures. These rules and procedures provide the detailed framework for the prison's operation. Therefore, prison rules and procedures provide the blueprints for ensuring the maintenance of basic human rights through delineation of entitlements and privileges and their removal. To ensure prison rules and operating procedures for private prisons are transparent and accountable, operators are required to submit draft rules to State authorities for approval and government monitors or auditors intermittently review performance specifications, which include, of course, the rules and procedures.

Harding suggests that while prison rules acknowledge human rights, they are fundamentally an administrative arrangement between the State and itself (Harding 1997: 53). Accordingly, they do not confer on prisoners the potential for litigation in cases where they believe their rights have been compromised. Notwithstanding this, they do provide a basis for legal challenge through review of administrative decisions provisions or through judicial review in the Supreme Court should due process fail in applying prison rules. For example, in the Supreme Court of Victoria, a prisoner from Fulham Correctional Centre successfully challenged the loss of visits privileges following his conviction for a prison offence. It was successfully argued that in convicting the prisoner the Corrections Manager (Operations) failed to follow due process as detailed in the *Corrections Act 1986* (Vic), in that he gave inappropriate notice and refused to allow a relevant witness to be called (*Henderson v Beltracchi* [1999] VSC 135).[4]

Prisoners are also protected by common law that has established that prison authorities have a duty of care to inmates (see *Cekan v Haines* (1990) 21 NSWLR 296). Violation of the duty of care entitles a prisoner to sue for damages. Examples of breaches of this duty of care include poor maintenance of machinery in prison workshops leading to accidents, faulty kitchen equipment or slippery floors. In discussing the legal position of prisoners in private centres, Davies suggests that breach of a statutory duty should entitle an inmate to seek a writ of *mandamus*, that is, 'a court order which requires a public officer or body to perform their statutory duty according to law' (Davies 1998: 40). However, as most Corrections Acts lack specific detail on service delivery standards and as correctional staff at private facilities are not government officials, prisoners would have considerable difficulties in successfully litigating for failure to protect rights under this option.

Inquisitorial and administrative mechanisms

The final and possibly the most immediate and effective methods for prisoners in private prisons to protect their rights is through internal prison mechanisms, such as complaints to Official Visitors and Ombudsmen, Freedom of Information access, independent reviews and internal audits. Internal review systems oversee the implementation of prison rules and ensure that the prison's operations replicate the process and outcomes detailed in departmental policy and procedures and that the level of service delivery is at a level appropriate to society's demands. As State legislation provides for access to such groups in public prisons, private prisons are contractually bound to provide identical access. Prisoner access to these agencies varies; however, the most common method is through privileged mail.[5] In Queensland, under reg 8 of the *Corrective Services Regulations* 1989, privileged mail recipients typically include the following:

- the Ombudsman (Commonwealth, State or Territory as relevant)
- the relevant State Minister for corrections
- the Commonwealth Attorney-General
- an Official Visitor
- the Registrar or Clerk of the Court
- the Commissioner of Police
- the Secretary of a Community Corrections Board
- the Director of Public Prosecutions
- the Human Rights and Equal Opportunity Commission
- the relevant Director/Commissioner, Freedom of Information
- the departmental permanent head

A further avenue for the protection of prisoners' rights in private prisons is effective monitoring by the purchaser of the service, namely, the State. Effective monitoring is not only crucial to ensure the State maintains responsibility for the administration and allocation of punishment but it also provides quality control through ongoing oversight of service delivery.

Internal review systems require, in part, a set of standards which should, among other things, detail expectations regarding protection of prisoners' rights. In Australian prisons, both public and private, these standards reflect and often make reference to international minimum standards as well as domestic expectations. However, as these standards are not enshrined in legislation, they are not legally binding on correctional authorities. Like public prisons, there is the same expectation that these standards will be maintained in private centres.[6]

Official Visitors

Every Australian prison, whether public or private, has at least one Official or Prison Visitor appointed by the relevant Minister under legislation.[7] Indeed, commonly there are three Visitors who visit on a rostered basis. Official Visitors are required to visit a prison at least twice per month and have unrestricted access to all parts of the prison and all documents held by that centre. While generally Official Visitors have access to all parts of the prison, the General Manager or Superintendents can issue instructions to restrict access should he or she feel the Visitor is at risk or prison security may be compromised. The Official Visitor's primary function is to investigate prisoners' complaints and issues, as well as to oversee prison conditions. While there is interstate variation, Official Visitors are selected on the basis of expertise relevant to corrections. Accordingly, their backgrounds include legal, Indigenous or community representatives. The role of Official Visitors is consistent in public and private prisons.

As in public prisons, prisoners in private prisons have access to the Ombudsman in cases where they believe they have been subjected to procedural unfairness or oppression (Harding 1997: 57). Each State with private prisons provides legislated access for the Ombudsman through the Ombudsman Acts and/or Corrections or Prisons Acts.[8] There is no distinction between representations made to the Ombudsman from public or private prisons. The Ombudsman will only intervene when the internal prison complaint process has reached its conclusion and the outcome remains unsatisfactory. Further, the Ombudsman will not address issues of staffing levels and physical conditions in the prison, as these are non-procedural and the responsibility of the Minister. The Ombudsman usually lacks power to enforce its recommendations.

Table 9.2 summarises total complaints made to the various State Ombudsmen from prisoners in private and public prisons during 1998 and 1999. As with most quantitative data on prisons and prisoners, a number of factors complicate a comparative analysis. In this instance, Remand and Reception centre complaints are primarily related to property issues or inappropriate treatment as part of the arrest and post-sentencing process as opposed to specific corrections issues.[9] Further, prisons with medium to low security classification prisoners have fewer issues, as prisoners in these situations tend to be more settled if on long sentences or near release.

Table 9.2. Ombudsman complaints and visits, 1998-99

State	Prison	Total complaints	Total visits	Complaints per 100[1]
Qld	Arthur Gorrie	66	2	10.87
	Borallon	28	2	5.69
	QCORR	649	22	22.29
Vic	Port Phillip	197	9	32.83
	MWCC	71	5	56.80
	Fulham	71	2	12.03
	CORE	353	2.1 av	21.95
NSW	Junee	27	1	4.50
	Public	407	1.65 av	6.52
SA	Mt. Gambier	NA[2]	1	NA
	DCS (public)	453	10	34.55

1   Average daily prison population was used in this calculation.
2   The South Australian Ombudsman does not distinguish between public and private centres in complaints data collection.

Notwithstanding these factors, an interesting feature of Table 9.2 is the high number of complaints from the Port Phillip Prison and the Metropolitan Women's Correctional Centre, both privately operated in Victoria at the time. These were the only two private centres with a complaint rate higher than the public centres. This is a clear reflection of the well-documented problems these two centres have had, including deaths in custody and excessive lock-downs. Clearly, Ombudsman complaints in these instances reflect the failure of these private entities to provide adequate prisoner protection.

Anti-corruption agencies

Prisoners are vulnerable to the influences of official corruption and, accordingly, may have fundamental entitlements abused. For example, corrupt officers could influence case management outcomes or prison labour could be used inappropriately for officer profit.

In New South Wales (NSW), under ss 7 and 8 of the *Independent Commission Against Corruption Act* 1988 and s 218 of the *Crimes (Administration of Sentences) Act* 1999, the Independent Commission Against Corruption has the power to investigate private prisons. In NSW at present, Junee Correctional Centre is the only private prison. To date, there have been no specific investigations into official corruption at that centre. However, major investigations have been concluded into case management practices for the entire NSW prison system and these have implications for Junee.

Unlike NSW, in Queensland, the Criminal Justice Commission (CJC) does not have powers to investigate complaints of official corruption in private prisons (Criminal Justice Commission 2000b: 1). The implications of this inability to investigate such allegations has direct relevance to a government's ability to maintain responsibility for the administration of punishment.

Recent allegations of theft, unauthorised manufacturing for personal profit and staff and management conflicts of interest in the industries section of Borallon Correctional Centre have significant implications for abuse of prisoners' rights (Queensland Legislative Assembly, 3 October 2000: 3293). While being repeatedly requested by the State Government to allow the Queensland Police Service and CJC to investigate these allegations, the then-provider, CCA, has declined such an investigation, instead initiating an independent audit.[10] Notwithstanding that prisoner labor is allegedly involved, as no formal charges have been laid and as the allegations of impropriety concern internal CCA company matters, the government decided that they lacked contractual or legislative power to intervene and rectify the situation.

Although these allegations appear to contravene several clauses of the contract and, therefore, the providers are in breach of contract, the government proved unable and CCA unwilling to instigate an appropriate investigation. The protection of prisoners' rights was consequently significantly compromised.

Freedom of Information

Freedom of Information (FOI) provisions for prisoners in private facilities do not vary from those in public facilities, as long as the information being requested relates to correctional as opposed to contractual matters. In this instance, 'contractual matters' are details of the contract between the purchaser (the State) and the provider. Should an inmate feel his or her entitlements are being diminished as a result of the contract, commercial-in-confidence provisions limit FOI access, although there is again some interstate variation.

Excessive use of commercial-in-confidence provisions to deny access to service agreements limits transparency and, accordingly, accountability. In Victoria, a long-running dispute over access to Victorian private prison contracts was resolved through an FOI application to the Victorian Civil and Administrative Tribunal in May 1999 (Audit Review of Government Contracts 2000; Freiberg 1999). In this instance, all details, apart from those concerning prison security, were released. In NSW, however, commercial-in-confidence provisions totally restrict public access to the service contract for Junee Correctional Centre. The initial reluctance of governments to release contract information appears to be waning. In Western Australia (WA), the contract for the Acacia private prison, including costs, is posted on the Ministry of Justice website, <www.justice.wa.gov.au/content/files/acacia.pdf>. In Queensland, the tender and contract documents for the recent re-tender of Borallon Correctional Centre were released at the completion of the letting process.[11] In this instance, costings were excluded despite the contract itself permitting them to be released.

Monitoring and audit

As previously indicated, there is no distinction between private and public prisons regarding an inmate's access to mechanisms for the protection of rights or entitlements. However, a distinguishing feature of the private correctional system which has the potential to improve protection of rights in private prisons is government monitoring and audit. Monitoring is the State-initiated process to oversee the operations of the private provider. The role of a State-appointed monitor, liaison officer or controller is distinct from a departmental auditor, with the former concerned with maintenance of contractual and legislated standards while the latter focuses on performance evaluation in public and private prisons (Harding 1997: 38).

Effective monitoring provides an additional dimension of accountability through rigorous and constant inspection of existing entitlements. It does not, however, replace or diminish the importance of other internal review mechanisms. Where the common review mechanisms are largely retrospective, usually initiated through inmate complaints, effective monitoring is pro-active, concerned with the day-to-day interpretation of prison policy and dealing with inmate issues as they occur, all of which is directed towards ensuring an appropriate level of service provision.

Ineffective monitoring, however, creates the potential for the State to partially transfer responsibility for the allocation of punishment to the private service provider by failing to oversee centre operations. For example, in managing and operating a centre, private providers are involved with every facet of prison life, from initiating and participating in hearing cases for breaches of prison rules and, possibly, deciding penalties for breach convictions, through to determining the quality of health services, food — the list goes on and on. Should monitoring fail, the State would have no responsibility for the allocation of punishment in the hearing of prison rule breaches or the sentence management process, for example. Further, should the provider reduce service delivery to maximise profit, the consequences of unfettered profit taking could, in the short term at least, remain unchecked. Should this occur, possible implications impinging on inmates' rights and entitlements are increases in prisoner-on-prisoner assaults and reduced out-of-cell hours, which are both symptomatic of insufficient staff, as well as reductions in the quality and amount of food, health care and so on.

The audit function has a far wider scope than monitoring and is not limited to private prisons. Prison audits are concerned with the quality of service provision, which includes the maintenance of suitable standards of service delivery impacting on prisoners' rights and entitlements. The audit role involves overall performance evaluation, as distinct from contract monitoring.

The efficacy of a prison system is to some extent determined by the quality of monitoring and audit. Arguably, the best example of an effective blend of monitoring and audit is in the United Kingdom. In this model, a controller is appointed by the director-general of prisons to oversee and report on each private prison's performance (Harding 1997: 90). The controller has power to conduct investigations at each private prison, including allegations of inappropriate behavior by custodial officers. Further, the controller also adjudicates in hearing prison rule breaches and administers appropriate disciplinary measures should they be required. In this instance, the private provider has no role in the internal prison discipline process other than initiating the charge. Thus, the State maintains responsibility for the allocation of punishment.

In UK prisons, the audit function lies with Her Majesty's Chief Inspector of Prisons. The strength of this office is its independence. The Inspector of Prisons reports directly to the Home Secretary, not the prison service and, accordingly, has no interest in matters other than the performance of the prison being audited. Audits are not limited by the potential for 'capture', in which the regulator becomes more concerned with ensuring that the interests of the service provider are protected than the outcome or performance of that provider (Harding 1997: 61-3). While providing an advisory service only, inspections are conducted both on an announced (regular and advised) and unannounced basis, with subsequent reports being publicly available. Further, the inspectorate completes thematic reviews of various prison functions, providing models of best practice.[12]

In Australia, there is considerable variation in private prison monitoring and auditing models with differential effectiveness, as will be identified.

New South Wales

Under s 242(1)-(8) of the *Crimes (Administration of Sentences) Act* 1999 (NSW), a 'Monitor' (originally known as a 'Liaison Officer') is appointed to Junee Correctional Centre. This officer was initially appointed to facilitate its opening and then to monitor performance and operator compliance with minimum standards as detailed in Schedule 1 to the management contract (Bowery 1999: 81). Originally located on-site, the role has since altered, with monitoring now occurring through random visits. The Liaison Officer is required to complete an annual compliance audit which reviews performance against a minimum standards checklist and includes interviews with management, officers and prisoners, centre inspections and review of records and consideration of reviews by other departmental stakeholders (NSW Department of Corrective Services 1999: 86). The Liaison Officer is required to publish the performance review in the Department's Annual Report. The Liaison Officer is not involved in breach of prison rule hearings and has no delegated powers to intercede in such matters other than reporting. Disputes are referred to external review sources. As the Liaison Officer is now off-site, the role is effectively that of a contract compliance auditor tasked with ensuring minimum standards are maintained.

Victoria

The regulation and monitoring of all Victorian prisons is the responsibility of the Commissioner of Correctional Services under s 8A of the *Corrections Act* 1986. In particular, it is the role of the Monitoring and Assessment Unit in the Commissioner's Office to evaluate prison performance against standards and inputs and to determine compliance levels. Further, for private prisons, s 9D of the Act provides scope for the Secretary of the Department of Justice to appoint a monitor to review service provision by the suppliers and/or their subcontractors on an as-needed basis from time to time. Additional monitoring is performed by the off-site Contract Administrator appointed by the Secretary of the Department of Justice. The Contract Administrator's duties include liaison between the government and the provider, preparation of monthly reports including the reporting of major developments and any adverse occurrences and managing contract disputes.[13] As in NSW, annual reviews of the private prisons must be published in the Commissioner's Annual Report. The level of reporting is, however, limited in terms of accountability as was indicated by the Victorian Auditor-General in a review of the correctional system.

[t]he limited range of information dealing with the industry communicated to the Parliament to date in the Department's annual report falls far short of the level necessary to effectively meet its accountability obligations relating to the operation of the prison system. (Audit Victoria 1999: para 5.12)

In Victoria, the Commissioner of Correctional Services has responsibility for the development of performance standards and outputs as well as a regulatory role in determining how successfully these are being achieved in both public and private prisons. Regulation involves a combination of monitoring and auditing. By being both the regulator and purchaser of contract correctional services, the initial organisational and reporting structures of the Commissioner's Office established a framework destined for capture, that is, where the regulator becomes more concerned with ensuring the success or continuation of the provider than the quality of service provision, having significant negative effects on the protection of prisoners' rights.

Port Phillip Men's prison operated by Group 4 opened in September 1997. In its first five months of operation, there were three deaths and 49 cases of self-mutilation and attempted suicide as well as an unacceptably high number of positive drug tests (Audit Victoria 1999: para 5.98). The situation did not improve with a major disturbance occurring on 11-12 March 1998, which resulted in 48 cells being unusable for a period in excess of ten days (Audit Victoria 1999: para 5.105; Audit Review of Government Contracts 2000: 25). A government-appointed Task Force reported that the problems were due, in part, to management failing to fulfill basic operational requirements with an ad hoc approach and a preparedness to present information that was incorrect (Audit Victoria 1999: para 5.109). As a result of this report, Group 4 was required to provide a 'cure plan'[14] and given 30 days to improve performance. Additionally, the accommodation service charge was reduced due to the reduction in bed space occurring as a consequence of the disturbance, although this was by only 0.2% of the annual accommodation service charge (Audit Victoria 1999: para 5.114). The Commissioner's Office subsequently reviewed the prison again in February 1998 and reported that only 11 of 19 service delivery outcomes had been achieved. However, a default notice was not issued until June 1998 (Audit Victoria 1999: para 5.115).

While recent data suggest that Group 4's performance at Port Phillip has improved (Audit Victoria 1999: para 5.119), the situation at the Metropolitan Women's Correctional Centre owned, managed and operated by CCA deteriorated to the point that, in spite of a series of default notices between May and June 2000, the Commissioner invoked the emergency powers provision (s 8F) of the *Corrections Act* 1986 and a default clause of the Prison Service Agreement and took responsibility for the management and operation of the prison until such time as the prison is stable and a long-term solution has been reached.[15] Whereas Group 4 finally introduced a range of remedial strategies, albeit only following repeated although apparently ineffectual punitive actions by the purchaser, CCA repeatedly failed to address deficient performance appropriately.

A review of incidents at the Metropolitan Women's Correctional Centre suggests that protection of prisoners' fundamental rights was limited. What is particularly disturbing is an upward trend in serious incidents that is the opposite to that occurring at Port Phillip.[16] For example, in 1998-99 there were 32 self-harm incidents as compared with 18 in the previous year. There were 48 prisoner-on-prisoner assaults in 1998-99 compared with 29 in the previous year (Audit Review of Government Contracts 2000: 29). Also reported were incidents of prisoners being excessively locked in their cells due to staff shortages, tear gas being used to control inmates and staff failing in one instance to identify an 'at-risk' inmate who had made repeated requests for assistance and who subsequently suicided (Prison Privatization Report International 1999 (No 32)).

While there were clear managerial deficiencies in the operation of both of these centres, a number of other factors contributed to the problems. For example, almost half of the entire Victorian prison population was relocated to private prisons over a short time span. In the case of Port Phillip, this occurred in only 12 weeks. Further, in an attempt to ensure a prison officer culture that reflected a new approach to penology, inexperienced officers were employed in preference to those with public sector correctional experience.

In an attempt to diffuse the situation following the Commissioner's takeover of the Metropolitan Women's Correctional Centre, CCA argued that the decision was politically motivated by a government opposed to privatisation and that a number of contributing factors were beyond their control, such as overcrowding (Prison Privatization Report International 1999 (No 32)). In 1998-99, the average prison utilisation rate was 108.8%, indicating that overcrowding would be a factor contributing to the incidents at the Metropolitan Women's Correctional Centre (Audit Review of Government Contracts 2000: 25).

In reviewing the Victorian prison system, Victoria's Auditor-General indicated several factors which contributed to prisoners' welfare being compromised (Audit Victoria 1999).

- The Contract Administrator noted that, despite failing to achieve necessary performance improvements following 'cure plans', the Commissioner's Office had been 'very accommodating' in commissioning issues beyond what could be considered reasonable (para 7.77). In this instance, the dissonance created by the purchaser also being the regulator resulted in capture, with the Commissioner's Office being overly generous in failing to initiate suitable penalties for poor performance. Poor performance was dismissed for too long as 'teething problems' (para 7.69).

- When penalties were initiated, they were minimal and not commensurate with the distress caused by the poor performance (para 7.72).

- Problems with internal communication such that it took up to two months for the Commissioner's reports to reach the Contract Administrator (para 7.62).

- Performance specifications were largely quantitative, in some cases, based on lowest levels in the public system or, for self-harm, assaults and positive drug tests, the highest rates in the public system (para 7.36). Accordingly, private operators were not under pressure to be innovative in developing new work practices to reduce self-harming levels or the incidence of drug use.

In both the Group 4 and CCA examples, the continued poor performance of the private providers was allowed to continue despite being in default of contractual obligations, thus compromising prisoners' entitlements. While initial teething problems are to be expected with any new centre's opening, the regularity of major incidents in the provision of fundamental responsibilities, such as providing a safe environment, indicates serious problems. Failure to respond appropriately, particularly at the women's prison, suggests that poor work practices had become endemic. In this example, a clearly deficient service provider combined with ineffective monit-oring and an audit system that, until recently, was captured negated the potential of the purchaser to be pro-active in maintaining prisoners' rights.

The situation in Victoria is being controlled, as exemplified by the Commissioner taking control of the Metropolitan Women's Correctional Centre. While these early performance deficits have compromised some prisoners' entitlements and rights, there are elements of the Victorian model which have improved service-wide provision and will continue to do so at an increased rate. For example, the development of health standards and monitors appointed to review the provision of health care in private prisons has improved the level of care. Further, with the refinement of performance indicators, 'competition by comparison' has been created between the private and public sectors, with the public system having to improve performance to remain competitive (Audit Review of Government Contracts 2000: 40). The public system has become more accountable (Audit Victoria 1999: para 7.81), thus improving the protection of prisoners' rights.

Queensland

The system of monitoring private prisons in Queensland has changed over time. Initially, both private prisons opened with State-appointed monitors operating on-site. At Borallon, managed and operated by CCA, this was under the title of a Contract Monitor while at Arthur Gorrie, managed and operated by ACM, the position was called the Contract Auditor (later replaced with two positions: Senior Liaison Officer and Liaison Officer).

While not mandatory, the contracts with both operators provided for the appointment of a person to monitor the performance of the contractor and/or audit any aspect of the centre and operations. Each provider was obliged to provide suitable accommodation and access to all books, registers and documents to allow compliance assessment. At Borallon, the Contract Monitor was initially the delegated authority for a range of activities including leave of absence approvals and adjudication in breaches of prison rules. These and other delegations were later transferred to the operator. In both centres, however, monitors were encouraged by the purchaser to provide a supportive as well as inquisitorial role, thus creating role dissonance ultimately leading to capture.

With the expansion of other contracted components in the Queensland model, such as community corrections centres, the role of the Borallon monitor in contrast with that of the liaison officers at Arthur Gorrie became multifaceted. Yet the duties remained with one person. This, combined with the delegation of various powers to the private centres, reduced the perceived need for a monitor's presence on-site, particularly at Borallon, which was operating at a very high standard. Accordingly, on-site auditing was replaced with intermittent inspection as part of the departmental compliance audit process. In this instance, there is no distinction between public and private prisons, as both are subject to compliance audit.

This audit process is of particular interest at Arthur Gorrie. As that centre is the State's primary remand and reception centre, prison classifications are assigned during the reception process. That is, inmates are assigned a security classification by a custodial officer employed by the private provider. When the centre opened, the Senior Liaison Officer, or delegate, was required to approve all classifications as determined by the sentence management team. In due course, however, it was determined by the Queensland Corrective Services Commission that the role of the liaison position was no longer required and the position removed with responsibilities transferred to the purchaser.

Currently, if the sentence is less than two years, the provider is not required to submit the recommended classification to the Department of Correctional Services sentence management team for approval as the General Manager has the delegated authority to make such decisions. For a sentence over two years, the recommended classification requires departmental sanction. Therefore, in sentences less than two years, private enterprise determines the initial sentence management process which clearly has major ramifications for a prisoner. An aggrieved prisoner, however, may appeal sentence classification decisions to the department (*Corrective Services Regulation* 2001, reg 4). As with all prisons in Queensland, audit of the prisoner classification and sentence management process occurs through an inspector's presence in classification meetings and case management reviews to ensure appropriate processes.

The audit and monitoring role in Queensland has recently been amended. In reviewing oversight of private providers, the Commission of Inquiry into Corrective Services suggested that 'self-reporting and good information analysis negate the need for on-site monitors' (Queensland Corrective Services Review 1999: 60). Accordingly, it was indicated that State responsibility for prisoners in private centres would be retained through effective performance measurement, output based contracts, comprehensive performance audit and off-site monitors. In the event of declining performance, an audit team may be placed at the centre until such time as the matter has been rectified (Queensland Corrective Services Review 1999: 61).

Draft legislation for the reconstituted contract monitoring role is included in the *Corrective Services Bill* 2000 and in the new contract for the management and operation of Borallon. Under the terms of this contract, the purchaser may appoint a monitor whose responsibilities include ensuring that service providers meet contract and statutory obligations. Monitors' duties are not, however, solely inquisitive. They are also required to encourage a 'partnering framework' through bilateral communication (personal communication, Department of Corrective Services audit office, 10 October 2000). The monitor is also required to provide operational support to the service providers and there is provision for as yet unidentified delegation of certain authorities. These delegations will not, however, include participation in prison discipline matters. To minimise the potential for capture, three monitors' positions have been established and a specific proce-dures manual is currently being developed. It is proposed that by being off-site and rotated, monitors will maintain the necessary independence from the two existing private providers.

South Australia

Of all States, the South Australian model offers the least invasive method of private prison performance monitoring and auditing. Privatisation of the Mt Gambier Correctional Centre was achieved administratively following the failure of enabling legislation. Accordingly, that centre retains a State-employed General Manager and a number of advisory staff, while Group 4 provides the operational staff. As the State retains management responsibility, monitoring is considered redundant.

Western Australia

Western Australia is the most recent State to privatise a component of its custodial correctional system with the letting of the Acacia Correctional Centre to CCA/AIMS on 21 December 1999. In doing so, WA has also introduced what is potentially the most rigorous of all monitoring and audit models.

In this model, the principal, that is, the chief executive officer of the Ministry of Justice must appoint a contract manager with all of the powers of that chief executive officer relating to the agreement and an on-site contract monitor responsible for overseeing prison operations

(*Acacia Prison Services Agreement,* cl 21). The contract requires monthly reviews of performance against minimum standards by a panel comprising the State-appointed contract manager, the contract monitor, a contractor representative and the contractor's Superintendent at the centre. Further, the contract establishes timeframes for incident reporting as well as dispute resolution procedures including the process of invoking default clauses for failing to maintain minimum standards.

In WA, all breaches of the Prisons Act at Acacia require adjudication by a Visiting Justice or CEO-appointed adjudicator who may be the contract monitor or a superintendent from a public prison. Thus, the private provider has no role in disciplinary proceedings apart from making the initial infringement report.[17] An additional safeguard requires custodial officers laying charges against inmates for breaches of the Prisons Act to have formal prosecution training. The separation of punishment from the provider combined with custodial officers trained in prosecution constitutes a substantially improved breach hearing process. These measures enhance the protection of the rights and entitlements of prisoners.

The final element of the WA model which provides improved protection of prisoners' rights is the appointment of an Inspector of Custodial Services. Appointed under the *Prisons Amendment Act* 1999, the role of the inspectorate is to 'bring independent external scrutiny to the standards and operational practices relating to custodial services within Western Australia' (Office of the Inspector of Custodial Services (WA) see *Annual Report 1999/2000*: 7). The inspectorate has audit responsibilities for all custodial facilities in WA as well as a mandate to undertake thematic reviews and comment on service standards. The operational methodology of the inspectorate is not dissimilar to that of Her Majesty's Chief Inspector of Prisons apart from the reporting structure. In WA, the Inspector reports directly to Parliament, having statutory autonomy. In this way, independence is maintained and the potential for capture is limited.

The implications for protection of prisoners' rights are profound. The introduction of a private prison in WA has provided a catalyst for considerable reform to the benefit of improved protection of prisoners' rights. The multifaceted approach to accountability, combined with the clear distinction between the allocation and administration of punishment, ensures the State retains its responsibility for corrections while improving accountability not only with the private provider through monitoring and structured review but in the public system as well with the introduction of the Inspector of prisons.

Conclusion

The introduction of private prisons in Australia has been the catalyst for significant reform in the evaluation of prison performance which, ultimately, has impacted on protection of inmate rights. The introduction of purchaser/provider contracts, which often include references to various UN standards and conventions, key performance indicators, minimum standards and output based evaluation, for example, are now universally accepted as defining performance expectations. Prior to privatisation, such expectations were often broad and ill-defined, thus limiting performance assessment and the accountability of the public sector.

While there is no doubt that performance measures have markedly improved, ultimately the success or otherwise of ensuring respect for the basic human rights of prisoners in public or private centres rests with the thoroughness of the audit and monitoring systems. Prisoners' rights in private prisons are no different from those in public institutions. However, should accountability fail, observers of private prisons are left to speculate about any abuse or profit taking at the expense of prisoners' rights. Not only must accountability be enshrined in legislation and, therefore, open, the purchaser must take immediate and appropriate action in any instance of inappropriate behavior. In instances where the public sector purchaser of correctional services has failed to take definitive measures to counter poor performance, the opportunity to maximise the potential benefits of private providers is lost, replaced by suspicion of operations and attention to prisoners' rights.

Notes

1   It should be noted that this percentage has reduced as the contract for the Metropolitan Women's Correctional Centre (Deer Park), formerly owned and operated by Corrections Corporation of Australia (CCA) in Victoria, was extinguished on 3 October 2000.

2   Privatisation of Mount Gambier Prison in South Australia was achieved administratively, with the Department of Corrections appointing a public sector manager with small support staff, while the prison is operated by Group 4.

3   In Queensland, s 189 of the *Corrective Services Act* 2000 sets out the power to make administrative policy and procedures for prisons.

4   Fulham is owned and operated by ACM.

5   Unlike standard prisoner mail, privileged mail cannot be searched except in the presence of the prisoner or read without the prisoner's written permission.

6   It is usual for Invitations to Tender documents to refer to UN Covenants and minimum standards. The minimum standards in the Acacia Prison Services Agreement highlight a number of principles, including that prisoners retain citizenship rights.

7   *Corrections Act* 1986 (Vic) s 35; *Corrective Services Act* 1988 (Qld) ss 23-26; *Crimes (Administration of Sentences) Act* 1999 (NSW) s 228; *Prisons Act* 1981 (WA) ss 54-55.

8   *Ombudsman Act* 1974 (NSW); *Parliamentary Commissioner Act* 1971 (WA); *Ombudsman Act* 1973 (Vic); *Parliamentary Commissioner Act* 1974 (Qld).

9   Personal communication, Senior Administrative Review Officer, Parliamentary Commissioner for Administrative Investigations, 4 October 2000.

10   CCA no longer holds the management and operation contract for Borallon Correctional Centre.

11   The contract was signed 1 October 2000 and released 4 October 2000.

12   Detailed on the Chief Inspector's website at <www.homeoffice.gov.uk/hmipris/hmipris. htm>

13   Prison Services Agreement for the Development, Ownership & Operation of the Men's Metropolitan Prison, executed July 1996, Commissioner of Correctional Services, p 121.

14   Detailed in the Prison Services Agreements as a plan proposed by the contractor to remedy a default.

15   The end result of this action has been that the centre has returned to government control.

16   For Port Phillip, 75 self-mutilations were reported in 1997-98 and 16 attempted suicides. In 1998-99 the figures were 40 and 9 respectively (Audit Review of Government Contracts 2000: 24).

17   *Acacia Prison Services Agreement*, Conformed copy only, between the State of Western Australia and Corrections Corporation of Australia Pty Ltd.

Impacts of Privatisation

Approximately three years prior to my arrest I was diagnosed with cancer, specifically Lymphocystic Lymphoma. As this disease remains active today I require ongoing medical treatment and until recently one could describe the treatment and management of my disease as adequate. The privatisation of the prison medical service requires inmates now to be transferred to Port Phillip prison for treatment. The incompetence and lack of professionalism of their operations, management and Health Services is the cause of ever increasing problems we experience in attempting to obtain adequate and proper medical treatment.

Victorian male prisoner

It seems to me that the private enterprise really try hard to make your stay as less traumatic as possible but the public servants just don't care at all and really give everyone a hard time ... You must take into account also the public system constantly tampers with mail ... we pay good money (our money) to use the phone and it is always breaking down. So the public system cannot even get a simple thing like that right ... Private gaols do a better job than the public ones. Many things eg riots, deaths, lying, bastardry, thievery does happen in the public area but they always sweep it under the carpet.

Victorian male prisoner

CHAPTER 10

Prisoners as Citizens: A View from Europe

Vivien Stern

Perceptions and treatment

Ted Conover is a journalist. He wanted to write about the prison system of New York State but made no progress using conventional methods. So he applied to become a prison guard. He was accepted and went through the training. After seven weeks, he qualified and started work at Sing Sing, the most unpopular posting in the system. Training school had taught him how prisoners were to be seen as 'the bad guys'. 'The scum of the earth' was how one senior office described them (Conover 2000: 3).

One week of the training was called 'range week', spent learning how to shoot. Recruits were taught that 'shooting at the ground in front of rioting inmates … could be highly effective, as it sprayed buckshot at several individuals instead of giving only one man the full force of a blast' (Conover 2000: 43).

In the last two weeks, a topic was 'Defensive Tactics'. The recruits learnt that '[j]abbing an inmate with straightened fingers in the windpipe … or the eyeballs … was said to be extremely effective. And in the case of the latter move, there was a good chance it would not even cause blindness' (Conover 2000: 51).

In many ways, Sing Sing is like prisons all around the world. People are locked up, deprived of freedom of choice, separated from their families, kept in a same-sex environment with many others from the same background. They are subject to rules aimed at regulating what they can have in their cells, whom they can write to, how long they have in the open air and how they can raise complaints about their treatment. Preventing them from escaping is a major determinant of the routines of daily life.

If some prisoners and staff were to be suddenly transplanted from, say, Sing Sing prison in upstate New York to the high security prison in San Jose, Costa Rica, they would know straightaway they were in a prison. They would know their way around. They would recognise the prisoner culture and the unwritten rules that govern it, the tacit agreements with the guards that allow the place to function, the methods prisoners find to make life more bearable.

But they would immediately realise they were not at home. They would be struck by a different approach to the relationship between the captives and the guardians than the one they were used to. They might be surprised, for example, to find themselves in a meeting room with the prison director discussing how they were all going to manage the next stage of building refurbishment and how it could be accomplished with minimum disruption to everyone's lives. They might notice in the way they were spoken to that they were in a culture that sees its prisoners in a different way. They would find themselves under the authority of a government that was trying, albeit not always successfully, to treat its prisoners as citizens, a prison administration that put all its staff through a human rights training course. They might be surprised to learn that a ruling by the Constitutional Court in 1993 gave both pre-trial and sentenced prisoners the right to vote.[1]

The way prisoners are seen in any society is likely to affect the way they are treated, how many of their rights as citizens are taken away when they lose their liberty, how far prison life is unlike life in outside society.

The view taken of prisoners in any culture is a complex interaction of many processes. A positive attitude to prisoners by those at the top, the authority figures, can be one element. In the summer of 1999, President Guterres of Portugal visited Tires prison on World Anti-drug Day, where he inaugurated a new drug free wing and launched a new program for drug addiction prevention in prison. The event received extensive coverage.

In July 2000, the Pope visited the overcrowded and dilapidated Regina Coeli prison in Rome (see the European Committee for the Prevention of Torture and Inhuman or Degrading Treatment or Punishment (CPT) 1997 for a description of the conditions at this prison). He spoke of a prison system with 'human features' and 'a penal system more in conformity with human dignity'.[2] In November

2000, the US Catholic Bishops issued a statement on crime and punishment, stressing the need for a more socially inclusive way of treating prisoners (Catholic Bishops of the United States 2000). The portrayal of prisons and prisoners in the media is another factor that affects the way prisoners are seen. The balance of the coverage is one barometer. It can show how much the public feels some sense of ownership of the fate of those who are incarcerated. How much coverage is given to abuses of prisoners' rights, prison suicides, the problems prisoners face on release? Do all commentators speaking about prisoners' problems have to make a disclaimer that victims are of course more important and apologise for being concerned about the treatment of prisoners?

Language and images are also significant. The Director General of the prison service of England and Wales recently called for more attention to be given to language (Narey 2000)[3]. In some prisons, he said, 'a minority of staff ... see prisoners not as people entitled to be treated with dignity but as some form of sub species'. It was, he said, not a sign of the culture he wanted to promote in British prisons to talk not of serving meals but of 'feeding, as if we were dealing with animals in a zoo'. He went on: 'I visited a prison just a few days ago and saw a notice on a door which said *No Entry While Feeding in Progress*. What does that convey about our attitude to prisoners?' (Narey 2000).

British television cameras are often permitted to film in prison. Such news items or documentaries show prisoners as normal, average, usually young working class men, just like young men next door or on the street. In the United States, the images are more of people handcuffed or wearing leg chains, dressed in abnormal orange jumpsuits. The advertisements in US prison service magazines aimed at selling security equipment often feature prisoners as unsmiling, villainous looking creatures. One such recent advertisement had the caption 'He could cut you up'. It went on to say, 'The cell block. The dining hall. The yard. Somewhere, there could be a hardened criminal concealing a sharpened weapon. Watching. Waiting. Hoping someone makes a wrong move, so he can make his'. The advertisement is for a telephone system that works so well that prison authorities will not have to worry about it. Thus they can concentrate on worrying about the prisoner with the weapon (August 1998, vol 60, *Corrections Today*: 19).

Public events are also significant in showing how a society views its prisoners, whether as people temporally abstracted from the community or as permanent outcasts. Every year in the United Kingdom, there is an art competition for prisoners and patients in secure mental hospitals. Prizes are awarded and the entries are on public display and for sale for several weeks on the top floor of a shopping mall in London.[4]

The East European experience

Nowhere are greater changes taking place in the treatment of prisoners than in the countries of the former Soviet bloc. In these States, the transition from communism to democracy had a profound effect on imprisonment. In communist times, prisoners were indeed enemies of the State. Zdenek Karabec, a former Director General of the Czech prison service, wrote:

> If offenders in totalitarian countries are labelled as enemies of the state, then state authorities consider themselves entitled to exercise power over them in any way ... (staff) were also encouraged in the notion that they were superior to the prisoners and had power over their lives. (Karabec 1995: 18)

Now that most of the formerly Soviet states are democratic, many have joined the Council of Europe (the latest to join are the former Soviet Republics of Armenia and Azerbaijan). Membership requires them to make a great leap and change their penal laws, their structures and their attitudes to people in prison. This process has shown very clearly the distinction between prisoners as non-persons and prisoners as citizens. In Soviet times, prisoners were not citizens in any sense. They were slave labourers. Their status was governed by law and regulations that gave them some rights but within a context of leaving the world of citizens and joining another world (Solzhenitsyn 1974). It is illustrative of this status that statistics on the incidence of tuberculosis in the Russian Federation are even now collected for two categories of person: citizens of the Federation and 'the rest'. 'The rest' includes prisoners, refugees and the homeless.[5] Many of the rituals of humiliation and depersonalisation found in most prison systems at some time were practised in the Soviet gulag. Prisoners' heads were shaved. Shapeless, pyjama-like uniforms were issued. Prisoners were required to turn and face the wall with heads lowered when visitors or authority passed by. Papers were stamped so that everyone would know on release that this is an ex-prisoner. The location of prisons and what went on in them was a State secret. There was no interchange with the normal services of the community. The doctors, nurses, psychologists all came from the Ministry of the Interior, the security service.

The amount of change in the region in the past decade has been enormous and has given a number of signposts to the rest of the world as to the requirements of prison systems in democratic societies that wish to conform to international human rights standards. Changes in prison rules in Russia, for instance, meant that in 1988 dietary punishment was abolished[6] (King 1994: 76). From 1992, putting prisoners in straitjackets was no longer allowed. The rules were changed to allow prisoners in special high security units and those awaiting sentence to be given bedding and to be allowed outside exercise every day. Freedom of conscience and the right to practise religion were recognised. Head shaving was stopped and beards and moustaches were permitted. Adult women were allowed to wear their own clothes. Access to a private doctor was permitted if the prisoner had the money to pay. Restrictions on correspondence were abolished. Family visits were increased. If telephones had been installed, prisoners were allowed to use them. Letters to legal authorities were not stopped or read. Neither visits nor parcels nor access to the prison shop could be withheld as a disciplinary punishment. Prisoners became entitled to 12 working days as paid holiday and, in certain circumstances, they could take these days outside the prison camp. Time spent in prison would count towards accumulating pension rights (Stern 1998: 78-9).

In Poland, radical reform over ten years took the Polish prison service from a Soviet-style system to a prison service receiving a very favourable report from the Council of Europe Committee for the Prevention of Torture (CPT 1998b), a report more favourable than ones on the United Kingdom or the Netherlands for instance (CPT 2000b; CPT 1998a).

The reform in Poland is a useful indication of the elements needed for a prison system that tries to respect the human rights of those it deprives of liberty. A major part of the reform was to open up the prisons to the progressive elements of society and to the churches. Secrecy was abolished and *bona fide* visitors of all sorts were encouraged — artists, journalists, charities, educationalists. The staff were required to accept and follow the new methods or leave. About one-third left (Stern 1998: 78-9).[7] Family contact was encouraged and home leaves greatly increased.

The West European experience

The changes in East and Central Europe are much influenced by European views about imprisonment. These countries are nearly all in the

Council of Europe or aspiring to join. A number in Central Europe are also applicant countries to the European Union. Hungary, Poland, Romania, the Slovak Republic, Estonia, Lithuania, Bulgaria, Czech Republic and Slovenia all hope to join. Broadly speaking, approaches to imprisonment in the world can be divided into three categories. First, there is a group of countries that does not accept the basic premise that underlies the international human rights standards governing the treatment of prisoners: 'that prisoners should be treated with humanity and with respect for the inherent dignity of the human person' (*International Covenant on Civil and Political Rights* (ICCPR) art 10). These countries do not see prisoners as continuing their citizenship with a view to eventual reintegration into society. The United States is the largest country in this group which includes Saudi Arabia and some other Middle Eastern States, Burma and Singapore.

Secondly, there is a group that accepts the human rights principles in theory but fails to deliver them in practice, either because of poverty or institutional incompetence. Many countries in Africa fail due to poverty,[8] while Brazil and others in Latin America fail due to institutional incompetence.[9]

Finally, there is the European group, subject to the requirements of the Council of Europe and the European Convention on Human Rights (ECHR). Those aspiring to join the European Union have to pass certain tests and prison conditions acceptable in a European context are part of these.[10] The European system of regional standard setting for prisons and monitoring their performance is the most developed in the world and it is worth considering it in some detail.

As did the UN human rights machinery, the Council of Europe grew out of the Second World War.[11] The monstrous human rights abuses of the time led to some conclusions about how States and the bulk of their peoples can mistreat minorities, groups they have historically mistrusted and people they have been taught are their enemies. The Council of Europe's founders were looking to encourage inclusive societies in which rights were respected and no one was seen as an internal enemy. They wanted to replace the notion of 'enemies' with the notion of fellow citizens who may have committed heinous acts but who must be kept within the framework of that society and assumed to be one day re-entering it as a free citizen again (see as an example Council of Europe, Committee of Ministers, 1987).

On the basis of the Council of Europe founding ethos and the European Convention on Human Rights, a corpus of documents on the treatment of prisoners has been developed. These include the European Prison Rules of 1973 as revised in 1987 and recommendations on the treatment of dangerous prisoners, on prison leave and on foreign prisoners.[12] The aim of all these documents has been to put flesh on the bones of the ECHR within a framework of European ideas about citizenship. Thus the commentary to the European Prison Rules stresses their basis in principles of humanity, morality, justice and respect for human dignity.

The CPT

The work on imprisonment of the Council of Europe was greatly deepened by the creation in 1989 of the Committee for the Prevention of Torture and Inhuman and Degrading Treatment or Punishment (CPT) (Evans & Morgan 1999a; 1999b). The Committee arises from the *European Convention for the Prevention of Torture and Inhuman and Degrading Treatment or Punishment*. Each State party to the Convention may nominate one member to the Committee. Members may be civil servants, psychiatrists, lawyers, prison officials, doctors or criminologists. The Committee is assisted by experts and neither Committee members nor experts are allowed to inspect their own country. Inspections are usually done by a small number of members with one or two experts. They have the right to come to any member State and inspect any place where people are detained by the State against their will: prisons, mental hospitals, immigration detention centres. They may ask for access to any such place at any time of the day or night and may also ask to see documents. The country to be visited is notified in advance and given the details of the places the Committee will visit a few days beforehand. However, this schedule can change in the course of a visit. The Committee usually begins its visit with meetings with the national authorities, human rights groups and nongovernmental organisations with an interest in and which have information about detention conditions in their country. The Committee makes a report to the government and the report is confidential. Almost always, however, the government gives permission for the report to be published, often together with its reply to the points made in the Committee's report.[13]

During the ten years they have been working, the CPT has uncovered and highlighted many abuses. When they visited the United Kingdom for the first time in 1991, they found living conditions in some prisons so bad that they decided they amounted to inhuman or degrading treatment (CPT 1991: 73-4). When they visited France in 1993, they condemned the practice of shackling women in labour to the hospital bed (CPT 1993: 38). In Switzerland in 1992, they condemned the placing of mentally sick prisoners naked in dark and squalid cells (CPT 1992: 17). In Portugal, they were horrified in 1994 by the sanitary arrangements in Linhó Prison: '... by the time thirty or forty prisoners had used the cesspit, newly arriving prisoners were confronted with a mound of excrement ... to which they added their own contribution' (CPT 1994: 32). In Italy the high levels of over-crowding in 1995 were found to amount to inhuman and degrading treatment (CPT 1995a: 32). They criticised the Netherlands heavily in 1998 for their treatment of high-security prisoners (CPT 1998a: 32-3, 65). The treatment of pre-trial prisoners in Sweden has caused them concern over several years and they have revisited several times to see if there have been improvements (CPT 1995b; 1999a).

From their experience of inspections, the CPT has in recent years begun to elicit principles for the treatment they expect if torture or inhuman or degrading treatment is to be prevented. Their latest Annual Report sets out what they expect for the treatment of women deprived of their liberty. Prisoners should only be searched by staff of the same gender and any search requiring prisoners to undress should be done out of sight of staff of the opposite gender. In principle, women should be held separately from men. However, where some gender association is occurring in prison, it can be positive, providing prisoners agree and are properly supervised. Babies should not be born in prison. Pregnant women should never be shackled or restrained to beds or other furniture (CPT 2000a: item 27).

On imprisonment generally, the CPT feels that overcrowding can be so bad that it is inhuman and degrading. All prisoners without exception must have at least one hour of exercise in the open air every day. The use of force against prisoners is a very important issue. After any use of force, prisoners should be immediately examined by a doctor out of hearing of prison staff. Results of the examination should be formally recorded and made available to the prisoner. A record should be kept of every instance of the use of force. Disciplinary procedures should provide prisoners with a right to be heard and to appeal against any sanction imposed. Prisoners placed in administrative segregation should be given reasons for it in writing (though reasons might not include details which threaten security). Solitary confinement can, in certain circumstances, amount to inhuman and degrading treatment (CPT 1999b).

These points derive from considerable analysis of the circumstances that give rise to ill treatment and the conditions that are conducive to it happening. They give an indication of what States and their prison administrations need to ensure is in place as a framework.

England and Wales

The CPT and the European institutions operate at the international level, verifying and giving guidance. National arrangements are the basis for ensuring prisoners get proper treatment. It is therefore perhaps useful to look in more detail at the arrangements in two European states and the way prisoners' rights are secured.

The United Kingdom is divided into three jurisdictions: Scotland, England and Wales, and Northern Ireland. Here I shall be concentrating on England and Wales. The question of prisoners' rights was much discussed in mid-2000 since the 1998 *Human Rights Act* was implemented in October 2000. The *Human Rights Act* incorporates the ECHR into British law. Its main effect is to allow cases to be brought to the UK courts that would formerly have had to go to the Court of Human Rights in Strasbourg, a very lengthy business for a complainant. There are many expectations that the *Human Rights Act* will affect the way prisoners are treated and give them some new rights. In April 2001, however, a challenge by prisoners, under art 3 of the ECHR First Protocol (right to free elections), to the refusal by the electoral registrar to register them as voters was unsuccessful (*R v Secretary of State for the Home Department, Ex parte Pearson and Martinez; Hirst v HM Attorney General* [2001] HRLR 39).

Such expectations are based more on hope than on precedent. The record of the European Court of Human Rights in cases brought by prisoners does not encourage such expectations. Cases brought under art 8 (right to respect for private and family life, home and correspondence) in the 1970s and 1980s established that prison authorities could not stop or read correspondence between prisoners and their lawyers.[14] In 1979, the Committee of Ministers decided that under art 12 (the right to marry), a prisoner has the right to marry and could not be prevented because he or she was in prison.[15] The largest number of cases has been about the release of life sentence prisoners. These cases, brought under art 5 (right to liberty and security of person), have led to substantial changes in the procedures for releasing those given non-mandatory life sentences.[16] Cases brought under art 3 (prohibition of torture or inhuman or degrading treatment) have not been successful (Livingstone & Owen 1999: 177, para 5.59).

The British courts have also not been groundbreaking. They have interpreted very cautiously the famous dictum by Lord Wilberforce: 'Under English law a convicted prisoner, in spite of his imprisonment, retains all civil rights which are not taken away expressly or by necessary implication'.[17]

Most of the cases brought by prisoners in the English courts are about the lawfulness of various parole release and recall arrangements. In 1992, a court ruling held that a prisoner on parole who was recalled to prison was entitled to be told the reasons for the recall and argue against the recall before the Parole Board.[18] In 1993, the courts ruled that since security classification was relevant to parole and since those in the highest security category, Category A, could not be considered by the Parole Board for release, prisoners should be given reasons for their security classification.[19] In 1997, Lord Woolf and others ruled that a prisoner had the right to the gist of the reports that were being given to the review body about security status.[20]

The rulings about the treatment of prisoners are less clear cut. In 1995, the courts decided that the 'compacts' between prisoners and the prison service, under which prisoners agree to undertake a program of activities and the prison service agrees to provide them, were not legally binding on the prison service.[21] However, in 1999, the courts ruled that a pregnant woman in prison was entitled to the same standard of obstetric care and observation as if she were at liberty.[22] In 1997, in a significant ruling, it was held that young offenders could not be held routinely in adult prisons whilst awaiting allocation after sentence.[23]

In 1997, the Court of Appeal decided that a convicted prisoner had no right to communicate orally with the media through a journalist, the loss of that right being part and parcel of a sentence of imprisonment. That judgment also covered searching correspondence with prisoners' lawyers, where the court decided that staff doing searches could read the correspondence to the limited extent necessary to check that it was what it purported to be and to make sure no illicit material was concealed.[24]

In 1999, the House of Lords overturned the judgment that prisoners could not communicate with journalists. The Lords decided that an indiscriminate ban on all visits to prisoners by journalists or authors in their professional capacity was unlawful. Prisoners had the right to talk to journalists to try and persuade them to investigate allegations of miscarriages of justice.[25]

In 2001, the House of Lords overturned previous judgments and ruled that the policy requiring prisoners to be absent during cell searches when the legal correspondence held by them in their cells is examined by prison officers is unlawful.[26]

Chief Inspector of Prisons

Law is important in Britain but mostly in respect of lawfulness of detention, how its length is decided and by whom. For the day-to-day treatment of prisoners, other mechanisms come into play.

An important institution in the England and Wales context is the Chief Inspector of Prisons. The Chief Inspector's office was set up in 1980. The remit of the Inspectorate is to inspect and report on prisons to the Secretary of State for the Home Department, in particular their conditions, the treatment of prisoners and the facilities available to them. Since it was established, the post has been filled for most of the time by substantial figures with a determination to make an impact. From 1987 to 1995, the Chief Inspector was Stephen Tumim, a judge. He became a thorn in the flesh of the incumbent government and on his retirement, they looked for a more compliant figure. At the end of 1995, they appointed General Sir David Ramsbotham, a former Adjutant General of the British Army. However, he was as outspoken and determined as his predecessor (Stern 1998: 240).

The Chief Inspector has a staff of about 22 people to carry out inspections and provide support services. The Inspectorate also employs specialist inspectors and researchers on a consultancy basis.[27] They carry out about 40 inspections a year. Apart from details about security matters the reports are published in full. The Inspectorate's separate publicity machine ensures that reports receive considerable coverage in the press.

Over the years, the Inspectorate has developed criteria by which to measure the conditions in the prisons it inspects. These criteria are described as the indicators of a 'healthy prison'. A 'healthy prison' is one in which:

• Every prisoner is safe.
• Every prisoner is treated with respect as a fellow human being.
• Every prisoner is encouraged to improve him or herself and given the opportunity to do so through purposeful activities.

- Every prisoner is enabled to maintain contact with their family and prepare for release, thereby reducing the likelihood of their re-offending. (HM Chief Inspector of Prisons 2000: 15)

The office of the Chief Inspector has done a great deal to highlight shortcomings of the prison management in England and Wales and there is a similar arrangement in Scotland, where the Chief Inspector is also an ex-military man.[28]

During his term of office, the former Chief Inspector managed to build up a strong body of support amongst parliamentarians and the public. Moves made by the Government therefore to blunt the edge of the Inspectorate by merging it with the more social work-oriented Inspectorate of Probation provoked considerable opposition and were eventually withdrawn (House of Commons *Hansard*, 2 October 2000, column 1202, UK Parliament).

Prisons Ombudsman

The Chief Inspector is a national office. So too is the office of the Prisons Ombudsman. The office of the Prisons Ombudsman was set up in 1995. The establishment of such an office was strongly recommended in the report produced by Lord Justice Woolf and others after the major riot at Strangeways Prison in Manchester in 1990 (Woolf & Tumim 1991 (Woolf Report): 418, para 14.342). The Ombudsman investigates complaints from individual prisoners who have tried the channels of complaint within the system and have failed to get a satisfactory response. In 1999-2000, the Ombudsman received 1937 complaints, of which 561 were eligible for investigation (Prisons Ombudsman 2000: 7). The largest single category of eligible complaints was about the fairness of disciplinary hearings. Where the Ombudsman finds that the disciplinary hearing has been unfair, he recommends to the prison service that the finding of guilt be quashed.

Boards of Visitors

The Chief Inspector and the Ombudsman are national offices. In addition, each prison has a Board of Visitors. Boards of Visitors are groups of citizens appointed by the Home Secretary to a particular prison in their locality. Each Board has between ten and 20 members. Board of Visitors must meet not less than eight times in 12 months. They must 'satisfy themselves as to the state of the prison premises, the administration of the prison and the treatment of the prisoners' (*The Prison Rules 1999*, Statutory Instrument 1999 No 728, Pt V, r 77(1)). They must draw to the attention of the Governor anything they are concerned about and report to the Secretary of State when they feel it is 'expedient' and must inform the Secretary of State immediately of 'any abuse which comes to their knowledge' (*The Prison Rules 1999*, r 77(3),(4)). They must also hear prisoners' complaints and requests, inspect the food and 'inquire into any report made to them ... that a prisoner's health, mental or physical, is likely to be injuriously affected by any conditions of his imprisonment' (*The Prison Rules 1999*, r 78).

Segregation of a prisoner for longer than three days also has to be authorised by a member of the Board of Visitors, though if they refuse, the prison governor can ask his superiors to authorise it under delegated powers from the Secretary of State (*The Prison Rules 1999*, r 45).

Boards of Visitors can be criticised for their lack of independence. Their members are appointed by the Home Secretary and can be removed by him. Yet they play an important part in bringing people from the outside world into the very heart of the prison. They can carry keys, speak to prisoners out of the hearing of prison staff and raise directly with the Home Secretary anything they feel is important enough.

Other reform agents

Also part of the UK prison monitoring environment are the non-governmental organisations (NGOs). There are several NGOs dedicated to monitoring prisons and highlighting abuses, such as the Prison Reform Trust, Inquest and the Howard League for Penal Reform. However, in recent years, it has been difficult for NGOs to find as authoritative a voice as the Chief Inspector or to find a message that is attractive to a media less interested in a penal reform agenda.

The last decade has been stormy for penal reform in the United Kingdom. The decade began with the riot at Strangeways Prison in Manchester, lasting 23 days and filling the TV screens of the world. An inquiry was carried out by Lord Justice Woolf as he then was and Stephen Tumim, then Chief Inspector. Their report set out a penal reform agenda based on a balance between security, control and justice. 'There must ... be justice in our prisons. The system of justice which has put a person in prison cannot end at the prison doors. It must accompany the prisoner into the prison ...' (Woolf & Tumim 1991: 373, para 14.19).

The Woolf Report started a reform movement which looked likely to succeed but was cut short by political changes. A harsher political climate was accompanied by a rapid increase in the numbers in prison from 40,000 to more than 65,000 in 1998.[29] Two serious escapes from high security prisons in 1995 were widely and dramatically publicised and led to a new emphasis on security at the expense of more rehabilitative programs. In order to try to retrieve some lost ground on rehabilitation, the prison system in England and Wales followed the path of the other English-speaking countries, such as New Zealand and Canada, and developed a new faith in the effectiveness of psychologically-based and heavily-marketed programs. A prisoner control system, based on moving to more privileges in return for good behaviour, was introduced (HM Prison Service 1995).

More recently prison numbers have kept rising and overcrowding pressures have reduced the chances of individual attention. Scandals continue. 27 prison officers have been brought to trial for abuse of prisoners (Travis 1999). Suicides are higher than ever before.[30] A young offender serving six weeks for petty theft was murdered by his cellmate the night before he was due to be released (Kelso 2000).

France

In France, too, scandals are on the agenda. The French public is the most sceptical about imprisonment of any public in Western Europe. Prisons have recently burst their way onto the French political scene. Early in 2000, a French doctor, Veronique Vasseur, published an account of her time as a prison medical officer in La Santé Prison in Paris. Her account of life there shocked the nation. She describes filthy cells infested with rats (Vasseur 2000: 40). She describes being called to a prisoner who complained he could not eat. X-rays showed he had swallowed a soupspoon, a fork, a bunch of five keys, 12 coins and a packet of razor blades (Vasseur 2000: 34). Most of the mattresses were full of lice (Vasseur 2000: 49). Vasseur describes treating dozens of prisoners with a skin disease, bread scabies, they got from eating mouldy bread, a disease seen in wartime but not often otherwise (Vasseur 2000: 37). A mentally ill prisoner goes berserk in the segregation block. She is called. There are only seven guards. They wait — they won't go in until there are eight. The eighth comes. They open the door. They hurl themselves in. She finds a bit of the prisoner in which to put the needle to give him an injection. She never sees his face (Vasseur 2000: 30).

In January 2000, a number of prominent prisoners, ex-ministers, civil servants and business people sent a petition to the Ministry of Justice complaining about prison conditions (Webster 2000). The French Parliament set up a commission to investigate prison conditions and the Minister of Justice, Elisabeth Guigou, set up another commission to be chaired by the president of the *Cour de Cassation* (the highest appeal court), to look at the external control of prisons (Dorozynski 2000: 465). This Commission was reminded by the Minister of Justice of the background, that the specific control of individual prisons was varied and sometimes defective, the visits of the judicial authorities were infrequent and the lack of real activity by the oversight commissions was regularly criticised (Ministre de la Justice 2000: 3).

The French system is very much in the European tradition where the legality of what goes on in prison is controlled by judges. In both the French and Spanish tradition, the system of the *juges d'application des peines* (JAP) is to be found. The system of specialist judges was established in 1958. They are expected to provide regular reports on the situation in the prisons (Faugeron 1991: 257) and also make a range of decisions about what happens to prisoners. They decide reductions in length of time in prison, the authority to leave the prison without an escort, length of time a prisoner is held in segregation, placement in semi-liberty or conditional release, placement on electronic monitoring and revocation of conditional release (Ministre de la Justice 2000: 93).

Each prison also has a *commission de surveillance*, a control commission, with members from the local authority including the mayor of the town where the prison is located (Faugeron 1991: 257).

Both these structures have been widely criticised over many years and the Commission report endorsed these criticisms. The Commission found that French prisoners' access to redress from wrongs had neither 'the accessibility, the visibility, nor the predictability' required by the French Constitution and the ECHR. Prisoners, the report concluded, did not have an access to the law equal to that of other citizens because they did not have access to an independent person to give an answer to their questions or a solution to their dispute. Many decisions of the prison administration were not open to question because they were subsumed under 'the needs of internal order'. The application of law in prisons could be considerably improved (Ministre de la Justice 2000: 6-7). Good outside control can only operate if there is in place a body of norms, a frame of reference, adequate protection for the individual against arbitrary treatment and the right to a fair hearing (Ministre de la Justice 2000: 5).

The Commission went on to recommend a new prison law for France, based on the idea that prisoners should have the status of a citizen, only deprived of freedom of movement. This would mean that new prison law should make it clear for the prison staff how they are to balance the competing aims of security and preparation for release. Starting from the concept of the prisoner as 'a detained citizen', the implication was that if the prisoner was to be moved from the relative freedom of the general prison to the segregation block, such extra deprivation of liberty should be governed not by regulations but by law (Ministre de la Justice 2000: 151-5).

Currently appeals to the administrative judges by prisoners have been refused on the basis that decisions made by the prison administration are measures of internal control and not susceptible to review. Prisoners have also had no method of appealing against the decisions of the JAP. This will have to change if the new French prison law is to be truly acceptable to international standards (Ministre de la Justice 2000: 156-7).

The report concluded that there is no point in having a good law if prisoners cannot use it (Ministre de la Justice 2000: 159). The Commission went on to recommend a new control system for French prisons. This should not be seen as in opposition to the prison system but for the benefit of the prisons, to make them appropriate to a democracy (Ministre de la Justice 2000: 4). Such a change would also bring other benefits. It would lead to a permanent debate on the quality of the prisons and the resources they need, as well as on respect for the law and how it is achieved, prison conditions and security, rather than the current bursts of public interest that arise only when there is a crisis.

This new system of control has some similarities with the English model. Adequate control, in the opinion of the Committee, needs three elements. The first is verification, that is, control by a body that ensures the prisons are run properly with due respect for law, and looks at the conditions of detention, relationships in the prisons, the buildings, the cells, the activities. This control should be independent of the prison administration (Ministre de la Justice 2000: 165-6).

The second form of control is called 'mediation'. This needs to occur close to the prison and those who live in it and should therefore be organised regionally. The mediators should be independent, permanent and qualified. Their role would be to receive prisoners' requests and complaints, in confidence. They would try to find a solution, to mediate between the prisoner and the administration (Ministre de la Justice 2000: 180-3).

The third line of control is proposed to be 'Delegates or Representatives', citizens able to visit freely, talk to whomsoever they wish and ensure openness. They should be volunteers from civil society (Ministre de la Justice 2000: 187-8).

Although it is not yet clear when the report of the Commission is to be implemented, its findings usefully show the latest thinking in Europe on a system that would implement European views on the status of prisoners and their position in law.

Conclusions

The basic principle which should underlie imprisonment in all countries who have signed up to the International Covenants is set out in art 10 of the ICCPR.

All persons deprived of their liberty shall be treated with humanity and with respect for the inherent dignity of the human person.

Added to this are the other rights: the right to life, the right to family life, the rights of the child, the right not to be discriminated against, the right to medical treatment on the same basis as a non-imprisoned person.

Bringing together the accumulated interpretations of the Council of Europe, the UN (through its publications), the work of the Special Rapporteur on Prisons of the African Commission on Human and Peoples' Rights and the CPT, some clear propositions emerge.

Torture is always forbidden. Prisoners are to be treated within a framework of the rule of law when something is to be done to them that affects their time in prison or their access to redress for problems with their conviction. There must be an independent complaints machinery. There must be external inspection of prisons. Women must be kept separate from men and juveniles from adults. Prisoners should be protected from diseases and from harm from other prisoners. Prisoners have a right to family life. Discrimination against women or against minorities is unacceptable.

When putting these requirements into practice, we can legitimately reach certain conclusions. Prison regimes should tend towards rehabilitation and re-insertion into society. It should be assumed that prisoners are all redeemable. There has to be a framework of law and regulation within which the authorities may discipline prisoners and restrain their liberty further. We can assume that catch-all disciplinary provisions such as 'any offence against good order and discipline' are not in accordance with natural justice. We can also assume that including a provision in the discipline code that it is an offence to make a false and malicious allegation against a prison staff member is unacceptable. It is reasonable to assume that removing family visits as part of the punishment system or increasing them as part of a progressive behavioural system is undesirable.

It is clear that prisoners must not be at the mercy of arbitrary power. There are enough experiments to show that even the most humane prison staff can lose their sense of right and wrong and common humanity when conditions in the prisons allow it. There must be independent avenues of redress.

Some commentators feel that the right to vote, to continue to be a member of a State pension scheme and to be eligible for State national insurance and other work-related benefits are part of a system where prisoners are seen as citizens. Women must be protected from sexual abuse and, in their treatment as mothers, should receive care as much like other citizens as possible. Children in prison should be treated first as children, with the prime consideration being their welfare.

How can an environment be created in which such treatment is what prisoners are accorded? To achieve such a consensus requires action on many levels: political, at the level of prison authorities, with the media, the churches, NGOs and lawyers.

Finally, there is the context. With the increase in incarceration in the United States, United Kingdom, Australia and New Zealand, it is perhaps appropriate to consider 'citizens as prisoners'. How many of our fellow citizens do we want to see locked up before we feel safe? In the United States, that figure now stands at two million, a rate of 682 per 100,000, even higher than Russia which stands at 678. In Australia and New Zealand too, prison growth has been substantial. What is the meaning of citizenship when so many are felt to be expendable?

Notes

1   Based on notes taken by author during a visit in March 2000.

2   'The Celebration of the Great Jubilee' in *L'Osservatore Romano*, weekly edition in English, 12 July 2000.

3   'Achieving Results', speech by Director General Martin Narey to the Prison Service Conference at Harrogate, 1 February 2000 quoted in *Prison Service News – Magazine of the HM Prison Service*, February 2000, p 4.

4   Information about the Annual Koestler Awards Exhibition is available on the HM Prison Service website at <www.hmprisonservice.gov.uk> under 'Prison Life'.

5   Information provided by Major-General Kononets, head of the Penitentiary Medical Services of the Russian Federation to a conference held in Sigtuna, Sweden, 4-6 October 2000.

6   Dietary punishment is still employed in the Special Housing Unit at Coxsackie prison for young offenders in New York State. See Conover 2000: 28.

7   In New South Wales, Australia, when a similar attempt was made to change the culture of a prison system, the department's finances did not permit it to offer redundancies to unsuitable staff and cultural change was blocked (Vinson 1982).

8   In some cases, a lack of resources in other parts of a country's criminal justice system results in large numbers of unconvicted prisoners being held on remand in prison. See for example a discussion of the situation in Malawi in *Prison Reform International Newsletter* 1996. See also South African Human Rights Commission 1998 and Penal Reform International 1999, both of which describe how a lack of resources is hampering the implementation of progressive reform policies.

9   See for example, Human Rights Watch 1998, which describes how the centralised organisation of the Brazilian prison system causes problems in itself. See also Amnesty International 1999 on violations against detainees in Brazil and Human Rights Watch 1997 on prison conditions in Venezuela.

10   In 1993, at the Copenhagen European Council, existing Member States identified certain economic and political standards which Central and Eastern European countries would need to attain as a pre-condition to accession to the European Union. A general introduction to the criteria is set out at <www.europa. eu.int/comm/enlargement/intro/criteria.htm and a specific example of their application in the context of prisons is given at <www.hrw.org/press/1999/ dec/turkey1210.htm>.

11   See the website of the Council of Europe at <www.coe.int> under 'A Short History'.

12   The rule and recommendations are available online at <www.coe.int.>

13   For more about the CPT, see <www.cpt.coe.int/en/about.htm>.

14   For example, *Golder v United Kingdom* (1979-80) 1 EHRR 524; *Silver v United Kingdom* (1983) 5 EHRR 347.

15   *Hamer (Alan Stanley) Against the United Kingdom*, Resolution of 2/4/81; Res No DH (81)5).

16   For example, *Thynne, Wilson and Gunnell v United Kingdom* (1991) 13 EHRR 666.

17   *Raymond v Honey* [1983] 1 AC 1 at 10.

18   *R v Secretary of State for the Home Department; Ex parte Georghiades* (1992) COD 412; (1993) 5 Admin LR 457.

19   *R v Secretary of State for the Home Department; Ex parte Duggan* [1994] 3 All ER 277.

20   *R v Secretary of State for the Home Department; Ex parte McAvoy* [1997] EWCA Civ 2888.

21   *R v Secretary of State for the Home Department and Governor of Her Majesty's Prison Risley; Ex parte Hargreaves, Briggs and Green* [1996] EWCA Civ 1006.

22   *Brooks v Home Office* [1999] 2 FLR 33.

23   *R v Accrington Youth Court: Ex parte Flood* [1997] EWHC Admin 783.

24   *R v Secretary of State for the Home Department; Ex parte Simms; R v Governor of Whitemore Prison; Ex parte Main* [1998] 2 All ER 491.

25   *R v Secretary of State for the Home Department; Ex parte Simms* [1999] 3 All ER 400.

26   *R v Secretary of State for the Home Department; Ex parte Daly* [2001] UKHL 26.

27   More information can be found at <www.homeoffice.gov.uk/hmipris/hmipris. htm>.

28   For more information on the role of the Prisons Inspectorate in Scotland, see <www.scotland.gov.uk/library/documents/glen-01.htm>.

29   In 1998, the average yearly prison population was 65,300 according to the Home Office: Research Development and Statistics Directorate, Research Finding No 118, *The Prison Population in 1999: A Statistical Review* (2000: 1).

30   During 1998-99, according to HM Prison Service, there were 82 self-inflicted deaths: *Annual Report* at <www.hmpriosnservice.gov.uk/corporate/reports.asp>.

PART THREE

Citizenship and Rights

CHAPTER 11

International Human Rights Law Applicable to Prisoners

Camille Giffard

Introduction

The objective of this chapter is to set out the main international human rights standards which Australia should respect and implement in relation to prisoners. It is designed to provide a basic context for readers to assess Australia's performance in practice, while increasing general awareness of the standards that should be implemented and which may be invoked before national and international bodies if they are not.

What is international human rights law?

International human rights law in its present form evolved primarily in response to the atrocities committed during the Second World War. It is designed to regulate the relationship between a nation state and its citizens or other persons under its authority. It creates obligations for the state towards these persons, places limits on its powers and sets out rules which should be present in the national legal system in order to provide protection from abuse. The behaviour of a state is kept in check by regulating the actions of its representatives: public officials. This is anyone who acts or carries out functions on behalf of the state, like a police officer, a judge, a state-employed teacher or doctor, or a prison warden.

Obligations under international human rights law are both positive and negative in nature. Some human rights standards may require public officials *not* to engage in certain types of conduct, for example beating a suspected offender in order to extract a confession. On the other hand, others may require a *positive* action, such as an obligation to enact legislation to protect the right to life, an obligation to carry out an effective investigation where an individual claims that he or she has been assaulted by a public official, or taking steps to protect a prisoner who is believed to be at risk from other prisoners.

Human rights standards and norms are generally articulated in formal documents drafted and agreed to by states, such as the *International Covenant on Civil and Political Rights* (ICCPR) or the *United Nations Convention Against Torture and Other Cruel, Inhuman or Degrading Treatment or Punishment* (UNCAT). These agreements, or treaties, are binding only on states that have formally consented to be bound by them.

Sometimes states will place conditions or limitations on their acceptance of the obligations in the treaty by making a reservation to its terms. For example, Australia made a reservation to article 10 of the ICCPR in August 1980, stating that it accepted the obligation to segregate juveniles and adults in detention only to the extent that it is considered beneficial to those concerned.[1] In order to establish exactly what standards a state must respect, it is important to check not only which treaties it has ratified but also if it has made any reservations. Australia has accepted relevant obligations primarily under the ICCPR, UNCAT, the *International Convention on the Elimination of All Forms of Racial Discrimination* (ICERD), the UN *Convention on the Elimination of all Forms of Discrimination Against Women* (CEDAW) and the *UN Convention on the Rights of the Child*. The focus of this chapter will be on the ICCPR and UNCAT.

In some countries, including Australia, the acceptance of a treaty does not automatically mean that it becomes part of the law of the land. Instead, legislation must be adopted which translates the treaty norms into national law. This is complicated by the federal nature of the Australian system, which requires implementation at both federal and State and Territory level. Both the Human Rights Committee (HRC re Australia 2000: para 14) and the Committee Against Torture (CAT re Australia 2000: para 7(a)) have made it quite clear, however, that the Commonwealth has overall responsibility for ensuring that its international human rights obligations are respected.

Human rights treaties do not exist in a vacuum and most are underpinned by international bodies and mechanisms that oversee respect for the standards they contain, seeking to ensure that they are not merely theoretical but actually implemented in practice. The Human Rights Committee, for example, supervises the application of the ICCPR, while the Committee Against Torture oversees respect for the UNCAT. Such supervisory bodies help to develop and interpret the norms and to explain what they mean when applied to real situations.

A number of these bodies are also authorised to receive complaints directly from persons who claim that their rights have been violated by a 'State Party' to the treaty. This complaint procedure is optional, however, even where a state is a party to the treaty and the supervisory bodies can only examine a complaint if the state in question has expressly accepted the procedure. Australia has accepted individual complaint procedures under the ICCPR, UNCAT and ICERD. Some human rights documents, like the *Standard Minimum Rules for the Treatment of Prisoners*, are not formally overseen by a supervisory body of their own but they are regularly relied on by other supervisory mechanisms to assist in the interpretation of more generally defined norms.

A further group of human rights mechanisms, the Special Procedures of the UN Commission on Human Rights, functions independently of treaty obligations. Instead of being limited to states that have explicitly accepted specific obligations, these mechanisms may supervise and receive relevant complaints about any state that is a member of the United Nations, including Australia. Generally speaking, these procedures are charged with monitoring human rights either from a thematic or a country-specific perspective and relevant complaints would include those that relate to the particular subject matter or country for which the procedure is responsible. There is no country-specific procedure for Australia but any of the thematic procedures could examine relevant complaints relating to this country. Most commonly of significance to prisoners would be the Special Rapporteur on Torture, the Special Rapporteur on Violence Against Women, the Special Rapporteur on the Independence of Judges and Lawyers and the Working Group on Arbitrary Detention.

How is international human rights law relevant to prisoners?

Australia's acceptance of international human rights obligations, in particular under the ICCPR and UNCAT, means that, in the way it and its representatives behave, it must respect those obligations or it may be acting unlawfully and thus subject to scrutiny by the international committees appointed to supervise state performance under those instruments. This applies as much to Australia's dealings with prisoners as to its actions towards any other person or group of persons.

The consequences of failure by a state to respect human rights standards depend on the particular obligations in question and the powers of the relevant enforcement mechanism. For example, they could involve a formal finding that human rights have been violated, a strong recommendation that those responsible for the violation be prosecuted and compensation provided to the person or group whose rights have been violated, or a request that the allegations be thoroughly investigated and the results communicated to the relevant international committee. Although the majority of monitoring committees may only make recommendations to states as to how they should repair the violation and cannot compel them to do so, states do not generally like to be publicly condemned for human rights violations and will often attempt to respond in some way to the recommendations.

Those who believe their human rights have been infringed in some way, including prisoners, can seek to take action both within the national legal system and, where this does not yield an effective remedy, at the international level. In the case of Australia, an action open to prisoners at the international level is the possibility of making an individual application (or 'communication') to the Human Rights Committee or the Committee Against Torture. It might also be appropriate to submit information to a special procedure of the United Nations, such as the Special Rapporteur on Torture or the Working Group on Arbitrary Detention.[2]

It is important not to have unrealistic expectations when making a complaint to a human rights body. Patience and perseverance are essential and the rewards are often small, in individual terms. Dealing with complaints can take a long time, sometimes as long as several years. As a rule, a genuine attempt must have been made to obtain a remedy within the national legal system before applying to the international bodies. This is known as 'exhausting domestic remedies'. Allegations must be carefully prepared, thoroughly explained and submitted in writing with specific details and as much supporting evidence as possible, although the Special Procedures tend to require less formality than the treaty bodies. Any deadlines given by a supervisory body must be respected or, if there are legitimate reasons why this is not possible, explanations and requests for extensions should be provided well in advance. Findings and recommendations, no matter how strongly worded, cannot be enforced. Nonetheless, a public condemnation by a human rights body can have significant impact on a state, can provide a measure of satisfaction to the individual complainant by vindicating the allegations made and can, where the state concerned demonstrates a willingness to co-operate with the international bodies, even contribute to changes in policy and legislation in response to difficulties highlighted by individual cases.

What does international human rights law say about prisoners' rights?

General human rights norms apply to everyone (ICCPR art 2). This means that although prisoners may be subject to additional limitations on those rights, they have the same human rights as other citizens. Some rights are more relevant or take on greater importance in a prison context than others, however, like the prohibition of torture and cruel, inhuman or degrading treatment or punishment, the right to liberty and security of person or the right to a fair trial. In addition to these general human rights norms, specific standards have also been formulated in relation to persons deprived of their liberty. In order to examine what international human rights law has to say about the rights of prisoners, the first step will be to identify and explain the general norms that are most frequently applicable to prisoners. These include rights which might have been violated prior to entering a custodial institution, like the right to a fair trial, but for which a prisoner might wish to seek a remedy while in custody. Subsequently, a closer examination will be made of the more detailed standards applicable specifically to prisoners.

General human rights norms

General human rights norms, with few exceptions, do not make specific reference to prisoners. They set out a relatively abstract right, like the right to liberty and security of person, a violation of which may then be claimed on the basis of a specific set of facts. A list of the main human rights contained in the ICCPR and of relevance to prisoners may be found in Table 11.1. Only those most commonly invoked by prisoners will be discussed below but it should be noted that any of these rights could potentially be relied on by a prisoner believing that his or her rights have been violated.

Many of the rights listed here are not absolute; some restrictions may be lawfully imposed by the state for a number of recognised reasons. This is true primarily of those rights which may be classified as 'freedoms': freedom of movement, freedom of thought, conscience and religion, freedom of expression, freedom of assembly and freedom of association. Restrictions on these freedoms are lawful where they are 'prescribed by law' (provided for in a piece of national legislation) and necessary to achieve one of a number of specified purposes. These vary slightly but generally refer to the protection of national security or public safety, the protection of public order, public health or morals or the protection of the rights and freedoms of others (see Human Rights Brief No 4 2001). In cases involving prisoners, the state will often argue that restrictions on a right are legitimate on grounds of national security or public safety but in all cases it is for the human rights body examining the matter to determine if a restriction is lawful. Some rights may *never* be restricted, even in times of war or public emergency, in particular the right not to be arbitrarily deprived of life, the right not to be subjected to torture or inhuman treatment, the right not to be held in slavery or servitude and the right to the non-retroactivity of criminal punishment (ICCPR art 4).

Under both the ICCPR (art 2.3) and the UNCAT (arts 13-14), State Parties have a general obligation to ensure that any person whose rights have been violated has an effective remedy for the violation, decided by a competent authority and enforceable if granted. In relation to Australia, the Human Rights Committee has expressed concern about the absence of an effective remedy in certain areas (HRC re Australia 2000: para 13), while the Committee Against Torture has done so in response to allegations that prison inmates complaining about their treatment in an institution may be subject to intimidation (CAT re Australia 2000: para 6(d)).

Right not to be arbitrarily deprived of life

Article 6 of the ICCPR sets out that everyone has the inherent right to life, which is to be protected by law and of which no one shall be 'arbitrarily' deprived.

What is meant by 'arbitrary' deprivation of life? Remembering that human rights are about state-individual relationships rather than those between individuals, it is generally understood to mean a deliberate act by a public official resulting in the taking of someone's life, including an act of omission in failing to prevent a killing which could have been prevented by a public official. According to the Human Rights Committee, states 'should take measures ... to prevent arbitrary killing by their own security forces ... [and] the law must strictly control and limit the circumstances in which a person may be deprived of his life by such authorities' (HRC General Comment No 6: para 3). A more elaborate articulation of this in the case of killings in connection with law enforcement may be found in two professional codes adopted under the auspices of the United Nations: the *UN Code of Conduct for Law Enforcement Officials* and the *Basic Principles on the Use of Force and Firearms by Law Enforcement Officials*.[3] They emphasise that the use of force should be exceptional and strictly controlled. Basic Principle 3 specifies that law enforcement officials (defined as 'all officers of the law who exercise police powers, especially the powers of arrest or detention') may use force 'only when strictly necessary and to the extent required for the performance of their duty'.

Table 11.1. Main rights of relevance to prisoners contained in the ICCPR

Article 2	All rights are to be ensured without discrimination of any kind
Article 6	Right not to be arbitrarily deprived of life
Article 7	Right not to be subjected to torture or to cruel, inhuman or degrading treatment or punishment
Article 8	Right not to be held in slavery or servitude or required to perform forced or compulsory labour
Article 9	Right to liberty and security of person
Article 10	Right of all persons deprived of liberty to be treated with humanity and with respect for the inherent dignity of the human person
Article 11	Right not to be imprisoned merely on the ground of inability to fulfil a contractual obligation
Article 12	Right to freedom of movement and freedom to choose one's own residence
Article 13	Right of a legal alien not to be expelled except in accordance with the law and following an opportunity to put his or her case against the expulsion
Article 14	Right to a fair trial
Article 15	Right to the non-retroactivity of criminal punishment
Article 16	Right to recognition as a person before the law
Article 17	Right not to be subjected to arbitrary interference with privacy, family, home or correspondence
Article 18	Right to freedom of thought, conscience and religion
Article 19	Right to hold opinions without interference and to freedom of expression
Article 21	Right of peaceful assembly
Article 22	Right to freedom of association with others
Article 25	Right and opportunity to take part in the conduct of public affairs, to vote and be elected and to have equal access to public service
Article 26	Right to equality before the law and to non-discrimination on any ground such as race, colour, sex, language, religion, political or other opinion, national or social origin, property, birth or other status
Article 27	Persons belonging to an ethnic, religious, or linguistic minority have the right, in community with other members of their group, to enjoy their own culture, to profess and practice their own religion and to use their own language

Article 6 of the ICCPR also requires states to protect the right to life *by law*, including through criminal legislation outlawing murder by private individuals. Although the obligation of the state to protect the right to life does not extend as far as an obligation to provide optimal living conditions, the Human Rights Committee is of the opinion that it does require states to adopt positive measures and that it should not be interpreted restrictively (HRC General Comment No 6: para 5). In particular, the state may be considered to have a special duty towards persons deprived of their liberty, such that failure to provide them with food or medical treatment, or to prevent suicide, may amount to a violation of art 6.[4]

In a prison context, protection against abuses in the use of force and the arbitrary deprivation of life take on significance in the maintenance of discipline, especially with regard to official responses to prison unrest or riots. The use of force in such circumstances should always be proportionate to the situation in order to avoid becoming arbitrary. The Committee Against Torture has expressed concern about allegations of excessive use of force by police forces and prison guards (CAT re Australia 2000: para 6(c)). Beyond the imposition of controls on the use of force by officials, however, the obligation to protect the right to life also creates a duty for officials not to knowingly tolerate abuses between prisoners. Should a prisoner be killed by another prisoner in circumstances indicating that officials were aware of the existence of a risk and in a position to prevent the killing yet failed to do so, this could raise an issue under art 6.

Prohibition of torture and cruel, inhuman or degrading treatment or punishment

The prohibition of torture is widely agreed to be the most untouchable of human rights. It can never be limited for any reason, even in time of war or public emergency. Because the prohibition is absolute, the central issue for someone wishing to make a claim that torture or inhuman treatment has occurred is always to establish that the treatment in question amounts to torture or inhuman or degrading treatment or punishment. There are no further qualifications that can make such treatment legal. So what exactly constitutes prohibited treatment?

Article 1 of UNCAT defines torture as:

> any act by which severe pain or suffering, whether physical or mental, is intentionally inflicted on a person for such purposes as obtaining from him or a third person information or a confession, punishing him for an act he or a third person has committed or is suspected of having

committed, or intimidating or coercing him or a third person, or for any reason based on discrimination of any kind, when such pain or suffering is inflicted by or at the instigation of or with the consent or acquiescence of a public official or other person acting in an official capacity. It does not include pain or suffering arising only from, inherent in or incidental to lawful sanctions.

From this definition it is possible to extract three essential elements which constitute torture:

1. the infliction of severe mental or physical pain or suffering
2. with the consent or acquiescence of the state authorities
3. for a specific purpose, such as gaining information, punishment or intimidation.

Torture is characterised and distinguished from other forms of ill-treatment by the severe degree of suffering involved and the require-ment for a purposive element. Forms of ill-treatment other than torture do not have to be inflicted for a specific purpose but there does have to be an intent to expose individuals to conditions which amount to or result in the ill-treatment (Giffard 2000: 12-13).

One complication in attempting to draw distinctions between different degrees of ill-treatment is that the severity of suffering has been interpreted as a subjective element. In making the assessment of severity, human rights bodies may take into account personal characteristics of the victim, such as sex, age, religious or cultural beliefs or state of health. This means that any decision is very much fact-driven. Furthermore, the Committee Against Torture has dealt with very few cases addressing the qualification of a particular form of treatment, while the Human Rights Committee has proved reluctant to make distinctions between torture and other forms of ill-treatment, preferring instead to make findings of violation of art 7 of ICCPR as a whole (HRC General Comment No 20: para 4). Distinct forms of treatment specifically of concern to prisoners which the Human Rights Committee has expressly stated may amount to prohibited treatment include prolonged solitary confinement (HRC General Comment No 20: para 6)[5] and corporal punishment (HRC General Comment No 20: para 5). Article 7 also explicitly prohibits the subjection of an individual to medical or scientific experimentation without his or her free consent. The Committee Against Torture has expressed concern at the use by prison authorities of instruments of physical restraint which may cause unnecessary pain and humiliation, including in the case of Australia (CAT re Australia 2000: para 6(b)).

Extensive analysis of Human Rights Committee jurisprudence may be found elsewhere (Nowak 1993: 126-41; Rodley 1999: 75-106). For the purposes of this chapter, what is important is to draw out the kind of subject matter which the Committee would examine in connection with art 7 and distinguish it as far as possible from that which would be considered under art 10, the article which deals specifically with the treatment of persons deprived of their liberty. Again, this is made difficult by the fact that, where there is an overlap in subject matter, the Committee tends to prefer to find that both articles have been violated.[6] Where it *has* made a distinction, it has usually opted to find a violation of art 10 but not art 7, thus establishing that art 10 covers conditions showing a less severe disregard for human dignity.

Although there is a significant overlap between the two articles, some distinctions may be drawn between them, both in terms of scope and of the approach adopted by the Human Rights Committee. In the first place, art 7 applies in all circumstances while art 10 only covers persons deprived of liberty. In practice, the focus under art 7 tends to be on specific and often severe incidents involving attacks on human dignity, whereas art 10 is relied on when addressing the general condition of a detention facility along with specific conditions of detention. It also has a lower threshold.[7] Finally, the obligation on the state under art 7 tends to be to refrain from certain types of treatment, while the obligation under art 10 is a more far-reaching, positive duty to ensure minimum standards regardless of economic difficulties (Nowak 1993: 188-9).

In addition to outlawing the treatment itself, the prohibition of torture and other forms of ill-treatment carries with it a series of positive obligations designed to contribute to the elimination of such treatment. The Human Rights Committee considers that it is not enough to prohibit the treatment by law but that measures must also be taken to ensure that complaint mechanisms are effective, that perpetrators are held responsible and that remedies are made available to victims (HRC General Comment No 20: para 14). These obligations are also expressly provided for in UNCAT (arts 12-15). Other safeguards which might be implemented include granting access to lawyers, doctors and family members, requiring that a register of detainees be kept and making confessions or other evidence obtained under torture inadmissible in court (HRC General Comment No 20: para 11), the latter also being a specific obligation under art 15 of UNCAT.

Right to liberty and security of person

Article 9 of the ICCPR provides that 'everyone has the right to liberty and security of person' and that 'no one shall be subjected to arbitrary arrest or detention'. It goes on to clarify that for a deprivation of liberty to be legitimate, it should take place 'on such grounds and in accordance with such procedures as are established by law' (art 9.1). It is clear that this is not an absolute right. A person *can* be detained but only where it is provided for, and in accordance with, the law. In addition, any person arrested is entitled to a number of procedural guarantees: they must be informed of the reasons for the detention (art 9.2); they must be brought promptly before a judicial officer and are entitled to trial within a reasonable time (art 9.3); they have a right to apply for review of the lawfulness of the detention by a court without delay (art 9.4) and a right to compensation if they have been unlawfully deprived of liberty (art 9.5).

Most significant in seeking to prevent the prolongation of situations of unlawful detention are the requirement that detainees be brought promptly before a judge and the right to seek a review of the lawfulness of detention. The former is designed to limit periods during which individuals are not allowed to communicate with persons outside the place of detention, such as their lawyer, family or doctor. The central debate revolves around the meaning of the term 'promptly', as even in countries which do not practise incommunicado detention as a matter of course, legislation usually permits restrictions on contacts with the outside world, including lawyers, on national security grounds or in relation to certain crimes committed by more than one person. Although the Human Rights Committee has not precisely defined the term, it considers at least that 'delays must not exceed a few days' (HRC General Comment No 8: para 2).

With respect to the right to seek a review of the lawfulness of detention, it is significant that this right should be exercised before a court and not merely a judicial officer. It should be noted that the right appears to relate to the *lawfulness* of the detention as distinct from the question of whether or not the detention was *necessary* (Rodley 1999: 338). Furthermore, it is specified that where a detention is found to be unlawful, the release of the person must be ordered. Consequently, the court before which the review is being sought must have the power to order the release of the individual, failing which the Human Rights Committee may find a violation of art 9.4.[8]

Detention can be arbitrary from the very beginning or it can become arbitrary at a later stage where, for example, a prisoner continues to be held after a term of imprisonment has been fully served.[9] Detention may become arbitrary if it continues beyond the period for which the state can provide appropriate justification.[10] A prisoner may wish to pursue a claim under art 9 in relation to events which occurred at the time of being taken into custody or which may be ongoing, for example, if a prisoner has spent an excessive amount of time in pre-trial detention.

Right to a fair trial

Article 14 of the ICCPR sets out a complex list of guarantees which must accompany any trial. The basic principle is that 'All persons shall be equal before the courts and tribunals [and] everyone shall be entitled to a fair and public hearing by a competent and impartial tribunal established by law' (art 14.1). Any prisoner involved in a court case in parallel to his or her imprisonment should be aware of these guarantees and, where relevant, might well be able to invoke the lack of fairness of the trial as a ground for challenging the legality of detention.

Table 11.2. Main fair trial guarantees contained in ICCPR article 14

Article 14.1	Right to equality before the law Right to a fair and public hearing before a competent, independent and impartial tribunal Requirement of publicity of proceedings and judgment except in limited specified circumstances Minimum guarantees of the accused in criminal trials:
Article 14.2	Right to be presumed innocent until proven guilty
Article 14.3	Right to be informed of the charge Right to adequate time and facilities to prepare a defence and to communicate with a lawyer of choice Right to be tried without undue delay Right to a defence, including to be tried in his presence, and to the free assistance of a lawyer if required Right to call and examine witnesses Right to the free assistance of an interpreter if required Right not to be compelled to testify against himself or to admit guilt
Article 14.5	Right to an appeal
Article 14.6	Right to compensation for miscarriage of justice
Article 14.7	Right not to be tried twice for the same offence

Standards applicable specifically to persons deprived of their liberty

The principal international standards specific to persons deprived of their liberty in the Australian context are art 10 of the ICCPR and the UN *Standard Minimum Rules for the Treatment of Prisoners* (Standard Minimum Rules or SMRs). Unlike the other human rights norms discussed previously, art 10 specifically and exclusively applies in circumstances involving the deprivation of liberty but, like the other norms, its provisions are still quite general. In contrast, the Standard Minimum Rules are very detailed but they are not formally binding on states. In practice, the two sets of standards are complementary because the Human Rights Committee has relied heavily on the Standard Minimum Rules to develop the scope of art 10. It expressly rejected an argument by a State Party that it was incompetent to examine the conditions of detention of an individual where these are referenced in relation to the Standard Minimum Rules, emphasising that the Rules 'constitute valuable guidelines for the interpretation of the Covenant' (HRC Communication No 632/1995 (1997): para 6.3). In expressing concern about prison conditions when examining State Party reports, both the Human Rights Committee and the Committee Against Torture have regularly recommended that they be brought into compliance with the Standard Minimum Rules.[11] At the time of adoption of the ICCPR, delegates in the UN General Assembly specifically stressed that the Standard Minimum Rules should be taken into account when interpreting and applying art 10 (Nowak 1993: 185).

ICCPR article 10

Article 10 of the ICCPR provides that all persons deprived of their liberty have a right to be treated 'with humanity and with respect for the inherent dignity of the human person'. It also specifies that accused persons should, except in exceptional circumstances, be separated from convicted persons and subject to separate treatment appropriate to their status as unconvicted persons. Accused juveniles should similarly be separated from adults, as should juvenile offenders, who should also be accorded treatment appropriate to their age and legal status. Australia currently has a reservation in place to art 10, stating that the obligation to segregate juveniles and adults, whether convicted or unconvicted, is accepted 'only to the extent that it is considered by the responsible authorities to be beneficial to the juveniles or adults concerned'.

Article 10 establishes that there is a minimum of humane treatment that must apply to conditions of detention (Nowak 1993: 183). The Human Rights Committee has emphasised that art 10 represents a level below which it is not acceptable to sink and that implementation cannot be dependent on resources (HRC General Comment No 21: para 4). The Committee has relied extensively on the Standard Minimum Rules in the interpretation of art 10. There is consequently a well-developed jurisprudence addressing a wide and detailed range of aspects of detention conditions. Because the Committee tends to examine general conditions of detention under art 10, most of its findings of violation both in relation to individual communications and in the examination of state reports refer to a combination of various factors. Such findings are more valuable in relation to individual communications because they explicitly qualify conditions as incompatible with art 10. In the context of the state reporting procedure, it is more common for the Committee to express concern at certain aspects of conditions of detention rather than to make an explicit finding of violation.

Factors which have consistently contributed to a finding of violation in individual communications include overcrowding and solitary confinement,[12] restrictions on contact with relatives or legal representatives,[13] and limitations on access to media.[14] The St Catherine Prison Cases (against Jamaica) found the following conditions to be in violation: inadequate opportunities to leave the cell, failure to provide a mattress, inadequate sanitation, inadequate ventilation, absence of natural light, inadequate food and water, and lack of medical assistance or denial of medical treatment.[15] The greater the number of factors present, the more likely it is that a violation will be found but violations have been found even in the presence of a single factor where that one was felt to be significant.[16]

In its observations concerning state reports, the Human Rights Committee has expressed concern in relation to overcrowding,[17] lack of sanitary facilities,[18] lighting,[19] food,[20] training of prison personnel,[21] inadequate facilities for visits by relatives and legal representatives,[22] medical care,[23] inequality of treatment,[24] non-separation of accused persons from convicted persons and juveniles from adults[25] and prolonged solitary confinement.[26]

Standard Minimum Rules for the Treatment of Prisoners

A number of documents have been adopted by the United Nations specifically in relation to persons deprived of their liberty. The principal text referred to here is the Standard Minimum Rules but other guidelines include the *Basic Principles for the Treatment of Prisoners*, the *Standard Minimum Rules for the Administration of Juvenile Justice* (known as the 'Beijing Rules'), the UN *Rules for the Protection of Juveniles Deprived of their Liberty* and the *Body of Principles for the Protection of All Persons Under any Form of Detention or Imprisonment*.

The Standard Minimum Rules are designed mainly to apply to prisoners who have been placed in a custodial institution following a judicial decision, whether convicted or untried (although particular rules apply to untried prisoners (SMRs 84-93)). Even where a person is being detained without charge, however, many of the same provisions will apply (SMR 95).

Although the Standard Minimum Rules themselves acknowledge that they set out what is 'generally accepted as being good principle and practice in the treatment of prisoners and the management of institutions' and that not all of the rules are 'capable of application in all places and at all times' (SMRs 1-2), the Human Rights Committee has observed that there are certain minimum requirements regarding conditions of detention which it considers 'should always be observed, even if economic or budgetary considerations may make compliance with these obligations difficult'.[27] The minimum conditions identified by the Committee with reference to the Standard Minimum Rules are minimum floor space and cubic content of air for each prisoner, adequate sanitary facilities, clothing which shall be in no manner degrading or humiliating, provision of a separate bed and provision of food of nutritional value adequate for health and strength (SMRs 10, 12, 17, 19, 20).

Furthermore, although the rules as a whole are not a legally binding document, some of the specific rules may reflect broader legal obligations that do have binding status and provide guidance in their interpretation. For example, SMR 31 states that 'corporal punishment, punishment by placing in a dark cell, and all cruel, inhuman or degrading punishments shall be completely prohibited as punishments for disciplinary offences', clearly restating the general prohibition against torture and inhuman treatment (Rodley 1999: 280-1). In its third report to the Human Rights Committee, Australia indicated that the principles in the Standard Minimum Rules were reflected in the *Standard Guidelines for Corrections in Australia*. These, though not binding on Australian States and Territories, provide assistance to legislatures and prison authorities in the drafting of rules (para 368).

Table 11.3. Principles of general application
elaborated upon by the Standard Minimum Rules

A register of prisoners must be kept in all places of detention, containing a number of required pieces of information: SMR 7
Different categories of prisoners should be kept separate: SMR 8
Accommodation must comply with certain conditions, in particular with regard to size, number of occupants, lighting, ventilation and sanitation: SMRs 9-14
Facilities should be provided for the maintenance of personal hygiene: SMRs 15-16
Clothing and bedding must be provided to a specified standard: SMRs 17-19
Food and water of adequate quality must be provided: SMR 20
Opportunities for exercise must be provided: SMR 21
Various medical services must be made available on a regular basis, including outside the institution if necessary: SMRs 22-26
Methods and procedures for discipline and punishment are strictly regulated, including through the absolute prohibition of certain forms of punishment: SMRs 27-32
Instruments of restraint may only be used in very limited circumstances and never as a punishment: SMRs 33-34
Prisoners must be informed of the rules of the institution and given an opportunity to make complaints: SMRs 35-36
Contacts with the outside world are to be allowed in certain forms, including through communication with family and friends: SMRs 37-39
Access to books should be permitted: SMR 40
Prisoners should be allowed to practice their religious beliefs as far as practicable: SMRs 41-42
Prisoners' property must be dealt with in accordance with specific rules: SMR 43
Notification of death, illness, or transfer must be passed on to relatives or the prisoner as appropriate: SMR 44
The removal of prisoners must respect certain conditions: SMR 45
Detailed rules exist as to the selection and functions of institutional personnel: SMRs 46-54
Regular inspections of the institution should be carried out by an appropriate authority: SMR 55

As the Standard Minimum Rules are very detailed, a full analysis is not possible here. However, the central themes can at least be highlighted. The rules are divided into two parts: rules of general application and rules applying to specific categories of prisoners.

With respect to *rules of general application*, the basic underlying principle governing the application of the rules and the treatment of prisoners is that of impartiality and non-discrimination (SMR 6). Leading on from this, the rules become more specific and precise, elaborating on the principles identified in Table 11.3.

Categories of prisoners to whom *specific rules* apply are prisoners under sentence, insane and mentally abnormal prisoners, prisoners under arrest or awaiting trial and civil prisoners. The rules relating to prisoners under sentence address issues surrounding the rehabilitative purpose of imprisonment and include detailed provisions on work and other activities. The rules relating to the other three categories of prisoners essentially deal with the special requirements of those groups.

Conclusion

International human rights law has developed an extensive body of standards for the protection of prisoners from abuses at the hands of officials. As a state that has acceded to these standards, Australia has a legal obligation under international law to respect them and to ensure that its representatives do the same. Those who believe their rights have been violated are entitled to pursue this before the national courts to the extent provided for in domestic legislation.[28] If they are not able to obtain an effective remedy at that level, they may seek to bring their case before one of the international bodies responsible for supervising respect for international standards, in particular the Human Rights Committee.

Notes

1   The 1980 reservation was withdrawn in 1984 and replaced with the following regarding art 10: 'In relation to paragraph 2(a) the principle of segregation is accepted as an objective to be achieved progressively. In relation to paragraphs 2(b) and 3 (second sentence) the obligation to segregate is accepted only to the extent that such segregation is considered by the responsible authorities to be beneficial to the juveniles or adults concerned.' See <www.unhcr.ch.tbs.doc.nsf>.

2   See for example Amnesty International/Law Society 2000 or Giffard 2000 for a discussion of these procedures. Further information may also be found on the website of the Office of the UN High Commissioner for Human Rights, where the procedures are based (www.unhchr.ch). See also Pritchard 1998.

3   The Human Rights Committee has occasionally referred to non-compliance with these texts in connection with prisons: see for example HRC re USA 1995: para 285.

4   See for example HRC Communication: *Guillermo Ignacio Dermit Barbato & Hugo Haroldo Dermit Barbato v Uruguay* Communication No 84/1981, UN Doc Supp No 40 A/38/40 (1983) (27 February 1981) at 124.

5   Solitary confinement has also been qualified as torture by the Committee Against Torture where the cells involved measured merely 60 by 80 cm, with no light or adequate ventilation and the inmate was obliged to stand or crouch at all times (CAT re Turkey 1993: para 52).

6   For example, violations of both articles were found in connection with an incident during which a prisoner was subject to severe beatings, his belongings destroyed, his clothes and sleeping mat drenched and no medical treatment was provided for the resulting injuries (HRC Communication: *Irvine Reynolds v Jamaica*, Communication No 587/1994, UN Doc CCPR/C/59/D/587/1994 (24 April 1997): para 10.2-10.4). A similar double violation was found in a case involving confinement in a grossly overcrowded cell, being obliged to sleep on a wet concrete floor and being unable to see family, relatives or a legal representative for eight months (HRC Communication: *St Catherine Prison Cases (Jamaica)*: Communication No 704/1996 (1998): para 71).

7   One case which provides a good illustration of the distinction is that of *Nicholas Henry v Jamaica*. Distinct violations were found of arts 7 and 10. The art 7 violation was found on the basis of very detailed descriptions of beatings and the resulting injuries, as well as the absence of evidence of an investigation. The art 10 violation was based on a failure to provide medical treatment for an ongoing medical condition in spite of a recommendation by a surgeon that an operation be carried out (HRC Communication: *Nicholas Henry v Jamaica*, Communication No 610/1995, UN Doc CCPR/C/64/D/610/1995 (21 October 1998): para 7.3). In *Anthony Finn v Jamaica*, a violation of both articles was found where the failure to provide medical care arose in connection with an incident of beating (HRC Communication: *Anthony Finn v Jamaica*, Communication No 617/1995, UN Doc CCPR/C/63/D/617/1995 (4 August 1998): paras 3.2 and 9.2).

8   For example, HRC Communication: *A v Australia*, Communication No 560/1993, UN Doc CCPR/C/59/D/560/1993 (30 April 1997): para 9.5.

9   For example, see Communication No 4/1977 (1980), p123, para 18; Communication No 5/1977 (1979), p 124, para 10; Communication No 138/1983 (1986), p 121, para 10.

10   (for example, HRC Communication: *A v Australia*, Communication No 560/1993, UN Doc CCPR/C/59/D/560/1993 (30 April 1997): para 9.4).

11   For example, see CAT re Kyrgyzstan 1999: para 6(e); HRC re Armenia 1998: para 13; HRC re Costa Rica 1994: para 11; HRC re Gabon 1996: para 23; HRC re Sudan 1997: para 15; HRC re Togo 1994: para 5; HRC re Zambia 1996: para 13, 25.

12   HRC Communication: *Allan Henry v Trinidad and Tobago*, Communication No 752/1997, UN Doc CCPR/C/64/D/752/1997 (10 February 1999): paras 7.4; 8.6.

13   HRC Communication: *Deon McTaggart v Jamaica*, Communication No 749/1997, UN Doc CCPR/C/62/D/749/1997 (3 June 1998): para 8.6; *Ms Carolina Teillier Arredondo (on behalf of Maria Sybila Arredondo) v Peru*, Communication No 688/1996, UN Doc CCPR/C/69/D/688/1996 (14 August 2000): paras 8.3, 8.4, 8.8-8.12, 10.4.

14   HRC Communication: *Ms Carolina Teillier Arredondo (on behalf of Maria Sybila Arredondo) v Peru*, Communication No 688/1996, UN Doc CCPR/C/69/D/688/1996 (14 August 2000): paras 8.3, 8.4, 8.8-8.12, 10.4.

15   Violations of art 10(1) were found in a series of cases concerning St Catherine District Prison, Jamaica, where the factors involved included being confined to a cell 23 hours a day, having no mattress, bedding or furniture, inadequate sanitation, no natural light, inadequate ventilation, food which was not palatable, lack of medical assistance and denial of medical treatment (HRC Communication: *St Catherine Prison Cases (Jamaica)*: Communications Nos. 720/1996 (1998), 719/1996 (1998), 707/1996 (1997), 705/1996 (1998), 704/1996 (1998) and 617/1995 (1998)).

16   For example, the deprivation of natural lighting except for one hour of recreation was sufficient for the Human Rights Committee to hold that the dignity of the

person had not been respected (HRC Communication: *Abdool Saleem Yasseen & Noel Thomas v Republic of Guyana*, Communication No 676/1996, UN Doc CCPR/C/62/D/676/1996 (31 March 1998): para 7.6).

17 HRC re Yemen 1995: para 254; HRC re Lithuania 1997: para 14; HRC re Morocco 1994: para 12; HRC re Ukraine 1995: para 4; HRC re Cameroon 1999: para 23; HRC re India 1997: para 26; HRC re Poland 1999: para 16.

18 HRC re Jamaica 1997: 13; HRC re India 1997: para 26; HRC re Nigeria 1996: para 285.

19 HRC re Jamaica 1997: 13.

20 HRC re Jamaica 1997: 13; HRC re Cameroon 1999: para 23; HRC re Nigeria 1996: para 285; HRC re Russian Federation 1995: para 5.

21 HRC re Jamaica 1997: 13.

22 HRC re Jamaica 1997: 13.

23 HRC re Cameroon 1999: para 23; HRC re Nigeria 1996: para 285; HRC re India 1997: para 26.

24 HRC re India 1997: para 26.

25 HRC re Latvia 1995: para 4; HRC re Lebanon 1997: para 17.

26 HRC re Luxembourg 1992: paras 7, 9.

27 (HRC Communication: *Albert Womah Mukong v. Cameroon*, Communication No 458/1991, UN Doc CCPR/C/51/D/458/1991: para 9.3; see also HRC General Comment No 21).

28 For detailed discussion of domestic remedies in Australia, see the chapters in this volume by Craig Minogue (ch 12) and John Rynne (ch 9).

CHAPTER 12

An Insider's View: Human Rights and Excursions from the Flat Lands

Craig WJ Minogue

This chapter examines the limits of domestic and international remedies for the violation of prisoners' human rights. It touches on four court actions where prisoners, of whom I am one, agitated human rights issues in the Supreme Courts of Victoria, South Australia and in the Federal and High Courts of Australia. Inmates acted for themselves in these cases and, in one case, human rights violations were found to have been committed. The resulting judgments, however, amounted to there being no enforceable human rights at law for State prisoners.

Prisoners' access to HREOC

In November 1996, I wrote to the Human Rights and Equal Opportunity Commission (HREOC), claiming that I was being denied the following basic human rights: having unimpeded access to the courts, being allowed to possess documentary evidence in a case against me and being able to consult with a lawyer at Barwon Prison. The wrongs I complained about amounted to violations of article 14 of the *International Covenant on Civil and Political Rights* (ICCPR).[1] It should be noted that the ICCPR is a Schedule to the HREOC Act of 1986. HREOC declined to hear my complaint, advising me that it did not have jurisdiction over State agencies in relation to 'human rights' matters. In a letter dated 6 May 1997, HREOC wrote:

> Under s 11(1)(f) of the [HREOC] Act ... the Commissioner has authority to inquire into any act or practice that may be inconsistent with or contrary to any human right. Under the Act, 'human right' is strictly defined, and relates to specific international instruments to

which Australia is committed and only deals with acts done or practices of Commonwealth agencies. *Your circumstances are that you are a state prisoner incarcerated in a state prison.* The Commissioner does not have any authority under the Act to conduct an inquiry into an act or practice of a state agency. For this reason, the Commissioner must decline your complaint ... (emphasis added).

I personally litigated this issue in the Federal Court.[2] I did this by mounting a Constitutional challenge to the validity of the HREOC Act (*Minogue v Human Rights and Equal Opportunity Commission* (1998) 54 ALD 389).

In 1998-99, approximately 20 per cent of all non-employment related complaints to HREOC were from prisoners. As the States are responsible for all prisons, the vast majority of 'human rights' complaints from prisoners are not accepted.[3] HREOC does have jurisdiction to investigate a prisoner's complaint if he or she is complaining about sex, disability or race discrimination. The reality, however, is that few prisoners' complaints relate to these issues. Prisoners are concerned about:

- Poor health care
- Physical and psychological violence from prison staff and police
- Strip-searching (see Appendix A below) and urine testing as a punitive tool of prison management
- Restricted access to legal documents, information about the law, lawyers and the Courts[4]
- Poor food which does not maintain health and which causes disease[5]
- Exploitation of prisoners by forcing them to buy their own food[6]
- Being held in cells with no natural light or fresh air[7]
- Being forced to work for the profits of national companies making consumer goods with no holiday or sick pay, no WorkCover, occupational health and safety coverage or workers compensation coverage[8]

These are the issues of concern to prisoners and all of these issues arise as a result of actions taken by State, not Federal, agencies.

In *Minogue v Human Rights and Equal Opportunity Commission* (1999) 166 ALR 129, HREOC argued that it did not have jurisdiction to hear my complaint and withdrew from the hearing, saying that it was inappropriate to debate the legalities of its own Act.[9] The Commonwealth Attorney-General intervened to oppose me. And the Victorian Branch of the International Commission of Jurists (ICJ) was given leave to intervene as *amicus curiae*. Counsel acting for the ICJ,

Tony Pagone QC (Vice President of the ICJ), and barristers Wendy Harris and Debra Coombs filed a written outline of submission that put the following matters to the Court.

- That 'the Commission always had jurisdiction to consider [my] complaints pursuant to those of its functions ... which are not tied or limited to Commonwealth ... acts or practices'.

- That 'there was ample indication in the material provided to the Commission by [me] that [my] human rights, as defined under the Act, may be or are being contravened, and that the actions of authorities at HM Prison Barwon in relation to [me] may be or are inconsistent with Australia's obligations under the Covenant'.

- That there would 'be no breach of any constitutional principle or mandate if the Commonwealth were to take action to secure [my] human rights and those in [my] position — it being clear that the combination of the wide powers vested in prison authorities under the *Corrections Act* [1986 Vic] and the limited protections for prisoners embodied in s 47 of that statute ... are wholly inadequate for this purpose and, indeed, permit action against prisoners in contravention of their human rights, contrary to the requirements of the Covenant [ie the ICCPR]'.

Ultimately, the matter was lost. I appealed but human rights law was not advanced and there remain no enforceable human rights at law for prisoners in relation to the actions of State Government agencies — the agencies that are most prevalent in the lives of prisoners.[10]

Prisoners' access to the civil courts

Before I initiated the action against HREOC, I was involved in assisting a fellow inmate, Hugo Rich, to litigate human rights issues against Barwon Prison and the Victorian correctional authorities.[11] Mr Rich was suffering from the same problems that first caused me to complain to HREOC, those problems being that prison authorities were refusing to allow access to documentary evidence in relation to criminal charges that had been brought against him and which he needed in order to prepare an appeal.

The court in *Rich* delivered an equivocating judgment. This was due in part to a poorly drafted application, the civil rules being new to us at that stage. The judge said he was 'not impressed' (*Rich v Groningen* (1997) 95 A Crim R 272 at 285) with the 'recent inventions' (at 284)[12] of the authorities at Barwon Prison in relation to the practice of turning away lawyers from visiting their clients, and he said that he thought they were acting outside their powers in restricting visits by lawyers against the statutory intention to allow visits at certain times (at 286). The judge's criticisms, however, were made under the cover of *obiter dicta* comments and were therefore worthless because *obiter dicta* comments are made outside the purview of a case and do not form part of the common law.

Some light was thrown on the poor standing of prisoners' human rights by the case of *Collins v South Australia* (1999) 74 SASR 200. In this case, Robert Collins, a prisoner acting on his own behalf, brought an action against the State of South Australia claiming violations of his human rights at the Adelaide Remand Centre. Justice Millhouse found that he was satisfied on the evidence that Collins' human rights had been violated and he thought it was strongly arguable that the scheduling of an international treaty to an enactment incorporated it into domestic law (at 209-210). His Honour, however, ultimately said, 'Much as I regret it, as a single judge I am not able to give force to the basic human rights set out in these conventions [ie the conventions scheduled to the HREOC Act]' (at 213).

Having started a new action in the High Court (*Minogue v Williams* [1999] FCA 1589 (Weinberg J)), I relied upon the decision in *Collins* to support my cause of action and I extended my legal arguments from that case.[13] The primary judge in *Minogue v Williams* did not accept the dicta in *Collins* and found that neither the High Court nor the Federal Court had jurisdiction to hear a human rights suit brought by an individual claiming violations of the ICCPR by a State agency. By order of the Court, the costs of the respondent (the prison manager) were awarded against me.[14] A lawyer supporting me as a media spokesperson (Barwon Prison authorities had banned me from contact with the media in relation to 'human rights issues')[15] remarked after this judgment, 'So, not only can the State violate your human rights, but now you have to pay them for the privilege!'

I appealed the decision in *Minogue v Williams* [2000] FCA 125. I argued that a schedule is a part of the Act itself and not an inferior portion of the Act (see *Re Foley; Channell v Foley* (1952) 53 SR (NSW) 31) and that the placing of material in a schedule is usually only a matter of convenience, most likely due to the amount or format of the material concerned.[16] I went on to argue that if there is a conflict between a section of an Act and positive provisions in the schedule, then it is very clear that 'the schedule must be read as overriding the provisions in the section' (Gifford & Gifford 1994: 79). I advanced detailed arguments in relation to issues of statutory construction and the place of schedules at law and I closed my submissions by saying:

> All individuals, subject to the jurisdiction of Australia, should be afforded the protection of the human rights provisions, in their plain English meaning, as they are found in the schedules of the HREOC Act without any limitations. And these provisions should be extended to all parts of this Federal State, accompanied by effective remedies for violations of those provisions. And it should not matter if you are a person in my position claiming human rights, or the Rights of the Child, if you are a 15-year-old Aboriginal boy in a Northern Territory Prison.

The Appeal Court in *Minogue v Williams* was not moved by my submissions and it disapproved the dicta in *Collins*, stating that the scheduling of international human rights treaties to the HREOC Act does not incorporate them into domestic law.[17] The Court, however, missed my point. I was not arguing incorporation, more basically I was saying that the body of the text in the schedules — text which contains positive provisions — should be given force and effect in law in relation to the plain meaning of the words used.

Having tried and failed to enliven a Federal jurisdiction for human rights remedies, I need to make a few points about the State jurisdiction. Section 47 of the *Corrections Act* 1986 (Vic) is headed 'Prisoners rights' and the provisions in that section are referred to as 'rights' (see Appendix B). At the first hearing of *Minogue v Williams*, the issue of *Corrections Act* rights was canvassed in some detail. The presiding judge posed a rhetorical question, asking if these were not 'hortatory rights' (*Minogue v Williams* [1999] FCA 1589, transcript of proceedings on 28 October 1999, p 25). When I later looked up the word 'hortatory' in the dictionary and found that it meant to urge or encourage a course of action, I posed a question, at first to myself, and later to the Appeal Court: 'Is the idea of *"hortatory right"'* not a self-evident oxymoron?'. In discussing the status of rights in the *Corrections Act*, the following exchange between the judge and counsel for corrections is indicative of their status.

> Judge: 'Is a contravention of section 47 an offence against the Act?'
> Counsel: 'I don't believe there is a provision which explicitly provides to that effect.'
> Judge: 'Yes, so that a prisoner could not himself institute proceedings for an offence ...'
> Counsel: 'That would appear to be the case, your Honour, yes.'
>
> (*Minogue v Williams* [1999] FCA 1589, (Weinberg J) transcript of proceedings on 28 October 1999: 26- 27)

It was my submission that *ubi jus ibi remedium* (where there is a right there is a remedy), but the issue of the rights for which there is no remedy was not resolved.[18] The reality is that without the considerable indulgence of a common law court at the State level, a violation of a prisoner's rights under the *Corrections Act* 'couldn't be run in any court' (*Minogue v Williams*, transcript of proceedings, 28 October 1999: 28). Counsel for my jailers said, 'Section 47 is a very clear legislative command about prisoners' entitlements ... [*but*] ... there's certainly no express conferral of a private right of action by the Act' (*Minogue v Williams*, transcript of proceedings, 28 October 1999: 33).

International redress

What international remedies are available to agitate prisoners' rights issues? In theory, Australia is internationally accountable for violations of the ICCPR, including by Federal, State or Territory governments under the provisions of the First Optional Protocol to the ICCPR. Article 1 of the Protocol states that Australia will 'recognize the competence of the [Human Rights] Committee'. The Commonwealth Attorney-General, Mr Daryl Williams, has made the current Commonwealth Government's position on this issue clear, and that is to deny responsibility.

A brief example will illustrate the political position. A Cambodian man, referred to as Mr A, entered Australia by boat in late 1989 as an asylum seeker. He was kept in detention for more than four years while his application for asylum went through the Courts, while at various times he was denied access to a lawyer. A Protocol complaint, called a 'communication', was lodged in Mr A's case with the Human Rights Committee. The communication claimed that Australia was in breach of its obligations under the ICCPR. The Committee found in April 1997 that Mr A's detention contravened the ICCPR and that the system of judicial review of Mr A's detention had been inadequate.

This was a strong finding against Australia, a finding that should have been met with concern by the Commonwealth Government. The Attorney-General's response, however, was to duck the finding. He said, 'The committee is not a court and does not render binding decisions or judgments. It provides views and opinions and it is up to countries to decide whether they agree with those views and how they will respond to them' (MacDonald 1997: 9). This is an interesting comment because in documents filed in *Minogue v Human Rights and Equal Opportunity Commission* by the Attorney-General, it was argued that HREOC and the Federal Court did not have jurisdiction to hear my human rights complaint, and it was disingenuously suggested that the appropriate place for me to make my 'plea' should be 'to the political branches of government rather than to the courts'.[19] I had made my plea to the Attorney-General in a letter dated 20 August 1997 but I was directed to the Human Rights Committee.[20] But as demonstrated in the case of Mr A, the Attorney-General will not necessarily act on the Committee's findings.

The Ombudsman

The 'Prisoners rights' section of the *Corrections Act* entitles prisoners to send and receive uncensored letters to and from the Ombudsman and to make complaints about their jailors, the police or other government officers. The Ombudsman is the only independent complaints handling authority for State prisoners. The primary function of the Ombudsman, as defined in s 13 of the *Ombudsman Act* 1973 (Vic), is to conduct investigations of administrative action. The Ombudsman has wide and independent powers of investigation and the Act contains persuasive powers, but these are rarely used. Informal approaches are preferred.

> Although under the *Ombudsman Act* [Vic] I have the power to formally obtain information from an authority, I find that it is far more expedient to obtain information from an authority on an informal basis where officers of authorities volunteer information regarding a complaint I have received.[21]

Informal inquires may be an expedient method of dealing with complaints; however, it has been my experience that prison and police officers do not confess guilt when their colleagues ask them to respond to an Ombudsman's inquiry. In my 15 years in prison, I have never personally heard of a prisoner's complaint being substantiated by the Ombudsman. In 1997-98, there were 787 complaints from prisoners to the Ombudsman in Victoria and of those, one was formally investigated and sustained. In 1998-99, there were 771 complaints, none of which was formally investigated. In 1999-2000, there were 562 complaints, only one of which was formally investigated and sustained.[22]

A complaint to the Ombudsman is so ineffective that prisoners and their advocates view it as not being worth the time and effort.[23]

Kate Lawrence is a lawyer with the North Melbourne legal centre, which represents many inmates. 'The Ombudsman's office is terribly ineffectual,' she says. 'Essentially what they do is go to the people you have complained about, get their story and say, "there is your answer". You already knew that. The fact that nothing happens can exacerbate frustrations. In terms of teeth, the Ombudsman is a gummy shark. Prisoners don't view it as a serious option'. (Mottram 2001: 3)

The Ombudsman's role is the vital one of safeguarding citizens from the excesses of government agencies, like the police and prisons. Yet lawyers are often quoted in the media expressing their dissatisfaction with the Ombudsman. For example, 'It is understandable that so far as my clients are concerned, the office of the Ombudsman is viewed as a waste of space ... If you are bashed in a police station and there are no witnesses you are wasting time going to the Ombudsman' (Mottram 2001: 3, quoting lawyer Dennis Heslin).

Conclusion: No legal remedies

So, in conclusion, HREOC, the Federal Court and the High Court do not have the jurisdiction to hear a complaint from a State prisoner; corrections law in Victoria confers rights but no remedies for their violation; the Ombudsman is not an effective remedy; and the Commonwealth Attorney-General will not necessarily accept findings against Australia by the UN Human Rights Committee.

This chapter has examined the limits of domestic and international remedies for the violation of prisoners' human rights. In short, there are no remedies. And sadly the situation is not getting better. A report was produced for the then-Human Rights Commission in 1986 (the year I first came to prison) by Professor Gordon Hawkins and his findings are as true today as they were 15 years ago. He wrote 'If one asks then, in conclusion, what rights prisoners in Australia can currently claim, the answer is virtually none at all; not even the basic necessities of life' (quoted in O'Neill & Handley 1994: 172).

In trying to sum up my experiences for this chapter, I reflected back to an early directions hearing in the Federal Court. The issues to be dealt with on the day fizzled out and the judge apologised to the parties. I jokingly replied, 'At least I've had a day out'. It was not much of a joke and more for the amusement of the judge and my playing on the ignorance of those who don't know the reality of a day out from prison. A lawyer who was acting as my media spokesperson wrote a few days later, 'It must be a different experience for you zipping along at 100kmh and seeing the horizon as opposed to the flat world of prison'. I wrote back:

There are no windows, and it is pitch black in the back of a prison van. And I get motion sickness, and the exhaust fumes that belch into the caged compartment in which I am locked, make me ill. Each time I go and come back from Court I very nearly throw-up. I get a one step glimpse as I get off the van and step through the back door of the Federal Court, and that's only of the media pack. If I am 'lucky' I can occasionally get a glimpse of people on the street if a scratch has been made in the layers of black paint on the windows. And I am sorry to say, but I don't yearn to be out there with you, frankly, resentment is all I feel. What comes to my mind are the echoes of inmates screaming at night as they are being bashed by prison guards, the polite turning away of lawyers and judges, and the fact that if a prisoner wants to run a court action against his or her gaolers to prevent human rights abuses, they have to do it themselves.

This is no day out, prefaced and concluded as it is by the borderline sexual assault of the strip-search; the prison guard ordering me to 'Lift your ball bag!' and 'Bend over and spread 'em!', so he can peer up my anus.

Yes, the prison environment is a very flat place, but that is not just limited to the topography, it also includes the operational philosophy and thinking — what there is of it — and the general lack of any real purpose. Engaging in the intellectual arena of the Federal Court is a nice change and I almost feel like a real person again, but ultimately they all turn away from me and shuffle back out to their chambers and I'm sent back to the flat lands.

Should I feel justified in my resentment? Who can tell? After all, I have tertiary level study by correspondence, television, my computer and books, and three meals a day — better than most nursing home residents, if you believe the media. Anyway, there are plenty of other people to ask. Perhaps those who are being sent to prison for stealing biscuits and orange cordial could add their voice to mine. But then again, who would hear us?

Notes

1   'All persons shall be equal before the courts and tribunals. In the determination of any criminal charge against him, or of his rights and obligations in a suit at law, everyone shall be entitled to a fair and public hearing by a competent, independent and impartial tribunal established by law' (ICCPR, art 14.1). 'In the determination of any criminal charge against him, everyone shall be entitled to the following minimum guarantees, in full equality: (b) To have adequate time

and facilities for the preparation of his defence and to communicate with counsel of his own choosing' (ICCPR, art 14.3 (partial). 'Everyone convicted of a crime shall have the right to his conviction and sentence being reviewed by a higher tribunal according to law' (ICCPR, art 14.5).

2   This action attracted a lot of media attention: see McCulloch 1998: 244.

3   In the HREOC Annual Report 1996-97, it is reported that the second largest group of complaints to the Commission was from prisoners. There is reference to the fact that it will not deal with the majority of these and that '[t]he Commission may only inquire into complaints from prisoners, however, if they are from persons imprisoned under federal laws' (HREOC 1997: 61). This raises interesting questions I am not able to explore fully here. Briefly let me say that s 120 of the Constitution says that offenders against the criminal law of the Commonwealth are to serve their sentences is State prisons. The clear implication is that a cooperative scheme is established between the Commonwealth and the States; however, the operation of prisons is a wholly State matter! The principal authority on s 120 in *Leeth v Commonwealth* (1992) 174 CLR 455 at 466 per Mason CJ, Dawson and McHugh JJ.

4   See *Minogue v Human Rights and Equal Opportunity Commission* (1998) 54 ALD 389; *Rich v Groningen* (1997) 95 A Crim R 272.

5   This was the factual issue in *Minogue v Williams* [2000] FCA 125 (Full Court).

6   In the three months November 1996 to February 1997, food items were sold to the 240 prisoners at Barwon Prison included: 3189 tins of fish, 1959 bags of rice, 1873 packets of noodles, 1238 tins of baked beans and spaghetti, 1217 dozen eggs, 685 tins of tomatoes, 518 bags of pasta, 274 bottles of pineapple & orange juice, 273 tomato paste twin packs, 233 tins of fruit, 218 bottles of chilli sauce, 161 boxes of cereal, 136 boxes of Salada biscuits, 114 bottles of cooking oil and 102 boxes of Cup-a-Soup.

The kitchen budget at the time was $420,000/year. At the same time, the inmates spent $120,000/year on food. Over 12 months, then, some 12,756 x 130g tins of fish were sold, which is 1658 kilos of fish. And some 7836 x 500g bags of rice were sold, which is 3918 kilos of rice. When cooked, rice increases in weight by at least 50 per cent. This means that prisoners are supplying themselves with eight tonnes of rice per year at Barwon Prison alone. I am sure that, throughout Australia, prison shops and canteens make millions of dollars from this trade in food.

7   In its 1995-96 Annual Report, under the chapter heading of 'Human Rights', subheading 'Human rights and the justice system', HREOC reported:

The Queensland Police Service (QPS) sought comments from the Commission in relation to a proposal to build a new underground watch house at Rockhampton. Following concerns about the underground character of the proposed facility and the possible psychological consequences such an environment might have on detainees and police staff, the Commissioner recommended that the QPS revise the building plans and seek expert advice from an environmental psychologist. This recommendation was adopted. The expert report revisited facility plans to ensure adequate natural light, fresh air, ventilation and access to the natural environment. The Commission also identified a range of consultative and other measures which would need to be observed in the development of the plans. (HREOC 1996: 50)

The matter was 'raised at [a] senior level with the Queensland Government' (HREOC 1996). Queensland's Anti-Discrimination Commissioner is reported as stating that the HREOC intervention in this matter, *inter alia*, resulted in 'improved accommodation for the staff' (HREOC 1996: 135).

It should be noted that the Melbourne Custody Centre has no natural light, poor ventilation, no fresh air or access to the natural environment. If a prisoner were to complain about this to HREOC, it would not have the jurisdiction to hear the complaint. In October 1998, a prisoner complained about the Custody Centre to the Victorian Ombudsman. The Ombudsman replied on 17 July 2000 that all was well and that the hard-pressed and hard-working police officers were doing their best.

8   On 18 May 1999, I wrote to the Victorian WorkCover Authority (Victoria) asking, 'If I injure myself at work in a prison industry am I covered by WorkCover? Can I make a claim like any other worker?'. John Vitorson, the Manager of the WorkCover Advisory Service, advised on 10 June 1999: 'In accordance with the s 5 of the *Accident Compensation Act* 1985 prisoners are not workers as there is no contract of service and no worker/employer relationship. Accordingly, a prisoner injured while performing work in prison has no entitlement to compensation under WorkCover.' I once refused to work and as part of my punishment I had legal documents and law books removed from me and was told by prison management, 'If you go back to work, you can have your computer, documents and books returned'. At the time, I was due to appear in the Full Federal Court in relation to *Minogue v HREOC* (1999) 166 ALR 129. A community lawyer, Amanda George, and lawyers from the office of the Australian Government Solicitors who were acting for the Commonwealth Attorney-General intervened with prison authorities and talked them around into allowing me access to legal documents, law books and my computer equipment for use in the appeal.

9   In *Commonwealth v Human Rights and Equal Opportunity Commission and Another*, the Court relied upon the dicta in *R v Australian Broadcasting Tribunal; Ex parte Hardiman* ((1980) 144 CLR 13 at 35-36) to question the fact that HREOC appeared in that matter by its counsel and solicitor and argued the case before the Court as an adversarial party. The Court went on to say that there was doubt about whether HREOC was entitled to pursue the adversarial course it did (*Commonwealth of Australia v Human Rights and Equal Opportunity Commission* (1995) 63 FCR 74 at 84).

10   The appeal is reported at *Minogue v Human Rights and Equal Opportunity Commission* (1999) 166 ALR 129 and elsewhere.

11   See *Rich v Groningen* (1997) 95 A Crim R 272. It should be noted that Hugo Alistair Rich, my close friend, was previously know as Olaf Dietrich, the successful applicant in the seminal judgment of *Dietrich v The Queen* (1992) 177 CLR 292. When Olaf/Hugo was preparing the arguments that were ultimately used in Dietrich, I played a small role in that I wore one of Edward De Bono's hats and was the naysayer, the critic of all the arguments he advanced (De Bono 1987). Some of the sessions were quite animated and sometimes bitter as I nitpicked at him for hours on end but the sessions would always end with a reference to the important case of *Powell v Alabama* 287 US 45 (1932), a case that the High Court accepted as an authority. The allusion to Powell's Case became a ritual. Hugo would pause at the doorway of our prison yard, look back to me and say, 'All I'm asking for is the same rights that a black man had in Alabama in 1932!'. Sometimes this was said with a laugh; at others, it was said with passion, moist eyes and a crack in his voice. Having tested the ideas as much we could in our H Division prison yard, we sent it off. I held out no hope of the High Court accepting the arguments. I was happy to be wrong.

12   '… it has all the hallmarks of an afterthought …'

13   *Minogue v Williams* was a suit brought by me against the General Manager of
        Barwon Prison in the High Court (Case No M8/99) claiming human rights
        violations and personal injury, different circumstances from those which gave rise
        to *Minogue v HREOC* [1998] 54 ALD 389. The matter was remitted to the Federal
        Court (becoming Case No VG406/99) for the jurisdictional question to be
        decided. I failed to convince the Court that I had enlivened the jurisdiction of the
        High Court pursuant to s 75(i) of the Constitution. See *Minogue v Williams* [1999]
        FCA 1589 (Weinberg J).

14   The order for costs against me was later made a moot point after I appealed the
        decision. After bar table negotiations, the public prison system agreed to drop its
        claim for costs and never to ask for costs if I were litigate against them in the
        future. See *Minogue v Williams* [2000] FCA 125 (Full Court) which details the
        capitulation of prison authorities on the costs issue.

15   Section 47(1)(n) of the *Corrections Act* 1986 (Vic) gives a prisoner 'The right to send
        and receive ... letters uncensored by prison staff'. However, s 47D, inserted in
        2001, authorises the prison governor to inspect and censor a letter he or she
        reasonably believes
        (a) is a threat to prison security; or
        (b) may be of a threatening or harassing nature; or
        (c) may be being used to further unlawful activity or purpose; or
        (d) contains indecent, abusive, threatening or offensive written or pictorial
        matter, or an indecent, obscene or offensive article or substance.
        Section 21(1) of the Act provides wide powers. 'The Governor of a prison is
        responsible for the management, security and good order of the prison and the
        safe custody and welfare of the prisoners'. (This power is, as a matter of practice,
        delegated by instrument to all prison staff.) Regulation 44(1) of the *Corrections
        Regulations 1998* (Vic) states that 'A prisoner must not ... (o) commit an act or
        omission that is contrary to the good order, management or security of the prison
        or the security of the prisoners'. What constitutes 'the good order, management or
        security of the prison' is a matter wholly for the prison staff to determine, and if
        that includes not being allowed to communicate with the media about human
        rights issues, then there is the power to restrict my communication in such a way.
        At this point, the comments of Dixon J in *Flynn v The King* should be recalled.

        ... if prisoners could resort to legal remedies to enforce gaol regulations
        responsibility for the discipline and control of prisoners in gaol would be
        in some measure transferred to the courts administering justice. For if
        statutes ... were construed as intending to confer fixed legal rights upon
        prisoners it would result in applications to the courts by prisoners for
        legal remedies ... and [this] should be avoided. (*Flynn v The King* (1949)
        79 CLR 1 at 8 per Dixon J)

16   Brett LJ (later Lord Esher MR) said in *Attorney-General v Lamplough*: 'With respect
        to calling it a schedule, a schedule in an Act of Parliament is a mere question of
        drafting — a mere question of words. The schedule is as much a part of the
        statute, and is as much an enactment as any other part' (*Attorney-General v
        Lamplough* (1878) 3 Ex D 214 at 229 per Brett LJ).

17   The schedules to the *HREOC Act* are *Convention Concerning Discrimination in
        Respect of Employment and Occupation, International Covenant on Civil and Political
        Rights, Declaration of the Rights of the Child, Declaration on the Rights of Mentally
        Retarded Persons* and *Declaration on the Rights of Disabled Persons.*

18   *Ubi jus ibi remedium* can also be translated: 'there is no wrong without a remedy':
        see Broom 1939: 118-136. See also the comments of Holt CJ in *Ashby v White*: 'It is
        a vain thing to imagine a right without a remedy; for want of right and want of

remedy are reciprocal' (*Ashby v White* (1703) 2 Ld Raym 938 at 953; 92 ER 126 at 136 per Holt CJ). See also Viscount Haldane for the Privy Council in *Board v Board*: 'If the right exists, the presumption is that there is a Court which can enforce it, for if no other mode of enforcing it is prescribed, that alone is sufficient to give jurisdiction to the King's Courts of justice' (*Board v Board* [1919] AC 956 at 962 per Viscount Haldane).

19   Outline of submissions filed on behalf of the Attorney-General, para 29.

20   Letter from Nicholas Grono dated 31 October 1997 for the Attorney-General.

21   Letter to me from the Ombudsman, Dr BW Perry, dated 3 July 2000.

22   *1999-2000 Annual Report of the Ombudsman* (Part C): 34-9. Complaints from prisoners to the Ombudsman represent 20 per cent of all complaints to that office (2000: 34). Prisoners' complaints were about (in this order of frequency): visits, medical issues, employment/funds, drug testing, lost and damaged property, classification/protection, mail/phones, disciplinary charges and hearings (2000: 35).

23   It is not unusual for complaints to the Ombudsman to take many months or years to be finalised. The reality is that most prisoners are not in custody long enough to see a complaint to the Ombudsman through to completion. In 1998-99, for example, 75% of male and 88% of female inmates received a sentence of 12 months or less (Private Prisons Investigation Panel (Vic) 2000: 12).

Appendix A
Strip-Searching of Prisoners

Barwon Prison in Victoria conducts 12,000 strip-searches a year on its 240 inmates. Extrapolating this ratio to the State's 3000 prisoners, then taking into account that other prisons conduct more strip-searching, the State probably conducts over 130,000 strip-searches on its 3000 inmates per year.* As a result of these 130,000 strip-searches, fewer than 130 items of contraband will be found and 90 per cent of these will involve tobacco being taken into non-tobacco areas such as prison hospitals and transport vehicles.

Refusal is not an option, as it is clear to all prisoners that force will be used until the individual complies or is physically unable to resist. Prisoners are required to remove all clothing one article at a time, then hand it to one of the two officers doing the search. The officers, wearing rubber gloves, physically search all clothing and throw it to the floor after searching. The prisoner stands in various stages of undress holding the next item of clothing until the officer has finished with each item. The process of removing ones clothes and having them searched usually leaves a prisoner standing naked in front of staff and other prisoners for some minutes. The officer orders the prisoner to:

1. Bend your head forward and run your fingers though your hair.
2. Bend your head back and open your mouth.
3. Remove any dentures if used.
4. Pull down your bottom lip.
5. Pull up your top lip.
6. Lift and wiggle your tongue.
7. Turn your head to the right and pull back your ear.
8. Turn your head to the left and pull back your ear.
9. Turn your head to the right (to allow the officers to look in your ear canal).
10. Turn your head to the left (to allow the officers to look in your ear canal).
11. Hold both your arms out and show the officers the front and back of your hands, between your fingers and your under arms.
12. Lift your scrotum (it is also possible to be required to peel back your foreskin).

13. Turn around, bend over and pull the cheeks of your buttocks apart. (Female prisoners are required to remove any sanitary device and squat to the ground twice as well as bending over and pulling the cheeks of their buttocks apart.)
14. Lift your right foot and wiggle your toes.
15. Lift your left foot and wiggle your toes.
16. Get dressed. (It is part of the procedure that you are told to 'Get dressed!' It is the last little insult to demonstrate just how powerless you are that they even instruct you to put on clothing.)

* These figures were released to Ms Judy Cox of Essendon Community Legal Centre Inc as part of a Freedom of Information application made to the Victorian Department of Justice: letter to Ms Cox from Frances Cataldo dated 8 February 1996.

Appendix B
Corrections Act 1986 (Vic) s 47

47(1)   Every prisoner has the following rights:

(a) if not ordinarily engaged in outdoor work, the right to be in the open air for at least an hour each day, if the weather permits;

(b) the right to be provided with food that is adequate to maintain the health and well-being of the prisoner;

(c) the right to be provided with special dietary food where the Governor is satisfied that such food is necessary for medical reasons or on account of the prisoner's religious beliefs or because the prisoner is a vegetarian;

(d) the right to be provided with clothing that is suitable for the climate and for any work which the prisoner is required to do and adequate to maintain the health of the prisoner;

(e) if not serving a sentence of imprisonment, the right to wear suitable clothing owned by the prisoner;

(f) the right to have access to reasonable medical care and treatment necessary for the preservation of health including, with the approval of the principal medical officer but at the prisoner's own expense, a private registered medical practitioner, physiotherapist or chiropractor chosen by the prisoner;

(g) if intellectually disabled or mentally ill, the right to have reasonable access within the prison or, with the Governor's approval, outside a prison to such special care and treatment as the medical officer considers necessary or desirable in the circumstances;

(h) the right to have access to reasonable dental treatment necessary for the preservation of dental health;

(i) the right to practise a religion of the prisoner's choice and, if consistent with prison security and good prison management, to join with other prisoners in practising that religion and to possess such articles as are necessary for the practise of that religion;

(j) the right to make complaints concerning prison management to the Minister, the Secretary, the Commissioner, the Governor, an official visitor, the Ombudsman, the Health Services Commissioner and the Human Rights Commissioner;

(k) the right to receive at least one visit which is to last at least half an hour in each week under section 37;

(l) the right to be classified under a classification system established in accordance with the regulations as soon as possible after being sentenced and to have that classification reviewed annually;

(m) subject to sections 47A and 47B, the right to send letters to, and receive letters from, the following people without those letters being opened by prison staff –

  (i) the Minister, the Secretary, the Commissioner or an official visitor;

  (ii) a member of Parliament;

  (iii) a legal practitioner representing the prisoner, or from whom the prisoner is seeking legal advice;

  (iv) the Ombudsman;

  (v) the Health Services Commissioner;

  (vi) the Human Rights Commissioner;

  (vii) any person authorised to act on behalf of a person listed in sub-paragraph (iv), (v) or (vi);

(n) subject to section 47D, the right to send and receive other letters uncensored by prison staff;

(o) the right to take part in educational programmes in the prison.

(2) A prisoner's rights under this section are additional to, and do not affect any other rights which a prisoner has under an Act other than this Act or at common law.

(3) Sub-section (1)(m) does not prevent the opening of letters in accordance with section 28(3) of the *Ombudsman Act* 1973 or section 86L(7) of the *Police Regulation Act* 1958.

Legal Assistance

I believe the main topic is legal aid and the lack of facilities to prepare a case if legal aid is refused for an appeal. Most sentence prisons don't have legal books to prepare for a case, no computers and other equipment needed for an appeal. Therefore you go to your appeal with no idea of what points of law to argue, nor any reference material to present to the court. I believe that if you are in need of legal assistance, and it is proven that you don't have the means to pay for it yourself, then you should automatically get legal aid (be it an appeal or whatever).

Victorian male prisoner

Legal visits are not conducted in secure environments. They are regularly interrupted and aborted under the direction of prison staff. Legal Aid regularly won't provide assistance. Duty Solicitors visit irregularly and only process Legal Aid applications. Community Legal Centres won't visit prisons, citing budgetary restrictions.

Unrepresented prisoners are provided with absolutely no access to Legislation or Common Law precedents. Even though all this material is now available freely on the internet, at any public library. (And this position is sanctioned by SA's Supreme Court!).

South Australian male prisoner

Being placed in country jails while still having outstanding court cases or appeal: the problems include the cost of ringing solicitors and the lack of legal books and the lack of opportunity to work on cases because the country jails want you to work regardless. We should be left in remand jails at our request because of the disadvantages of being taken to jails that don't have the books. And phone calls are way too expensive to talk with barristers or solicitors!

Victorian male prisoner

CHAPTER 13

Segregation

David Robinson

Introduction

Segregation of prisoners for disciplinary or security reasons is among the most severe lawful measures available to a prison service. It raises important issues in relation to prisoners' rights.

This chapter considers segregation in Australian prisons. It examines relevant legislation, policy and practices in State and Territory correctional systems and evaluates them by reference to international human rights standards. Particular reference is made to the UN *Standard Minimum Rules for the Treatment of Prisoners* (Standard Minimum Rules or SMRs). The chapter considers the provisions authorising segregation, the duration and conditions of segregation and processes for accountability and review.

Definitions

The term 'segregation' is difficult to define with precision. The terminology varies considerably between jurisdictions, although 'separation' and 'separate confinement' are among the most commonly used terms in legislation and regulations. Precise definitions of these terms are not contained in relevant legislation.

All Australian correctional agencies advised the author that 'solitary confinement' is neither authorised nor practiced in their respective systems.[1] However, it would be erroneous to conclude that this in itself indicates a measured approach to segregation on the part of Australian prison systems. Rather, it is more likely that it reflects a perception that 'solitary confinement' only covers the most extreme and all-encompassing forms of segregation. While there does not appear to be a universally agreed definition of 'solitary confinement', Western Australia's (WA's) Ministry of Justice referred to a 'generally accepted' view of solitary confinement as involving 'isolation from all other people, sensory deprivation, reduction of diet and no access to entitlements such as visits, telephone calls and other privileges available to prisoners'.

For the purposes of this chapter, 'segregation' covers the following practices:

- individual confinement in cells or other designated locations within the facility for specified periods for security or disciplinary reasons,
- 'lockdowns' during which the entire inmate population or sections of it are confined to their cells or particular parts of the facility,
- separate confinement of certain classifications of prisoners for their own protection.

This chapter does not examine maximum security classification of prisoners in detail. In most Australian jurisdictions, the legal regime for maximum security classification is quite separate from that for separate confinement for disciplinary or security purposes. However, in some circumstances, maximum security arrangements may amount to segregation as described above and some examples are considered. The chapter does not address routine arrangements for separation of prisoners on the basis of age or gender.

Legal authority for prisoner segregation

International standards

International standards do not absolutely prohibit segregation of prisoners, either as a disciplinary measure or for security purposes. However, they set limits on the circumstances in which it can be applied. They indicate that measures of this type should only be applied sparingly and where it is justified in the circumstances. The Standard Minimum Rules refer to 'justifiable segregation'.

> Imprisonment and other measures which result in cutting off an offender from the outside world are afflictive by the very fact of taking from the person the right of self-determination by depriving him of his liberty. Therefore the prison system shall not, except as incidental to justifiable segregation or the maintenance of discipline, aggravate the suffering inherent in such a situation (SMR 57).

However, with regard to solitary confinement, the most severe form of segregation, international standards take a stricter approach. The

UN *Basic Principles for the Treatment of Prisoners* provide that 'efforts addressed to the abolition of solitary confinement as a punishment, or to the restriction of its use, should be undertaken and encouraged' (Principle 7).

Segregation and other disciplinary measures are subject to requirements of reasonableness and necessity. The Standard Minimum Rules provide that discipline shall be applied with firmness, but with no more restriction than is necessary for safe custody and well-ordered community life' (SMR 27). This means that there must be an element of proportionality between segregation and the prison offences that may provoke it. Segregation must not be permitted in circumstances where it is an excessive response to offending behaviour by prisoners. Disciplinary provisions should include measures that are less severe than segregation and should require the use of those measures in circumstances where they represent a more appropriate alternative to segregation.

The disciplinary procedures that may lead to segregation must meet certain requirements of transparency and natural justice as set out in SMRs 29 and 30.2 and Basic Principle 26.

- Disciplinary procedures in prisons must be set out in law or regulations covering:
  - the types of conduct that constitute disciplinary offences
  - the types and duration of punishment that may be applied
  - the authority competent to impose punishment
- No prisoner is to be punished except in accordance with the terms of such law or regulation.
- Prisoners shall be informed of the alleged offence.
- Prisoners shall have the right to be heard before disciplinary action is taken, including a proper opportunity of presenting a defence.
- The competent authority shall conduct a thorough examination of the case.

State and Territory provisions

All jurisdictions except Tasmania have legislation or regulations authorising the separate confinement of prisoners for security purposes.[2] Generally, they provide that such orders may be made for the safety of the prisoner concerned or other prisoners or for the security and good management of the prison. Tasmania is the only jurisdiction in which the legislation does not provide specifically for separate confinement of prisoners for security or management purposes. Instead, Tasmania's regime of separate confinement is based on s 6 of the *Corrections Act* 1997 (Tas), which gives the Director of Corrective Services general responsibility for the order and control of prisons.

The legal authority for prison lockdowns is less explicit. State and Territory legislation does not contain provisions dealing specifically with lockdowns. Prison authorities rely on general provisions allowing measures for the control and management of correctional facilities. Most corrective services agencies advise that lockdowns are ordered in times of inmate unrest, to facilitate searches for contraband or illegal substances or to undertake preliminary investigations following a death in custody. There are also other circumstances in which they may be ordered. According to the New South Wales (NSW) Department of Corrective Services, partial lockdowns may occur due to staff shortages in particular locations within a correctional centre. The Queensland Department of Corrective Services advised that some prisons routinely lock down for one afternoon each week for staff training. In WA, lockdowns are sometimes ordered during industrial action or urgent staff briefings. The Northern Territory (NT) Correctional Services Commissioner advised that 'lockdowns only occur for one of the following reasons, staff shortages in particular locations, scheduled staff training and in cases of extreme emergency'.

In all jurisdictions, it is a legal requirement that prisoners be entitled to attend disciplinary proceedings against them and be given an opportunity to present a defence. Some jurisdictions specifically provide in legislation for prisoners' entitlements to call witnesses and conduct cross-examination. In the NT, Tasmania, Queensland and WA, legislation stipulates that prisoners are not entitled to legal representation in disciplinary proceedings.[3] Victoria goes further than most jurisdictions in setting standards for disciplinary processes. Clause 9 of the *Victorian Correctional Policy and Management Standards* (Office of the Correctional Services Commissioner, Department of Justice, 1996) requires that prison managers ensure an 'effective, just, fair, consistent and expeditious procedure' for dealing with matters of a disciplinary nature.

Duration and conditions of segregation

International standards

Segregation must not be so severe that it amounts to 'torture' or 'cruel, inhuman or degrading treatment or punishment'. The *Convention Against Torture and Other Cruel, Inhuman or Degrading Treatment or Punishment* (UNCAT) prohibits intentional acts by public officials that fall within these categories. This prohibition also appears in art 7 of the *International Covenant on Civil and Political Rights* (ICCPR). Segregation must also be consistent with the requirement that persons deprived of their liberty be treated 'with humanity and with respect for the inherent dignity of the human person' (ICCPR art 10.1). The UN Human Rights Committee, which has responsibility for the ICCPR, has confirmed that solitary confinement can violate arts 7 and 10.1 when prolonged.[4]

The Standard Minimum Rules prohibit placement in a 'dark cell' as a form of punishment (SMR 31). They also prohibit punishment by close confinement or reduction of diet unless the medical officer has examined the prisoner and certified in writing that he or she is fit to sustain it (SMR 32.1).

Conditions of segregation must meet the minimum standards required of all prisoner accommodation (SMRs 10 and 14). Prisoners are to be allowed to communicate with family and friends through correspondence and visits (SMR 37). This requirement applies irrespective of whether the prisoner has been placed in segregation. Additionally:

> Prisoners subject to close confinement as a form of punishment must be visited daily by a medical officer, who is obliged to advise the prison director if he or she considers that this punishment should be terminated or modified in the interests of the prisoner's health (SMR 32.3).

European jurisprudence on prisoners' rights also merits consideration in the context of segregation. While it does not have the same status for Australia as that of the UN Human Rights Committee, its interpretations of analogous provisions in the European Convention on Human Rights provide valuable insights. Furthermore, the jurisprudence concerning freedom from torture and inhuman or degrading treatment is considerably more developed under the European system than the UN system.

In determining whether confinement measures amount to inhuman or degrading treatment, the European Commission of Human Rights has said that regard must be had to the surrounding circumstances, the stringency of the measure, its duration, the objective pursued, its effects on the person concerned and whether a basic minimum of possibilities for human contact has been left to the individual concerned.[5] In the case of *Krocher and Moller v Switzerland* the Commission said the essential question was 'whether the balance between the requirements of security and basic individual rights was not disrupted to the detriment of the latter'.

The European Commission has said that absolute sensory isolation coupled with absolute social isolation amounts to inhuman treatment that cannot be justified by any security considerations.[6] However, the Commission distinguished this total isolation from the situation where a prisoner is denied association with other prisoners for security, disciplinary or protective purposes but is still allowed contact with prison officers, medical personnel, lawyers and visitors, as well as contact with the outside world through television and other media. The Commission does not consider that this amounts to inhuman or degrading treatment or punishment.[7]

Some of the international standards governing conditions of segregation have been incorporated into the *Standard Guidelines for Corrections in Australia*. The Standard Guidelines do not have the status of law but are intended as guidance on the application of the Standard Minium Rules and related international standards in Australian correctional systems. The Standard Guidelines (1996 edn) provide:

5.33 Prolonged solitary confinement, corporal punishment, punishment by placement in a dark cell, reduction of diet, sensory deprivation and all cruel, inhumane or degrading punishments must not be used.

5.34 When prisoners are confined in a separate area to facilitate the withdrawal of privileges as a disciplinary measure, the Manager and a representative of the Medical Officer should visit them daily and must advise the central administration if they consider the termination or alteration of the punishment necessary on grounds of physical or mental health.

State and Territory provisions

Duration of segregation

See Table 13.1.

Table 13.1. Maximum periods of segregation for security and disciplinary purposes in Australian prison systems

Jurisdiction	Segregation for safety & security purposes	Segregation for disciplinary purposes
NSW	Max 14 days by order of prison governor; max three months by order of Commissioner subject to extension of up to three months at a time. [1]	Max three days by order of prison governor; max 28 days by order of a Visiting Justice.[2]
NT	No period specified in legislation or regulations.	Max seven days.[3]
Queensland	Max seven days for special treatment orders unless the Chief Executive approves otherwise. [4]	Max seven days.[5]
SA	No period specified in legislation or regulations.	Max 30 days during investigation into an alleged offence by the prisoner.[6]
Tasmania	No period specified in legislation or regulations.	Max 48 hours for a disciplinary offence; max 30 days if formally charged and found guilty of prison offence.[7]
Victoria	No period specified in legislation or regulations. May only be separated from other prisoners while the safety of the prisoner or other persons, or the security, good order or management of the prison is at risk. [8]	Max 14 days for each offence, not exceeding 30 days in total.[9]
WA	Max 30 days, subject to extension by the issue of a new order.[10]	Max 72 hours in normal cell for a minor offence by order of prison superintendent; max seven days in a punishment cell for each offence, not exceeding 21 days in total, by order of a Visiting Justice.[11]

1. *Crimes (Administration of Sentences) Act* 1999 (NSW) ss 13, 14.
2. *Crimes (Administration of Sentences) Act* 1999 (NSW) ss 53, 56.
3. *Prisons (Corrective Services) Act* 1980 (NT) s 33.
4. *Corrective Services Act* 2000 (Qld) s 38. Note: under s 47(1), a prisoner may be accommodated in a maximum security facility for up to six months.
5. *Corrective Services* Act 2000 (Qld) s 91.
6. *Correctional Services Act* 1982 (SA) s 36(2)(a).* The SA Department for Correctional Services confirmed that the corrective services legislation does not allow for segregation as a disciplinary penalty but only as a measure to be applied during investigation of alleged offences.
7. *Corrections Act* 1997 (Tas) ss 59, 61.
8. *Corrections Regulations* 1998 (Vic) s 22.
9. *Corrections Act* 1986 (Vic) s 53(4).
10. *Prisons Act* 1981 (WA) s 43.
11. *Prisons Act* 1981 (WA) ss 77, 78.

Conditions of segregation

In some correctional facilities segregated prisoners are accommodated in separate cells or units maintained for that purpose. In NSW, prisoners separately confined for security purposes (as distinct from disciplinary confinement) are kept in 'segregation cells'. Only when a prisoner in a segregation cell has also been found guilty of a disciplinary offence can the Governor determine that the contents of a cell (television, radio etc) should be removed. In Queensland, prisoners on separate confinement or special treatment orders are accommodated in the detention units of correctional facilities which consist of ensuite cells with attached individual exercise yards. According to the Department of Corrective Services, these prisoners 'have some capacity to verbally interact with staff and other prisoners'.

In some jurisdictions, there are specific legislative requirements for the physical conditions in which segregated prisoners are accommodated. For example, the *Prisons Act* 1981 in WA also sets out requirements for the size, ventilation and lighting of cells used for separate confinement for both security and disciplinary purposes. The Act provides that cells used for these purposes:

> shall be of such a size and so ventilated and lighted that a prisoner may be confined in that cell without injury to health and every prisoner in separate confinement shall have the means of taking air and exercise for not less than one hour each day at such times and for such other periods as the chief executive officer may direct. (*Prisons Act* 1981 (WA) s 43(3))[8]

Other State and Territory provisions generally emphasise the least restrictive approach possible in the regime for those prisoners separately confined for safety or security purposes. These prisoners are entitled to have access, as far as possible, to the range of conditions, facilities and privileges that apply to other prisoners. This includes access to food, exercise, medical care, visits and other matters. In some jurisdictions, the legislation, regulations or correctional centre policy manuals establish minimum standards relating to accommodation and access to exercise and open air.

However, prisoners who are separately confined as a penalty for having committed prison offences are generally subject to a harsher regime. For example, in NSW separate confinement for prison offences may be accompanied by loss of privileges which include participation in hobbies and leisure activities, access to radio or television, use of library facilities, ability to purchase goods, keeping of approved personal property, use of telephone, contact visits and weekend leave and day leave (*Correctional Centres (General) Regulation* 1995 (NSW) reg 170). In WA, prisoners separately confined as a punishment have access to showers only 'as the superintendent directs'. There is no access to radio or television and visits are not permitted except at the discretion of the superintendent (Director-General's Rule 3U, Western Australia Ministry of Justice, 1990). In Queensland, prisoners under separate confinement for disciplinary reasons may be subject to forfeiture of privileges.[9] However, under the *Corrective Services Act* 2000 (Qld), all prisoners are entitled to legal visits and to one personal visit each week (s 122). As these are legislative entitlements rather than privileges, they cannot be forfeited or withdrawn.

Complaint and review processes

International standards

International standards require that prisoners have access to complaint and review processes on matters concerning their treatment in prison.

The Standard Minimum Rules require that every prisoner on admission be given written information about:

- the regulations governing treatment of prisoners
- the disciplinary requirements of the institution
- the method by which prisoners may seek information and make complaints
- any other information necessary to enable the prisoner to understand his or her rights and obligations and to adapt to prison life (SMR 35.1).

It is also a requirement that prisoners be allowed to make complaints to the central prison administration, judicial authorities or other proper authorities (SMR 35.2). Prisoners' complaints must not be subject to censorship. Complaints are to be acknowledged without undue delay and dealt with promptly (SMR 35.4).

The *Body of Principles for the Protection of All Persons under Any Form of Detention or Imprisonment* require that prisoners against whom disciplinary action is taken have the right to appeal to higher authorities against such measures (Principle 26).

Independent monitoring of prison systems is also required under international standards. The Standard Minimum Rules require that penal institutions and services be subject to regular inspection by qualified and experienced inspectors appointed by a competent authority. Their role is to ensure that these institutions are administered in accordance with existing laws and regulations (SMR 55).

State and Territory provisions

State and Territory prison systems allow for prisoners to complain about segregation and other aspects of their treatment in prison. Complaints can be made through a range of avenues. Correctional authorities advise that prisoners are given full access to available complaint avenues both within the prison system itself and outside including the Ombudsman and Official Visitor schemes operating in a number of jurisdictions. For example, in Victoria the *Corrections Act 1986* provides that prisoners have the right to make complaints concerning prison management to the Minister, the Secretary of the Department of Justice, the Governor, an Official Visitor and the Ombudsman (*Corrections Act* 1986 (Vic) s 47(1)(j)). The legislation also stipulates that they have the right to send letters to and receive letters from the Ombudsman without them being opened by prison staff (*Corrections Act* 1986 (Vic) s 47(1)(m)) except as permitted by ss 47A and 47B (added in 2001).

Official Visitor schemes also play an important role in the monitoring and oversight of prison systems. According to the Victorian Ministry of Justice, Official Visitors are permitted unrestricted access to their respective prisons and are able to communicate freely with all staff and prisoners. In Queensland, orders for the 'special treatment' of prisoners through segregation in excess of one month must be reviewed by an Official Visitor at intervals not exceeding one month (*Corrective Services Act* 2000 (Qld) s 39(1)). The legislation in Queensland also provides for Official Visitors to undertake reviews of maximum security orders (*Corrective Services Act* 2000 (Qld) s 50(1)).

In most States and Territories, prisoners subject to segregation orders have certain rights of review under legislation. In NSW, a prisoner on segregation or being held in protective custody for a period exceeding 14 days may apply for a review by the Serious Offenders Review Council (*Crimes (Administration of Sentences) Act* 1999 (NSW) s 19(1)). The Council may order the suspension of the segregation or protective custody or the removal of the inmate to a different correctional centre (*Crimes (Administration of Sentences) Act*

1999 (NSW) s 20(1)). In the NT, prisoners have the right to appeal to the Director of Corrective Services against a penalty imposed at a misconduct hearing, including an order for separate confinement (*Prisons (Correctional Services) Act* 1980 (NT) s 34). In Queensland, the review is to be conducted by a corrective services officer who is of more senior status than the officer who made the original decision (*Corrective Services Act* 2000 (Qld) s 89(1)). Tasmanian prisoners may appeal to the Director of Corrections (*Corrections Act* 1997 (Tas) s 60).

In Victoria, on the other hand, there is no right of appeal against punishment by separate confinement. The Victorian *Corrections Act* 1986 states 'A decision or purported decision of a disciplinary officer under this section cannot be appealed against, reviewed, challenged or called in question in any court' (*Corrections Regulations* 1998 (Vic) s 50(9)). In WA, there is no specific right of appeal against segregation, although a prisoner may appeal to the Supreme Court via a writ claiming a denial of natural justice.[10]

An evaluation of prisoner segregation in Australia

Any evaluation of segregation practices in Australian prisons must acknowledge the complexity of the issues involved. Professor Nigel Rodley echoed the views of many commentators when he said, in relation to solitary confinement, '[t]he task of balancing humane treatment with exceptional security needs is a difficult one' (Rodley 1999: 296). Issues that need to be considered include whether the confinement is necessary to meet reasonable disciplinary require-ments or to ensure the safety of prisoners. Another important issue is whether the confinement is applied through transparent and approp-riately regulated processes that preclude arbitrary and vindictive decisions.

An evaluation must also take into account the voices of prisoners. A number of prisoners have written about their experiences of segregation, for the purposes of this chapter. While their claims (like those of the correctional authorities) have not been independently verified or investigated, they provide an important perspective in the examination of this subject. The harshness of the segregation regime, as described by some of them, does not sit well with international stan-dards, including the requirement that persons deprived of their liberty be treated 'with humanity and with respect for the inherent dignity of the human person' (ICCPR art 10.1). Two prisoners described the regime in G Division at Yatala Labour Prison in South Australia.

Prisoners in G Division spend at least twenty-one and a half hours in their cells on any given day, due to many 'staff shortages' there are days where prisoners receive no exercise in the yards, at which time prisoners remain secured in cell, this is a frequent and ongoing matter of concern to all.

The G Division complex is an oppressive, harsh and restrictive environment, prisoners ... are, at most, kept separated from other long-term prisoners ... prisoners are unable to form allegiances to save management any 'power structure' from prisoners and they can manage such prisoners ...

Long–term prisoners within G Division over a period of six months suffer from bouts of depression and have inconsistent bouts of 'highs and lows' which is not addressed by professional services which may ameliorate the individuals circumstances, which, at most, is caused, by

(i)   [being] kept apart from other prisoners
(ii)   no physical contact with anyone during separation
(iii)   restricted privileges (comparison to general prison population)
(iv)   no changes to prisoner environment
(v)   prisoner has no recourse to prisoner personnel administration
(vi)   unprofessional and abusive conduct by prison personnel
(vii)   no employment, no hobbies and restricted privileges afforded to prisoners
(viii) judicial rights limited to prisoners to have long-term separation reviewed.

South Australia male prisoner in a submission to HREOC

As I write this submission I am being held in solitary confinement for organising an unauthorised gathering with other prisoners and inciting them to have a passive sit in. This is contrary to the good order and security of the institution.

We arrived in G division, the punishment block. I was dragged out backwards and carried in. I was strip-searched again and given a canvas dress to put on. I was then placed into a cell with two canvas blankets.

While in G division I have been allowed to have regulated phone calls and visits. I have been allowed a shower and change of underwear daily. I have been out to the yard almost on a daily basis. I am always locked away alone and do not have any contact with other prisoners. I have been given clothes and bedding and am fed three times a day. I am able to turn the light in the cell on or off. Also I can ask the staff to turn on a radio which is in the wall.

If I comply with the rules and regulations of G division my privileges increase in accordance with the regime I am under.

South Australia male prisoner in a submission to HREOC

An evaluation must also acknowledge the weight of research and professional opinion concerning the serious effects of excessive use of separate confinement or isolation. In its recent report to the UN Committee Against Torture, the WA Deaths in Custody Watch Committee cited a number of research studies in this area.

Medical and psychiatric literature on the adverse effects of isolation on prisoners demonstrates that it amounts to cruel, degrading and inhuman punishment. Isolation constitutes a major source of stress for a prisoner. Isolation deprives the individual of social company and familiarity and generally leads to feelings of helplessness ... [R]esearch has consistently demonstrated that even without assaults, isolation produces anxiety, depression, aggression and other behavioural deficits, including self-mutilation and suicide ideation ... (Western Australia Deaths in Custody Watch Committee 2000: para 2.5.2, citing Saporta & Van der Kolk 1992: 151-81 and Seligman & Maeier 1967: 1-9)

It is not possible in this brief chapter to examine comprehensively all aspects of prisoner segregation in Australia in terms of compliance with international law. However, a number of important observations can be made in relation to legislative and policy regimes and the manner in which they have been applied. The above overview of State and Territory provisions indicates that they incorporate, in varying degrees, most of the requirements of international human rights instruments dealing with prisoners' rights. However, it also reveals several significant gaps.

The absence of a right of appeal against punishment by separate confinement in Victoria contravenes the Standard Minimum Rules.

In Tasmania, the absence of specific provisions governing the regime of separate confinement for security purposes is cause for concern. The reliance on general provisions relating to the maintenance of order and control in prisons confers an extremely wide discretion on the Director of Corrective Services. There are no clear limits under legislation or regulations on the duration of separate confinement orders and very little accountability.

Monitoring

The fact that segregation facilities are inherently more private and isolated than mainstream facilities can result in lower levels of scrutiny and accountability, a fact that was acknowledged by Professor Richard Harding, WA Inspector of Custodial Services, in his March 2001 report on the special handling unit at Casuarina Prison in Western Australia.

Segregation areas are, by their very nature, less visible than other parts of maximum security prisons. The frequent thoroughfare of lawyers or program staff or official visitors tends to have a beneficial impact on mainstream conditions; but these movements are attenuated in 'prisons within prisons'. Without scrutiny, conditions can deteriorate badly (para 3.1).

In a balanced report which also documented some positive aspects of segregation conditions and procedures, Professor Harding high-lighted deficiencies in various areas of prisoner treatment and service provision. They included inadequate access to exercise and recreational facilities (paras 3.11-14) and food that did not meet minimum standards of nutrition and hygiene (paras 3.6-10). Inconsistent and punitive treatment by prison officers was also a concern for prisoners.

With regard to the prisoners held under s 36, a view that was commonly expressed by the officers was that the length of their segregation was a matter for management. They did not think of themselves as case managers, professionals having input into outcomes, but rather as custodians. Indeed, the whole manner of communication with these prisoners epitomised this – dealing with them through the hatch ... (para 1.21).

Some prisoners complained of 'mind games' that officers played – meaning the withholding of privileges one day or the granting of that same privilege to another prisoner or the failure to take forward a request or to unlock the door into the outer courtyard for those in solitary confinement, and so on. Lack of consistency between officers exacerbated these things. Most prisoners said that complaints about such matters were ignored. Generally, prisoners thought that the officers were uninterested in their welfare and more concerned about their own affairs, rosters, overtime, award conditions and so on (para 2.12).

The report made a number of recommendations aimed at improving conditions and increasing accountability in the segregation facilities at Casuarina Prison. They included establishment of a Case Manage-ment Review Committee to monitor the progress of all officers held in these areas and improved record-keeping in relation to 'major events' such as the use of restraints and chemical agents and the incidence of self-harm (para 6.6).

Indefinite separation

Even where separate confinement is regulated by law, it is not always interpreted and applied in a manner consistent with international standards. An example is the imposition of indefinite confinement in violation of legislative provisions that specify maximum periods for such orders. Indefinite confinement may violate the prohibition of 'cruel, inhuman or degrading treatment or punishment' and the requirement that persons deprived of their liberty be treated 'with humanity and with respect for the inherent dignity of the human person' (ICCPR arts 7 and 10). As noted above, the UN Human Rights Committee has found violations of both requirements in cases involving prolonged confinement.

One of the most notable examples of indefinite confinement in Australia's prison system concerned the Woodford Correctional Centre in Queensland. The practice of confining prisoners indefinitely in the maximum security unit of that facility received considerable publicity when it was challenged in 1999.

> Imagine someone places a narrow bench and plastic mattress in a soundproof bathroom and locks you in there, indefinitely. Once or twice a day three big guys come in, shackle you at the wrists and order you to strip, squat and cough. They escort you down a featureless corridor and into an enclosed yard about the same size as your bathroom/cell for one hour of 'exercise'. When they take you back they watch you strip and squat again. Food is shoved through a slot. You eat it sitting on your bed. You are woken every two hours during the night when an officer shines a torch in your face for the 'head-count'. Once a month you can see immediate family in a tiny cubicle through reinforced plastic. Occasionally a prison doctor calls through the slot to ask if you are ill. A camera in the corner follows your every move. Prison guards in a computerised control room watch you while you sleep, while you use the toilet or have a shower or sit weeping on the bed. (Fletcher 1999: 274)

In 1999, seven prisoners initiated legal proceedings challenging the practice of indefinite confinement in the maximum security unit at Woodford (*Farr v Queensland Corrective Services Commission* [1999] QSC 86). The court found that indefinite confinement was not authorised by the *Corrective Services Act* provision dealing with 'special treatment orders'. Justice Moynihan said that s 39 set clear parameters on those orders. 'It does not authorise open-ended special treatment. An order for special treatment should be for a specific portion of time' (*Farr v Queensland Corrective Services Commission* [1999] QSC 86 at [12] Moynihan J).

Just prior to this decision, legislation was passed providing that Queensland prisoners may not be kept in maximum security for more than six months without a new order by the Chief Executive of the

Department of Corrective Services (*Corrective Services Act* 1998 (Qld) s 43A(3)). While this was considered an improvement, the legislation has still been the subject of criticism.

> Prisoners are now entitled to a review after six months in the unit, but that review is not independent or external. There is no obligation on the department to take account of psychiatric or other medical factors or to consider the purpose being served by placement of prisoners in the regime. (Fredericks 1999 quoting Karen Fletcher, Queensland Prisoners Legal Service)

Even where maximum periods are specified in legislation, these can be circumvented by the imposition of repeated extensions. The Queensland Prisoners Legal Service advised that, in many cases, prisoners under special treatment orders have been held in a situation of absolute isolation for many months at a time, even though the maximum period for such orders is seven days (email to author dated 19 March 2001). In recent comments on the equivalent NSW provisions, the Indigenous Social Justice Association noted '... the three month renewals have virtually no limit and as a consequence of that we have had people in segregation for years' (letter to author dated 10 May 2001).

Administrative segregation

Another area in which legal provisions governing prisoner segregation are applied inappropriately arises from the distinction between administrative and disciplinary segregation. Provisions governing separate confinement for security purposes are sometimes invoked as a form of de facto punishment, thus avoiding the procedural requirements and safeguards associated with disciplinary confinement. Judicial challenges to administrative segregation often fail because courts are reluctant to second guess the decisions of prison management on matters concerning the security and good order of the facility. In a detailed analysis of the subject, Matthew Groves (1996) considered the systematic misuse of administrative discretion to impose de facto punishment against which prisoners have little or no effective recourse. After examining the statutory powers used to place prisoners in administrative segregation and the principles by which judicial review applications are resolved, including grounds of review such as unreasonableness and failure to satisfy procedural requirements, he concluded that prisoners in these circumstances have little chance of obtaining redress in the courts.

Protection

In some correctional facilities, conditions in protection cells are of an even lower standard than in other cells. Protection prisoners do not always have the same access to programs and services available to other prisoners. During an inspection of Long Bay Prison in March 2000, the then federal Human Rights Commissioner, Chris Sidoti, expressed concern about conditions in protection cells at that facility (although it should be noted that in other aspects of its conditions and programs for prisoners Long Bay was considered a model by comparison with other facilities). The NSW Commissioner for Corrective Services acknowledged these problems and subsequently reported to the Human Rights Commissioner on some positive initiatives being piloted to address it. They include in-cell service provision by inmate development staff and specific program packages delivered through CD-Rom, distance education and other means.

In 1999, the standard of accommodation for protection prisoners was scrutinised by the Victorian Auditor-General (Audit Victoria 1999). The audit report noted that the percentage of protection prisoners in Victoria had been increasing steadily and had reached 23% of all inmates at the time of the audit (Audit Victoria 1999: para 6.37). The report found that prison facilities were having difficulty keeping pace with the increasing numbers of protection prisoners and that this was reflected in the standard of their accommodation.

> The importance of adequate planning is reinforced by the fact that the Commissioner's Office has found it necessary to resort to double bunking and the placing of mattresses on cell floors to accommodate additional prisoner numbers, especially in protection units (double bunking can be described as the accommodation of 2 prisoners in cells designed to accommodate 1 prisoner only). As pointed out by the Commissioner's consultant, there has been a steady increase in the number of protection prisoners and capacity pressures would soon be experienced. It is also highly questionable whether the accommodation of prisoners on mattresses on the floor and folding beds can be regarded as ideal practice. (Audit Victoria 1999: para 6.41)

Lockdowns

Prison lockdowns represent a significant dimension of segregation that is not adequately dealt with in current provisions. State and Territory legislation does not make specific reference to lockdowns or the circumstances in which they can be imposed. Correctional authorities do not regard lockdowns as being covered by existing provisions on separate confinement but by general provisions concerning the management and control of prisons. This means that prison lockdowns are, to a large degree, unregulated. It effectively removes lockdowns from the accountability requirements that apply to separate confinement. It makes it much more difficult to challenge the decision to order a lockdown, its duration and the conditions associated with it. The lack of clear standards in relation to lockdowns is underlined by the wide variety of circumstances in which they are applied, ranging from cases of 'extreme emergency' to staff training and briefings. The readiness of some correctional authorities to order lockdowns on a routine basis to accommodate the day-to-day administrative concerns of the facility, as distinct from a necessary response to prison security, must cause concern. It does not sit easily with the principle that these measures should be applied sparingly and that prison regimes should seek to minimise differences between prison life and life on the outside. 'The regime of the institution should seek to minimize any differences between prison life and life at liberty which tend to lessen the responsibility of the prisoners or the respect due to their dignity as human beings' (SMR 60.1).

The Indigenous Social Justice Association has described the weekly use of lockdowns in one New South Wales facility.

[W]ith respect to the Metropolitan Remand and Reception gaol, I can assure you that lockdowns have been a major problem and that lockdowns still occur on a weekly basis for custodial officer training purposes. This is part of what is termed the 'structured day' for the custodial officers. (letter dated 10 May 2001)

The inadequacy of the legal regulation of prison lockdowns was starkly illustrated by the lockdown imposed at Casuarina Prison in December 1998. The lockdown was ordered in response to a riot that occurred at the prison on Christmas Day. Prisoners suspected of involvement in the riot were confined to cells for 23 hours per day for an extended period following the incident (section 43 prisoners). Other prisoners were subject to slightly less onerous lockdown conditions but were still denied access to the main prison compound and were not able to undertake work and education. In 1999, the WA Ministry of Justice commissioned an inquiry into the incident (Smith, Indermaur & Boddis 1999). The inquiry concluded that the lockdown was punitive and an excessive response to the security issues arising from the incident. The following extracts from the report highlight the severity of the lockdown and some of the questions it raises in terms of the rights of the prisoners concerned.

> For most prisoners interviewed by the Inquiry team the focus of concern was ... the perceived unfairness of the 'lock-down' introduced immediately after the riot. In particular, the stated policy of "no tolerance" was seen by many prisoners as a form of 'pay back' ... [I]t was a concern to the Inquiry team that few efforts were made to ameliorate the effects of the restrictive regime in ways that would not have compromised security or control. (Smith, Indermaur & Boddis 1999: para 6.1.3)

> There is some concern that the 'lock-down' is excessive and there is at least the perception that it is being employed as a form of punishment. There is also a substantial concern, voiced by a number of prisoners that the more restrictive regime is creating grievances of unfair and arbitrary treatment ... The justification for the restrictive regime was for safety and security. Given this it seemed possible to implement a series of actions that would not compromise safety and security but would ease the disadvantages to prisoners. For example, allowing a slightly longer exercise period and providing televisions for those prisoners without access to them. For prisoners under section 43 confinement, access to one or two telephone calls per week to their family. In general, a greater degree of communication with prisoners, and a concern for the effect of the confinement on them, may have been helpful. (Smith, Indermaur & Boddis 1999: para 6.10.1)

The inquiry recommended that management responses to events of the type that occurred at Casuarina should not include measures severely curtailing access to services to the detriment of prisoners. It also recommended that consideration be given to trading an extra day off the sentence for every day the prisoner is subjected to a severely restricted regime such as a lockdown (Smith, Indermaur & Boddis 1999: para 9.3.4.8).

Contribution to self-harm and deaths in custody

> I recently have just been released from an isolation cell, known here as IOU or Intensive Observation Unit [at Casuarina Prison], which forms part of three 'punishment areas' ... I was placed within a cell containing nothing (literally!). Initially I was walked in, handcuffed, surrounded and escorted by 5 officers ... I was walked to the opposite end of the cell to the door and was told to 'stick ya' nose in the wall, whereupon I was uncuffed and assisted (?) in placing my palms flat against the wall, forcibly ... After being strip-searched and the subject of some jokes and humiliation for the officers' amusement ...

Being my first time in a position like this, I didn't know what to expect, how long I was going to be there ... anything.

I sat on the bed (?) that had no mattress, only cold hard steel mesh frame ... [T]his cell contained nothing, except a foam cup, a button operated sink/basin and a toilet with no seat or lid, and a quarter roll of toilet paper.

Just because a prisoner is in punishment is no reason to alter the medical schedule, whatever the medication. I wasn't even given a Ventolin pump. Good thing I didn't have an asthma attack huh?

A prisoner in a punishment cell is still a person, although not treated as one by officers ... In these times, I didn't think these things and conditions existed anymore!!!

A prisoner should still be given basics ... whilst in a punishment cell. A prisoner doesn't even get phone calls (out), visits or even contact with other prisoners, apart from the occasional knock on the wall! TV, radio, newspaper ... in fact contact to anybody other than a prison officer is not allowed. Boredom is something you get used to.

WA male prisoner in a submission to HREOC

The incidence of self-harm by segregated prisoners raises questions concerning compliance with international standards, in particular the requirement that all accommodation for prisoners be consistent with their health needs (SMR 10). For prisoners who are at risk of self-harm, the level of risk can be exacerbated by the experience of isolation. This issue was also covered by the Victorian Auditor-General's 1999 inquiry, which endorsed the findings of a taskforce on suicide and self-harm in Victorian prisons condemning the isolation of suicidal prisoners as 'an unacceptable practice' (Audit Victoria 1999: para 8.236). The Auditor-General was critical of observation cells used to accommodate at-risk prisoners in a number of facilities, noting that in many instances these cells were stripped of all amenities contrary to the recommendations of authoritative research. The report described the conditions of observation cells at the Metropolitan Women's Correctional Centre and Dhurringile and Barwon Prisons in Victoria.

These observation cells were totally bare as all objects capable of being used to inflict self-harm had been removed. In contrast, new authoritative research suggests that stripping cells of all amenities contributes to a suicidal person's thoughts of loneliness, isolation, marginalisation and hopelessness. In audit opinion, it is difficult to imagine why any prisoner would voluntarily alert staff to their intention to attempt suicide or inflict self-harm if the final outcome was for the prisoner to be placed in an observation cell. (Audit Victoria 1999: para 8.237)

The Auditor-General concluded that alternative methods of accommodating at-risk prisoners should be explored (Audit Victoria 1999: para 8.238).

Segregation practices have been acknowledged as contributing to the high rate of Indigenous deaths in custody. Recommendation 181 of the National Report of the Royal Commission into Aboriginal Deaths in Custody proposed:

> that Corrective Services should recognise that it is undesirable in the highest degree that an Aboriginal prisoner should be placed in segregation or isolated detention. In any event, Corrective Services authorities should provide minimum standards for segregation including fresh air, lighting, daily exercise, adequate clothing and heating, adequate food, water and sanitation facilities and some access to visitors. (Royal Commission into Aboriginal Deaths in Custody 1991: rec 181)

In a 1996 assessment of implementation of the Royal Commission's recommendations, the Human Rights and Equal Opportunity Commission (1996b) noted that all jurisdictions with the exception of Queensland claimed full implementation of recommendation 181. However, it also cited the WA Deaths in Custody Watch Committee's claim that in most prisons the proportion of Aboriginal inmates in segregation far exceeded their representation in the prison as a whole (Human Rights and Equal Opportunity Commission 1996b: 190-1).

The Commission documented Indigenous deaths in custody during the period under review, several of which involved segregated prisoners.

> An Aboriginal investigator in the case of the 35-year-old man who died at Townsville Prison ... described the segregation cells as filthy, dingy and without adequate sanitation facilities.
>
> In the case of the 17-year-old juvenile who died at Lotus Glen Prison ... the deceased had the AIDS virus and was consequently placed in isolation. The conditions of the isolation were adequate and complied with the above recommendation [rec 181]. However, it was questionable whether isolation was appropriate. While prison officials informed the Coroner that other prisoners would not be disposed towards sharing a cell with the deceased, a visitor to the prison reported that inmates spoke otherwise.
>
> A 17-year-old juvenile who died in Yatala Prison on 27 January 1995 ... was placed in a maximum security cell in an adult prison. For a juvenile with a short sentence (nine months) isolation of this nature cannot be justified.
>
> (Human Rights and Equal Opportunity Commission 1996b: 190-1)

In its 2000 report to the UN Committee Against Torture, the WA Deaths in Custody Watch Committee documented the continuing high rate of Indigenous deaths in WA prisons, which it described as the highest in Australia per head of population (Western Australia Deaths in Custody Watch Committee 2000: 1). The Committee claimed that legislative provisions governing isolation for disciplinary and security purposes were applied excessively, with prison officers often ignoring statutory limitations on the period of isolation and that the provisions allowing segregation for the security and good management of the prison were often used as a form of de facto punishment (Western Australia Deaths in Custody Watch Committee 2000: paras 2.5.1-8).

> Some prisoners are placed under the s 43, Rule 3U/Rule 6C regime before being charged. They were told that they were being placed on the Close Supervision regime, but it was the same as punishment regime, with no access to phones, non-contact visits and one hour of exercise a day.

> There is further provision in Rule 3N of the Director-General's Rules that if the Executive General is of the opinion that management, control or security requires it, a prisoner may be placed in isolation in Special Handling Units (SHU) … although the Rule states that prisoners are to wear restraints when on outside visits, in practice they wear restraints whenever they leave their cells. Sometimes prisoners are left in restraints while locked in their cell. (Western Australia Deaths in Custody Watch Committee 2000: para 2.5.8)

These and other abuses were cited to support the Committee's conclusion that in Western Australian prisons there are frequent violations of the UN Convention Against Torture arts 1 (torture) and 16 (cruel, inhuman or degrading punishment or treatment) (Western Australia Deaths in Custody Watch Committee 2000: 1-2).

Conclusion

As acknowledged above, a comprehensive analysis and evaluation of prisoner segregation in Australia is beyond the scope of this chapter. However, from this brief examination of the relevant legal provisions and their application, one cannot escape the conclusion that Australia's record in this area is a mixed one. There is considerable variation across Australian prison systems in the level of protection for the rights of prisoners subject to segregation. In some jurisdictions, legislators and policy-makers have made considerable efforts to encourage just and humane regimes of prisoner segregation and they are to be commended for that. However, in a number of jurisdictions, there are serious gaps in legal protection such as the absence of a right of appeal against disciplinary segregation. The lack of clear regulations governing the use of prison lockdowns is a common feature in all prison systems in Australia. However, it is at the level of the day-to-day application of both administrative and disciplinary segregation that the greatest concerns arise. Inadequate conditions in isolation cells at some facilities, excessive and arbitrary use of segregation in reported cases, the link between segregation practices and self-harm and the prima facie evidence of racial discrimination in the implementation of segregation all highlight the need for greater accountability in this area. These issues raise important questions of compliance with international human rights standards. They demand urgent and concerted action by Australian governments and prison systems.

Notes

1   The author wrote to each correctional authority late in 1999 seeking information on the use of segregation. The following responses were received and this chapter reports on the information provided. Letters dated 2001 responded to a draft of this chapter provided for comment. Western Australia Ministry of Justice 20 February 2000 & 15 February 2001; New South Wales Department of Corrective Services 18 January 2000, 26 September 2000 & 19 February 2001; South Australia Department for Correctional Services 1 February 2001; Queensland Department of Corrective Services 19 January 2000 & 8 March 2001; Northern Territory Correctional Services Commissioner 16 November 1999.

2   *Crimes (Administration of Sentences) Act* 1999 (NSW) ss 13-14; *Corrective Services Act* 2000 (Qld) s 38; *Prisons Act* 1981 (WA) s 43; *Correctional Services Act* 1982 (SA) s 36; *Corrections Regulations* 1998 (Vic) reg 22; *Correctional Services Determination No 1* (NT) s 3(21))

3   *Prisons (Correctional Services) Act* 1980 (NT) s 32(7); *Corrections Act* 1997 (Tas) s 59(12); *Corrective Services Act* 2000 (Qld) s 89(3); *Prisons Act* 1981 (WA) s 76(1).

4   HRC Communications: *Larrosa v Uruguay* Communication No 88/1981, UN Doc A/38/40 (1983); *Marais v Madagascar Marais v Madagascar*, Communication No 49/1979, UN Doc A/38/40 (1983). See also HRC General Comment No 20 (1992) para 6.

5   Appl 6038/73, *X v Federal Republic of Germany*, Coll 44 (1973), p 115 (119); Appl 6166/73, *Baader, Meins, Meinhof and Grundmann v Federal Republic of Germany*, Yearbook XVIII (1975), p 132 (144-146); Appls 7572, 7586 and 7576/76, *Ensslin, Baader and Raspe v Federal Republic of Germany*, Yearbook XXI (1978), p 418 (454-460); Report of 16 December 1982, *Krocher and Moller v Switzerland*, D & R 34 (1983), p 24 (51-55.

6   Appls 7527/76, 7586/76 and 7587/76, *Ensslin, Baader and Raspe v Federal Republic of Germany*, Yearbook XXI (1978), p 418 (456).

7   Report of 25 January 1976, *Ireland v United Kingdom*, B.23/1, p 379; Appls 7572/76, 7586/76 and 7587/76, *Ensslin, Baader and Raspe v Federal Republic of Germany*, *Yearbook* XI (1978), p 418 (456); Appl 8317/78, *McFeeley v United Kingdom*, D & R 20 (1980), p 44 (82); report of 16 December 1982, *Krocher and Moller*, D & R 34 (1983), p 24 (53), and Appl 10263/83, *R v Denmark*, D & R 41 (1985), p 49.

8   Similar wording is used in s 82, which deals with punishment by confinement.

9   The Queensland Department of Corrective Services advised that privileges would be determined in the proposed *Corrective Services Regulation* 2001 (Qld), which was due to be submitted to Cabinet for consideration 'in the near future'.

10   In relation to review processes, the WA Ministry of Justice advised '... Magistrate Paul Heaney has just completed a review of adjudicatory processes in relation to prison offences and made a number of recommendations for change, which may affect this situation. They are currently under consideration by the Offender Management Division' (15 February 2001).

Prison Discipline

I had to do four days for a breach. The breach area consisted of four cells two on each side facing each other. One cell was called the 'cage'. This was a particularly scary cell because no light came into this cell. The windows were caged so it can't be seen out of. Mostly difficult women were put into this cell. (By 'difficult' I mean women the officers could not control.)

The other cells were plain as they consisted of a bed base, shower with no shower curtain and window in which the officers would view you showering. Sometimes there would be mattresses and sometimes not. These particular cells weren't clean at the best of times. The door between the cells on the other side was always locked when women were in the breach cells, so there was no communication with other inmates.

Meals would be brought up on trays – quite often cold and mostly finger food so they didn't have to supply cutlery. Women are limited to what they could have in the cells as for the most part all privileges are relinquished whilst on breach. Books, pens, pencils and paper are not allowed. If you are lucky, there may be a bible in the cell. Toiletries are also not permitted in the cell. It is at the officers' discretion and availability as to whether you shower or not and have access to clean clothing once again at their discretion. Also at the officers' discretion is the availability of hygienic sanitary pads and meds.

Exercise is also at the discretion of the officers and is also subject to their availability. If the officers don't like you for whatever reason, usually being in the breach cells is an opportune time to square up on inmates. And there isn't a lot that can be done about it. There is very limited access to medical staff unless you are on medication which was brought around three times a day. Once again it's at the officers' discretion as the only communication available is via an intercom situated on the wall which was a direct line to the officers' station.

Usually visits with family would be suspended for the duration of your stay in the DU. I personally was not denied legal visits. I was denied medical attention on one occasion. Although it wasn't a serious medical emergency, my request to see the sister was denied.

On breach I was also denied newspapers and contact about the outside world. I was not allowed to use the telephone or write letters, or contact my family in any way.

Queensland female prisoner

Of my 25 years behind bars, I have done about three and a half years in solitary confinement and I have been confined under Administrative Regimes for nearly four years in total, so for about seven and a half years all together. I am currently under Administrative Regime for doing a tattoo. I do not know how long it will be for, but I have lost my job, have lost my wages, have no recreation and no normal privileges. I will not go into all my other lock downs, but generally they involved either fighting (with pen and paper) to help others, or breaking a minor rule.

WA male prisoner

As far as prisoners in detention units are concerned, they do not have access to TV, radio, books or any other means they can entertain themselves. The key factor here is the boredom, which is a very unhealthy condition. It also varies in different jails. Normally the older, government-run jails, for instance Goulburn in NSW, Alice Springs Prison in the Northern Territory, to name just a few, are the worst offenders for inhuman conditions.

Queensland male prisoner

The fundamental problem associated with maximum security 'management' units is not their design or structure (although they are inevitably spartan and oppressive facilities), it is the management practices of the prison officers who run them. Such repressive practices derive from a mindset whereby the purpose of the unit dictates the way the prisoners in them are treated. As time progresses the nature of these units justifies their continued operation: the prison officers torment and oppress the prisoners in the unit until they rebel, then they have to oppress them because they're rebelling, which also causes their continued separation as 'management problems'.

Victorian male prisoner

Down the back – the Special Handling Unit – it's a big fear. It's for punishment. It's the main punishment area. Fearful of the way you're treated, you're completely stripped of everything. There's a bed down there. You're strapped to it completely naked. It's only supposed to be for twelve hours but one guy was in there for three days.

WA male prisoner

CHAPTER 14

Prisoners' Right to Health and Safety

Michael Levy

Introduction

International human rights instruments related to prisoners' health and safety begin with the requirement that everyone deprived of his or her liberty is to be treated with humanity and with respect for the inherent dignity of the human person (art 10.1 of the *International Covenant on Civil and Political Rights* (ICCPR)). The UN *Standard Minimum Rules for the Treatment of Prisoners* (SMR) make the prison medical officer partly responsible for ensuring humane conditions. SMR 26(1) provides:

> The medical officer shall regularly inspect and advise the director upon:
> a) The quantity, quality, preparation and service of food;
> b) The hygiene and cleanliness of the institution and the prisoners;
> c) The sanitation, heating, lighting and ventilation of the institution;
> d) The suitability and cleanliness of the prisoners' clothing and bedding;
> e) The observance of the rules concerning physical education and sports, in cases where there is no technical personnel in charge of these activities.

The provision of health care is expected to meet four standards.

1. Access to a healthcare worker (with support of a fully equipped hospital service).
2. Equivalence of care to that available in the community.
3. Respect for the principles of confidentiality and patient's consent to treatment.
4. Adequate preventive health care.[1]

Constraints on the delivery of an appropriate health service to Australian prisoners fall into three principal categories.

5. We lack information on the health status of inmates.
6. We lack guidelines for minimum health care standards.
7. Health care providers are administratively dependent on custodial authorities.

There is a lack of reliable information about the health of Australian prison inmates. While a number of single-issue surveys have been undertaken in Australian prisons (Awofeso, Harper & Levy 2000; Butler et al 1997; Awofeso & Levy 1999; Fasher et al 1997), only one comprehensive survey of prisoners' health has been completed: the New South Wales (NSW) Inmate Health Survey of 1996 (Butler 1997).[2]

While some results may be generalised from NSW to the Australian prisoner population (eg oral health), most results will be more specific to the population under investigation (eg Hepatitis B and C prevalence). The main health issues described in the survey results were substance abuse, mental health including intellectual disability and communicable diseases. Above all, prisoners have multiple concurrent and therefore complex health problems.

Yet the health of prisoners has attracted little attention in the general community and perhaps even less in the medical community. Comparative studies of health services offered to Australian prisoners are not available. States and Territories provide a patchwork of services based more on historical idiosyncrasy than on need. Even proven needs and reasoned responses in one jurisdiction have not been successfully translated across State/Territory borders.

This chapter reviews the health and safety measures in Australian prisons by reference to the four standards, listed above, established in relevant human rights instruments. It concludes with a broader evaluation of the prospects of meeting these standards and the basic rule that every prisoner should be treated with humanity in a context of increasingly retributive sentencing practices. At the same time, we must bear in mind Tomasevski's warning.

> The existing ethical and human rights principles and standards rarely specify entitlements of prisoners in health care. Most problems related to the health care of prisoners cannot be solved by conventional human rights practice of identifying practices that constitute violations of individual rights. Prisoner health is characterised by overlapping considerations of health, security and professional safety (Tomasevski 1992: xvii).

Access to health care

Internationally agreed standards provide '[p]risoners shall have access to health services available in the country without discrimination on the grounds of their legal status' (*Basic Principles for the Treatment of Prisoners*, Principle 9).

The issue of access to health services presents a number of challenges to those responsible for inmate health care. Not only do prisoners have poorer access to health services in the community prior to incarceration (Glaser & Greifinger 1993) but also, when they return to the community, they may encounter difficulties in obtaining medical care and social services (Warren et al 1994). Given these realities, imprisonment, perversely, provides an opportunity to address the health needs of a group that is difficult to access in the community.

The custodial authority ultimately controls physical access to the clinic. Prison officers usually control locks on doors. This complex situation presents a paradox. Many prisoners are living close to a health facility for the first time in their lives and have the time to access it but access is dependent upon staff responsible primarily for security and so access can be compromised by local administrative conditions.

The research literature on the health benefits of incarceration is limited to:

- pregnancy (Martin et al 1997),
- access to HIV therapies (Inciardi 1996; Edwards et al 2001),
- tuberculosis treatment (Greifinger, Heywood & Glaser 1993), and
- diabetes care (MacFarlane 1996).

The principle of independence

The Australian Medical Association recommends that health care for prisoners should be provided independently from the custodial system (Smith 1999). Integration of health care within the corrections administration exposes the health professional to the risks of collusion, co-option and control. Custodial authorities would be expected to give health a low priority in contrast to 'control and security'. In this situation, neither the health nor the custodial systems can provide the inmate with an independent health advocate.

> The provision of health services to prisoners is necessarily modified by them being prisoners as well as patients. The attempt to dissociate these two roles, and the corresponding roles of health professionals in

providing health care to their patients while implementing prison rules, marks all efforts to reform prison health.

... international standards relating to prison health, particularly those adopted by the health profession, increasingly plead for the dissociation of the prison administration from the prisoners' health care (Tomasevski 1992: xviii).

Given that the health of prisoners impacts on that of the general community, the disposition of a health ministry should be more favourable toward the prisoner population. Also, prison health finds a place within the national health priorities; on every health indicator, inmates are sure to be more needy. In the final analysis, prisoner health is a health, not a security, issue. Therefore, it is critical that policies and practices come from, and contribute to, this health paradigm.

Under any circumstances, the health service should not report to the custodial authorities on the health status of an inmate without the informed consent of that inmate.

Australian arrangements

The NSW system is unique in that the provider of most health services is the Corrections Health Service. This Service is fully funded by the NSW Health Department and accountable solely to the Minister of Health.

Some other jurisdictions contract prisoner health care out to the health system. In South Australia (SA), the Department of Human Services contracts its prison health responsibility to the Royal Adelaide Hospital. In the Northern Territory (NT) and Tasmania, prisoners receive health services that are contracted by the custodial authorities from mainstream health services.

Western Australia (WA) and Queensland, on the other hand, provide health services from within the custodial authority, making the prison Governor the effective employer of the health service staff. In Victoria, with over 50% of prison beds privatised, health service standards and policies remain the responsibility of the Health Department but health services provision is part of the contracted services to be provided by the four different private operators.

Prison hospitals were a feature of older prisons but these facilities rarely serve the modern application of ambulatory health care. Newer prisons should contain plans for a health facility at the conception stage. Certainly, there are clinics within Australian prisons that do serve the needs of inmates, health staff and custodial officials adequately (examples in NSW are the clinic at the Metropolitan Reception and Remand Centre opened in 1997 and the refurbished clinic at the Glen Innes prison farm).

Access to community-based services

Overwhelmingly, medical attention to ill prisoners is provided by services brought into the prison. Larger prison systems are providing specialist referrals, while the smaller prisons either transfer inmates requiring specialist attention to a central (metropolitan) correctional centre or refer them to community services.

Access to health services in the community is restricted in a number of ways. The physical constraints imposed by gates, mortar and bricks can mean that emergency transport entry and egress can be adversely affected. Hospital inpatient accommodation for almost all inmates (certainly those with a higher security classification) requires a custodial guard at all times. Outside referral becomes increasingly difficult as the security classification of the particular inmate rises. This is because of the arrangements necessary to ensure the secure transfer of the inmate. A regrettable consequence of this situation is the reticence of some community health services to accept prisoners as inpatients and even as outpatients.

Referrals to private practitioners are provided subject to security and escort provisions being satisfactory. Where a private health service is provided, the inmate will be expected to pay. Some items such as spectacles and dentures may only be provided subject to a consideration of issues such as the inmate's pre-determined earliest release date; non-urgent procedures would usually be deferred to the post-release period.

Access to alternative medicines and non-conventional health care providers is dealt with on a case-by-case basis, with no consistent policy across systems in different jurisdictions. Access is not authorised in WA while elsewhere access is dependent upon the prisoner paying.

Discharge and follow-up

There are increasing efforts being devoted to discharge planning for inmates. At the simplest level, a discharge summary is prepared and provided to the ex-prisoner's health carer with the inmate's consent. A NSW proposal, yet to be trialed, will involve Community Controlled Aboriginal Health Services contacting Indigenous inmates prior to their release and, jointly with Corrections Health Service and the community-based health providers, developing a post-release health plan.

Finally, when an inmate is released, efforts to stream ongoing health issues toward the health system and away from the criminal justice system may impact on the notorious 'revolving door' whereby re-incarceration is an assumed given for all the custodial systems in Australia. One approach to be trialed in NSW will involve health staff following inmates with an ongoing mental health or drug addiction problem into the community during the immediate post-release period.

The hesitancy with which community-based health services currently engage ex-prisoner clients needs to be overcome, preferably in the pre-release period. Thus a dual directional flow of health personnel can co-ordinate their efforts through the pre- and post-release periods.

Health workers

Health workers in the custodial setting work in a unique professional environment (Wilmott 1997; Lessenger 1982:). It needs to be acknowledged that some prisoners use health-related issues to manipulate their circumstances (Doyle 1998). Professional risks are profound, as was revealed in one inquiry conducted by the NSW Independent Commission Against Corruption (1998). That inquiry reported on a specific case of professional misconduct by a nurse providing false statements to support the early parole of an inmate (her boyfriend).

Health professionals have few opportunities to acquire specialised training. Only a limited number of specialised courses in prison health care train health care professionals working, or intending to work, with prison inmates (Bertrand & Harding 1993). Prison-based nursing has experienced substantial development as a sub-specialty of nursing. The NSW College of Nursing has developed a Graduate Diploma in Correctional Nursing to commence in 2001. Medical students are being offered opportunities to test their ethical and clinical skills in the correctional environment. The Graduate Medical Program at the University of Sydney has established a formal agreement with the Corrections Health Service to this end.

Health workers employed by the custodial authority are at distinct risk of having divided loyalties – between the service that employs them (locally, the prison Governor) and the inmates, whose care is entrusted to them (Smith 1999). Under these circumstances, it is too easy to have medical decisions overruled for security reasons.

Within the custodial paradigm, experience shows that only issues of concern to the occupational health and safety of prison officers gain any prominence. There is potential conflict in the role of the health professional working in prison. Depending on the structure of the system, not only the needs of the inmate must be served but also those of the custodial system. Certification of fitness, whether it is for work or for punishment, carries the potential for conflict.

Equivalent care

Health personnel, particularly physicians, charged with the medical care of prisoners and detainees have a duty to provide them with protection of their physical and mental health and treatment of disease of the same quality and standard as is afforded to those who are not imprisoned or detained.

Principles of Medical Ethics relevant to the Role of Health Personnel, particularly Physicians, in the Protection of Prisoners and Detainees against Torture and Other Cruel, Inhuman or Degrading Treatment or Punishment, Principle 1.

A number of issues – constitutional, administrative and ultimately political – conspire against the provision of excellent health services for all Australian prisoners. The responsibilities of the different tiers of government devised at the time of Federation, and their subsequent interpretation, has left Australian prisoners poorly cared for.

While the Commonwealth Government took a major role in devising standards of access to healthcare and funding services with the Medibank and Medicare legislation since the 1970s, these developments were denied Australian prisoners. The result is a mish-mash of services which respond in a variable manner to real, perceived or historically determined needs, and always subservient to the security and good order imperatives of the custodial authority.

In the absence of national leadership, each jurisdiction has a health service that has evolved to meet local imperatives. Section 120 of the Australian Constitution allowed the States and Territories to retain full responsibility for all prisoners. Offenders convicted under federal law serve their sentences within the jurisdiction of sentence. As at March 2000, there were 676 federal sentenced prisoners in Australia. Yet the Commonwealth makes no demands of State and Territory prison systems as to the minimum standards of treatment of federal prisoners. Medicare disentitlement of prisoners further distances the Commonwealth from the interests of prisoners.

Mental health

The treatment of mental illness among prisoners illustrates the distance between the care expected in the community and that provided in prison. The prevalence of mental illness among prisoners is higher than in the general community. In a submission to the recent NSW Parliamentary Select Committee Inquiry on the Increase in Prisoner Population, the Department of Corrective Services stated that 13% of female inmates in NSW have an intellectual disability, 21% had attempted suicide and 40% have a diagnosis of personality disorder (Department of Corrective Services NSW 2000: 22).

Along with pre-existing morbidity, the stress associated with incarceration may contribute to the initial presentation of mental illness among prison inmates. Moreover, a factor contributing to the increase in the number of inmates in Australian prisons has been the de-institutionalisation of mental patients (Doyle 1998), with inadequate funding of community mental health services and without commensurate controls on the intake of persons into custody.

Sexual abuse is a common antecedent to inmate ill health: 48% of female prisoners and 16% of male prisoners reported that an adult had involved them in sexual activity before the age of 16 years (Butler 1997: 86).

SMR 82 provides:

1. Persons who are found to be insane shall not be detained in prisons and arrangements shall be made to remove them to mental institutions as soon as possible.
2. Prisoners who suffer from other mental diseases or abnormalities shall be observed and treated in specialized institutions under medical management.

In all States and Territories, inpatient care of persons scheduled under mental health legislation is the responsibility of the Departments of Health. Only Tasmania and NSW still have forensic units within correctional centres. The other jurisdictions maintain secure facilities external to prisons. Both Tasmania and NSW are planning to alter the arrangements for forensic psychiatric management in the near future.

Confidentiality and consent

Clinics in older prisons are often located in areas that were not originally designed for health care provision. Not surprisingly, they are inadequate and often inappropriate areas for health workers and clients alike. Confidentiality cannot be guaranteed in these surroundings, especially when the custodial authorities insist on observing all clinical interactions. Local operating orders will dictate whether a prison officer has to be physically present in the clinic or even in the examination room. In NSW, there is a rule that inmates can only be examined in the presence of a custodial officer. This has been guided as much by security concerns for health care staff as for prevention of corruption (Independent Commission Against Corruption 1998: 58).

Medical records are maintained for all inmates. Custodial authorities can access these records with the informed consent of the inmate. Similarly, transfer of health information between jurisdictions requires the authority of the inmate. In contrast, mental health records may be released to health authorities without the inmate's consent.

The formal consent of the inmate is required for health service provision, as in the community. Health care providers may enforce medications under conditions that are stringently monitored by bodies such as the Mental Health Review Tribunal. However, it must be questioned whether, in his or her disempowered position, the inmate can exercise truly informed and free consent.

Prevention

It is in the context of preventive health care and, more broadly, provision of a safe environment that Australian prisons most profoundly fail prisoners, their families and the community as a whole. The failure to respond appropriately to substance abuse, communicable diseases and risks of self-harm and death in custody puts the entire community at risk.

Substance abuse

The entire area of substance abuse is fraught with the inherent contra-diction between health and law enforcement: while it is recognised in theory that drug-dependent persons need medical assistance, by the very consumption, possession and purchase of drugs they pertain to criminal law enforcement rather than health. (Tomasevski 1992: 67)

The 1996 Inmate Health Survey in NSW reported that 90% of male inmates and 66% of female inmates had a past history of injecting, 40% were injectors at the time of incarceration and 24% of females and 20% of male inmates reported heroin use while in prison.[3] Of those who did inject in prison, just under 10% were initiated into injecting during a period of incarceration. A total of 69% of users shared injecting equipment while in prison. A total of 70% of inmates were tobacco smokers (Butler 1997: 79).

A SA study reported that 36% of inmates injected while in prison (Gaughwin et al 1991). A Victorian study reported that six out of a group of 36 (17%) recently released inmates shared injecting equipment for the first time in their drug-using careers while they were in prison (Crofts et al 1995).

Correctional systems focus almost entirely on the supply side of illicit substance use in prisons. Interception of injecting equipment and contraband substances is a daily event. Drug testing of inmates (Wartofsky 1981) usually through urinalysis, is carried out as:

- random checks,
- targeted tests (where a suspicious event has been identified), and
- 'program' tests (eg where an inmate is 'earning' a community visit or seeking reclassification 'downward' (ie from a maximum security prison to a medium security prison)).

SA is the only Australian jurisdiction to apply differential sanctions for cannabis and opiates. The imposition of uniform sanctions for any illicit substance that is detected is thought to encourage the use of opiate narcotics over cannabis because metabolites of the latter are detectable for longer periods (four to six weeks for cannabis compared with two to three days for heroin) (Gore, Bird & Ross 1996; Gore, Bird & Strang 1999).

Methadone has been provided to some prison inmates in NSW since 1986 (Byrne & Dolan 1998: 1744). In 2000, the number of inmates enrolled on the prison methadone program was between 900 and 1200.

Adoption of methadone maintenance by other jurisdictions has been slow. SA introduced a methadone maintenance program in 1999, Tasmania has recently introduced methadone maintenance and it has been piloted in Queensland. While Victoria is expected to adopt methadone maintenance therapy in the near future, recent practice has been to deny long-term inmates this therapeutic option. WA offers methadone maintenance to HIV+ inmates and to pregnant inmates. There is no proposal to offer methadone to inmates in the Northern Territory (however, it should be noted that methadone is not a community option in the NT at present either).

Additional therapeutic options such as l-alpha-acetylmethadol (LAAM), Naltrexone and Buprenorphine are currently only available to a small number of inmates in NSW.

Liquid bleach in the form of domestic cleaning material has been available to inmates in NSW since 1993 (Dolan, Wodak & Hall 1998). The understanding is that the bleach is provided to clean injecting equipment, although its efficacy, particularly for Hepatitis C disinfection, is questionable. All other States and Territories, except SA, have a policy of making bleach available to inmates, although the application of this policy is variable.

No Australian jurisdiction currently supports the provision of clean injecting equipment to prisoners, despite needle-syringe exchange achieving high levels of community acceptance since 1988. There is support for similar initiatives in the prison environment from Swiss, German and Spanish programs (Nelles et al 1998). However, political and industrial objections have been overwhelming to date. The death of a NSW prison officer in 1994 after he was injected with HIV-infected blood by a prisoner in 1991 (Jones 1991: 884) is cited by the Prison Officers Vocational Branch (NSW) as an argument against the introduction of safe injecting equipment into Australian prisons.[4] This is despite the large number of injecting implements and amounts of illicit drugs confiscated as well as the yield of 'dirty urines', all indicating a high level of ongoing use of illicit drugs in prison. A recent investigation in a NSW prison into possible exposure of inmates to blood-borne viruses through shared injecting equipment had over 150 inmates seek assistance over a three-day period.

The danger of the current policy to control the supply side of illicit drug use is the number of fatal and near-fatal overdoses in prisons. In NSW in the 12 months from July 1999, health staff responded to 52 narcotic overdoses. In the six-year period July 1994 to June 2000, of 143 deaths in custody in NSW, 25 (17%) were from drug overdoses. While deaths from other causes (suicide, murder) are decreasing, overdose deaths are increasing. Overdose deaths are becoming the commonest cause of deaths in custody – but whether these are accidental or intentional (self-inflicted or murder) is often impossible to discern.

Delays in summoning assistance in the face of an overdose could lead to unnecessary deaths. Police in the community have been given discretionary powers not to take evidence at the scene of non-fatal overdoses so as to encourage early notification and minimise the risk of overdose deaths. Custodial officers in NSW have been given a similar policy directive. Whether this encourages earlier notification in the prison environment is yet to be assessed.

Release of former narcotic-users into the community, unable to assess their level of physiological tolerance to narcotics, is one of the greatest tests of incarceration as a social policy. The reasons for this are complex but the lack of preparedness of former inmates to face the dangers of resuming previous habits following a period of sporadic use or abstinence, would be a major contributor. A recent UK study reported death rates of up to 80 times community levels for former inmates in the fortnight following release (Harding-Pink 1990; see also Seaman, Brettle & Gore 1998; R Robertson 1998). Similar results are reported from Victoria among women released from prison (Davies & Cook 1998).

Communicable diseases

Prisoner populations have a higher prevalence of Hepatitis B and C and HIV, with little opportunity for protecting themselves or others should they wish to use the harm minimisation practices available in the community. Blood-borne viruses (Butler et al 1997; Butler et al 1999) and tuberculosis (Butler & Levy 1999) pose particular risks to inmates and the general community. Voluntary HIV and Hepatitis screening is offered to inmates in all jurisdictions except the NT, where screening is compulsory.

Data on HIV prevalence among Australian prisoners reflects the success of HIV control programs in the general community. The prevalence of HIV among persons entering Australian prisons between 1991 and 1998 was consistently under 0.5% (McDonald et al 1999). However, there is strong epidemiological evidence of both HIV (Dolan & Wodak 1999) and Hepatitis C (Haber et al 1999: 31-3; Post et al 2001) transmission within Australian prisons.

Safer sex practices, promoted widely in the community, are denied inmates in all jurisdictions bar NSW. Condoms have been freely available in NSW prisons since 1995. WA, SA and Victoria have adopted this strategy in principle but are yet to allow inmates to actually access them because of concerns on the part of custodial staff that condoms could be used as weapons. While such a denial would be strongly challenged in the community, no such demands have yet been voiced on behalf of inmates.

The level of homosexual sex among Australian prisoners is poorly reported and the distinctions between consensual and non-consensual sex, while difficult to define in the community, are even more blurred in prison. Regrettably, sex is a tradeable commodity in prison, one used to acquit debts or to secure protection. As a measure of the poor state of information in this matter, incidences of sexual activity as low as 1% and as high as 25% have been reported (Heilpern 1998: 7).

A recent development, the compilation of genetic data banks for forensic purposes, is creating a situation where inmates are now reluctant to submit a sample for pathology testing for fear of forensic evidence being taken. Even routine examinations such as the collection of stool samples and throat swabs during a food-borne outbreak have been refused by inmates for this very reason. All this makes the practice of public health and health protection in the prison environment extremely difficult.

It is perhaps in this area of disease control that the current management of Australian prisons poses the greatest direct threat to the general community. The lack of effective transfer of evaluated programs across jurisdictions means that inmates continue to be unnecessarily exposed to life-threatening conditions. These threats are readily transferred into the general community. This has been described as 'cruel and unusual punishment' (Crofts 1997: 116).

Deaths in custody

The issue of deaths in custody has a special relevance to Australian prison systems. Rates are consistently higher than those reported for any other system in the world. The Australian Institute of Criminology reports annually on prison mortality. In fact, this is the only 'health' issue that has warranted a national data collection!

Inmate deaths from all causes are twice that of a comparable population in the community. For specific causes, the disparity is greater: 19 times higher for drug-related deaths and murder is six times more prevalent (Essential Equity 1999). Regrettably, as stated earlier, the rate of death from drug overdoses in prison is now surpassing other causes.

Clearly, Australian prisons do not provide adequately for the safety of inmates. With the building of newer custodial facilities and the decommissioning of older prisons, the 'engineering approach' to deaths in custody (reducing the number of hanging points) may have some effect. Prediction of, and response to, at-risk individuals is improving as the clinical skills of health practitioners and case management by custodial staff develop.

The Royal Commission into Aboriginal Deaths in Custody was one response to the high number of deaths in Australian police lock-ups and prisons. While the focus was on Aboriginal and Torres Strait Islander inmates, the major finding that the rate of deaths related directly to the rate of incarceration provided a system-wide focus for penal reform in Australia.

The Royal Commission made many recommendations of relevance to prisoners' health including:

- the need for health services to be available for Aborigines in police custody (rec 127)
- the need for improved and systematic communication of information between mainstream and Aboriginal health services (rec 250)
- quality of health services available to Aborigines to be community standard (rec 251)
- evaluation of Aboriginal health services to be based on effectiveness and efficiency (rec 260)
- the need for Aboriginal involvement in health promotion campaigns targeting Aborigines (rec 282).

(Royal Commission into Aboriginal Deaths in Custody 1991)

In the years since the Royal Commission's Report, the proportion of Aboriginal inmates has continued to climb. The response to this insidious process must be a planned reduction in prisoner numbers with an emphasis on the differential incarceration of Aboriginal and Torres Strait Islander citizens.

Conclusions

The issue of health care provision for prison inmates cannot be separated from basic philosophical considerations of the role of mass incarceration and deprivation of liberty. A society that applies a punitive (retributive) model of justice can easily justify that the ill health of the inmate is merely an extension of that punishment; 'serves him right', 'they do not deserve to be treated' are refrains of the ill-informed proponents of this system of justice (Wolfgang 1998). 'Prisoners either get better than they deserve or deserve as bad as they get' (Berkman 1995: 1617).

Most criminal justice systems in Australia subscribe to a rehabilitative model of justice, even if political expediency promotes the retributive model through the mass media to the general public. While the rehabilitative model starts to offer some direction to health care providers, there is a tendency to adopt enforced treatments as an option (Burt 1993). Thus therapeutic options available to the psychiatrist, physiotherapist or general practitioner will still embrace the options of enforced drug treatment for schizophrenia and enforced abstinence for substance abuse and tuberculosis. These options are considered disreputable in the general community but are still seen as credible options to be used on prison inmates. The rehabilitative model of justice proposes that there are limits to its capacity to reform 'hardened criminals'. It is, therefore, not unreasonable to argue that there are limits to the health services to be provided to inmates, the range of services to be provided to which 'class' of inmates and even the quality of services to be provided (Schneiderman & Jecker 1996; Cameron-Perry 2000; Finlay 1998).

The restorative model of justice offers health care providers the greatest opportunity to apply their professional skills to a population at risk. By accepting a position that crimes are a violation of person and relationships, it is possible to accept that the prisoner has had to bear a share of the burden. The patterns of disease manifest among Australian prisons attest to this. The restorative approach to repair, reconciliation and reassurance offers much to the health care provider.

Notes

1   See generally SMRs 22-26; *Basic Principles for the Treatment of Prisoners*, Principle 9; *Body of Principles for the Protection of All Persons under Any Form of Detention or Imprisonment*, Principles 24, 26; *Principles of Medical Ethics relevant to the Role of Health Personnel, particularly Physicians, in the Protection of Prisoners and Detainees against Torture and Other Cruel, Inhuman or Degrading Treatment or Punishment*.

     There is a lack of data to support meaningful comparisons of prison health services within Australia and with overseas prison systems. The Helsinki Institute of Crime Prevention (HEUNI) has published the primary source of information on prison health services in western Europe and Canada (Tomasevski 1992). Internationally, only four countries have been independently assessed as having prison health services that are superior to community standards: Hungary, the Netherlands, Scotland and Spain. Norway is noted for having the best integration of prison health services with those in the community; the local health authority provides all services to prisoners. There are also concerns regarding the organisation of health services in the United Kingdom (Smith 1999) and France (Dorozynski 2000).

2   The Inmate Health Survey was repeated in NSW in 2001. Victoria, South Australia (SA) and the ACT may use similar instruments for data collection in the near future.

3   Almost all prison use of heroin is injected, even among inmates who previously smoked heroin.

4   Submission to the NSW Drug Summit, NSW Government, 1999.

Health Care

It's my personal opinion that jail medical treatment is very poor and that the longer you are in the system, the harder it is to obtain medical attention. A popular treatment for anything ranging from a headache to a heart attack is Panadol. I know of many horror stories from various women in the system who have been given wrong diagnosis from both doctors and medical staff (ie sisters). Unfortunately, we are not open to getting a second opinion, because there is no one else. In the 3 yrs and 9 months that I have been in the system, I would rate the current medical system as 4 out of 10.

Many health issues and concerns have been raised at this centre as the services are non-existent. There is no medical services on the weekend — this includes the sister. The women have fought long and hard to have the sister come over to the women's division on a regular basis. The centre would not entertain the idea of having a female doctor come in. The reason given was that they couldn't afford it and that we should be grateful that the doctor gives time from his private practice to attend the centre.

Queensland female prisoner

I am on methadone and an asthmatic, which are both very easy to get treatment for. Asthma via Ventolin which is provided after asking the medics, who visit the units three times daily, breakfast, noon, early evening, providing also prescribed medication which is actually quite hard to get. Initially you fill in a form (as with everything!) and can wait between 2 days to 2½ weeks is the longest I've personally had to wait to see a doctor, and that was regarding chronic stomach pains. So waiting to see the doctor on duty can depend on a few things: workload, staff-levels and if the doctors feel it is urgent ... I generally have excellent health, so I have very little to do with the jail infirmary. The dispensing of methadone is most times good, with very few problems, although you will always come across something sometime, but that's to be expected.

WA male prisoner

The medical conditions are satisfactory in most of the places that I have seen. The field of improvement could be in the early detection of depression in prisoners, which would greatly reduce suicide rates in prisons. Two other fields which have room for definite improvement are dental service (where there are long waiting lists even in emergency or painful cases) and the time required to see a specialist.

Queensland male prisoner

One other thing is our access to a dentist. We had one come to the jail every 2 weeks but this stopped and we now have to go to Wolston Prison to get dental care. Where we have a problem is that we have had to wait 4 weeks and longer to see him and some guys have toothache. Sometimes guys, myself included, have had to wait 6 weeks or more before we see him.

Queensland male prisoner

The one problem that is universal is that we can only see a dentist if we have something wrong. Generally there isn't enough time for the dentist to do checks or cleaning.

Tasmanian male prisoner

The current waiting time to see a doctor is over 14 days. All other illnesses are treated by nurses. Serious illness ie falling over and not moving type illnesses result in an ambulance trip to hospital. The only way to get urgent medical treatment is to have a life-threatening disease.

NSW male prisoner

When I was seen by the doctor soon after my transfer from Risdon, I asked for an appointment to be made for a colonoscopy. I had been advised in Hobart to undergo this procedure, but postponed it because of the approaching transfer. I assume my medical records were sent from Risdon.

Some four weeks later I was informed at the morning count that I was to go to St Vincent's Hospital immediately for a colonoscopy. I queried this, because the procedure requires preparation: some hours' fast and a substance to drink to empty the bowel. Medical staff indicated that I should attend the appointment anyway.

At the hospital I was told the procedure could not be done, as my bowel was not empty. I was returned to the prison, where the director of medical services apologised and said another appointment would be made.
Six weeks later I raised the subject with the doctor. He made inquiries and ascertained that the appointment had not been rebooked.

It is perhaps worth noting that, while I feel certain that my fundamental good health means a serious condition is unlikely, two doctors have told me that the symptoms are consistent with those of bowel cancer. A more prompt action would therefore seem appropriate.

Victorian female prisoner

CHAPTER 15

Crime Victims and Prisoners' Rights

Sam Garkawe

Introduction

Since the 1970s, there has been much support on behalf of crime victims[1] for better treatment and greater consideration of their views at all stages of criminal justice processing.[2] In the last two decades in particular, this advocacy has also been concerned with the final stages of the criminal justice system where decisions regarding prisoners are made. This has resulted in many governments introducing a number of initiatives to provide crime victims with certain 'rights'[3] in relation to decisions about the prisoners responsible for their victimisation. For example, initiatives in New South Wales (NSW) since 1996, examined in detail in the next section, provide crime victims with rights in relation to various criminal justice decision-making stages and processes that affect prisoners. These include bail hearings, sentencing decisions, the classification of prisoners within the prison system and various restorative justice programs that involve incarcerated prisoners. However, probably the most contentious aspect of this trend, and the one which will be the main focus of this chapter, is that in many jurisdictions certain crime victims have been provided with the opportunity to make submissions during the parole hearing of 'their' prisoner.[4] This might allow the views of victims to influence the Parole Board's decision whether or not to release a prisoner or to impose conditions on release.

These developments may cause concern among civil libertarians and prisoners' advocates, as it would appear at first glance that allowing crime victims to have rights in relation to prisoners is likely to have a detrimental effect on prisoners' rights. This chapter aims to assess the validity of these reactions and to evaluate the policy options available to ensure that there is a reasonable and fair balance between the rights of victims and the rights of prisoners. One section of this chapter describes the main general arguments for and against providing crime victims with greater rights in the criminal justice system. The following section then critically examines in detail these arguments in relation to parole proceedings. As part of this analysis, the policy options pertaining to the issue of victims' submissions during parole proceedings are assessed. The chapter concludes by examining some possible benefits from the perspective of prisoners of allowing for victims' rights. It is suggested that, provided care is taken in introducing victims' rights, the potential benefits outweigh any dangers for prisoners.

Many, if not all, of the victims' initiatives in Australia referred to above and throughout this chapter have been strongly influenced by the 1985 UN *Declaration of Basic Principles of Justice for Victims of Crime and Abuse of Power* (the UN Declaration). The first two paragraphs of art 6 of the UN Declaration have been particularly significant and are thus worth stating in full.

> The responsiveness of judicial and administrative processes to the needs of victims should be facilitated by:
>
> (a) Informing victims of their role and the scope, timing and progress of the proceedings and of the disposition of their cases, especially where serious crimes are involved and where they have requested such information;
>
> (b) Allowing the views and concerns of victims to be presented and considered at appropriate stages of the proceedings where their personal interests are affected, without prejudice to the accused and consistent with the relevant national criminal justice system;

Two important points concerning the above provisions need to be noted at the outset, as they are relevant to a number of significant recurring themes throughout this chapter. First, a clear distinction needs to be made between the rights of victims to certain information regarding the criminal justice system, as set out in paragraph (a) above, and their right to have their 'views and concerns ... presented and considered at appropriate stages of the proceedings', as set out in paragraph (b). The latter category of rights is often referred to as victims' 'input' or 'participation' rights. The most important difference between these two types of rights is that different qualifications apply to each right. In particular, the UN Declaration suggests that the right of victims to certain criminal justice information should only apply in cases of 'serious' offences and where the victim actually requests the information. These limitations are more to do with ensuring that the State is not placed under too onerous an obligation in order to satisfy such rights, rather than any civil liberties concerns.

On the other hand, victims' 'input' or 'participation' rights are to be 'without prejudice to the accused'; in other words, they are subject to the civil liberties of accused (and convicted) persons. Note that paragraph (b) also specifies that such rights have to be consistent with the 'national criminal justice system'. In countries such as the United States, the United Kingdom and Australia, this means the adversarial system of criminal justice which has been structured on the basis of a contest between the State and the offender. Introducing the possibility for crime victims to have rights in such systems not only carries with it potential civil liberties issues but also impacts upon State resources. Allowing for victims' input or participation is likely to add to the burden on the State due to the direct costs of these additional procedures as well as the extra training required for the criminal justice officials who must implement them.

The second major issue emerging from paragraphs (a) and (b) of art 6 of the UN Declaration is that victims' rights will often affect, and thus must frequently be balanced against, the other key stakeholders in the criminal justice system – namely the offender[5] and the State (which represents the interests of the public and taxpayers).[6]

Andrew Karmen provides a useful framework by categorising victims' rights by reference to whose expense is potentially at stake. He discusses in detail three categories of victims' rights:

1. those gained only at the expense of offenders
2. those gained only at the expense of what Karmen refers to as the 'system' (ie the State)[7]
3. and finally those gained at the expense of both the 'system' and offenders (Karmen 1996: 339-48).

It is possible to match up this classification with the type of victims' rights envisaged by the UN Declaration. The right to certain information contemplated by art 6(a) falls into Karmen's second category of victims' rights, as they are gained at the expense of the system/State and do not raise civil liberties concerns.

However, the input or participation rights contemplated by art 6(b) generally fall into his third category, as they are gained at the expense of both the system or State and the offender. This analysis reinforces the difference between victims' information rights and their input or participation rights.

Case study: NSW initiatives which provide crime victims with rights in relation to prisoners

Since 1996, NSW has probably been the most active Australian jurisdiction in developing the rights of crime victims during criminal justice processing.[8] This is particularly the case in relation to victims' rights with respect to decisions regarding prisoners, stemming from three major initiatives in the latter half of the 1990s.

The first was the enactment of the *Victims Rights Act* 1996 which included a 'Charter of Victims Rights' (Pt II of the Act) providing crime victims with certain rights.[9] The second was the enactment of the *Sentencing Amendment (Parole) Act* 1996 that, together with the *Victims Rights Act* 1996, formed part of a package of victim-related legislation.[10] The third initiative is the several non-legislative based restorative justice programs introduced in recent years by the NSW Department of Corrective Services (the Department) that, as will be shown, may impact on the rights of prisoners.

How have these developments provided rights for victims and how may these rights impact on the rights of prisoners?

Bail proceedings

Section 6 of the *Victims Rights Act* 1996 provides victims with the right to information about special bail conditions and the outcome of bail applications (s 6.12 and s 6.13 respectively). These rights to information fall into the category of rights gained at the expense of the State as found in art 6(a) of the UN Declaration. The rights do not present any problems in terms of prisoners' rights because they do not affect prisoners' entitlements to apply for and be granted bail. However, s 6.11 is more controversial as it provides for the right of victims to 'put their need *or perceived need* [emphasis added] for protection from the accused before a bail authority' (*Victims Rights Act* 1996 (NSW) s 6.11). This 'input' or 'participation' right falls into the category of rights gained at the expense of the State and the offender (art 6(b) of the UN Declaration). It clearly can affect the rights of prisoners, as victims' own subjective views of the alleged threat against them may persuade bail authorities not to grant bail. This also seems to militate against the presumption of innocence that should apply to unconvicted persons.

Sentencing hearings

The NSW Charter of Victims Rights provides that victims are, upon request, entitled to be informed of the outcome of criminal proceedings and any sentence imposed on an offender (*Victims Rights Act* 1996 (NSW) s 6.5(d)). This right to information, categorised as a right gained at the expense of the State, again does not present any difficulties from a prisoners' rights perspective. However, the right of victims to have a victim impact statement presented to sentencing authorities 'to ensure that the full effect of the crime on the victim is placed before the court' (*Victims Rights Act* 1996 (NSW) s 6.14),[11] being an input or participation right, is more controversial. Despite laws allowing victims to present victim impact statements during sentencing existing in practically all Australian jurisdictions (O'Connell 1999: 88-92), they clearly remain a controversial issue within victimology[12] and in terms of the civil liberties of offenders.[13]

The classification of prisoners within the prison system

Certain changes to the classification of prisoners within the prison system are another area where the views of victims may impact on prisoners' rights. 'A victim should, on request, be kept informed of the offender's impending release or escape from custody, or of any change in security classification that results in the offender being eligible for unescorted absence from custody' (*Victims Rights Act* 1996 (NSW) s 6.15).

Again, as this is a right of victims to information which is classified as a right gained at the expense of the State, it does not present any civil liberties concerns. However, the *Crimes (Administration of Sentences) Act* 1999 (NSW) establishes a system which entitles victims to make submissions with respect to decisions on whether 'serious offenders' (as defined in s 3(1)) are eligible for unescorted leave of absence.[14] These provisions which provide for input or participation rights of victims again have implications for prisoners' rights. This is because such victim submissions may influence the relevant authority either to disallow, defer or place more stringent conditions on any external leave granted to a prisoner.

Parole decisions

Section 6.16 of the *Victims Rights Act* 1996 (NSW) states:

> A victim should, on request, be provided with the opportunity to make submissions concerning the granting of parole to a serious offender or any change in security classification that would result in a serious offender being eligible for unescorted absence from custody.

Two important restrictions on the above right should be noted. The first is that it only applies to victims of 'serious offenders' and not to victims of all offenders who might be eligible for parole. However, the Department has taken the view that other victims should also have the opportunity to make a submission.[15] The second is that it applies only when victims of 'serious offenders' request the opportunity to make a submission with respect to a parole hearing. There is thus no requirement for the Department to inform such victims of a forthcoming parole hearing in the absence of a specific request.

The *Sentencing Amendment (Parole) Act* 1996 (NSW), the second important enactment referred to above, implemented a system that enabled the Department to comply with both this right and with s 6.15 of the *Victims Rights Act* 1996 (NSW).[16] Under s 256 of the *Crimes (Administration of Sentences) Act* 1999 (NSW), a 'Victims Register' has been established, enabling victims[17] to register their interest in receiving notice that the offender may be paroled.[18] The *Crimes (Administration of Sentences) Act* 1999 (NSW) also establishes 'an elaborate and comprehensive procedural scheme'[19] allowing victims of serious offenders[20] registered with the Victims Register to make submissions to the Parole Board concerning the possible parole of the prisoner.

Restorative justice initiatives in relation to incarcerated prisoners

Restorative justice, a growing trend in Australia,[21] can be thought of as either an alternative or a supplement to the formal criminal justice system. One of the main arguments in favour of restorative justice is that the rights of victims are enhanced through their greater opportunity to participate directly in decision-making.[22] Recent restorative justice programs established by the Department constitute the final area where rights accorded to victims may impact upon prisoners' rights (Booby nd).[23] The development of a restorative justice philosophy is reflected by the dramatic change in the mission statement of the Department which, until 1997-98, was:

> To protect the community and reduce offending behaviour by providing a safe, secure, fair and humane correctional system which encourages personal development (New South Wales Department of Corrective Services, *Annual Report 1997-98*).

This mission statement was amended in 1998-99 to read:

> To provide a safe, secure, fair and humane correctional system which reduces offending behaviour, *promotes restitution by offenders to victims*

of crime and reparation to the community [emphasis added] (New South Wales Department of Corrective Services, *Annual Report 1998-99*).

Examples of restorative justice programs established by the Department include conferencing between victims and incarcerated prisoners and their respective families and other support persons, 'protective mediation'[24] programs between victims and incarcerated prisoners and 'victim awareness' modules or courses for incarcerated prisoners.[25]

The fact that an incarcerated prisoner has successfully participated in such a program may assist his or her parole application (*Crimes (Administration of Sentences) Act* 1999 (NSW), s 135(2)(f)).[26] The problem with this from a prisoners' rights perspective is that the opposite may well be the case. Failure to participate or complete a program may reflect negatively on a prisoner's record and diminish the chances of an early release. Where a program relies in whole or in part on the consent and/or willingness of the victim to participate, then it is clear that the victim's views and approach may well affect the rights of prisoners.

Given that restorative justice provides victims with a more direct voice in criminal justice decision-making, it can be seen as most analogous to providing victims with input or participation rights,[27] thus placing it in the category of rights gained at the expense of the State and offender. Thus civil liberties issues will need to be considered.[28]

This brief overview shows that in NSW, the rights of victims may affect prisoners' rights at several stages of criminal justice processing. But should the trend towards greater victims' rights be accepted uncritically? Do victims' rights negatively impact on the balance that needs to be struck between victims' and prisoners' rights? These issues must first be seen as a part of the more overall issue of the appropriate role of victims in an adversarial criminal justice system and what rights victims should have in such a system. The next section briefly examines the main arguments for and against victims having a greater role in the criminal justice system before the subsequent section returns to the specific issue of victims and parole proceedings. Note that a detailed discussion of the arguments in relation to the other stages or processes of the criminal justice system is beyond the scope of this chapter. However, the general arguments in the next section and the more specific following arguments in relation to parole hearings do have a considerable degree of relevance to these other stages or processes.[29]

Should crime victims have a greater role in the criminal justice system?

The issue of the role of victims in adversarial criminal justice systems is one of the most difficult and controversial questions in criminal justice today.[30] Many victim advocates and supporters, citing the UN Declaration and other international instruments as persuasive documents,[31] have argued for greater rights for victims in the criminal justice system. Such rights include the right to obtain information concerning criminal justice decisions and processes, the right to services, the right to protection from harassment and retaliation and the right to compensation and reparation. More controversial victims' rights proposals are the right to be present, have their views made known and to participate at relevant stages of the proceedings. Probably the most prominent victims' right discussed in the media and in academic literature that has come to fruition has been the right of victims in the United States (US Department of Justice 1998: 107),[32] Canada (Ruby 1994: 399-401), New Zealand (*Victims of Offences Act 1987* (NZ) s 8(1)) and Australia to present a victim impact statement during the offender's sentencing hearing. On the other hand, a proposal that has not yet eventuated at the time of writing is the 1982 suggestion to amend the US Constitution in order to guarantee that victims 'shall have the right to be present and to be heard at all critical stages of judicial proceedings'.[33] This comprehensive proposal to constitutionally entrench the rights of victims is still very much a live issue in the United States.[34]

However, not all the above changes and proposals have been welcomed and there has been much debate among civil libertarians, academics, defence lawyers and others concerned with the potential for victims' rights to interfere with the defendant's rights and thus subvert the proper functioning of the criminal justice system. These arguments have been confined to input or participation rights of victims. In general, most writers have been supportive of information rights for victims or, more generally, victims' rights gained at the expense of the State.[35]

Those who argue against participation rights for crime victims point to the fact that the purpose of the criminal justice system is to decide the guilt or innocence of the accused and, if he or she is guilty, an appropriate penalty. Such decisions must be made with objective fairness so that there is a degree of consistency in the prosecution and punishment of offenders. In other words, like cases should be treated similarly and should not be dependent upon whether individual victims are prepared to participate or provide input or not. It is also asserted that the input of victims should not really be a factor in these decisions because victims may be motivated by a desire for revenge and/or retribution or, alternatively, by a desire to forgive and forget regardless of the seriousness of the crime. In light of such emotional responses according to the individualised opinions or views of victims, the provision of formal or substantive victims' rights is problematic in terms of the proper functioning of the criminal justice system. Some writers also argue that greater victim involvement is merely a guise to foster a more retributive criminal justice system, as its effect will be to deny more defendants bail, increase penalties for offenders and lessen the chances of prisoners being released earlier on parole (Elias 1993: 90-7).

The counter viewpoint presented by victims' advocates is that the present system unfairly and unjustly excludes the victim who is, after all, the person actually harmed by the crime. This exclusion leaves victims feeling powerless and alienated from the system. As a result, they may decline to report crimes.[36] Where they do become involved as witnesses, they may suffer 'secondary victimisation'.[37] To overcome these problems, many victims' advocates argue, victims need to have a greater role in the system. Providing them with rights is the best means to achieve this.

Perhaps a more sophisticated argument refers to the specific interests that victims have in criminal proceedings, such as their need for information, compensation, protection, privacy, freedom from unfair cross-examination and their psychological need for a just verdict and, if applicable, an adequate sentence (Garkawe 1994: 601-3). Because these interests of victims are likely to be affected by decisions made during the criminal process, the laws of 'procedural fairness'[38] suggest that they should at least have the right to be heard before such decisions are made. Proponents of this perspective tend also to view the above civil liberties concerns as exaggerated, arguing that victims' rights and defendants' rights can reasonably co-exist. Alternatively, they argue that the introduction of victims' rights, even if they do detract from defendants' rights, are necessary and just in order to restore a fair balance between the rights of victims, which have previously been so neglected, and those of accused persons.

It is possible to continue the above arguments with claim and counter-claim. For example, in answer to the need for victims to have more input into proceedings, one may argue that such involvement will be likely to be counter-therapeutic as it will increase victims' stress, inconvenience and expense and perhaps raise false expectations which cannot be fulfilled. There is also little evidence that this is what victims themselves want.[39] On the other hand, proponents of victims' input argue that, provided victims are made fully aware of these possible difficulties, they should have the choice of being involved, and to deny them this choice on the grounds of these potential problems is paternalistic and unjust.

How do these arguments apply in parole hearings?

Assessing the arguments in the context of parole hearings: To what extent should victims have rights?

A number of approaches can be adopted in relation to the particular issue of victims' rights in parole hearings. An example of an extreme position which rejects any role for victims at this stage is that of Robert Elias.

> At [parole] hearings, victims may oppose release, claiming that punishment should last longer, based on the harm done by the crime … Why should victims have the right to participate? … As with sentencing legislation, graduations of harm are already built into parole rules. Why should victims supersede those rules with their own view of the appropriate punishment? (Elias 1993: 97)

It is the writer's opinion that this view is unsatisfactory as it seems to assume that victims' desire for retribution is the only possible reason for their involvement and that, as a result, they will demand denial of parole or the imposition of more stringent parole conditions. This assumption is difficult to test in practice and some writers disagree that the majority of victims in fact seek retribution (Karmen 1996: 163-6). Given that crime victims come from all walks of life and from all sections of society, each being affected differently by crime, and do not form a homogenous group, it is inherently problematic to determine their collective opinions. Moreover, there does not appear to be any empirical evidence as to whether victims' submissions have made any difference to the rate of parole orders or to parole conditions.[40] In fact, as a matter of logic, it is possible to envisage that some victims may wish for the prisoner's immediate release as an expression of forgiveness or an acknowledgement of reconciliation. Alternatively, the victim may foresee improved chances of compensation if the prisoner is released and takes up employment.[41]

A further argument against victims' input into parole decisions is that few victims have actually shown a desire to provide input or otherwise participate. For example, a study by Julie Gardner in South

Australia indicated that very few victims were interested in being actively involved in parole decisions (5.6%). Most wished to have no involvement (53.2%), a significant number merely wanted to be informed of the decision (30%) and a small minority only wanted to be consulted (11.2%) (Gardner 1990: 50). Anecdotal evidence in NSW also suggests that only a small percentage of victims who are informed of a forthcoming parole hearing actually proceed to make a submission.[42] However, while this evidence indicates that few victims may take up any right to be involved in parole decisions, it does not answer the question of whether the right should be available for those victims who do wish to be involved.

The opposite position is to unconditionally accept victims' rights in relation to parole hearings, including the right of victims to make submissions.

> Although a prisoner's behaviour while incarcerated should be considered in parole decisions, the nature of his conduct while at large is vital. No one knows better than the victim how dangerous and ruthless the candidate was before he was subjected to the scrutiny of the parole board ... Victims have a legitimate interest in seeing not only that their attackers are appropriately punished but also that they are not released prematurely to harm others. (Harrington et al 1982: 84)

This view is also problematic because it again seems to assume that victims' desire for retribution is the only possible justification for their involvement and that they will always oppose parole or demand stringent conditions. Furthermore, it ignores the civil liberties impacts on the rights of prisoners of unrestrained subjective victims' views being presented at parole hearings. The statutory scheme allowing for victims' submissions to parole hearings found in the NSW *Crimes (Administration of Sentences) Act* 1999 (NSW), by not providing for any restraints on what victims can say in their submissions, seems to accept this position. The major safeguard for offenders in relation to the contents of a victim's submission is that the submission can only be provided in one of two ways. First, the submission can be in writing, in which case prisoners may dispute the contents and would generally also have the right to cross-examine the victim. Alternatively, provided the Parole Board gives its approval, the victim can present sworn oral evidence that is subject to cross-examination (*Crimes (Administration of Sentences) Act* 1999 (NSW), ss 147 and 190). Generally, however, the procedural and evidentiary safeguards in relation to such submissions appear to be weak.[43] It is thus the writer's opinion that the NSW scheme does allow for subjective victims' views (provided they are genuinely held) to be presented to the Parole Board. This in turn does have the potential to sway the Board unfairly to delay the release of a prisoner or to apply more stringent conditions to their release.

Between these opposing positions is a third and more detailed approach to the issue that is favoured by this writer. While this approach does allow for victims to have rights in relation to parole proceedings, in the writer's opinion it does strike an appropriate balance between these rights and those of prisoners.

It is first essential to differentiate between those categories of victims' rights that are gained at the expense of the State and the other two categories that involve civil liberties issues. The first category includes providing victims with the right to *information* concerning criminal justice decision-making processes and outcomes.[44] Most commentators, even those who are critical of victims' participation rights, agree that these rights are desirable and should be encouraged.[45] Not only is this seen as fair, it also helps to overcome victims' feelings of powerlessness, and research has shown that it is what they wish.[46] Most importantly, these rights do not present any major problems in terms of the rights of the defendant, offender or prisoner. Thus, victims should have a right to know the results of bail, sentencing and parole hearings, as well as what conditions have been attached. Many of the 'rights' found in the NSW Charter of Victims Rights are precisely directed towards this goal.

Much more difficult and controversial issues arise when it comes to the question of victims' input or participation rights, such as the right of victims to present a submission to a parole hearing. As we have already seen, these are classified as victims' rights gained at the expense of both the State and the offender. Both of the extreme approaches outlined above seem to suggest that the only reason for a victim wishing to be involved is the desire for retribution. However, while some arguments against this view have been referred to above, focusing on the victim's reasons for wishing to be involved is, in the writer's opinion, erroneous. The decisive issue should be whether the evidence that the victim wishes to present is *legally relevant* to the particular decision being made. It is thus asserted that if the victim has any *legally relevant* and *verifiable* factual evidence that has a bearing upon a determination before the decision-maker, then the evidence should be put before that decision-maker. This is because it is preferable that decision-makers have the full evidence before them so they can make as informed a decision as possible.

But how do we determine whether the evidence of the victim is 'legally relevant'? The vital question is whether the views of the victim actually contribute to the objective decision-making process of the decision-maker. If these views add something factual that is verifiable and which is not known to the decision-maker, then it is the writer's opinion that they should be provided to the decision-maker. On the other hand, if it is a view or opinion based upon the victim's subjective instincts rather than having any verifiable factual basis, then it is argued that the view is not legally relevant to the decision and thus should *not* be provided to the decision-maker. This is not an easy distinction to make in many circumstances, as illustrated below.

How might these principles work in the case of parole hearings? In 1996, as a forerunner to the enactment of the *Sentencing Amendment (Parole) Act* 1996 (NSW), the NSW Law Reform Commission (the Commission) conducted a public inquiry into, among other matters, victims' input into parole hearings. While most of the submissions favoured allowing victims to present submissions to parole hearings (New South Wales Law Reform Commission 1996c: 266), the Commission did assess the arguments for and against victims' submissions as a matter of principle. It concluded that there should be a right for victims to make submissions to the Parole Board as 'they potentially constitute matter relevant to the Board's determination whether to make a parole order' (New South Wales Law Reform Commission 1996c: 265). In other words, it believed that victims' submissions were legally relevant.

On what grounds did the Commission find this to be the case? The Commission first stated that the Parole Board makes a parole order only when it determines that the 'release of the prisoner is appropriate having due regard to the principle that the public interest is of primary importance'. [47] It then argued that the 'victim is an integral part of the public interest and may have information relevant to it which is otherwise unavailable to the [Parole] Board' (NSW Law Reform Commission 1996b: 447). Examples of information that the Commission thought might fall within this category were:

> threats made to harm any person; the victim's fears relating to the offender's behaviour on release; evidence of the circumstances of the crime not on record before the Board; and evidence of the offender's behaviour during the time in custody. (New South Wales Law Reform Commission 1996c: 265)

Each of these categories of information needs to be assessed separately to determine whether it can properly be described as legally relevant evidence. The categories of 'threats made to harm any person', 'evidence of the circumstances of the crime not on record before the Board' and 'evidence of the offender's behaviour during the time in custody' are clearly interrelated. What these categories contemplate is evidence of threats made to victims or their family and supporters or other negative behaviour of the prisoner[48] that may well constitute new evidence not otherwise before the Parole Board. Most of the time it must be acknowledged that evidence of threats made or other negative behaviour of prisoners would have come to the attention of the authorities well before the parole hearing. If brought up in previous court or prison disciplinary proceedings, this information should constitute part of the Parole Board's records. It may well arouse the strong suspicion of the Parole Board if victims or their family or their supporters bring this kind of evidence to light at this late stage. Of course, the Parole Board and the prisoner would be entitled to question and assess the *bona fides* of such evidence. Clearly, the older this evidence, the more the Parole Board may doubt its authenticity. However, the important point is that it is possible to imagine circumstances where victims or their family or supporters were reluctant to make a report at the time of the threat or negative behaviour of a prisoner.[49] In these limited circumstances, such threats or other negative behaviour might constitute new evidence for the Parole Board and would thus be properly described as 'legally relevant'. Provided the evidence is verifiable and adequate procedural and evidentiary safeguards are put in place, then this writer's approach supports such evidence being presented to the Parole Board.

The other category of evidence mentioned by the NSW Law Reform Commission was 'the victim's fears relating to the offender's behaviour on release'. This category is even more controversial and perhaps represents where the major differences lie between victims' advocates and those who take a more civil liberties approach. It also illustrates the difficulties in deciding what is legally relevant.

Civil libertarians would argue that the victim's opinion on whether the prisoner should be released is not legally relevant evidence, as it is not based upon verifiable objective facts. Instead, they would assert that it is based on subjective matters such as victims' own fears, their perception of the trustworthiness of the prisoner and whether they have forgiven the prisoner. These are precisely the types of emotional responses arising from individualised opinions or views of victims that civil libertarians argue subvert the proper functioning of the criminal justice system. The counter-argument is that the views of the victim are in fact legally relevant as victims form an important part of the 'public interest' or 'protection of the community' that Australian legislation normally lays down as the primary criterion for Parole Board decisions.[50] For example, the Parole Board in NSW is obliged to have regard to 'the likely effect on any victim of the offender, and on any such victim's family, of the offender being released on parole' (*Crimes (Administration of Sentences) Act* 1999 (NSW), s 135(2)(c)).

Which of these two contrary positions should prevail? In the writer's opinion, a distinction needs to be drawn between objective facts on which the victim's opinions are based and their subjective opinions based on those facts. Objective facts may be legally relevant using the criteria discussed above. However, to assert that the subjective opinions of victims are legally relevant is far more problematic. It may be difficult to argue that their views or opinions add very much to the decision-making processes of the Parole Board or will include facts or other material not previously before the Parole Board. In terms of the issue as to whether a prisoner should be released, the Parole Board normally has before it much material. This includes the opinions of the prisoner's psychologist (and possibly a psychiatrist's opinion), the full history of the prisoner's behaviour in prison, including any programs undertaken, police records, the sentencing judge's comments and any report of a probation or parole officer. Many of these opinions will be provided by people who are specially trained to present their views on a person's predicted future behaviour and who are more likely to have been in recent sustained contact with the prisoner. Thus it is the writer's opinion that as far as the decision to grant parole to a prisoner is concerned, the victim's subjective views and opinions should not be presented to the Parole Board.

However, where the victim's views may be of some relevance in a small minority of cases is where the *conditions* of parole are being determined. This is because the victim's views may contribute to the decision-making process by alerting the Parole Board to a situation making it appropriate to add special conditions to release on parole. A simple example would be where a victim submits that he or she has relocated to a small town or a rural area and would be fearful if the offender were to move there too. It is true that, in the majority of cases, the Parole Board would be expected to include a condition of parole that the offender not contact the victim or members of the victim's family (Fox & Freiberg 1999: 772). However, there may be some cases where the Parole Board, without some indication from the victim, might not know where the victim is living and thus has no opportunity to consider imposing a special, protective condition.

In summary, the type of victims' submission that should be presented to a Parole Board would include any verifiable and objective factual material concerning possible threats or other negative behaviour of the prisoner not already available to the Parole Board. Additionally, the views and perspectives of victims as to how they would feel if the prisoner were granted parole and what special conditions they might wish to be attached to the parole order could be accepted.[51] Restricting victims' submissions to such matters may not be a simple task. Victim support personnel, particularly those who staff Victims Registers, need to be aware of these issues and understand the dangers for both prisoners (in terms of their rights) and victims (in terms of the possibility of cross-examination and/or their submission being rejected) of inadmissible material being presented. They need to play a central role in helping victims with their submissions and in explaining to them in a sensitive and patient manner why some matters should not be included and why in the majority of cases the submission will be unlikely to have any legal effect. This should minimise any potential false expectations a victim may have.

Will the above proposals allowing limited victims' submissions to be placed before a Parole Board, necessarily lead to a diminution of prisoners' rights? Recent empirical evidence concerning the effect of victim impact statements on sentencing, despite some differences, can constitute a relevant analogy. Some of this evidence indicates that there is little to fear from victims' input into sentencing decisions. In a recent article, Erez points to research that shows that in the vast majority of cases the use of victim impact statements had no effect on the result. In the small minority of cases where victim impact statements seemed to have an effect, 'the data revealed that the sentence was as likely to be more lenient as it was to be more severe than initially thought' (Erez 1999: 548).

It is suggested that a similar pattern would emerge if empirical studies were conducted on the effect of victims' submissions to Parole Boards. First, in the majority of hearings, there would be no victim's submission. Where there are victims' submissions, it is asserted that in a substantial preponderance of these cases they would make no difference to the final result. Finally, in the small minority of cases where they do make a difference, it is true that in some cases parole would be denied or more stringent conditions imposed on release. On the other hand, as mentioned earlier, in some cases it is possible to envisage the reverse being the case.

Erez further argues that in the small number of cases where the victim impact statement has made a difference to sentence, this has furthered the interests of justice (Erez 1999: 548). It would be possible to assert likewise that similar conclusions would be reached in those cases where victims' submissions have made a difference to parole decisions. Where it is factual and verifiable evidence of the victim that has made a difference, then this is just and fair as all the victim's submission has done is to provide the decision-maker with more complete facts. Where the victim's views influence parole conditions, then this is a relatively small price for the prisoner to pay, and more stringent conditions of parole are likely to be justified in view of the balance that needs to be struck between victims' and prisoners' rights.

Conclusion

Given the safeguards for victims' submissions that have been suggested above and the important proviso that these submissions be subject to adequate procedural and evidential guarantees, it is submitted that the threat to prisoners' rights of victims' submissions at parole hearings is minimal. This does not deny the strong need for ongoing research on the effect of these changes on both victims and prisoners, including empirical research on what difference (if any) victims' submissions have made to parole decisions.

This chapter has focused on the possible negative implications of victims' rights on prisoners' rights. It may be further asserted that allowing victims to enter the equation constituted by prisoners and those who manage them may also benefit prisoners. The most significant potential benefit is that it may make prisoners more aware of the harm they have caused and their own responsibility for that harm. This awareness may trigger behavioural change and assist rehabilitation. This is particularly the case with the restorative justice initiatives referred to above, where there is scope for crime victims and offenders to work together for the benefit of all involved.

The notion of personal responsibility and the benefits it can provide for prisoners is perhaps worth concluding with. It is true that many prisoners and prisoners' rights advocates often argue that prisoners themselves are victims. This has a number of possible dimensions. Prisoners might have been crime victims themselves by, for example, being abused as children. Some may have offended in response to being victimised, for example, by domestic violence (Miers 2000). Many may be considered victims of a society that is rife with racism, poverty, inequality, unemployment and other problems.

They may also be victims in a more immediate and direct sense when assaulted in prison (Heilpern 1995). Their families clearly are 'secondary' victims if they are deprived of their breadwinner's income.[52]

While there is clearly truth in each of these perspectives and society needs to tackle these issues, they should not cloud the fact that prisoners should take responsibility for the harms they have inflicted. Anecdotal evidence suggests that many prisoners are not prepared to acknowledge this simple fact.

> the single most prominent feature of an offender's personality observed by the professionals is their view that they have no victims. Many will argue for themselves to be seen as victims, most deny they leave chaos and trauma in their wake ... Not addressing this aspect of a person's offending is as misguided as pretending that drug use has nothing to do with delinquent behaviour. (D Thompson 1999: 4)

If this is in any way true, the trend towards greater victims' rights in relation to prisoners may well be the most significant development in recent years in terms of prisoners' rehabilitation. This potential advantage of victims' involvement for both victims and prisoners seems to have encouraged many Corrective Services Departments to embrace restorative justice initiatives and acknowledge that they have a responsibility to help crime victims.[53] Victims' rights in relation to prisoners, if established within appropriate limits and with adequate safeguards, may well open up a whole new range of exciting possibilities which criminal justice policy makers and prisoners' advocates should not ignore. It is thus submitted that the potential benefits of victims' rights outweighs any dangers for prisoners and is thus not something that prisoners' advocates should fear. Rather, it is something they should welcome.

Notes

1   The definition of a 'crime victim' is a complex issue, often a matter of social construction and ultimately dependent upon one's perspective. For the purposes of this chapter, a narrow definition – similar to that found in most victim compensation legislation – will be used. This is that a 'crime victim' is a natural person who has been directly affected by an act or omission that the law has deemed illegal or, in the case of homicide, it is those individuals in close relationships with the deceased. It is acknowledged that this is a restricted definition, excluding the possibility of non-human entities being victims. Furthermore, some argue that many prisoners are victims as well. See the Conclusion to this chapter for a discussion of this point.

2   The promotion of this position has been most prevalent in (but not exclusive to) common law countries with adversarial systems of justice, due to the exclusion of crime victims as parties to court proceedings and the consequential powerlessness they feel. This advocacy has led to the formation of the discipline of 'victimology' that started as an offshoot of criminology and can arguably now be considered a separate discipline. For a recent overview of issues and services in Australia with respect to crime victims, see Cook, David & Grant 1999.

3   O'Neill & Handley argue 'the word "right" only has specific meaning in relation to the context it is used' (O'Neill & Handley 1994: 23). They refer to three senses in which the word is often used. The first is the widest, a claim derived from an unspecified moral standard or rule of law. The second, used in this chapter, is a claim recognised though not necessarily enforceable in law. The final sense is the narrowest sense (often referred to by lawyers as the only legitimate form of a 'right'), where the claim is not only recognised by the law, but also enforceable within the legal system (O'Neill & Handley 1994: 23).

4   These have generally been confined to victims of more serious crimes. In the United States, for example, '[i]n the past two decades, the passage of laws requiring victim input at parole has been one of the greatest advances in victims' rights, with 43 States now providing this right' (US Department of Justice 1998: 127).

5   This is despite art 6(b) specifying that victims' participation rights must be 'without prejudice to the accused'. The UN Declaration, unlike a treaty, covenant or convention, is not a binding instrument at international law. Furthermore, even if it were, most countries' legal systems (including Australia's) do not require their domestic law to comply with their international obligations. Therefore, states are generally free (subject to any domestic constitutional restraints) to introduce victims' participation rights, which may diminish the rights of accused persons/offenders.

6   Note that it is beyond the scope of this chapter to examine issues relating to whether the granting of various victims' rights may cast too onerous a burden on the state, given that such an exercise would involve a detailed financial accounting of the costs of the criminal justice system.

7   The words 'system' and 'State' are interchangeable in this context, as Karmen refers mainly to the added burden of providing these rights on the officials and agencies of the criminal justice 'system' which all generally add to the obligations and expense of the State. See Karmen 1996: 344, Table 7.2.

8   During the 1980s, all Australian jurisdictions issued 'Declarations' or 'Charters' of Victims' Rights which were administrative guidelines published in brochure form only and issued by the various Attorney-Generals' Departments to all government agencies dealing with victims of crime. Not surprisingly, these were highly influenced by the UN Declaration. In the 1990s, four jurisdictions placed their 'Declarations' or 'Charters' on a statutory footing: see *Victims of Crime Act* 1994 (ACT) s 4; *Victims of Crime Act* 1994 (WA) Schedule 1; *Criminal Offence Victims Act* 1995 (Qld) ss 6-18; *Victims Rights Act* 1996 (NSW) s 6. However, with the establishment of the NSW Victims of Crime Bureau as a monitoring body to ensure the rights contained in the *Victims Rights Act* are provided to victims, and the enactment of the *Sentencing Amendment (Parole) Act* 1996 (NSW), NSW has arguably moved ahead of other Australian jurisdictions.

9   These are not rights in the narrow legal sense (see note 3 above) because the legislation does not provide any mechanisms for their legal enforcement and authorities failing to provide the listed rights are not subject to any penalty. For

this reason, to the writer's knowledge, there is no case law that deals directly with the Charter. However, a breach of these 'rights' can lead to disciplinary charges being brought against the official involved (*Victims Rights Act* 1996 (NSW) s 8).

10   The third part of this package was the *Victims Support and Rehabilitation Act* 1996 (NSW) that overhauled the NSW victim compensation scheme.

11   See also *Crimes (Sentencing Procedure) Act* 1999 (NSW) ss 26-30, which put this provision into effect.

12   See, for example, *International Review of Victimology* (1994) 3(1 & 2) 17-165, a special symposium devoted to the issue of victims' participation in sentencing.

13   For a small sample of critical perspectives on the use of victim impact statements, see Henderson 1985; Hinton 1996; Hall 1992; McCarthy 1994 and Richards 1992. For some case law regarding murder trials where the use of victim impact statements by the deceased's family in deciding sentence has been rejected, see *Booth v Maryland* 482 US 496 (1987) and *R v Previtera* (1997) 94 A Crim R 76.

14   See Division 7 (ss 66-71) of the *Crimes (Administration of Sentences) Act* 1999 (NSW). Note that this system was also established in order to comply with *Victims Rights Act* 1996 (NSW) s 6.16 (set out in the text below).

15   Personal telephone conversation on 13 November 2000 with Norman White, Community Liaison Officer, NSW Victims Register. Note, however, that this accords with the legislative framework pursuant to *Crimes (Administration of Sentences) Act* 1999 (NSW), s 135(2)(c). This obliges the Parole Board, in making decisions on the release of any prisoners (not just 'serious offenders'), to have regard to 'the likely effect on any victim of the offender, and on any such victim's family, of the offender being released on parole'.

16   This Act amended the *Sentencing Act* 1989 (NSW), which has recently been repealed. Many of the provisions relevant to this chapter have been re-incorporated into the *Crimes (Administration of Sentences) Act* 1999 (NSW).

17   A 'victim of an offender' for the purposes of the Victims Register is broadly defined and not restricted only to victims of 'serious offenders'. It includes victims of the offence for which the prisoner has been sentenced or a family representative where the victim is dead or under any incapacity (*Crimes (Administration of Sentences) Act* 1999 (NSW), s 256(5)).

18   This is the information that must be provided to victims pursuant to *Victims Rights Act* 1996 (NSW) s 6.15. As at 30 June 2000, there were 516 registered victims with respect to 401 prisoners (personal telephone conversation on 13 November 2000 with Norman White, Community Liaison Officer, NSW Victims Register).

19   New South Wales Law Reform Commission 1996c: 265. Note that prior to the enactment of this scheme, crime victims, like any member of the public, could provide a submission to the Parole Board. This is the situation that exists in most, if not all, other Australian jurisdictions. Where this statutory scheme is an advance is that it recognises the special status of victims and provides a structured system for registered victims of 'serious offenders' to receive notice beforehand of a forthcoming parole hearing.

20   Other victims would still be entitled to certain information concerning prisoners pursuant to *Victims Rights Act* 1996 (NSW) s 6.15. But they are not entitled to make submissions to the Parole Board under *Victims Rights Act* 1996 (NSW) s 6.16. However, if such a victim finds out about an impending parole hearing and wishes to make a submission, generally he or she may do so.

21 This is true particularly in the area of juvenile justice, where most States have now introduced legislative based conferencing involving young offenders, victims and their respective families and supporters; see the *Young Offenders Act* 1993 (SA), the *Young Offenders Act* 1994 (WA), the *Juvenile Justice Legislation Amendment Act* 1996 (Qld), the *Young Offenders Act* 1997 (NSW) and the *Youth Justice Act* 1997 (Tas).

22 Whether restorative justice actually benefits crime victims is a matter for debate (Garkawe 1999).

23 These programs have been established at the initiative of the Department and do not presently have any legislative basis.

24 Defined as 'a process whereby a trained mediator assists the victim and the offender to negotiate an agreement which sets out the conditions of any future contact, or establishes that no contact will occur': Booby nd: 38.

25 For a good description of such programs in South Australia, see D Thompson 1999.

26 This may also be relevant to other prisoners' issues, such as their classification within the prison system and their chances of various forms of limited release.

27 It needs to be kept in mind, however, that restorative justice is a consensual process and thus victims (and offenders) do not have the right to demand that a restorative justice session or program take place.

28 For an exploration of these issues in relation to conferencing (now the most prominent form of restorative justice in Australia), see Warner 1994.

29 For example, after discussing the arguments in relation to the introduction of victim impact statements, Andrew Ashworth states that 'the arguments would be no weaker in relation to several other key stages of decision-making', specifically mentioning bail proceedings and decisions regarding parole (Ashworth 1993: 508).

30 For an analysis of the key issues, see Sebba 1996 and Crawford & Goodey 2000. The latter in particular indicates that one of the outcomes of this debate is a preparedness to search for and discuss other possible methods of criminal justice resolution, most obviously restorative justice.

31 Such as European Committee on Crime Problems (1985).

32 All US States, the Federal government and the District of Columbia have enacted laws allowing for victim impact statements at sentencing.

33 This was first proposed by the President's Task Force on Victims of Crime (see Harrington et al 1982: 114). For a detailed analysis and critique of this and later proposals, see Lamborn 1987.

34 At the time of writing, a further proposal for a constitutional amendment is before the US Congress; see Senate Joint Resolution 6 cited in Beloof 1999: 707-8.

35 This is mainly because they do not involve civil liberties issues. Andrew Ashworth refers to a basic dichotomy between victims' procedural rights and what he terms their 'service' rights. The latter include not only the right to certain information but also the right to call upon emotional and practical support in the period following the offence, the right to be treated with respect, sympathy and understanding by criminal justice officials and the right to compensation in cases of victims of criminal violence (Ashworth 1993: 499).

36 This is referred to in the criminological literature as the 'dark figure' of crime and, while estimates vary as to the size of this figure, most conclude that it is a very high figure indeed. The main source of such a conclusion is the comparison between official police crime statistics and victimisation surveys.

37   This is where victims suffer from insensitive and uncaring treatment by criminal justice professionals and others in the aftermath of their victimisation. This term is commonly used in the victimological literature: eg Paterson 1996: 227-31.

38   This is the recent term for the common law doctrine formally known as 'natural justice' and used most often in the administrative law context. It is best described by Mason J in the following terms:

> ... when an order is to be made which will deprive a person of some right or interest or the legitimate expectation of a benefit, he [sic] is entitled to know the case sought to be made against him [sic] and to be given an opportunity of replying to it. (*Kioa v West* (1985) 60 ALJR 113 at 126 per Mason J)

39   For example, Julie Gardner's survey of crime victims in South Australia found that most either wanted no involvement with the criminal justice system or wanted only to be informed of developments. The only exceptions where the majority of victims did want to be actively involved were, not surprisingly, in the identification of suspects and in attending court as witnesses, these being areas where victims are traditionally called upon and are expected to participate (Gardner 1990: 49-50).

40   The NSW Parole Board does not collect statistics on the percentage of Parole Board hearings where victims provide a submission, let alone the effects of such submissions: personal conversation on 13 November 2000 with Graham Egan, Secretary of the NSW Parole Board.

41   In such circumstances, the victim may request that the offender's parole conditions include compensation to the victim.

42   It is estimated that in no more than 20 per cent of parole hearings for serious offenders where there is a victim registered on the Victims Register was a victim submission forthcoming. This drops to only 2-3 per cent for 'non serious offender' victims: personal conversation on 13 November 2000 with Graham Egan, Secretary of the NSW Parole Board.

43   The NSW Parole Board is not bound by the rules of evidence, is generally open to the public and is to conduct its proceedings with "as little formality and technicality as fairness to any affected person" allows (*Crimes (Administration of Sentences) Act* 1999 (NSW), Sch 1, s 11). The legislation does not specify what the standard of proof is before the Board will accept any fact or matter that may be detrimental to the prisoner's application. However, the Board is bound by the rules of procedural fairness (*Baba v Parole Board of NSW* (1985) 5 NSWLR 338; *Todd v Parole Board* (1986) 6 NSWLR 71), which is unlikely to be enough to reassure civil libertarians and prisoners' advocates that the safeguards are sufficient. However, the safeguards for prisoners in other Australian jurisdictions appear to be even weaker. For example, in Victoria the rules of natural justice do not apply to proceedings of the Parole Board (*Corrections Act* 1986 (Vic) s 69(2)). On a broader level, in jurisdictions other than NSW, prisoners do not appear to have the right to a public hearing if a Parole Board rejects or defers parole following the expiration of the prisoner's non-parole period. For example, *Sentence Administration Act* 1995 (WA) s 27 provides that prisoners are entitled to be notified of a rejection or deferral of parole and can make a written submission to the Parole Board. It does not provide for the Board to conduct a hearing.

44   Other rights that may be included in this category are found in Karmen 1996: 344, Table 7.2. Refer also to the views of Ashworth 1993, summarised in note 35.

Note that information provided to victims beyond that contemplated by art 6(a) of the UN Declaration, such as the prisoner's place of detention, where the prisoner will reside after being released and details of their treatment or participation in prison programs, may raise civil liberties concerns. Releasing such information may breach the prisoner's privacy and may be used by some victims or their families to harass the prisoner or the prisoner's family. A Canadian review recommended that the privacy rights of prisoners should prevail in the absence of victims' genuine security needs (*Correctional Law Review* 1987: 14-15).

45 For example, Robert Elias concedes that victims should have the right to know when an offender is to be released (Elias 1993: 97).

46 This was the main conclusion of an extensive survey of victims' experiences of the criminal justice system in Great Britain in Shapland, Willmore & Duff 1985.

47 This language is in fact replicated in s 135(1) of the *Crimes (Administration of Sentences) Act* 1999 (NSW).

48 This could also include the family or the supporters of the prisoner, where the prisoner consents to or encourages their behaviour.

49 Similar reasons as to why many victims do not report crimes in the first place could be envisaged, such as fear of retaliation, psychological denial of the crime and thinking the matter too trivial at the time.

50 For example, in NSW the term 'public interest' is used (see *Crimes (Administration of Sentences) Act* 1999 (NSW), s 135(1)). In WA, the phrase 'paramount consideration to the protection and interest of the community' is used (*Sentence Administration Act* 1995 (WA) s 18).

51 The distinction between victims' submissions being able to affect the conditions of parole, as opposed to the decision to grant parole, also applies in the United Kingdom under the 1990 *Victim's Charter: A Statement of the Rights of Victims of Crime* (see Johnson 1995).

52 'Secondary' is a common expression used in the victimological literature to describe those people who are financially or psychologically dependent on the 'primary' victim (the one who was directly violated by the crime).

53 For example, note the change in the mission statement of the Department, referred to above.

Preparing for Release

While judges have increased their sentences, the administrative and quasi-judicial decisions that should be made during a prisoner's time in custody to help progress a prisoner through the prison system and prepare him or her for eventual release, either at the end of a total sentence or after having become eligible for parole after a number of years, are increasingly not being made. Release on parole can sometimes be delayed for years. In this internal part of the imprisonment process, which, to some extent, is out of sight of the media, and where there is not even the assurance of judicial independence, the same pressures are felt even more.

If a particular prisoner has been given a high public profile and is expected to receive close, often uninformed attention by the media, with the risk of possible political intervention, administrative decisions that can be interpreted as preparing that prisoner for eventual release are very difficult, and are often not made, or deferred, for many years. The result is some prisoners are less prepared for release than they should be, even though their total sentences may be about to expire.

Kep Enderby QC (2000)
'The Politics of Imprisonment: Is Democracy
always in accord with Justice?'
(Spring 2000) 3 *Dissent* 48-51 at 49

In 1995 I made application to attend the Sexual Offender's Treatment program. Later I was told I had to do the program to address my offending behaviour. In 1996 I was transferred to a centre which does not run the program at all. This effectively stopped me from addressing my offending behaviour. In subsequent sentence management meetings my security classification was deliberately held at a 'medium' level, because I had not addressed my offending behaviour. I was not allowed to attend the program, so I was caught in a 'Catch 22' situation. From 1996 to 1998, I was not allowed to progress through the system because I had not attended a program to address my offending behaviour. It mattered little to them that the program was unavailable where I was and they continually refused to transfer me to a facility where the program was available.

Queensland male prisoner

Now I have not received my parole because I said I will do any program you ask but I will not change my plea. The sex offender programs immediately ask you to say you are guilty (which I know they don't have any legal rights to do so) and you are immediately classed as in denial. That's what they tell the board and they don't give parole until you do the program. Hence I have spent an extra 2 years in gaol at taxpayers' expense. The programs people also try and question you on charges that were either dropped or the judge has directed the jury to return a not guilty verdict.

Victorian male prisoner

TH was released in May last year, after serving 4½ years of a 5-year sentence. He had been denied parole & remissions, & had not even been given a Leave of Absence (LOA) for one day. I had written a number of letters on his behalf to various agencies in the hope of getting some form of early release & had stressed that he needed to be given 7 days notice of his release date to enable him to comply with his bank's requirements to be given 7 days notice of his intention to draw some money from his Special Purpose Account. He had nowhere to go on his release and did not know Brisbane at all as he was from the Sunshine Coast, but could not go back there.

The Dept issued a letter to the jail saying that TH was to be released in 6 days time … & that he was to be afforded every opportunity to prepare for his release, by being able to arrange his affairs.

This did not happen!! On the day of his release, he was told he was going home that day, and within the hour was gone. He didn't even have a shirt to wear and had to borrow one from another prisoner. A letter to me from TH is a self-explanatory and a tragic record of his release.

> The day those bastards just chucked me out, they dropped me off at Browns Plains a place I never even been to. When I asked the driver where the dole office was, he said that he didn't know and just drove off. Can you imagine how I felt at that moment? Well I can tell you mate that I was scared shitless.

> Anyway, after lugging my stuff around for about an hour I finally found it, and all the hassles I had getting money off them with all the questions I had to answer. Most of them I didn't know, like your tax file no., your residential address, how far are you willing to travel to work, all that kind of shit you know. I just wouldn't have a clue what to tell them. After about 3 hours I was finally out of there, but my troubles weren't finished with yet because I still didn't know where the fucking hell I was. So I just waited in a bus stop for a bus to Brisbane …

When I finally got to Brisbane I just walked around for a while totally lost, there was just so many people around the streets and I felt as if every one of them was looking at me. So I jumped in a cab and asked him to take me to a place I could stay for the night. He took me to a hostel which cost $30 a night. The room was a small as a fucking cell, but strangely enough I sort of felt at home, you know.

That first night mate, all I could think about was how I could be put back inside ... No wonder so many people go back to jail with the great release plan they have for them ...

TH's concern at merely being dumped on the side of the road in Brisbane was fuelled by what had happened approximately a year earlier to another inmate acquaintance, AB. AB was released equally as suddenly one Friday afternoon & driven to Brisbane. He did not know Brisbane at all, but was told to go to the CES to get some money. Unfortunately, when he arrived there the CES was closed & would not re-open until the Monday morning. AB spent his first 3 nights of freedom sleeping in a park in Brisbane, a recipe for total disaster and a severe condemnation of the release system ...

There is a precursor-to-parole period of work release to a work release centre available to those so granted as part of their parole package. However, for inmates being released after having served full-time (a group who are ever increasing in the current political climate in this State) or who are being released on remissions, there is no such service available. The only help is through Centrelink's payment of a part-dole cheque immediately on release.

Two of the factors which are extremely important to prisoners are certainty & hope. The system being used in Queensland fails on both counts. A prisoner & his family are entitled to advance knowledge, with some certainty, of the date he is to be released. To merely be given a moment's notice to pack & get going is absolutely disgraceful ...

The other factor, hope, is removed because the prisoner is not given an opportunity to prepare job prospects for his release.

Queensland male prisoner

CHAPTER 16

Prisoners and the Right to Vote

Melinda Ridley-Smith & Ronnit Redman

At the end of the day, the state and federal governments expect an ex-prisoner who has served a sentence of five years or longer to readapt to a society that the ex-prisoner had no say in at all ...

New South Wales prisoner in a submission to the
Human Rights and Equal Opportunity Commission

Introduction

A significant legal and political incident of being a citizen in a democratic society is the right to vote. In Australia, however, some citizens are disenfranchised. A prisoner, subject to Australia's laws and affected by the policies and decisions of the government, may lose his or her citizenship rights to have a say in society and instead be relegated to the status of 'non-person', alienated from shaping the future political community in which he or she will live. The denial of one of the fundamental incidents of citizenship – the right to vote – thus serves not only to deny the prisoner the tangible civil and political rights of citizenship but also the more symbolic social rights of a sense of membership in the community (Rubenstein 1995; Kaiser 1971).

This chapter reviews the origins of denying prisoners the right to vote, the actual voting rights afforded prisoners in Australia and the status of voting rights for prisoners under international law. It considers both formal disqualifications on prisoners' franchise and administrative or informal barriers to the effective exercise of the vote. Both can constitute significant limitations on a prisoner's ability to participate in the political process. The chapter concludes with an analysis of reform efforts in Australia and available avenues by which barriers to the franchise might be challenged.

Background to the denial of voting rights to prisoners

A prison sentence results in a range of adverse legal consequences and disabilities, both readily apparent and of a more subtle nature (Damaska 1968).[1] These include restrictions on various civil and political rights. Under current Australian law, many prisoners are denied the right to vote.

The traditional denial of a prisoner's civil rights upon conviction has its origins in the concept of 'civil death'. In feudal England, the common law doctrine of 'attainder' meant that a person convicted of treason or a felony lost all civil rights such as the right to inherit, to own or deal with property and the right to sue. The status of 'attainder' also carried with it the notion of the 'corruption of the blood' which extended to deny others the right to inherit property by or through the convicted person. At law, that person was dead: *civiliter mortuus*. This concept of 'civil death' can be traced to Roman and Greek practices. It is also well known to the civil law system, having developed in medieval times in many continental countries (Damaska 1968: 350-6).

Imprisonment as a punishment is a relatively recent development. It was part of the movement away from public and physical punishment towards more social penalties. Yet this trajectory is not so simple as, while capital punishment can be seen as the ultimate form of physical punishment, 'civil death' can be seen as the ultimate form of social punishment. Rather than the extinction of the person, it involves the extinction of the legal person (Orr 1998: 66). It was intended to mark the loss of honour of the convicted person, to form part of his or her social degradation and humiliation (Orr 1998: 68). In feudal societies, the ultimate physical and ultimate social punishments coexisted.

The denial of civil rights was therefore often justified as being part of the punishment. Just as serious crime entails the physical removal from society by imprisonment, it also results in the social removal from society by the denial of civil rights. The idea is that society is entitled to strip the prisoner of his or her civil rights as part of the 'symbolic' form of punishment. That person is marked as someone without honour, without the right to participate in public life (Orr 1998: 68-9).

A related justification was that serious crime involves the rejection of 'the social contract', the rights and responsibilities of living in a society and participating in public life. Where a person is convicted of a crime, he or she is said to have deliberately or knowingly breached the social contract. Having rejected some rights and responsibilities of society, it follows that he or she should be denied enjoying or exercising other rights and responsibilities of that society, including the right to participate in the electoral process (Orr 1998: 69).

One other justification appears to arise from the concept of 'corruption of the blood' and the notion that a convicted person is somehow 'tainted'. This justification would appear to be the basis for the argument that there is a need to maintain the 'purity' of the election process, to guard the polls from 'unsafe elements'. This justification is particularly evident in US jurisprudence (Orr 1998: 63-4).

A number of criticisms may be made of the traditional justifications given for denying prisoners the right to vote (eg Australian Law Reform Commission 1987: 50-1) and these justifications must also be scrutinised in light of contemporary theories of sentencing and punishment.

The denial of civil rights is out of step with a modern rehabilitative approach.[2] If a principal aim of punishment is to rehabilitate the prisoner and to facilitate the prisoner's positive 're-entry' into society on release, the denial of civil rights such as the right to vote, serves no useful purpose. In fact, the denial of the right to vote would seem to work contrary to rehabilitation. It serves only further to alienate the prisoner from society, from the continued observation and affirmation of his or her civil and political responsibilities. It reinforces a sense of non-citizenship, disempowerment and isolation (Orr 1998: 69). It reinforces the status of the prisoner as 'non-person' (Kaiser 1971: 215).

It is also difficult to maintain the justification for its deterrent or disincentive value.[3] The potential loss of civil rights cannot be considered to have any real deterrent effect. It is very unlikely that it adds in any significant respect to the far more likely deterrent value of the threat of imprisonment and the loss of other tangible rights and freedoms that this entails (Orr 1998: 69).

There are also problems with arguing that the modern practice of denying a prisoner his or her civil rights, including the right to vote, is justified for its inherent retributive or punitive value. Even if it is arguable that denial of civil rights has punitive value in its symbolic expression of community condemnation, Orr has argued that this can only *really* occur if the punishment is symbolically connected with the offences for which it is exacted, that it is in some way proportionate or related to the offence. For example, the denial of the right to vote might be considered to be a proportionate or related response to *electoral* offences (Orr 1998: 70). However, even if the denial of voting rights can be seen to reflect a legitimate contemporary interest in retributive justice, the *automatic* application of disenfranchisement runs counter to this aim. If denial of the franchise is to reflect contemporary notions of sentencing, then the conscious application of a judicial discretion in relation to its value or utility as a punishment in any given case must be applied.

In sum, the denial of the right to vote is something of a 'hidden' punishment, applied automatically by operation of law (Fitzgerald & Zdenkowski 1987: 33; Australian Law Reform Commission 1987: 51). As a 'hidden' corollary of crime, it is difficult to argue that it adds much as either a symbolic form of punishment, as an expression of community condemnation or as a deterrent.

Finally, the denial of the right to vote to prisoners is not consistent with other restrictions placed on the right to vote. Other such restrictions on the right to vote are based on the person's capacity to participate properly in the electoral process and to exercise the right responsibly. These restrictions are based on factors such as age or unsoundness of mind. The restriction on prisoners' rights to vote cannot be justified in this way. Conviction and imprisonment do not impair one's ability to make rational and responsible voting choices.

Voting rights of Australian prisoners

This section considers the voting rights of inmates in Australian prisons. We first consider the various statutory regimes and administrative arrangements under which some prisoners are disqualified from voting. We then turn to examine the legislative provisions and practical arrangements that govern the exercise of the right to vote for those prisoners who are not disqualified. Both formal disqualifications and the circumstances under which a right to vote may be exercised can lead, in effect, to prisoner disenfranchisement and both are considered to be restrictions on the right to vote.

Disqualifications from voting for Australian prisoners

The Commonwealth and each State and Territory has legislative restrictions on qualifications to vote for convicted prisoners.[4] No jurisdiction disqualifies prisoners on remand. The length of sentence which gives rise to voter disqualification ranges in length from five years or more (the Commonwealth, the Australian Capital Territory, Queensland, Victoria) to 12 months or more (New South Wales, Western Australia) to any sentence of imprisonment (Tasmania). Only South Australia has no voter disqualification for convicted prisoners

(Orr 1998: 60, fn 29).[5] Table 16.1 lists the disqualification provisions across Australia.

In Australia, voting is compulsory and for those who are eligible to vote, enrollment on the electoral roll is mandatory. The mechanism for disqualification is generally through a prisoner not being entitled to have his or her name on the electoral roll.

There are some practical difficulties associated with ensuring that prisoners who are disqualified are removed from the relevant rolls and ensuring that those who are no longer disqualified are re-enrolled. Some legislative provisions are designed to facilitate the information flow between prisons and electoral officials. In relation to Federal elections, for example, s 109 of the *Commonwealth Electoral Act 1918* (Cth) requires the Controllers-General of State and Territory prisons to forward a list of prisoners sentenced for a term of five years or more to the Australian Electoral Commission (AEC) for disen-rollment. Two specific problems might be noted.

Table 16.1. Provisions relating to prisoners' disqualification

Jurisdiction	Provision	Categories of disqualification
Federal	*Commonwealth Electoral Act* 1918 s 93(8)(b) & (c)	Persons serving a sentence of five years or more Persons convicted of treason or treachery and not pardoned
ACT	*Electoral Act* 1992 (ACT) s 72(1)	Persons serving a sentence of five years or more Persons convicted of treason or treachery and not pardoned
Queensland	*Electoral Act* 1992 (Qld) s 64(1) & (2)	Persons serving a sentence of five years or more Persons convicted of treason or treachery and not pardoned
NT	*Electoral Act* 1979 (NT) s 27(1)	Persons serving a sentence of five years or more Persons convicted of treason or treachery and not pardoned
NSW	*Parliamentary Electorates and Elections Act* 1912 (NSW) s 21(b)	Persons serving a sentence of 12 months or more and in prison serving that sentence
Tasmania	*Constitution Act* 1934 (Tas) s 14(2)	All persons in prison under any conviction at time of Tasmanian election
Victoria	*Constitution Act* 1975 (Vic) s 48(2)(a) & (b)	Persons convicted of treason or treachery and not pardoned Persons convicted and under sentence for offence punishable by imprisonment for five years or more
WA	*Electoral Act* 1907 (WA) s 18(b) & (c)	Persons convicted of treason Persons serving a sentence or yet to serve a sentence of imprisonment for one year or more
SA	*Electoral Act* 1985 (SA) s 29	No disqualifications

First, in jurisdictions such as Victoria[6] where the legislation disqual-ifies prisoners under sentence for offences *punishable* by a term of five years or more, prison officials are not usually aware of the maximum term to which a prisoner could have been subject but only the actual term to which he or she was actually sentenced. In practice, then, officials inform the relevant electoral offices only of those prisoners actually serving terms of five years or more; prisoners serving shorter terms, although technically disqualified, will not be removed from the roll.

Secondly, only relevant now in relation to Victoria, some legislation refers to persons 'under sentence'. This would include persons released on parole or subject to non-custodial orders. In practice, unless a person subject to such a sentence is actually incarcerated or when he or she has finished the custodial portion of the sentence, it is unlikely that disqualification will result in removal from the electoral roll. This is because the AEC relies on information from prisons to make deletions from the roll (Orr 1998: 58). The AEC advises that its legal advice is to the effect that the current Commonwealth wording disqualifying prisoners 'serving a sentence' does not include early release or parole prisoners or those under a suspended sentence. These persons are therefore considered eligible to vote (AEC letter to Human Rights and Equal Opportunity Commission, 17 August 2000).

The consequence of these difficulties is that some persons who are technically disqualified will remain on the electoral rolls (for example, in Victoria where a person is given a suspended sentence) and some persons who are no longer disqualified (for example, in Queensland where a prisoner is on parole) may remain disenrolled. It is difficult to ascertain precisely how many people fall into these categories[7] but it is nonetheless plainly undesirable to have a situation in which a right as important as that of the franchise is subject to this degree of potential uncertainty in administration.

Arrangements for the exercise of the franchise for prisoners qualified to vote

The opportunity to exercise the vote effectively is an integral part of the right. For non-disqualified persons serving custodial sentences, segregated from the mainstream of social and political life, the effective exercise of the right to vote is often problematic. These prisoners include convicted persons serving terms less than that required for disqualification and prisoners on remand.

The AEC and each of the State and Territory electoral commissions were surveyed in relation to how the right to vote is facilitated for those prisoners who are eligible to vote.[8] Each of the State and Territory prison authorities were also surveyed.[9] A range of questions was asked of both the electoral commissions and prison authorities as to the arrangements made by which prisoners eligible to vote are in fact able to vote. The responses in respect of Federal, State and Territory and Aboriginal and Torres Strait Islander Commission (ATSIC) elections are set out below.[10] In addition, comments were sought from prisoners in relation to the actual operation of voting in prisons via a leaflet distributed in prisons and through consultation with an advocacy group representing prisoners (Justice Action).[11] These comments are also set out.

Federal elections

The AEC advised that when a federal election is announced, it liaises with each of the prison authorities.

The AEC may make arrangements with the Controller-General of Prisons for a State or Territory for the taking of votes of prisoners. Where such arrangements are made, an electoral visitor must visit the prison to take the votes of prisoners in that prison (*Commonwealth Electoral Act* 1918 (Cth) s 226A). Such arrangements are described as a 'mobile polling service'. Where a mobile polling service is to be provided by the AEC at a prison, the relevant Divisional Returning Officers will contact the prison directly to make the necessary arrangements. It appears that mobile polling services are provided to prisons where a significant number of prisoners are eligible to vote.[12]

Where mobile polling services are not available, the relevant Divisional Returning Officers will write to the prison enclosing postal vote application forms so that prisoners have access to postal voting. All eligible prisoners can vote as postal voters. A prisoner may also apply to become a 'general postal voter'.[13] If a prisoner has registered as a general postal voter, he or she will receive postal vote material and ballot papers at his or her nominated postal address following the announcement of the election. However, not all prisoners may be aware of or wish to become a general postal voter so postal vote application forms are sent out to prisons in any event.

In relation to generally encouraging voter registration of prisoners, the AEC provides to prisons the appropriate forms for prisoner enrolment on the electoral roll at the time an election is announced. The AEC also advised that for the most recent Federal election, it produced and distributed a poster in prisons nationally, informing prisoners as to who was eligible to vote, the need to enrol to vote and the process for postal voting (letter to HREOC dated 17 August 2000). In addition, NSW prisons were provided with information kits also aimed at informing prisoners of their eligibility to vote, the process for enrolment, the process for postal voting and other 'how to vote' information such as how to fill out ballot papers correctly. The AEC noted that prisoners also have access to the AEC's usual media campaign through print, television and radio, encouraging all eligible voters to enrol and vote. Telephone interpreter services are also available.

State and Territory elections

The majority of State and Territory electoral commissions advised that for State and Territory elections, postal voting is the only form of voting available to prisoners.

The relevant State/Territory electoral commission distributes postal voting application forms to the prisons in that State or Territory when an election is announced. It appears that, in some cases, the State/Territory electoral commissions take some active steps to publicise at the prison which prisoners are eligible to vote and to encourage those prisoners to enrol and vote. Some prison authorities also advised that efforts are made to advise prisoners of their eligibility and to facilitate enrolment and voting.[14]

However, a number of State/Territory electoral commissions advised that no specific information or special steps are taken to inform prisoners of their right to vote in a State/Territory election or to encourage them to enrol and vote. Reliance was instead placed on the usual media campaign to the public in the lead up to an election and the general telephone help lines. The Tasmanian Electoral Office advised that State elections are run in conjunction with the AEC and that the processes do not differ, save for different disqualification requirements (telephone conversation with author, 12 December 2000).

Other elections

The AEC advised that it undertakes the management of the ATSIC regional council elections.[15] Voting in ATSIC elections is not compulsory but if a prisoner is eligible, being either Aboriginal or Torres Strait Islander, then he or she must be enrolled on the Commonwealth electoral roll in order to vote. That prisoner must therefore not be disqualified from voting so as to have been removed from the Commonwealth electoral roll. For ATSIC elections, the AEC provides both mobile polling services and postal voting. As to information provided to prisoners, the AEC advises that Regional Returning Officers arrange to visit prisons, inform prisoners of the elections and their voting rights and encourage enrolment and voting.

Prisoners' experiences

It is not surprising that, given the isolation of the prisoner population and other incidents of incarceration, there is some considerable distance between policies and practices to facilitate the franchise and the situation 'on the ground' in prisons.

A number of themes run through prisoners' comments in response to a general invitation issued by the Human Rights and Equal Opportunity Commission (HREOC): 'that doesn't actually happen here', 'it all happens too late' and 'there isn't enough 'information' appear to be recurring elements of prisoners' experience with the franchise. For example, one prisoner commented that although 'we received information about elections and referendums via prison notice boards ... we were not given enough information to make up our minds how to vote'. One prisoner said that, although the facilities to vote normally exist, 'unless you are a well educated prisoner, you do not vote'. Complaints recorded by Justice Action alleged no voting material was visibly displayed in a number of NSW prisons in respect of the 1999 election[16] and that, in broad terms, prisoners were not given the 'opportunity to participate'.

This can sometimes result in prisoners being fined for not voting when they are eligible. For example, one female prisoner commented that:

> women often believe that along with the rest of their rights they don't have the right of voting either ... [the] majority of women don't understand what is required of them, to fill in [postal voting] forms, let alone the complexities of voting in general. Due to the fact that adequate information isn't provided to women in jails, many women are being fined due to misinformation received. (Queensland female prisoner in a submission to HREOC)

Again, in respect of qualifications to vote, one Victorian prisoner commented that the information appeared to be that persons serving sentences of five years or more were permanently disqualified from voting.

In relation to the mechanics of voting, one prisoner commented to the Commission that a postal vote application form was removed from its envelope when it arrived in the prison and, when a replacement was sent, it arrived too late to be lodged. The same prisoner considered challenging his disqualification on another occasion but felt that any review of a decision not to re-enrol him would have come too late.[17] Another NSW prisoner wrote that in the last State election postal voting forms were not delivered, despite his prior registration as a postal voter.

Justice Action's experience with the effective exercise of prisoners' voting rights is that there is a considerable distance between policy and implementation.[18] In their view, much remains to be done before prisoners can be in a position to cast an informed and free vote. They point out that voting involves the entirety of the process from enrolment, to the receipt of information about candidates and parties, to the actual casting of the vote. They stress that prisoners, by virtue of their incarceration, form a distinct target group with special requirements that need to be specifically addressed by electoral commissions and by political parties.

Justice Action makes a number of suggestions for change including better consultation with prisoners, the employment of consultant ex-prisoners to advise on the best way of communicating on electoral matters, enrolment of prisoners at the time of reception, the appointment of a liaison person within each prison and better communication between electoral commissions and correctional authorities. They see current practice of placing electoral information on notice boards as an important information strategy but one that must be used in conjunction with other methods, particularly with inmate development committees or similar prisoner consultative structures.

While the above material is anecdotal and is not the result of an extensive survey of prisoner views and experiences across Australia, it is broadly true that the implementation of the franchise for prisoners is not consistent and depends on a range of factors, including the size and nature of the prison, the attitude of correctional staff, the degree of commitment of prisoners and the legislative and policy regime under which elections are conducted.

It is also particularly interesting to note that a number of prisoners use the language of citizenship and participation when considering their disenfranchisement. One Tasmanian prisoner thought the right to vote should be extended to prisoners and other detainees 'as we are still people'. Another referred to the 'human privilege' to 'take care and interest in the affairs of other human beings' and another commented that most women prisoners 'have no concept of the government and what it means to society and their role in it' (submissions to HREOC).

Prisoners' voting rights under international law

A number of international instruments are relevant to prisoners' suffrage; chiefly the *International Covenant on Civil and Political Rights* (the ICCPR) which imposes binding treaty obligations on state parties, as well as the *Standard Minimum Rules for the Treatment of Prisoners* (the Standard Minimum Rules or SMRs) which provide further guidance on the content of international standards with respect to prisoners. This section considers the scope of international law in relation to the voting rights of prisoners. The final section analyses the Australian position described above in light of the international position.

Article 25 of the ICCPR deals with the political rights of citizens and recognises and protects the right of individuals to participate in the structures and processes of public affairs.[19] Article 25 provides:

> Every citizen shall have the right and the opportunity, without any of the restrictions mentioned in article 2 and without unreasonable restrictions:
>
> (a) To take part in the conduct of public affairs, directly or through freely chosen representatives;
>
> (b) To vote and to be elected at genuine periodic elections which shall be by universal and equal suffrage and shall be held by equal ballot, guaranteeing the free expression of the will of the electors;
>
> (c) To have access, on general terms of equality, to public service in his country.

As the Human Rights Committee (HRC) has stated in its General Comment No 25 adopted in 1996, 'Article 25 lies at the core of democratic government based on the consent of the people and in conformity with the principles of the Covenant'. It is at the heart of the political rights that the Covenant enshrines.

Despite the centrality of art 25, the Human Rights Committee has noted that 'the right provided for by art 25 is not an absolute right and that restrictions on this right are allowed as long as they are not discriminatory or unreasonable'.[20] The Human Rights Committee has indicated that it is 'aware that under the legislation of many countries offenders may be deprived of certain political rights' and that 'accordingly, art 25 of the Covenant only prohibits "unreasonable" restrictions'. However, 'in no case ... may a person be subject to sanctions solely because of his or her political opinion (article 2(1) and 26)'.[21]

The limits on art 25 – first by reference to discrimination and secondly by reference to reasonableness – are discussed below.

Further, the requirement that the rights in art 25 be capable of effective exercise is also considered.

Non-discriminatory restrictions

Concerning the principle of non-discrimination, General Comment No 25 points out that, in relation to the rights protected by art 25, 'no distinctions are permitted between citizens in the enjoyment of these rights on the ground of race, colour, sex, language, religion, political or other opinion, national or social origin, property, birth or other status' (HRC General Comment No 25 1996: para 3). Indeed, art 25 is explicit that the distinctions mentioned in art 2 of the ICCPR, which ensures individuals the protection of the rights in the ICCPR without discrimination, are not to fetter the rights and opportunities conferred by art 25.[22] For example, in relation to distinctions drawn by reference to a ground enumerated in art 2, the Human Rights Committee was clear in *Weisz* that 'in no case ... may a person be subject to sanctions solely because of his or her political opinion'.[23]

The status of being a prisoner is not a ground which is explicitly included in art 2 but it is arguably an 'other status' analogous to those listed. The common features of the specified grounds are that they are or historically have been commonly used to distinguish among people so as to favour one group over another in their opportunities to access means of survival and advancement or to participate fully in social and political life. They are all invidious grounds for making such distinctions because they do not reliably and universally measure ability or capacity (Human Rights and Equal Opportunity Commission 2000: 93).[24] Prisoners have historically constituted a distinct group subject to particular forms of discrimination.

If it can be argued that prisoner status is an 'other status' within the meaning of art 2, then discrimination against prisoners *solely* because of this status is not permitted. However, the Human Rights Committee's acceptance that the denial of political rights to prisoners can be legitimate under art 25 undermines the suggestion that prisoner status can be an 'other status' for the purpose of art 2.

There is another important aspect to the non-discriminatory application of art 25. As Orr points out, Indigenous people are heavily over-represented in Australian jails (Orr 1998: 75ff). Disqualifications on voting and restrictions on the capacity to exercise the vote will disproportionately impact on the Aboriginal population, a group which historically has been discriminated against in Australia with respect to the franchise (Brooks 1993). The right to vote in art 25 of the ICCPR must be available without discriminatory restrictions and this is rein-forced by art 5 of the *International Convention on the Elimination of All Forms of Racial Discrimination* (ICERD) which, together with art 1, prohibits racial distinctions having the purpose *or effect* of nullifying or impairing the equal exercise of various human rights, including the right to vote. To the extent that legislative disqualifications and admin-istrative restrictions disproportionately impact on Indigenous prisoners, they are discriminatory and may breach art 25 as well as ICERD.

Reasonable restrictions

Concerning the question of 'unreasonable restrictions', the Human Rights Committee stresses that any conditions which govern the exercise of the rights in art 25 must be established by law and must be based on objective and reasonable criteria (HRC General Comment No 25 1996: para 4). In particular, the right to vote must be established by law and may be subject only to 'reasonable restrictions such as setting a minimum age limit for the right to vote' (HRC General Comment No 25 1996: para 10).[25] The Human Rights Committee requires that States set out and explain legislative provisions that deprive citizens of their right to vote. It reiterates that the grounds for this deprivation should be both objective and reasonable (HRC General Comment No 25 1996: para 14).[26]

The Committee gives some content to the notion of reasonableness in this context by suggesting that it would be unreasonable to restrict the right to vote on the ground of physical disability or to impose literacy, educational or property requirements on the franchise (HRC General Comment No 25 1996: para 10). Specifically, the Human Rights Committee states that:

> if conviction for an offence is a basis for suspending the right to vote, the period of such suspension should be proportionate to the offence and the sentence. Persons who are deprived of liberty but who have not been convicted should not be excluded from exercising the right to vote. (HRC General Comment No 25 1996: para 14)[27]

This interpretation of art 25 is clearly at odds with the suggestion made above that being a prisoner could amount to an 'other status' because, if this were the case, then a restriction on the franchise *solely* by reason of this status would not be permitted and it is not necessary to go further to consider the reasonableness of any restriction. However, the Human Rights Committee appears, in General Comment No 25 and elsewhere, to deal with restrictions on the franchise for prisoners under the 'unreasonableness' limb rather than the arguably more protective 'non-discrimination' limb.[28] While the current state of Human Rights Committee jurisprudence appears to be that reasonable restrictions on qualifications for the franchise itself are permissible if they are proportionate to the offence and the sentence, it is suggested that the denial of the franchise to prisoners per se may be in breach of art 25. This suggestion is made on two bases: first, that disqualification is in breach of the non-discrimination limb of art 25; and secondly, that disqualification can never amount to a reasonable restriction. The latter basis draws on the argument made by Orr who suggests that the only permissible restrictions under art 25 are those which attach to the mechanics of enrolment and voting but not to the right to vote itself (Orr 1998: 62).

The effective exercise of the right to vote

Finally, the preceding discussion elaborating the Human Rights Committee's views on permissible exclusions from the rights set out in art 25 does not exhaust the reach of the article. Article 25 explicitly refers to both 'the right *and the opportunity*' to exercise these rights and the Human Rights Committee is concerned not only with the conferral of the rights on particular classes of citizens but with the substantive capacity of citizens to exercise these rights. States must do more than simply confer the right to vote in a non-discriminatory way. The Human Rights Committee's view is that 'States must take effective measures to ensure that all persons entitled to vote are able to exercise that right' (HRC General Comment No 25 1996: para 11).

Thus, the Human Rights Committee considers that art 25 requires the facilitation of registration to vote, the absence of obstacles to registration, the imposition of reasonable residence requirements only, the strict enforcement of penal laws prohibiting interference with registration or voting, and voter education and registration campaigns to 'ensure the effective exercise of art 25 rights by an informed community'. Those necessary conditions for the effective exercise of an informed right to vote – freedom of expression, assembly and association – must be fully protected and positive measures to overcome specific difficulties such as literacy must be taken (HRC General Comment No 25 1996: para 12).

While General Comment No 25 is useful in fleshing out the meaning of art 25, it does not comprehensively state whether particular restrictions on voting are 'reasonable and objective'. The Standard Minimum Rules provide some further guidance in relation to appropriate restrictions on the rights of prisoners to participate in civil society and political life. The general tenor of the Standard Minimum Rules is that imprisonment should not hinder reintegration into society after imprisonment and should not inflict punishment beyond that of the deprivation of liberty (SMR 57). In particular, SMR 60 requires the minimisation of differences between prison life and life outside prison which tend to lessen the respect due to prisoners' dignity as human beings.

> The treatment of prisoners should emphasise not their exclusion from the community but their continuing part in it ... steps should be taken to safeguard, to the maximum extent compatible with the law and the sentence, the rights relating to civil interests, social security rights and other social benefits of prisoners. (SMR 61)

Article 10 of the ICCPR provides that the basic aim of a prison system shall be the reformation and social rehabilitation of prisoners. The *Basic Principles for the Treatment of Prisoners* also state that, except for those limitations which are demonstrably necessitated by imprisonment, the human rights and fundamental freedoms in the ICCPR are to be retained by all prisoners (Principle 5). Further, 'favourable conditions shall be created for the reintegration of the ex-prisoner into society under the best possible conditions' (Principle 10).

Clearly, as it relates to prisoners, some restrictions on the franchise will be permissible where they are necessary incidents of incarceration. For example, some restrictions on freedom of assembly would be necessary. However, any such restrictions must be reasonable and proportionate and should impinge as little as possible on a prisoner's right to exercise an informed vote. It is also insufficient for a State simply to assert the necessity of a particular restriction. Any limitation must be *demonstrably* necessary.

The Australian position and proposals for change
Analysis of the Australian position

The survey of restrictions on the franchise for prisoners in Australia above reveals two main issues. First, there remain disqualifications on the franchise at Federal and State and Territory level for some prisoners. Secondly, the actual implementation of the right to vote for those prisoners who are not disqualified is uneven, despite some clear attempts to ensure that prisoners are able to exercise their rights effectively.

In relation to legislative disqualifications from the franchise, we consider that there is no justification for the continued retention of such restrictions. We agree with the criticisms of the traditional justifications for disenfranchisement set out in the first section of this chapter and consider that the restrictions find scant support in contemporary notions of punishment. They run counter to rehabilitative goals and serve only to alienate prisoners further from a society from which they have already been segregated and marginalised.

We also consider that Australia may be in breach of its international obligations under the ICCPR in relation to these disqualifications. On the broader interpretation of art 25 suggested above, it is difficult to see how any such restrictions can be non-discriminatory where the rationale for their retention is unclear. Even where the rationale is articulated, it is our view that the disqualifications are insupportable for any policy or practical reason.

If this broad interpretation is not accepted (and the above discussion suggests that it is out of step with the current jurisprudence of the Human Rights Committee), it remains arguable that even on a view of art 25 which would allow 'reasonable' and 'proportionate' restrictions on qualifications to vote, Australia is in breach of art 25. It is recognised that the denial of the franchise based on the *length* of a prisoner's term is to some extent related to the seriousness of the offence and could be argued to be proportionate to the offence and the sentence. We are of the view, however, that such an argument cannot be sustained. In Australia, disqualification is automatically applied by operation of law, regardless of the nature of the offence. There is no sentencing discretion to ensure that there is in fact a proportionality between the disqualification and the circumstances of the offence. In Victoria, where the *maximum term* is the basis for disqualification, the disqualification may be entirely unrelated to the circumstances of the actual offence. Finally, a disqualification which, depending on when elections are held, may or may not result in the loss of the opportunity to vote, and which can vary considerably between jurisdictions, is an arbitrary one and cannot be seen as being reasonable and proportionate (Orr 1998: 82).

Further, where disqualifications may have a racially discriminatory effect, as in Australia, they may be in breach of international obligations under ICERD in respect of racial discrimination.

In relation to the implementation of the franchise for non-disqualified prisoners, the research undertaken for this paper indicates a mix between useful and appropriate policies and initiatives to facilitate the vote and patchy implementation of these initiatives on the ground. Many of the suggestions of prisoners and their advocates concerning prisoner consultation and liaison, enrolment on intake and the continual flow of information about the political process are worthy of detailed consideration by the authorities in consultation with prisoners. It is critical to remember that the political process is not simply a matter of placing a mark on a voting form every few years but an ongoing debate that requires an informed and aware electorate. Prisoners as citizens are part of this electorate and their participation in this debate must be carefully attended to and fostered. The advice we received from some authorities that no special steps are taken to provide information about election issues to prisoners, as prisoners have the same access to information as all electors, is clearly insuff-icient and does not address the particular needs and difficulties facing a particularly vulnerable and isolated group of voters. Reliance, for example, on general telephone help lines is inappropriate in the context of prisoners' generally restricted access to telephones.

Again, without due attention by authorities to the full and timely flow of information to prisoners about political issues generally and elections in particular, as well as the opportunity to participate fully in political discourse through access to the full range of media (television, radio, print and internet), internal discussion, debating groups and guest speakers, it is our view that Australia could potentially be in breach of its obligations under art 25 in this regard.

Political reform proposals

Over the last three decades, there have been numerous calls for repeal of the provisions restricting the voting rights of prisoners, at both Federal and State levels. In 1978, the Royal Commission into NSW Prisons concluded:

> A citizen's right to vote should depend only on his ability to make a rational choice. Loss of voting rights is an archaic leftover from the concepts of 'attainder' and 'civiliter mortuus' and has no place within a penal system whose reform policies aim to encourage the prisoner's identification with, rather than alienation from, the community at large. All prisoners should be entitled to vote at State and Federal elections. Necessary facilities should be provided for them to exercise their franchise. (Nagle 1978: 303-4, rec 177)[29]

However, despite the recommendations of various commissions, committees and reform bodies that these provisions be abolished, there appears to have been little substantive response from the relevant legislatures to repeal the provisions.[30]

Further, it should not be thought that there is any clear push for reform and abolition of the restrictions on prisoners' rights to vote. Following the 1993 Federal election, the Joint Standing Committee inquiry into that election recommended that the franchise be extended to all prisoners. However, following the 1996 Federal election, the Committee noted that whilst that recommendation was agreed to by the government and included in amending legislation, it was withdrawn in the face of community opposition (Joint Standing Committee on Electoral Matters 1997: 48).[31] The Joint Standing Committee then recommended that the restrictions in fact be expanded so that *all* persons serving a prison sentence for *any* offence against the law of the Commonwealth or of a State or Territory be disqualified from enrolment or voting in Federal elections.[32] Amending legislation to this effect (Electoral and Referendum Amendment Bill (No 2) 1998 (Cth)) was subsequently introduced into Parliament but defeated in the Senate by the Opposition, the Democrats and the Greens.

Following the 1998 Federal election, the Joint Standing Committee noted that previous proposals for reform, either to extend or to further limit prisoners' franchise, had both been opposed and defeated. It concluded: '[a]lthough the majority of this Committee concurs with the previous Committee's recommendation, it believes that current legislation should stand until there is sufficient and widespread public support for a change' (Joint Standing Committee on Electoral Matters 2000: 89-90).

Of course, even if the Federal legislature did repeal the disqualification provision in the Federal legislation, the State/ Territory restrictions would not necessarily be affected.[33] One way to achieve a uniform scheme across Australia would be for the Federal legislature to use the constitutional external affairs power to adopt the political rights in art 25 of the ICCPR and override any State restrictions on prisoner enfranchisement. Such a proposal would, of course, rely on the political will of the government of the day (as well as a favourable interpretation by the High Court in the inevitable challenge) and no such legislative proposal has ever been made at a Federal level.[34]

Potential avenues for change

This to-and-fro movement has led Jerome Davidson to comment that if 'the status of prisoner disenfranchisement is to be relieved of the perpetual motion of the political pendulum, it must be questioned in another realm' (J Davidson nd: 4). Without this, prisoners' voting rights will greatly depend upon the prevailing political culture and goodwill of the various legislatures. Davidson's paper deals in depth with the 'other realm' of domestic constitutional guarantees and these will be considered briefly below. We will thereafter survey one 'other realm': the realm of international remedies.[35]

Davidson argues that the requirements in ss 7 and 24 of the Australian Constitution requiring MPs and Senators to be 'directly chosen by the people' must be taken to 'require a franchise wide enough to remain consistent with the contemporary meaning of "representative democracy"' (J Davidson nd: 9). By reference to art 25 of the ICCPR, Davidson concludes that the Constitution requires 'universal and equal suffrage among Australian citizens without unreasonable restrictions' (J Davidson nd: 10). Thus, limitations on the franchise which are either based on considerations concerning the ability of a person intelligently to participate in the electoral process or limitations which are 'reasonable' will be constitutional (J Davidson nd: 11). Davidson's view is that s 93(8)(b) of the *Commonwealth Electoral Act* 1918 (Cth) cannot be said to fall within either of these categories of limitations and is therefore 'inconsistent with the Constitutionally-entrenched requirement for representative government and is not a valid law of the Commonwealth' (J Davidson nd: 20).

While Davidson's argument has much to commend it, it is confined to the *Commonwealth Electoral Act* and would not necessarily affect the various disqualifications in State legislation.

Two avenues worth considering on a non-constitutional domestic level might be the use of the *Racial Discrimination Act* 1975 (Cth) (the RDA) to challenge Federal and State/Territory disqualification provisions and the use of the *Human Rights and Equal Opportunity Commission Act* 1986 (Cth) (the HREOC Act) to complain about discretionary restrictions on the franchise.

The RDA is the domestic enactment of the ICERD and prohibits racial distinctions which have the purpose *or effect* of nullifying or impairing certain human rights (s 9 of the RDA and art 5 of ICERD) as well as containing a general prohibition on indirect discrimination (s 9(1A) of the RDA). In the context of over-representation of Aboriginal people in the criminal justice system, it is arguable that the disqualification provisions are contrary to the RDA (Orr 1998: 75ff).

The HREOC Act allows complaints to be made about acts or practices which breach human rights.[36] This does not include complaints being made about the actual terms of a piece of legislation itself

(*Secretary, Department of Defence v HREOC* (1997) 78 FCR 208).[37] The HREOC Act does not render such an act or practice 'unlawful' and the only remedy available is a report that the act or practice breaches human rights and the tabling of this report in Parliament.

Given the difficulties inherent in achieving change through domestic political processes and the uncertainties involved in asserting domestic statutory and constitutional guarantees, it is important to consider any international remedies that may be available to disenfranchised prisoners. The law and practice of international human rights in this context are outlined elsewhere in this book but two main avenues should briefly be noted here.

First, the Human Rights Committee considers periodic reports from State parties on the implementation of the ICCPR and requires them to report on the rules governing the right to vote and the application of the rules. It also requires states to describe any factors which impede the exercise of the right to vote and positive measures taken to overcome these factors (HRC General Comment No 25 1996: para 13). These reports are publicly accessible and open to scrutiny. The Human Rights Committee then publishes its Concluding Observations on those reports. This process provides an avenue for international scrutiny of domestic action. The Human Rights Committee does consider the views of non-governmental organisations in assessing State party reports and in preparing its Concluding Observations.

Secondly, it is important to remember that art 25 of the ICCPR confers individual rights on citizens and that violations of these rights may give rise to claims under the First Optional Protocol to the ICCPR. Australia ratified this protocol in 1991 and it provides individuals with an avenue of petition to the Human Rights Committee when they have exhausted their domestic remedies. The Human Rights Committee notes that a violation of the rights in art 25 would allow for such a claim to be made (HRC General Comment No 25 1996: para 2).

Conclusion

The shape of a political community is determined by the collective will of its members, expressed through the exercise of a free choice and informed and constituted by an ongoing dialogue about the issues that face that community. For a society to be truly democratic, this dialogue must include all of its members and a society might be judged on the extent to which it enables the most isolated of its members to participate in these processes. Restrictions on the franchise for prisoners, from legislative disqualifications to formal and informal barriers to effective participation in political discourse and the voting process, undermine this dialogue and diminish our democracy.

Notes

1   Damaska classifies the adverse effects of conviction as follows: citizenship and political activity; military matters; restrictions on freedom; standing in the community; restrictions on public office, profession and employment/ occupation; participation in the administration of justice; activities independent of employment; and property, contracts, inheritance, family and lawsuits (Damaska 1968).

2   Murphy J made the following comment in his dissenting judgment in *Dugan v Mirror Newspapers Ltd* (1978) 142 CLR 583 (a High Court decision concerning whether the common law principles as to 'civil death' applied so that a person convicted in NSW of a felony could not maintain an action for a civil wrong).

      The main objection to recognizing the civil death principles as existing common law principles is that in treating persons as non-persons, that is, de-humanizing them, the principles violate the fundamental standards of human rights and are inconsistent with the rehabilitative goals of our criminal justice system. As this Court has the choice of accepting or rejecting the principles, I would refuse to recognize the doctrine of civil death as part of the existing common law.' (at 611, per Murphy J)

3   The Joint Standing Committee on Electoral Matters articulated the deterrence value of disenfranchisement thus:

      While rehabilitation is an important aspect of imprisonment, equally important is the concept of deterrence, seeking by the denial of a range of freedoms to provide a disincentive to crime. Those who disregard Commonwealth or State laws to a degree sufficient to warrant imprisonment should not expect to retain the franchise. (Joint Standing Committee on Electoral Matters 1997: para 4.56)

      See similar comments in the dissenting reports submitted by Senator the Hon Sir J Carrick, Hon MJR MacKellar and CW Blunt to the Joint Select Committee on Electoral Reform 1986.

4   The franchise in Australia is generally extended to all citizens over the age of 18 who are not disqualified by reason of unsound mind. British subjects enrolled to vote before 26 January 1984 are also eligible. See *Commonwealth Electoral Act 1918* (Cth) s 93(1)(b).

5   Note, too, that from 1979 until 1995 the *Electoral Act 1979* (NT) gave all Northern Territory prisoners the right to vote in Territory elections.

6   And, prior to 1995, the Commonwealth (Fitzgerald & Zdenkowski 1987: 15ff; submissions by the Australian Electoral Commission to the Joint Standing Committee on Electoral Matters inquiry into the 1993 election (submissions 91 and 141) on the practical difficulties of administering the former regime (held by the Committee Secretariat and the National Library of Australia)). The Victorian Electoral Commission has advised that it is proposed to amend the Victorian provisions to bring them into line with the Commonwealth legislation (telephone conversation with author 30 August 2000).

7   Orr estimates that at least 4952 people and probably closer to 9000 people were disenfranchised from the Commonwealth ballot in mid-1996 (Orr 1998: 74ff). Most electoral commissions were not in a position to provide statistics on disenfranchised prisoners, as they do not hold statistics for persons enrolled to vote prior to their incarceration or the total number of persons disqualified. The New South Wales (NSW) Department of Corrective Services, in a letter to HREOC dated 18 September 2000, provided the following statistics for NSW prisons in the 1998 Federal election: of 6691 inmates, 1880 were not eligible to vote. For the 1999 NSW state election: of 7017 inmates, 3387 were not eligible to vote. As to voting itself, Justice Action's figures based on AEC statistics from the 1996 Federal election suggest that between 2% and 33% of prisoners at various prisons in NSW voted (statistics supplied by AEC dated 26 August 1998, files of Justice Action).

8   The following responses were received: AEC letter dated 17 August 2000; State Electoral Office of NSW letter dated 3 August 2000; Electoral Commission Queensland letter dated 7 August 2000; Victorian Electoral Commission letter dated 6 September 2000 and information provided by telephone on 30 August 2000; State Electoral Office of South Australia letter dated 1 August 2000 and information provided by telephone on 16 October 2000; Western Australia Electoral Commission letter dated 11 August 2000; Northern Territory Electoral Office letter dated 14 August 2000; ACT Electoral Commission letter dated 8 August 2000; Tasmania Electoral Office information provided by telephone on 12 December 2000.

9   The following responses were received: Department of Justice, Office of the Correctional Services Commissioner of Victoria letter dated 10 October 2000; Department for Correctional Services of South Australia information provided by telephone on 27 July 2000; Ministry of Justice, Prison Services of Western Australia letter dated 7 August 2000; Correctional Services, Office of the Commissioner of Northern Territory letter dated August 2000; Department of Corrective Services of NSW letter dated 18 September 2000.

10   For the purposes of this chapter, information was not obtained in relation to prisoners voting in local government elections.

11   This advocacy group has been involved in the campaign for the enfranchisement of all prisoners and in resisting any rollback in the right of prisoners to vote. They were particularly active in resisting the *Electoral and Referendum Amendment Bill (No 2)* 1998 (Cth), which would have denied all prisoners the franchise. They are also active on an ongoing basis in relation to the effective exercise by prisoners of their right to vote.

12   For the 1998 Federal election, mobile polling booths were provided at the Metropolitan Remand and Reception Centre, Bathurst, Cessnock and Goulburn Correctional Centres in NSW (letter from the NSW Department of Corrective Services).

13   Section 184A of the *Commonwealth Electoral Act* 1918 (Cth) provides for electors to apply for registration as a general postal voter and sets out the grounds on which such registration may be made. One of the grounds is where the elector is detained in custody (*Commonwealth Electoral Act* 1918 (Cth) s 184a(2)(d)).

14   For example, see the responses from the NSW State Electoral Office and the NSW Department of Corrective Services. The NSW State Electoral Office sends material for display in NSW prisons which sets out the right of eligible prisoners to vote. The prisons distribute this material to prisoners and also display supplementary

departmental posters, make party 'how to vote' material available, make staff available to assist prisoners in voting and advertise deadlines for postal voting.

15   However these elections are carried out under different legislation and procedures to federal elections (*Aboriginal and Torres Strait Islander Commission Act* 1989 (Cth)). We note that, given the over-representation of Aboriginal people in jails, ATSIC elections are an important aspect of the voting rights of prisoners. Unfortunately space does not permit further specific analysis of ATSIC elections.

16   See also correspondence from Justice Action dated 26 September 1998 summarising complaints that material was not displayed in all prisons (files of Justice Action). Note, however, that while authorities concede that in some cases problems with display of material or postal votes have occurred, they contend that in other cases where complaints have been made investigation has found that problems were rectified or had not occurred (correspondence on files of Justice Action).

17   See also letter from Justice Action dated 18 September 1998 concerning complaints from prisoners that enrolment forms were not received until after close of rolls (files of Justice Action).

18   Information based on interviews with Brett Collins, Kilty O'Gorman and Michael Strutt of Justice Action, 23 October 2000. Apart from its broader campaigns around the franchise, Justice Action's specific strategies to address voting issues in prisons include: provision of information sheets on voting at election times to be distributed within prisons, requests for candidates to visit prisons, requests for collection of adequate statistical data concerning prisoner voting and encouraging prisoners to request how to vote information.

19   Note that the art 25 rights are conferred on 'citizens', not 'persons' (see discussion in Nowak 1993: 445ff).

20   HRC Communication: *Debreczeny v Netherlands*, Communication No 500/1992, UN Doc CCPR/C/53/D/500/1992 at para 9.2 (1995).

21   HRC Communication: *Luciano Weinberger Weisz v Uruguay*, Communication No 28/1978, UN Doc CCPR/C/OP/1 at 57 (1984).

22   The drafting history of art 25 indicates that it was initially proposed that the words 'irrespective of race, colour, national origin, social position, property status, social origin, religion or sex' be inserted in art 25. It was later decided that, to avoid repetition, the reference to the non-discrimination clause in art 2 would be made (Bossuyt 1987: 472). HRC General Comment No 18 (1989) states that art 25 (among other articles) refers specifically to art 2 because of the 'basic and general character' of the non-discrimination principle (para 3). See also the discussion in Nowak 1993: 456ff.

23   HRC Communication: *Luciano Weinberger Weisz v Uruguay*, Communication No 28/1978, UN Doc CCPR/C/OP/1 at para 15 (1984).

24   It is also arguable that the list of 'grounds' in art 2(1) is not exhaustive and that, even if being a prisoner cannot be construed as an 'other status', differentiation on this ground could still fall within art 2(1).

25   The drafting history indicates that the clause 'without unreasonable restrictions' was adopted to refer to matters such as the minimum age for voting or the exclusion of mentally ill persons (Nowak 1993: 473).

26   See the stress laid by the Human Rights Committee on the notion of 'reasonableness' in HRC Communications: *Marshall v Canada*, Communication

No 205/1986, UN Doc CCPR/C/43/D/205/1986 (1991); *Luciano Weinberger Weisz v Uruguay*, Communication No 28/1978, UN Doc CCPR/C/OP/1 (1984).

27 Nowak suggests that 'in view of the practice in most States ... [it is] to be assumed that ... the exclusion of persons who have been finally and conclusively convicted in court of certain crimes are to be deemed reasonable restrictions' (Nowak 1993: 446). He also suggests, however, that restrictions on pre-trial detainees would be unreasonable (Nowak 1993: 446).

28 Note, however, that the Human Rights Committee's interpretation of 'discrimination' is not itself absolute. Thus, for example, General Comment No 18 specifies that not every differentiation of treatment will constitute discrimination if the criteria for such discrimination are reasonable and objective and aim to achieve a legitimate purpose under the ICCPR (HRC General Comment No 18 1989: para 13). It is noted that art 2(1) refers to 'distinctions' and not 'discrimination'. However, it has been argued that art 2(1) is really only referring to unjustified distinctions – ie discrimination (McKean 1983: 146-50). The relationship between the 'discrimination/distinction' and 'unreasonable restrictions' aspects of art 25 is complex and cannot be further pursued here.

29 See also Criminal Law and Penal Methods Reform Committee of South Australia 1973: 129-30, rec 3.22.4(b); Joint Select Committee on Electoral Reform 1986: 33-6, rec 23; Australian Law Reform Commission 1987: 49-54 (see especially the summary of the various arguments for and against abolishing voting restrictions on prisoners at 50-1); Joint Standing Committee on Electoral Matters 1994: 143-4.

30 In South Australia, the legislature did act on the 1973 recommendation of the Criminal Law and Penal Methods Reform Committee of South Australia to abolish voting restrictions in South Australian law. However, the majority of legislative changes have been aimed at minimising inconsistency between the various provisions and facilitating how the provisions work in practice, rather than at repealing the provisions themselves.

31 In relation to political and community debate and the media reaction in Australia to reform efforts, see further Orr 1998: 72ff.

32 Based on the rationale quoted above in note 3, the Committee recommended that s 93(8)(b) of the *Commonwealth Electoral Act* 1918 (Cth) be amended to provide that a person serving a prison sentence for any offence against the law of the Commonwealth, or of a State or Territory, is not entitled to enrol or vote at Federal elections (Joint Standing Committee on Electoral Matters 1997: 48, rec 24).

33 The current disqualification provision in the Queensland, Northern Territory and ACT legislation draws upon the entitlement to be enrolled under the *Commonwealth Electoral Act* 1918 (Cth). Accordingly, changes to the Federal legislation may flow through to these jurisdictions if their legislation remains in its current form.

34 See the suggestion made by Orr, citing Fitzgerald & Zdenkowski 1987: 38-9, and the conclusion that such uniform laws are 'unlikely to be forthcoming' (Orr 1998: 81).

35 These other realms are not, of course, mutually exclusive. In particular, it is clear that developments in international law must be taken into account in the interpretation of domestic law (see for example *Mabo v Queensland (No 2)* (1992) 175 CLR 1 at 42 per Brennan J and discussion in Davidson nd: 9ff). Note further

that the remedies discussed here focus on challenging legislative disqualifications to the franchise and this has been the main focus of reform efforts in the domestic political arena to date. These arguments are equally applicable, however, to challenging policies or administrative arrangements which, in effect, deny or restrict access to the franchise or full participation in the political process.

36   Note that this is generally confined to the acts of the Federal government and there is generally no jurisdiction over State prisoners (ie prisoners sentenced for offences against State or Territory law) (eg *Minogue v Human Rights and Equal Opportunity Commission* (1998) 54 ALD 389). Such prisoners constitute the majority of prisoners in Australia.

37   Note, however, that HREOC can examine a federal 'enactment' and make recommendations for reforms needed for consistency with international human rights undertakings (HREOC Act s 11(1)(e)).

CHAPTER 17

Prisoners as Citizens

David Brown

Introduction

Late in the year 2000, millions of people around the world followed the US Presidential election cliff-hanger. They were introduced to the mysteries of the 'hanging chad' and left wondering at the absence of both a federal electoral agency and a uniform ballot paper and the fact that the electoral processes in the vital State of Florida appeared to be in the partisan hands of a brother of one of the two candidates. They watched aghast as the US Supreme Court in *Bush v Gore* 531 US 98 (2000) demonstrated that its decisions could be read off in advance on straight party political grounds, mocking the actual practice of the separation of powers. Meanwhile, a massive disenfranchisement of potential voters passed largely unnoticed. While the Florida electoral college vote and the entire election hung on a few hundred votes, 436,900 Florida citizens, predominantly black, were denied the vote because of a prior conviction for a felony.

Figures provided by The Sentencing Project, an independent private research organisation promoting criminal justice policy analysis, indicate that 46 US States currently prohibit inmates from voting while serving felony sentences, 32 prohibit felons from voting while on parole, 14 disenfranchise all ex-offenders who have completed their sentences and ten of these disenfranchise ex-felons for life (Human Rights Watch 1998). Disenfranchisement occurs even when the offender was convicted of a relatively minor crime or was not imprisoned.

The impact of the disenfranchisement of prisoners is staggering. The Sentencing Project estimates that 3.9 million Americans, one in every 50 adults, have currently or permanently lost their voting rights as a result of felony convictions. This includes 1.4 million people who have completed their sentences (Human Rights Watch 1998).

Nationally, 1.4 million African American men, or 13% of the male African American population, are disenfranchised, a rate seven times the national average. The Sentencing Project further estimates that at current rates of incarceration, three in ten of the next generation of African American men can expect to be disenfranchised at some point in their lifetime and that, in States that disenfranchise ex-offenders, around 40% of African American men may permanently lose their right to vote. Florida, the State in the eye of the electoral storm, is one of the States which disenfranchises ex-offenders and there 31% of African American men are disenfranchised. The figure is the same in Alabama, 29% in Mississippi and 25% in Virginia, indicating the racially based gerrymander that flows from these policies.

There is a strong argument that to deny prisoners the vote is a feudal hangover, a form of 'civil death' entirely out of place in a modern democracy. To deny the right to vote to ex-offenders is a permanent denial of citizenship, offensive to democratic principles, religious notions of redemption and secular notions of rehabilitation alike. The franchise is a fundamental cornerstone of democratic systems of government. Article 25 of the *International Covenant on Civil and Political Rights* (ICCPR) provides that 'every citizen shall have the right and opportunity ... without unreasonable restrictions ... to vote ... at genuine periodic elections which shall be by universal and equal suffrage'.

Australia, while avoiding the US excesses of disenfranchising ex-prisoners, does not comply with art 25, quite apart from our lack of commitment to one vote one value (Brooks 1993). Under Commonwealth law, prisoners serving sentences of five years or more are disenfranchised. State provisions vary: Queensland, Victoria, the Northern Territory and the ACT follow the Commonwealth position. New South Wales (NSW) and Western Australia deny the vote to anyone serving a sentence of one year or more. In South Australia, all prisoners are entitled to vote and in Tasmania, none. In practice, there are all sorts of problems for those prisoners entitled to vote in actually exercising that right, in getting access to the ballot box (see generally ch 16, this volume and Orr 1998).

Attempts by the writer to interest Australian newspapers in the issue of the disenfranchisement of felons in the United States, even with the newsworthy 'hook' of the outcome of the US presidential election hanging in the balance, were entirely unsuccessful; indeed of insufficient interest even to warrant the courtesies of replying to emails or bothering to communicate a rejection. Approaches to usually sympathetic individual journalists were fruitless. A similar lack of interest was evident in 1998 when the Howard Government attempted in the Electoral and Referendum Amendment Bill (No 2) 1998 to deny all prisoners the right to vote. The attempt was defeated in the Senate by the combined votes of the ALP, Democrats, Greens and Senators Harradine and Colston.

Why is it that there is so little interest in even discussing, let alone remedying, the denial of a fundamental right in modern democracies, the franchise, to prisoners and ex-prisoners? A cryptic answer might be that provided in the title of Bruno Latour's *We Have Never Been Modern* (Latour 1993). Indeed, feudal remnants such as the notion of 'civil death' and a variety of practices it spawned are clearly evident in relation to prisoners. In addition to the current Australian government's attempt to remove the franchise altogether for serving prisoners in Federal elections, there are common State practices such as the denial of the right to serve on juries to ex-prisoners and more recent additions such as the 1996 NSW statutory provision (*Victims Support and Rehabilitation Act* 1996 (NSW) s 24(4)) by which 'convicted inmates' were made ineligible to receive victims' compensation for 'an act of violence if it occurred while the person was imprisoned', despite the fact that the incidence of assault in prisons is much higher than in the general community. What this last example shows is that the issue is not just the persistence of feudal remnants but their constant refreshment.

Going backwards: From Kable to Dugan

Indeed, the doctrine of 'civil death' throws up examples which illustrate not just 'uneven development' or 'remnants', in short the notion of a stubborn persistence of the pre-modern, but of its overt resurrection in the common law of democratic states in conditions of late modernity. The saga of Susannah and Henry Kable in the late 18th century stands in counterpoint to the Australian High Court decision in *Dugan v Mirror Newspapers* (1978) 142 CLR 583; (1978) 53 ALJR 166.

In the opening pages of his *The Rule of Law in a Penal Colony: Law and power in early New South Wales*, David Neal traces the engaging story of first fleet convicts, Susannah Holmes and Henry Kable (Neal 1991). Susannah and Henry met in Norwich Castle jail after both had been sentenced to death for (separate) housebreaking. Both had their capital sentences commuted to that of transportation to America after the judge petitioned the king, in the manner described so richly by Douglas Hay in his famous essay in *Albion's Fatal Tree* (Hay 1975). In the more crowded and less segregated atmosphere of late 18th century prisons, Susannah and Henry's acquaintance led to a liaison and thence to the birth of a son in 1786. They applied for permission to marry in jail but it was denied. Meanwhile, transportation to America ceased with the American revolt and in 1786, the year of the birth, a fleet of ships was prepared to transport 750 convicts to Botany Bay in the colony of NSW on the east coast of Australia, where Cook had landed some 16 years earlier.

The fleet was short of women prisoners and Susannah and child, along with other women convicts from Norwich jail, were transferred to the hulk Dunkirk at Plymouth on 5 November 1786. But the captain of the hulk refused to accept the baby on board and the baby was left in the hands of the Norwich jailer, a Mr Simpson, who had accompanied the women prisoners. Simpson was evidently a humane fellow and one of some determination and resourcefulness. He travelled with the baby to London and laid in wait outside the home of Lord Sydney, the Home Secretary, accosting the peer as he left his abode and pleading the case not only for the reunion of mother and child but of father as well. Lord Sydney agreed and Henry Kable was in turn transferred from Norwich and, after ten days' separation, the family was reunited. Somehow, this heart-rending story attracted the attentions of the press and much was made of 'John Simpson, the humane turnkey' and of the alacrity with which Lord Sydney attended to the 'happiness of even the meanest subject in the kingdom' (Neal 1991: 5). Such stories touched a philanthropic nerve and Lady Cadogan organised a public subscription which yielded 20 pounds which, as Neal points out, was 'twice the annual salary of a labourer at that time, and four times the value of the goods Susannah had stolen – enough money to buy clothes and other items for their new life in New South Wales' (Neal 1991: 5).

The voyage took eight months, the ships arriving in Sydney Harbour in January 1788. Susannah and Henry were married in February in one of the first marriage ceremonies in the new colony. However, the parcel of goods bought with the subscription money and loaded in Plymouth seemed to have disappeared on route. So on the first of July 1788:

> [A] writ in the names of Henry and Susannah Kable was issued from the new Court of Civil Jurisdiction in New South Wales. The writ recited that the parcel loaded on to the Alexander had not been delivered to the Kables in Sydney despite many requests, and sought delivery of the parcel or its value. It named the ship's captain, Duncan Sinclair, as defendant (Neal 1991: 5).

In what was the first civil case ever heard under English law in the Australian colonies, a verdict was entered for the plaintiff in the sum of 15 pounds. Henry Kable became a constable and then chief constable in the new colony before moving on to become a merchant and ship owner. As Neal notes, this case was extraordinary in many ways. Not least of these was that having been convicted of a capital felony, Susannah and Henry were clearly covered by the common law doctrine of civil death, suffering 'attainder' and 'corruption of the blood', which would have prevented them from bringing a civil action in England. Neal notes that at first they were described in the writ as 'New Settlers of this place' but this had been crossed out and nothing substituted. He notes that:

the fact that Henry and Susannah were convicts and the legal consequences of that fact must have been obvious to some of those concerned; maybe the description 'New settlers' was too close to a fabrication, and hence this part of the writ was altered to maintain a discreet silence. (Neal 1991: 6)

Staples puts the point more forcefully, asking:

how was it that Sir Garfield Barwick's 'fundamental' relationship between a felon and a free man was breached in the full view of the whole colony and in a court constituted by the deliberate direction of Governor Arthur Phillip to try the grievance of two felons in his charge. Their status could not have escaped the notice of a single person in the settlement. They went before educated men. How was it that Sinclair at least whose mind was surely attuned to this minor crisis was not advised of or did not take the point which would have saved him in the High Court of Australia in 1978, one hundred and ninety years later?

The answer may perhaps lie in this: the rule, if its suggestion was known, was regarded by the mass of Englishmen as unjust, even absurd, inappropriate in the conditions of the colony and in any event totally inconsistent with the practice of the authorities in permitting the transportees to equip themselves to some degree with property to sustain themselves in their new place of confinement. Thus the community repudiated the rule at the outset (Staples 1981: 31).

Staples' reference to the High Court 190 years later is a reference to *Dugan v Mirror Newspapers* ((1978) 53 ALJR 166) in which the doctrine of civil death was held to apply in NSW in the late 1970s to prevent convicted capital felon Darcy Dugan suing for defamation. The trial judge, the NSW Court of Appeal and the High Court by six to one all

upheld the applicability of the doctrine of civil death in NSW in 1978.
Barwick CJ said:

> If the Court decides that the common law in England, properly
> understood, did deny a prisoner in the situation of the applicant the
> right to sue during the currency of the sentence and that law was
> introduced into and became part of the law of the colony, there is no
> authority in the Court to change that law as inappropriate in the
> opinion of the Court to more recent times during which capital felony
> remained ... I can see no basis on which it could be said that a law
> which in its time was fundamental to the relationship to the
> community of those convicted of capital felony was not suitable to the
> community of the colony, both at its inception and in 1828. (*Dugan v
> Mirror Newspapers Ltd* (1978) 53 ALJR 166 at 167 per Barwick CJ)

Murphy J, the sole dissentient, described the doctrine of civil death
as 'anachronistic' (*Dugan v Mirror Newspapers Ltd* (1978) 53 ALJR 166
at 176).

The main objection to recognizing the civil death principles as existing
common law principles is that in treating persons as non-persons, that
is, dehumanising them, the principles violate the fundamental
standards of human rights and are inconsistent with the rehabilitative
goals of our criminal justice system. (*Dugan v Mirror Newspapers Ltd*
(1978) 53 ALJR 166 at 177 per Murphy J)

The NSW legislature partially overturned the doctrine in 1981 by
passing the *Felons (Civil Proceedings) Act* 1981 (NSW) (Zdenkowski
1981; Zdenkowski & Brown 1982).

David Neal uses the Kables' story to reflect on the 'rule of law'
debate, revisiting Edward Thompson's famous conclusion to *Whigs
and Hunters* (EP Thompson 1975: 258-69). Neal identifies the key
elements of the rule of law as 'general rules laid down in advance,
rational argument from those principles to particular cases and, at
least in a developed form, a legal system independent of the executive
for adjudication of disputes involving the general rules' (Neal 1991:
67). Echoing Thompson's view that 'the rule of law itself, the
imposing of effective inhibitions upon power and the defence of the
citizen from power's all-intrusive claims, seems to me an unqualified
human good' (EP Thompson 1975: 266), Neal argues that 'the rule of
law tradition gained a foothold' with the Kables' case.

> The case meant that exercise of power in the penal colony would be
> open to scrutiny against a legal standard, not the standards of prison
> discipline or martial law, or the arbitrary standard of the governor.
> This did not mean that power would always be exercised lawfully;

power was used brutally and illegally by convicts against one another, by settlers against Aborigines, by police against Aborigines, by masters against assigned convicts, by magistrates against suspects and so on. The point is that the rule of law offered a check against 'power's all-intrusive claims'. While the foothold was small, the guarantees against abuse were also small. But people in the colony soon saw the possibilities for exercising and augmenting their power over one another in a legitimate way: through the courts. (Neal 1991: 190)[1]

However such 'footholds' can be covered over in the sands of time, as the *Dugan* case shows. The doctrine of 'civil death', 'repudiated' according to Staples in *Kable* in the context of the fledgling NSW penal colony, is declared 'fundamental to the relationship to the community of those convicted of capital felony' in 1788 (*Dugan v Mirror Newspapers Ltd* (1978) 53 ALJR 166 at 167 per Barwick CJ) and still in operation in 1978 by Barwick CJ of the Australian High Court. Once again it is tempting to see in the shift between *Kable* and *Dugan* the lingering effect of the 'convict taint' and the 'criminal class', immanent feudal relics waiting to burst forth in suitable modernist conditions. But conceptions of immanence tend to obscure the extent to which various ideologies and practices of exclusion are historically specific and variable, as shown by the formal re-institution in 1820 in NSW of the common law of attaint, as discussed in ch 6 in this volume and by Kercher (Kercher 1995). Such exclusionary practices are not only rediscovered but also refashioned and recreated, clothed in a popular legitimacy: a legitimacy stitched up in contemporary sentiments of desert, forfeiture, impurity and exclusion, evident especially in the United States in popular support for the death penalty, mandatory sentencing regimes and a politics of highly racially inflected mass incarceration.

'Convict taint' and the campaign for trial by jury in NSW

David Neal notes that Susannah and Henry Kable went on to have 11 children in all. By 1840, 52 years after their arrival in the first fleet, 'those of Henry and Susannah's progeny who owned a house worth more than 200 pounds and were male were eligible to sit on juries and vote for the first representative assemblies'. Indeed, 'Henry himself could have served as a juror, voted or even stood for the new Legislative Council' (Neal 1991: 189). But the 'taint' of Henry's convict origins did not just dissipate naturally in the new penal colony nor was it simply ignored as the doctrine of civil death had been in the first civil case in 1788.

While most contemporary debate about the jury system is conducted in the language of its practicality, rationality, expertise, economy or efficiency as a legal institution, its heritage in England and in the infant NSW penal colony can only be understood in terms of politics and the organisation of power. For as Neal points out:

> The jury issue provided the arena of conflict for rival theories of citizenship. The jury issue, with its powerful rhetoric about the Magna Carta and the rights of British subjects, translated from an issue of direct power via the jury box into a symbolic one which did serve to qualify the Emancipists for their share of political authority in the colony. (Neal 1991: 187)

The struggle for trial by jury was played out between the first governors, the English government and the Colonial Office, and the Emancipist (ex-convict) and Exclusivist (free settler) factions (Neal 1991: 167-87). The penal colony's early courts consisted of panels of military officers and the assessors of the Civil Courts. These were partial to the military. The Magistracy proved to be the initial base for the Exclusivists. In the absence of a parliament, the courts were a major political forum.

> The undemocratic state of New South Wales, together with the vexed question of the emancipists' civil status, heightened the political significance of the jury issue in the penal colony. Property qualifications – applicable to both jury service and the right to vote – could be relied upon as a measure of civic virtue in England. That was not true in New South Wales – at least according to the Exclusives – because many emancipists easily satisfied the property qualification. The Exclusives would have to rely on the convict taint as a mark of disqualification. The jury issue became a crucial test of status, especially as the prospect of a colonial legislature came closer ... Competence to serve on juries meant competence to vote for and to be a member of the representative political institutions which would eventually be granted to the colony (Neal 1991: 169-70).

The centrality of the trial by jury issue can be seen from the fact that it 'stood at the head of the Emancipists' first-ever petition to the king' in 1819. By 1833, trial by jury was extended to all criminal cases and in 1839 the option of trial by military panel was abolished. 'The convict taint would not operate to disqualify emancipists from the political franchise' (Neal 1991: 186).

Contemporary jury service and the persistence of 'convict taint'

While the colonial emancipists gained the right to sit on juries, that right and mark of citizenship is not available in an unqualified form to current ex-prisoners. The Australian States vary somewhat but NSW is typical in the disqualifications found in Schedule 1 to the *Jury Act* 1977 (NSW). These include those who at any time within the last ten years have served a sentence of imprisonment, within the past three years have been detained in a detention centre or who are currently bound by an order of the court (*Jury Act* 1977 (NSW) Sch 2, s 6(b)). Admittedly, these disqualifications lapse in time but only the last, currently bound by an order of the court, manifests an absence of the lingering traces of 'convict taint'.

In a recent case in which the High Court finally declared the pernicious practice of jury vetting as carried out in Victoria over many years illegal, a majority of the judges seemed little concerned that the process of jury vetting operated, by the back door, to exclude those with prior criminal convictions from jury service well beyond the existing statutory exclusions.

In *Katsuno*, on the basis of a list provided by the Chief Commissioner of Police, a peremptory challenge was exercised by the Crown to exclude a potential juror with non-disqualifying prior convictions for minor offences 25 and 20 years earlier (*Katsuno v The Queen* (1999) 73 ALJR 1458). The High Court was unanimous in finding that the provision of information by the Chief Commissioner of Police to the Director of Public Prosecutions (DPP) was impliedly prohibited by ss 21(3) and 67(b) of the *Juries Act* 1967 (Vic). Despite the finding of illegality, a majority (Gleeson CJ, Gaudron, Gummow and Callinan JJ) went on to hold that the use of the information by the DPP, obtained in contravention of the *Juries Act*, in making peremptory challenges did not constitute a failure to observe the requirements of the criminal process in a fundamental respect and dismissed the appeal. '[O]nce it is accepted that a peremptory challenge may be made for any reason, whether good or bad, it follows that the challenge made to the potential juror in this case cannot be viewed as a defect in the criminal process' (at 1467) and the breaches of the *Juries Act* were held not to cause a miscarriage of justice. The breaches of the Act 'took place at a point anterior to the actual selection of the jury and did not deny the accused his constitutional right to trial by jury' (*Katsuno v The Queen* (1999) 73 ALJR 1458 at 1469 per Gaudron, Gummow and Callinan JJ).

McHugh J and Kirby J entered strong dissents. Kirby J pointed out that the effect of the arrangement between the Chief Commissioner and the Crown was an 'enlargement of the categories of disqualification beyond those which Parliament has created' (*Katsuno v The Queen* (1999) 73 ALJR 1458 at 1483 per Kirby J). The first offence of the excluded juror occurred when he was a juvenile, had no current effectiveness and could not be treated as a conviction by law, yet it was treated as relevant to the juror's suitability to serve on a jury. The second occurred more than 20 years previously and was not a formal conviction in that sentence was suspended. Kirby J pointed out that:

> Upon the basis of the returns of the Sheriff illustrated by this case, approximately 8 per cent of the citizens eligible for jury service had some form of past conviction. If, whatever the exact detail of the matter (the seriousness of the conviction, its antiquity and irrelevance), persons are to be effectively removed from jury service on the basis of the bald statement contained in the Chief Commissioner's list – even when considered with the associated documentation – it is for Parliament to enlarge the disqualifications. It may not be done by the back door arrangement between police and prosecutors extraneous to the Act. (*Katsuno v The Queen* (1999) 73 ALJR 1458 at 1483 per Kirby J)

The majority judgments illustrate both a lack of concern with the importance of jury service as a mark of citizenship and the continued pertinence of notions of 'convict taint'.

Citizenship and exclusion

The stories told thus far contain mixed messages about citizenship, 'convict taint' and 'civil death'. Susannah and Henry Kable managed to avoid the Norwich gallows after conviction for capital felony, were transported *en famille* to Australia and, upon arrival, successfully prosecuted the first civil case in the NSW penal colony unhindered by the operation of the civil death doctrine. Henry and his male children lived to enjoy the full rights of citizenship, including the right to sit on juries and to vote, and prospered financially, although the *Elections Act* 1893 (NSW), in another reversal of the sort (see ch 6 in this volume), excluded a large group of convicted prisoners from the then-universal male franchise.

Note the gender exclusion here in relation to Susannah, an exclusion achieved not through convict taint but through being a woman and the requirement of property qualifications for full rights of citizenship. It would be well over a century after Susannah's arrival before her female descendants would be entitled to vote. Here is the far from universal underside of the historical development of categories of citizenship, which for many years to come in NSW and throughout Australia excluded Indigenous people completely and women partly from full citizenship, to say nothing about the racially based exclusions from citizenship of 'aliens' in the form of the White Australia Policy lasting until the mid-20th century. In relation to juries, a property qualification in the form of compilation of jury rolls from lists of ratepayers persisted in NSW until 1947 and it was only after the passage of the *Jury Act* in 1977 that women came en masse onto juries in that State.

In 1978, Darcy Dugan was unsuccessful in his civil action for defamation after the High Court decided by six to one that the doctrine of civil death for capital felonies had been received into NSW, had never been expressly repealed and that therefore Mr Dugan was civilly dead and had no right to sue at common law. Prisoners in NSW can only vote if they are serving sentences under 12 months and ex-prisoners cannot serve on juries for a period of ten years after release. Prisoners cannot, subject to limited exceptions, claim criminal injuries compensation for injuries sustained in assaults upon them while in prison. In 1999 in *Katsuno* a majority of the High Court did not seem to think it objectionable that a person was excluded from jury duty on the basis of non-disqualifying convictions as a juvenile over two decades earlier (*Katsuno v The Queen* (1999) 73 ALJR 1458 at 1458). And, as noted in the introduction, in the United States millions of ex-prisoners, or 'ex-felons' to use the formal antiquated terminology, are denied the vote to little apparent consternation.

Citizenship is central to some of 'our' most foundational colonial struggles 'from penal colony to free society' yet, as shown in the small number of examples discussed, it is far from universal and is replete with exclusions. Exclusions which at least in relation to prisoners are not withering away in the long march of enlightenment civilisation, as a Whig history would have it, but in some instances are being revived and resurrected, given new and brutalist forms. But in relation to prisoners, exactly how important are notions of citizenship? Is it a useful conceptual vehicle for the promotion of prisoners' rights and for the promotion of improvements in the conditions of imprisonment?

Citizenship, lawbreaking and punishment

Citizenship is usually defined formally as a membership or group status, the group being variably defined as a political community, nation state or civil society. The key components of citizenship are rights, duties, participation and identity and the various theories of citizenship tend to place emphasis on certain of these components at the expense of others. The theories or models of citizenship can be roughly divided into two main tendencies: liberal and republican/communitarian. Liberal theories of citizenship tend to emphasise rights, duties and responsibilities (rights in the more left-wing versions of liberalism; duties and responsibilities in the more conservative liberalism). Republican and communitarian traditions tend to emphasise participation, particularly participation in civil society. Identity is central to some communitarian traditions and also to nationalist conceptions of citizenship. Radical democratic theories provide not so much a theory of citizenship as a critique of liberal and communitarian positions, emphasising what Delahunty describes as 'the politics of voice, difference and justice' (Delahunty 2000: 46; see also Marshall 1992; Faulks 2000; Isin & Wood 1999).

Many of the commentaries on and discussion of theories of citizenship seek to identify the differences between liberal, communitarian, republican, democratic and other approaches. But what is perhaps of more interest for a discussion of prisoners and citizenship is their commonalities. Most, if not all, theories and models of citizenship emphasise principles of equality, freedom, participation, identity and so on, frequently according a different meaning or emphasis to these terms. But theories of citizenship typically fail to provide an explicit account of how citizenship, membership of a political or civic community, is acquired and lost. In this respect, they tend to presuppose membership and the boundaries or limits of the relevant community and then go on to describe the content of citizenship – what membership entails or should entail. This question of boundaries or limits – of admission to and exclusion from citizenship – would seem to be the central one when it comes to considering punishment.

In 1994, an ANOP Opinion Poll on Community Knowledge and Understanding of the Constitution, Citizenship and Civics was conducted as part of a Civics Expert Group Report to the Keating Labor Government (Civics Expert Group 1994). In response to the question 'What is a good citizen/what sort of things does a good citizen do?', the three leading answers were: 'Obey laws (62%); 'Show care and consideration for others' (38%); and 'Be involved in community activities' (30%) (Civics Expert Group 1994: 156). That by far the most common answer to the question about what is a good citizen focussed on obedience to law raises the question of how the relationship between citizenship, law-breaking and punishment is popularly viewed and understood. If, in the view of many, 'good citizens' are those who obey the law, this suggests a public ambivalence about the citizenship status of those who break the law.

One of the leading writers on citizenship, TH Marshall, emphasised equality and the need for the social democratic state to promote an equality of opportunity undermined by the market in a class based society. 'Citizenship is a status bestowed on those who are full members of a community. All who possess the status are equal with respect to the rights and duties with which the status is endowed' (Marshall 1992: 8). This begs the question who are 'full members' of the community and, more specifically, whether prisoners are 'full members'. Popular opinion as reflected in the ANOP survey suggests that 'full membership' of a community may be viewed as linked to and even dependent upon obedience to the law. This view gives rise to arguments that, by virtue of the offence committed, the individual who has been convicted and imprisoned thereby forfeits any claim to citizenship and to be the bearer of rights.

The most extreme version of this argument is apparent in the death penalty, where the forfeit is not only of citizenship but of the very right to exist. Less extreme versions involve the loss or forfeit of particular rights or incidents of citizenship, such as the franchise or the right to be a legal subject in general or for particular purposes. At a lower level and in relation to the more concrete and specific issues associated with prison conditions, which tend to be seen as more important than the symbolic issues by prisoners themselves, the key arguments are those of the 'they deserve nothing', 'they are being pampered in motel conditions while their victims suffer' sort. These are essentially contemporary tabloid media versions of Jeremy Bentham's 'principle of lesser eligibility' whereby prisoners should always be held in conditions worse than those of the honest, non-criminal poor.

The 'forfeit' argument is evident in the notion of civil death and has its roots in an amalgam of retributivist desert, conceptions of impurity, taint and pollution, the visceral attractions of revenge and the desire to exclude and render 'other'. An increased emphasis on the 'duties and responsibilities' part of the rights, duties and responsibilities criteria, stressed in various neo-liberal variants of conservative liberalism, have perhaps given some succour to the 'forfeiters'. As perhaps has some of the conservative communitarians' emphasis on community, religion, family and nation, an appeal to an organic consensus open to populist, nationalist and ethnic based excesses. Setting the extreme versions of exclusion and denial of full membership of a community and hence of citizenship aside, the more prevalent position is what Vaughan calls 'conditional citizenship' (Vaughan 2000: 26). By this he means that prisoners are more typically 'partial citizens', neither enjoying full citizenship nor entirely outside it. Punishment:

> is used on those who are conditional citizens, people who may be moulded into full citizens but who are, at present, failing to display the requisite qualities expected of citizens. This is one of the great animating impulses behind modern punishment, the desire to convert people into proper citizens rather than excluding them as with transportation, or making a spectacle of them, as with capital punishment. Yet for punishment to be meaningful, it must entail that some rights and privileges are forgone; the process of inclusion cannot be total. (Vaughan 2000: 26)

Vaughan's view that some rights and privileges must be forgone for punishment to be meaningful would be challenged by prisoners' advocates, those who see citizenship in universal forms and many who cite the oft-quoted liberal doctrine that 'people are sent to prison *as* punishment, not *for* punishment'. On this view, the only qualified as against absolute rights would be those that are necessarily qualified as a consequence of the irreducible conditions of imprisonment, such as the freedom of movement. Yet clearly in practice the 'pains of imprisonment' involve far more than merely restrictions on freedom of movement, as the whole history of the origins and development of the prison, the sociology of imprisonment and penology show. As David Garland and Peter Young have argued:

> Individual penal sanctions condense a number of different relations and it is necessary to acknowledge this, if an analysis capable of supporting political action is desired. An offender who is sentenced to imprisonment becomes the object of a relation of force (resistance will be met with physical coercion and violence 'if necessary'), which is at one and the same time legal (it is an authoritative order of the court, the prison is a legally authorised place of detention, its officers have legal powers at their disposal, the law specifies that prisoners shall not have the rights and capacities available to other citizens, etc.); political (the basis and limits of that authority and that force are ultimately political, as is the definition and enforcement of the criminal law; the form of the sanction is politically conditioned, etc.); ideological (the

prison carries specific symbolic connotations which mark the prisoner, his act and his family; prison architecture and practices carry particular signifiers – isolation, work, reward, discipline, obedience, etc.); and economic (the prisoner will be made to labour, his family will be financially disadvantaged, his work record and national insurance contributions will be interrupted, he will have difficulty regaining employment, the 'free' labour-market will be deprived of his labour, he will be deskilled, etc.). Of course, if the offender happens to be female, she will be subjected to a number of differential practices (as indeed will male 'sex offenders'), indicating the pertinence of sexual relations in this realm … Clearly then the penal sanction of imprisonment is a complex condensation of a whole series of relations. (Garland & Young 1983: 22-3)

The complex and condensed nature of these various relations does not, except at the most formal legal level, translate into a simple status of citizen or non-citizen. Vaughan's characterisation of prisoners as 'partial' or 'conditional' citizens is arguably a much more accurate rendering of their situation than the either/or of universal citizen/ non-citizen 'outlaw'. The notion of 'partial' citizen also has the advantage of calling attention to the fluid and unfinished nature of the prisoner's status and ability to participate in public discourse as a fully fledged democratic subject; a subject in the process of becoming.

Certain forms of punishment, such as exile and transportation, were consciously intended to temporarily or permanently expunge citizenship. This was the punishment. The position of imprisonment in modern societies is more ambivalent. Many of the chapters in this collection have illustrated the 'conditional' or 'partial' nature of current prisoners' claims to full citizenship. The discussion above of limitations on prisoner suffrage, right to serve on juries and ability to be a full legal subject, indicates the continued pertinence of notions of convict 'taint' or 'stain'.

Conclusion

We are left then with somewhat of a paradox in relation to the issue of prisoners as citizens. However desirable in a utopian sense, the current prospect of prisoners enjoying full or universal citizenship is unlikely. Not only because it would be politically preposterous to conservatives and populists who demand that some form of 'forfeit' attach to conviction, what Pratt calls 'emotive and ostentatious punishment' (Pratt 2000: 417), ranging from the extreme of capital punishment through to the more mundane subterranean forms of disqualification and denial. But also because forms of modernist penality and notions of rehabilitation are premised on the idea of personal improvement, to be achieved through calculated regimes of graded and partial citizenship within which incentives and rewards can operate, especially under the tutelage of neo-liberal notions of responsibilisation and offender contractualism. Universal or 'full' citizenship of prisoners is also unlikely because, whatever a formal legal status might imply, sociologically and in reality, the complex and condensed relations involved in imprisonment do not simply play upon or constitute a unitary legal subject, the citizen-prisoner.

As a political aim, partial or conditional citizenship should be rendered fuller and more complete. In that push, the emphasis should be placed not on the formal legal status of prisoners or on a particular unitary identity of prisoners but on the necessary conditions under which prisoners might participate fully in a democratic citizenship. Such participation includes the ability to challenge the legal processes that led to their imprisonment and to call attention to and reflect upon the social and economic conditions in which their offending and criminalisation occurred. That reflexivity needs also to encompass the various strategies – institutional, cultural and personal – of denial and neutralisation of often patently anti-social and damaging behaviour, hyper-masculinity and cultures of violence and predatory assault and sexual assault which sometimes led to imprisonment and which are reproduced and amplified under current prison conditions.

The conditions under which prisoners can participate in a democratic citizenship lie in a discursive citizenship, an ability to participate in the public realm. Such participation is premised on acts and a language of recognition, the articulation of a voice and access to public means of communication of those voices. The voices should be plural precisely because, as many feminists point out, imprisonment is far from all of a piece. Its histories, meanings and experiences differ on racial, gender and other fault lines; Indigenous prisoners, women prisoners and other specific groups such as non-English speaking prisoners and those with disabilities have specific interests and voices which are not helpfully essentialised into a unity, particularly as often represented by white, masculine-dominated vanguardist organis- ations (see Zdenkowski & Brown 1982: 355-64; Brown 1998; and, on the particularities of Australian penality for Indigenous people, Finnane & McGuire 2001 and Hogg 2001).

Russell Hogg and I have argued previously against seeing prisoners as inhabiting a fixed location, defined largely by their relation to the means and forces of production (Brown & Hogg 1985), an approach that characterises prisoners as therefore essentially 'unproductive' (Mathiesen 1974: 173-7). Mathiesen and others use this economic criterion to postulate an essential if not yet realised unity between workers and prisoners. Along with Laclau and Mouffe (1985: 181), we argue that there are multiple ways of constituting subject positions in attempting to create a proliferation of new and different political spaces in a series of constantly shifting alliances with various social movements (Brown & Hogg 1985: 63-8). As other chapters in this volume have illustrated, the point of entry, connection or concern with prison issues arises from a plurality of positions and identities. These include the specific and differential meanings, experiences and problems of Indigenous prisoners, women prisoners, those suffering from intellectual or physical disabilities, drug-addicted prisoners, prisoners with specific health needs, transgender prisoners, non-English speaking prisoners, prisoners subject to forms of administrative segregation, prisoners who lack basic levels of literacy, prisoners in private prisons and so on. The social movements, community support groups, government and non-government organisations and families which take up prison related issues are fluctuating, multi-vocal and diverse.

To be able to voice these diverse concerns, to participate in a 'discursive citizenship' in the public realm, prisoners must be secured under regimes which are healthy, not conducive to or tolerant of violence; conditions which promote contact with family and friends and the various associations of civil society; conditions which promote the maximum ability to participate in public discourse through access to all forms of media, including the internet; conditions which encourage participation in meaningful literacy, education, work skills and other programs; and conditions which do not permit the isolation and segregation of prisoners for the purposes of punishment or convenience, except on justifiable grounds which can be tested against clearly articulated legal standards.

The extent to which claims of citizenship advance these conditions is a moot point. Claims of citizenship can lead to the assertion of false unities, obscuring significant differences between different groups in terms of the conditions of criminalisation and the histories and experiences of imprisonment. More significantly, citizenship is often asserted in universalist forms which bear little relation to the denied and contested nature of key elements of citizenship; as we have seen in relation to prisoners for example, with reference to the vote, legal subjectivity and ability to sit on juries. As argued above, theories of citizenship are strong on affirmations of equality, freedom and participation but weak in that they fail to provide an explicit and concrete account of how citizenship (membership of a political or civic community) is acquired and lost. This failure is particularly acute in relation to prisoners, leaving much citizenship theory sounding abstract and rhetorical, disconnected from popular and political discourse where the 'forfeit' argument plays strongly to disqualify or disentitle prisoners from full citizenship.

If there is any advantage to claims of citizenship over claims of rights, it might lie paradoxically in their indeterminate and incomplete nature. At a popular level, claims of rights are readily comprehended but also easily characterised as claims of particularistic self-interest. A democratic citizenship is less a place, a status, a possession or a demand, and more a process: a process through which participation in a public discourse takes place; a process through which identities are recognised, equalities asserted, differences acknowledged and voices communicated and heard.

Note

1   For a range of assessments of Thompson's and Neal's arguments, see Zdenkowski & Brown 1982; Merritt 1980; P Anderson 1980: 197-207; Fine 1984: 169-89; Hirst 1980; A Davidson 1991; Byrne 1993.

APPENDIX

Correctional authorities' responses to prisoners' submissions

With the approval of correctional authorities in all States, with the exception of New South Wales (NSW),[1] and in the Northern Territory, brochures were distributed to prisons inviting prisoners to make submissions to this project for selective extraction in this book. They were invited particularly to respond to questions about health care, the use of segregation and the right to vote.

Prisoners in four States raised issues that caused such concern to Human Rights and Equal Opportunity Commission that they were drawn, anonymously, to the attention of the correctional authorities for a response.

The authorities in NSW confirmed that Lithgow prisoners are locked down every second Monday so that staff can participate in training.

The Victorian authorities confirmed prisoners' accounts of detention in police lock-ups upon sentencing and explained that, with the prison system operating at around 116% capacity, delays in transferring sentenced prisoners from lock-ups to prisons are inevitable, especially as Victoria prioritises the transfer of more vulnerable prisoners, whether remanded or sentenced, to prisoners where protection and appropriate programs and services can be provided. As in Western Australia (WA), where overcrowding is also an endemic problem, Victoria plans to open new prisons in the near future.

The Victorian authorities also detailed the health care arrangements in the State's two private prisons — Fulham and Port Phillip — and the range of complaint mechanisms available to prisoners.

The WA authorities described measures taken to ameliorate the sterility of crisis observation units for prisoners to be judged at risk of suicide.

The Queensland authorities explained that assessed risk to the community is a principal reason some prisoners are unable to participate in staged release programs such as day release, home leave and work release in advance of release.

Prisoners in all four States were critical of sex offender treatment programs on three principal grounds.

1. A pre-requisite for participation is an admission of guilt.
2. Some programs are not 'recognised' and some prisons do not offer programs.
3. Successful completion is a necessary criterion for release on parole.

All four States confirmed prisoners' accounts to some extent. With respect to the first criticism — levelled especially by prisoners who maintain their innocence — the following explanations were provided:

*   In Victoria, 'as a matter of practice the Sex Offender Program assumes that anyone found guilty of a sexual offence is guilty though there is no policy document requiring an offender's admission of guilt'.
*   Prisoners who deny their offences will not be accepted into the Sex Offender Programme in WA. However, such prisoners can undertake an alternative program specifically designed for them.
*   In Queensland, it is not necessary for the individual to express remorse or make a total admission of guilt. However, 'it is important that they acknowledge some involvement in the crime'. An 'acknowledgement of personal involvement' is a pre-requisite to participation.

All four States described their programs and explained reasons they are not available as widely as demand or need would have them or always in good time for individual prisoners. Regrettably, neither WA nor Queensland advised what proportion of offenders unable to access a program in good time were, as a result, unable to qualify for parole on or near their earliest release date.

The Queensland authorities confirmed some prisoners' accounts of uncertainty about release dates and short notice of release advising that in some cases the calculation of remission taking into account loss of remission, the intervention of new sentences and other factors make certainty of release dates difficult to achieve in some cases much in advance of release.

Note

1   Some prisoners in NSW learned of the project through the magazine *Framed* published and distributed by Justice Action.

Bibliography

Books, chapters, articles and reports

Allen, D (1990) 'Prisoners' rights' in J Wallace & T Pagone (eds), *Rights and Freedoms in Australia*, Freedom Press.

Allen, J (1994) *Rose Scott: Vision and Reform in Feminism*, Oxford Univ Press.

Amnesty International (1999) *Brazil: "No One Here Sleeps Safely"* – *Human Rights* Violations *Against Detainees*, AI Index AMR10 September 1999: Amnesty International: <http://web.amnesty.org/ai.nsf/Index/AMR 190097999?OpenDocument&of=COUNTRIES/BRAZIL>

Amnesty International/Law Society (2000) *The United Nations Thematic Mechanisms* – *Update 2000*, AI Index: IOR40/020/2000, <http://web.amn esty.org/ai.nsf/Index/IOR400202000?OpenDocument&of=THEMES\UN>

Andersen, J (2000) 'Women Drank Urine in Cells', *Townsville Bulletin*, 21 June, p 3.

Anderson, P (1980) *Arguments within English Marxism*, Verso.

Anderson, T (1989) *Inside Outlaws* – *a prison diary*, Redfern Legal Centre Publishing.

Ashworth, A (1993) 'Victim Impact Statements and Sentencing' [1993] *Criminal Law Review* 498.

Astudillo, P (2000) 'Australia: Private prisons to remain in Victoria despite government takeover of women's jail', *World Socialist Web Site*, 13 October 2000: <http://wsws.org/articles/2000/oct2000/pris-o13_prn.shtml>

Atkinson, A (1979) 'Four Patterns of Convict Protest' 37 *Labour History* 28.

Audit Victoria (1999) *Victoria's Prison System: Community Protection and Prisoner Welfare*, Special Report 60, Auditor-General's Office, Melbourne.

Audit Review of Government Contracts (2000) *Contracting, privatisation probity & disclosure in Victoria 1992-1999, Vol 2, Case Studies*, (Professor B Russell) Government of Victoria.

Australian Bureau of Statistics (1998) *Crime and Safety, Australia*, ABS Cat No 4509.0, Commonwealth of Australia.

Australian Bureau of Statistics (1999) *Australian Social Trends 1999*, ABS Cat No 4102.0, Commonwealth of Australia.

Australian Bureau of Statistics (2000) *Corrective Services, Australia*, ABS Cat No 4512.0, Commonwealth of Australia.

Australian Bureau of Statistics (2001a) *Corrective Services, Australia*, June Quarter, ABS Cat No 4512.0, Commonwealth of Australia.

Australian Bureau of Statistics (2001b) *Prisoners in Australia 2000*, ABS Cat No 4517.0, Commonwealth of Australia.

Australian Institute of Criminology (1978) *Minimum Standard Guidelines for Australian Prisons*, Australian Institute of Criminology.

Australian Law Reform Commission (1987) *Sentencing: Prisons*, Discussion Paper No 31, Australian Law Reform Commission.

Australian Law Reform Commission (1992) *Multiculturalism and the Law*, Report No 57, Australian Law Reform Commission.

Awofeso, N, SE Harper & MH Levy (2000) 'Prevalence of exposure to hepatitis C virus among prison inmates' 172 *Medical Jnl of Australia* 94.

Awofeso, N & MH Levy (1999) 'Should hepatitis C antibody-positive inmates be vaccinated against hepatitis A virus?' 170 *Medical Jnl of Australia* 338.

Coffey, J (1999) 'A Baby Should Never Be Born Like This', *The Eye*, 7–20 October, pp 37-38.

Baird, J (1999) 'Bid To Stop Killer's Parole', *Sydney Morning Herald*, 10 June, p 6.

Barry Papers MS 2505/41/58, National Library of Australia.

Behrendt, J & L Behrendt (1992) 'Recommendations, Rhetoric and Another 33 Aboriginal Deaths in Custody: Aboriginal Custodial Deaths Since May 1989' 2(59) *Aboriginal Law Bulletin* 4.

Behrendt, J & C Cunneen (1994) 'Report to the National Committee to Defend Black Rights: Aboriginal and Torres Strait Islander Custodial Deaths Between May 1989 and January 1994' 3(68) *Aboriginal Law Bulletin* 4.

Beloof, D (1999) *Victims in Criminal Procedure*, Carolina Academic Press.

Benda, BB (1991) 'Undomiciled: A study of drifters and other homeless persons, their problems and service utilization' 14(3) *Psychosocial Rehabilitation Jnl* 39.

Berkman, A (1995) 'Prison health: the breaking point' 85 *American Jnl of Public Health* 1616.

Bertrand, D & T Harding (1993) 'European guidelines on prison health' 324 *Lancet* 253.

Biles, D & V Dalton (1999) 'Deaths in private prisons 1990-99: A comparative study', *Trends and Issues in Crime and Criminal Justice* No 120, Australian Institute of Criminology.

Bird, G (1993) 'Power, Politics and the Location of the "Other" in Multicultural Australia', paper at *Multiculturalism and the Law*, 3-6 May, Melbourne, Australian Institute of Criminology: <www.aic.gov.au/conferences/multiculturalism/index.html>

Bird, G & M McDonell (1997) 'Muslims in the Dock: A Transgressive Narrative of Law and Life' 3(2) *Australian Jnl of Human Rights* 111.

Bird, G, (1999) *Law and Cultural Diversity*, National Centre for Cross Xultural Studies in Law, Southern Cross University, Lismore.

Booby, R (nd) 'Restorative Justice: A Paper Surveying the International Applications of a Restorative Justice Approach to Crime and Recommending the Establishment of Pilot Programs by the NSW Department of Corrective Services', NSW Probation and Parole Service.

Bossuyt, MJ (1987) *Guide to the "Travaux Preparatoires" of the International Covenant on Civil and Political Rights*, Martinus Nijhoff.

Bowery, M (1999) *Private Prisons in NSW: Junee – a four year review*, Research Publication No 42, NSW Department of Corrective Services.

Boyle, J (1985) *The Pain of Confinement – Prison Diaries of Jimmy Boyle*, Pan Books.

Broadhurst, R (1997) 'Aborigines and Crime in Australia' in M Tonry (ed) *Ethnicity, Crime and Immigration: Comparative and Cross-National Perspectives, Crime and Justice* — a Review of Research, Vol. 21, Univ of Chicago Press.

Brooks, A (1993) '"A paragon of democratic virtues?"' The development of the Commonwealth franchise' 12 *Univ of Tasmania Law Review* 208.

Broom, H (1939) *A Selection of Legal Maxims*, 10th edn, Sweet & Maxwell.

Brown, D (1990) 'Putting the Value Back into Punishment' 15(6) *Legal Service Bulletin* 239.

Brown, D (1991) 'The State of the Prisons in NSW under the Greiner Government: Definitions of Value' 4 *Jnl of Justice Studies* 27-60.

Brown, D (1998) 'Penality and Imprisonment Australia' in RP Weiss & N South (eds) *Comparing Prison Systems*, Gordon and Breach.

Brown D, D Farrier, S Egger and L McNamara (2001) *Criminal Laws*, 3rd edn, Federation Press, Sydney.

Brown, D & R Hogg (1985) 'Abolition Reconsidered' 2(2) *Australian Jnl of Law and Society* 56.

Burt, RA (1993) 'Cruelty, hypocrisy, and the rehabilitative ideal in corrections' 16 *Intl Jnl of Law and Psychiatry* 359.

Butler, T (1997) *Preliminary Findings of the Inmate Health Survey of the Inmate Population in the New South Wales Correctional System*, Corrections Health Service.

Butler, T et al (1997) 'Hepatitis B and C in New South Wales prisons: prevalence and risk factors' 166 *Medical Jnl of Australia* 127.

Butler, T et al (1999) 'Seroprevalence of markers for hepatitis B, C and G in male and female prisoners — NSW 1996' 23 *Australian and NZ Jnl of Public Health* 377.

Butler, T & M Levy (1999) 'Mantoux positivity among prison inmates - New South Wales, 1996' 23 *Australian and NZ Jnl of Public Health* 185.

Byrne, A & K Dolan (1998) 'Methadone treatment is widely accepted in prisons in New South Wales' 316 *British Medical Jnl* 1744.

Byrne, PJ (1993) *Criminal Law and the Colonial Subject, New South Wales, 1810-1830*, Cambridge Univ Press.

Cameron-Perry, JE (2000) 'Debate about medical treatment of life prisoners' 321 *British Medical Jnl* 510.

Carcach, C & A Grant (1999) 'Imprisonment in Australia: Trends in Prison Populations and Imprisonment Rates 1982-1998', *Trends and Issues in Crime and Criminal Justice* No 130, Australian Institute of Criminology.

Carter, KW (2001) 'The Casuarina Prison Riot: Official Discourse or Appreciative Inquiry?' 12(3) *Current Issues in Criminal Justice* 363.

Castieau diaries, Mss 2218, National Library of Australia.

Catholic Bishops of the United States (2000) *Responsibility, Rehabilitation, and Restoration: A Catholic Perspective on Crime and Criminal Justice. A Statement of the Catholic Bishops of the United States*, issued by United States Conference of Catholic Bishops, 15 November: <www.nccbuscc.org/sdwp/criminal.htm>

Chesterman, J & B Galligan (1998) *Citizens Without Rights — Aborigines and Australian Citizenship*, Cambridge Univ Press.

Chesterman, J & B Galligan (1999) *Defining Australian Citizenship – Selected Documents*, Melbourne Univ Press.

Civics Expert Group (1994) *Whereas the people ... Civics and Citizenship Education*, Australian Government Publishing Service.

Civil Liberties Organisation (1996) *Behind the Wall: A Report on Prison Conditions in Nigeria and the Nigerian Prison System*, Civil Liberties Organisation.

Clarkson, G (1981) *Report of the Commission on Allegations in Relation to Prisons under the Charge, Care and Direction of the Department of Correctional Services and Related Matters*, 11 December, South Australian Government Printer.

Conover, T (2000) *Newjack: Guarding Sing Sing*, Random House.

Cook, B, F David & A Grant (1999) *Victims' Needs, Victims' Rights: Policies and Programs for Victims of Crime in Australia*, Research and Public Policy Series No 19, Australian Institute of Criminology.

Coper, M (1987) *Encounters with the Australian Constitution*, CCH Australia, Sydney.

Correctional Law Review (1987) *Victims and Corrections*, Ministry of the Solicitor-General.

Correctional Services Commissioner (Vic) (2000) *Correctional Services Commissioner's Report on Metropolitan Women's Correctional Centre's Compliance with its Contractual Obligations and Prison Services Agreement*, Victorian Government Printer.

Corrective Services Ministers' Conference 1995 (1996) *Standard Guidelines for Corrections in Australia*, Corrective Services Ministers' Conference.

Council of Europe, Committee of Ministers (1987) *Recommendation No R(87)3*: http://cm.coe.int/ta/rec/1987/87r3.htm

Crawford, A & J Goodey (eds) (2000) *Integrating a Victim Perspective within Criminal Justice: International debates*, Ashgate Publishing.

Criminal Justice Commission (2000a) *Prison Numbers in Queensland: An examination of population trends in Queensland correctional institutions*, Criminal Justice Commission.

Criminal Justice Commission (2000b) *Queensland Prison Industries: A Review of Corruption Risks*, Research and Crime Prevention Division, Criminal Justice Commission.

Criminal Law and Penal Methods Reform Committee of South Australia (1973) *Sentencing and Corrections*, Report No 1, July, Government of South Australia.

Crofts, N (1997) 'A cruel and unusual punishment' 166 *Medical Jnl of Australia* 116.

Crofts, N et al (1995) 'Risk behaviours for blood-borne viruses in a Victorian prison' 29 *Australian and NZ Jnl of Criminology* 20.

Cunneen, C (1995) 'Ethnic Minority Youth and Juvenile justice: Beyond the stereotype of ethnic gangs' in C Guerra & R White (eds) *Ethnic Minority Youth in Australia*, National Clearinghouse for Youth Studies.

Cunneen, C & D McDonald (1997) *Keeping Aboriginal and Torres Strait Islander People out of Custody: An Evaluation of the Implementation of the Recommendations of the Royal Commission into Aboriginal Deaths in Custody*, Office of the Aboriginal and Torres Strait Islander Social Justice Commissioner, Human Rights and Equal Opportunity Commission.

Dalton, V (2000) 'Australian Deaths in Custody and Custody-related Police Operations 1999', *Trends and Issues in Crime and Criminal Justice No 153*, Australian Institute of Criminology.

Dalton, V & C Carcach (1997) *Five Years on – Trends in Aboriginal and Torres Strait Islander Deaths in Custody and Incarceration*, Commonwealth of Australia.

Daly, K & R Immarigeon (1998) 'The Past, Present, and Future of Restorative Justice' 1(1) *Contemporary Justice Review* 21.

Damaska, MR (1968) 'Adverse legal consequences of conviction and their removal: A comparative study' 59 *Jnl of Criminal Law, Criminology and Political Science* 347.

Danaher, G, T Shirato & J Webb (2000) *Understanding Foucault*, Allen & Unwin.

Davidson, A (1991) *The Invisible State*, Cambridge Univ Press.

Davidson, J (nd) 'Resurrecting the civil dead: Challenging the constitutional validity of prisoner disenfranchisement', unpublished.

Davies, J (1998) 'The effect of prison privatisation on the legal position of prisoners', 6 *Australian Jnl of Administrative Law* 34.

Davies, S & S Cook (1998) 'Women, imprisonment and post-release mortality' 14 *Just Policy* 15.

Dawes, MJ (1997) Dying in Prison: A Study of Deaths in Correctional Custody in South Australia 1980-1993, unpublished PhD thesis, Flinders Univ of South Australia.

De Bono, E (1987) *Six Thinking Hats*, Penguin.

Delahunty, G (2000) *Citizenship in a Global Age*, Open Univ Press.

Denoff, MS & PA Pilkonis (1987) 'The social network of the schizophrenic: patient and residential determinants' 15(1) *Jnl of Community Psychology* 228.

Department of Corrective Services Qld (2000) *Profile of Female Offenders Under Community and Custodial Supervision in Queensland*, Department of Corrective Services.

Department of Corrective Services NSW (2000) Submission cited in Select Committee on the Increase in Prisoner Population, *Interim Report*, NSW Parliament.

Devlin, A (1998) *Invisible Women: What's Wrong with Women's Prisons?*, Waterside Press.

Dinitz, S (1981) 'Are Safe and Humane Prisons Possible?' 14 *Australian and NZ Jnl of Criminology* 3.

Doan, V (1995) 'Indo-Chinese Youth: Issues of culture and justice' in C Guerra & R White (eds) *Ethnic Minority Youth in Australia*, National Clearinghouse for Youth Studies.

Dodson, M (1998) 'Linking international standards with contemporary concerns of Aboriginal and Torres Strait Islander peoples' in S Pritchard (ed) *Indigenous Peoples, the United Nations and Human Rights*, Federation Press.

Dolan, KA & AD Wodak (1999) 'HIV transmission in a prison system in an Australian State' 171 *Medical Jnl of Australia* 14.

Dolan, KA, AD Wodak & WD Hall (1998) 'A bleach program for inmates in NSW: an HIV prevention strategy' 22 *Australian and NZ Jnl of Public Health* 838.

Dorozynski, A (2000) 'Doctor's book shames French prisons' 320 *British Medical Jnl* 465.

Doyle, J (1998) 'Prisoners as patients: The experience of delivering mental health nursing care in an Australian prison' 36 *Jnl of Psychosocial Nursing* 25.

Dreyfus, H & P Rabinow (1982) *Michel Foucault: Beyond Structuralism and Hermeneutics*, Harvester Wheatsheaf.

Easteal, P (1992) The *Forgotten Few: Overseas-Born Women in Australian Prisons*, Australian Government Publishing Service.

Edwards, A (1995) *Women in Prison*, Crime and Justice Bulletin, NSW Bureau of Crime Statistics and Research, Sydney.

Edwards, S et al (2001) 'Issues in the management of prisoners infected with HIV-1: the King's College Hospital HIV prison service retrospective cohort study' 322 *British Medical Jnl* 398.

Electoral and Administrative Review Commission (1993) *Report on Review of the Preservation and Enhancement of Individuals' Rights and Freedoms*, Brisbane.

Elias, R (1993) *Victims Still: The Political Manipulation of Crime Victims*, Sage.

Enderby, K (2000) 'The Politics of Imprisonment: Is democracy always in accord with justice?' 3 *Dissent* 48.

Erez, E (1999) 'Who's Afraid of the Big Bad Victim? Victim Impact Statements as Victim Empowerment and Enhancement of Justice' [1999] *Criminal Law Review* 545.

Essential Equity (1999) *Comparative Mortality in NSW Prisons*, NSW Corrections Health Service.

European Committee on Crime Problems (1985) *Recommendation No R(85)11 on the position of the victim in the framework of criminal law and procedure*, Council of Europe.

Evans, M & R Morgan (1999a) *Preventing Torture: A Study of the European Convention for the Prevention of Torture and Inhuman or Degrading Treatment or Punishment*, Clarendon Press.

Evans, M & R Morgan (1999b) *Protecting Prisoners: The Standards of the European Committee for the Prevention of Torture in Context*, Oxford Univ Press.

Evans, R & W Thorpe (1992) 'Power, Punishment and Penal Labour: Convict Workers and Moreton Bay' 98 *Australian Historical Series*.

Evatt, E (2001) 'Realising Human Rights" Utilising UN Mechanisms' in S Garkawe, W Fisher & L Kelly (eds) *Australian Indigenous Human Rights*, Sydney Institute of Criminology Monograph Series No 14, Sydney pp 187-214.

Farrington, DP & D West (1990) 'The Cambridge study in delinquent development: a long term follow-up of 411 London males' in H Kerner and G Kaiser (eds) *Criminality: Personality, Behaviour, Life History*, Springer Verlag.

Fasher, AM et al (1997) 'The health of a group of young Australians in a New South Wales juvenile justice detention centre: a pilot study' 33 *Jnl of Paediatric Child Health* 426.

Faugeron, C (1991) 'Prisons in France: Stalemate or Evolution?' in D van Zyl Smit & F Dunkel (eds) *Imprisonment Today and Tomorrow*, Kluwer.

Faulks, K (2000) *Citizenship*, Routledge.

Findlay, M (1982) *The State of the Prison*, Michellsearch.

Fine, B (1984) *Democracy and the Rule of Law*, Pluto Press.

Finlay, IF (1998) 'Managing terminally ill prisoners: reflection and action' 12 *Palliative Medicine* 457.

Finnane, M (1997) *Punishment in Australian Society*, Oxford Univ Press.

Finnane, M & J McGuire (2001) 'The uses of punishment and exile: Aborigines in colonial Australia' 3(2) *Punishment and Society* 279.

Fitzgerald, J & G Zdenkowski (1987) 'Voting rights of convicted persons' 11(1) *Criminal Law Jnl* 11.

Fitzroy Legal Service (2000) 'Prisoners' in *The Law Handbook*, Fitzroy Legal Service.

Fletcher, K (1999) 'The Myth of the Supermax Solution' 24(6) *Alternative Law Jnl* 274.

Foucault, M (1977) *Discipline and Punish: The Birth of the Prison*, Penguin.

Fox, R & A Freiberg (1999) *Sentencing: State and Federal Law in Victoria*, 2nd edn, Oxford Univ Press.

Fredericks, K (1999) 'Supermax Prisoners Win Challenge', *Green Left Weekly*, 11 August.

Freiberg, A (1999) 'Commercial Confidentiality and Public Accountability for the Provision of Correctional Services' 11(2) *Current Issues in Criminal Justice* 119.

Freiberg, A & S Ross (1999) *Sentencing Reform and Penal Change – The Victorian Experience*, Federation Press.

Gardner, J (1990) *Victims and Criminal Justice*, Office of Crime Statistics, Series C, No 5, Attorney-General's Department (SA).

Garkawe, S (1994) 'The Role of the Victim during Criminal Court Proceedings' 17(2) *Univ of NSW Law Jnl* 595.

Garkawe, S (1999) 'Restorative justice from the Perspective of Crime Victims' 15 *Queensland Univ of Technology Law Jnl* 40.

Garland, D (1990) *Punishment and Modern Society*, Clarendon Press.

Garland, D (1996) 'The Limits of the Sovereign State – Strategies of Crime Control in Contemporary Society' 36(4) *British Jnl of Criminology* 445.

Garland, D (2001) 'The Meaning of Mass Imprisonment' 3(1) *Punishment and Society* 5.

Garland, D & P Young (1983) *The Power to Punish*, Heinemann.

Gaughwin, MD et al (1991) 'HIV prevalence and risk behaviours for HIV transmission in South Australian prisons' 5 *AIDS* 845.

George, A (2000) 'Women Prisoners as Customers: Counting the Costs of the Privately Managed Metropolitan Women's Correctional Centre', paper at *Women in Corrections: Staff and Clients*, 31 October–1 November, Adelaide, Australian Institute of Criminology.

Giffard, C (2000) *The Torture Reporting Handbook*, Human Rights Centre, Univ of Essex: <www.essex.ac.uk/torturehandbook>

Gifford, DJ & K Gifford (1994) *How to Understand an Act of Parliament*, 8th edn, Law Book.

Glaser, JB & RB Greifinger (1993) 'Correctional health care: a public health opportunity' 118 *Annals of Internal Medicine* 139.

Goffman, E (1961) *Asylums: Essays on the social situation of mental patients and other inmates*, Anchor Books.

Gomien, D, D Harris & L Zwaak (1996) *Law and Practice of the European Convention on Human Rights and the European Social Charter*, Council of Europe Publishing.

Gore, SM, AG Bird & AJ Ross (1996) 'Prison rights: mandatory drugs tests and performance indicators for prisons' 312 *British Medical Jnl* 1411.

Gore, SM , AG Bird & JS Strang (1999) 'Random mandatory drugs testing of prisoners: a biased means of gathering information' 4 *Jnl of Epidemiology and Biostatistics* 3.

Grabosky, P & J Braithwaite (1986) *Of Manners Gentle: Enforcement Strategies of Australian Business Regulatory Agencies*, Oxford Univ Press.

Grant, D (1992) *Prisons: The Continuing Crisis in New South Wales*, Federation Press.

Greifinger, RB , NJ Heywood & JB Glaser (1993) 'Tuberculosis in prison: balancing justice and public health' 21 *Jnl of Law, Medicine and Ethics* 332.

Groves, M (1996) 'Administrative Segregation of Prisoners: Powers, Principles of Review and Remedies', 20 *Melbourne University law Review* 369.

Gudjonsson, GH et al (1993) *Persons at risk during interviews in police custody: The identification of vulnerabilities*, Research Study No 12, Royal Commission on Criminal Justice, HMSO.

Haber, PS et al (1999) 'Transmission of hepatitis C within Australian prisons' 171 *Medical Jnl of Australia* 31.

Hall, G (1992) 'Victim Impact Statements: Sentencing on Thin Ice?' 15 *NZ Universities Review* 143.

Hampton, B (1993) *Prisons and Women*, Univ of New South Wales Press.

Harding, R (1997) *Private Prisons and Public Accountability*, Open Univ Press.

Harding-Pink, D (1990) 'Mortality following release from prison' 30 *Medicine, Science and Law* 12.

Harrington, LH et al (1982) *President's Task Force on Victims of Crime – Final Report*, US Government Printing Office.

Hartley, J (1996) *Popular Reality*, Arnold.

Hawkins, G (1986) *Prisoners' Rights: A Study of Human Rights and Commonwealth Prisoners*, Human Rights Commission, Occasional Paper No 12, AGPS, Canberra.

Hay, D (1975) 'Property, Authority and the Criminal Law' in D Hay et al (eds) *Albion's Fatal Tree*, Allen Lane.

Hayes, SC (1997) 'Prevalence of intellectual disability in local courts' 22(2) *Jnl of Intellectual and Developmental Disability* 71.

Hayes, SC & D McIlwain (1988) *The Prevalence of Intellectual Disability in the NSW Prison Population: An Empirical Study*, Criminology Research Council.

Heilpern, D (1995) 'Sexual Assault of New South Wales Prisoners' 6(3) *Current Issues in Criminal Justice* 327.

Heilpern, D (1998) *Fear or favour – sexual assault of young prisoners*, Southern Cross Univ Press.

Henderson, L (1985) 'The Wrongs of Victims Rights' 37 *Stanford Law Review* 937.

HM Chief Inspector of Prisons (2000) *Annual Report of HM Chief Inspector of Prisons for England and Wales 1998-1999*, HMSO.

HM Prison Service (1995) *Instruction to Governors 74/1995 Incentives and Earned Privileges*, HMSO.

HM Prison Service (1999) *1998/1999 Annual Report*: <www.hmprisonservice.gov.uk/corporate/dynpage.asp?page=26>

Hinton, M (1996) 'Guarding Against Victim-authored Victim Impact Statements' 20(6) *Criminal Law Jnl* 310.

Hirst, J (1983) *Convict Society and its Enemies: A History of Early New South Wales*, Allen & Unwin

Hirst, P (1980) 'Law, Socialism and Rights' in P Carlen & M Collison (eds) *Radical Issues in Criminology*, Martin Robertson.

Hogg, R (2001) 'Penality and modes of regulating indigenous peoples in Australia' 3(3) *Punishment and Society* 355.

Hogg, R & D Brown (1998) *Rethinking Law and Order*, Pluto Press.

Howe, A (1994) *Punish and Critique: Towards a Feminist Analysis of Penality*, Routledge.

Hudson, B (2000) 'Criminology, Difference and Justice: Issues for Critical Criminology' 33(2) *Australian and NZ Jnl of Criminology* 168.

Hughes, R (1988) *The Fatal Shore: a History of the Transportation of Convicts to Australia 1787-1868*, Pan Books.

Human Rights and Equal Opportunity Commission (1991) *Racist Violence: Report of the National Inquiry into Racist Violence in Australia*, Australian Government Publishing Service.

Human Rights and Equal Opportunity Commission (1996a) *Annual Report 1995-96*, Human Rights and Equal Opportunity Commission.

Human Rights and Equal Opportunity Commission (1996b) *Indigenous Deaths in Custody 1989-1996*, Human Rights and Equal Opportunity Commission.

Human Rights and Equal Opportunity Commission (1997) Annual Report 1996-97, Human Rights and Equal Opportunity Commission.

Human Rights and Equal Opportunity Commission (2000) *Age Matters: A report on age discrimination*, Human Rights and Equal Opportunity Commission: <www.humanrights.gov.au/human_rights/older_Australians/age_matters.html>

Human Rights Brief No 4 (2001) *Lawful Limits on Fundamental Freedoms*, Human Rights and Equal Opportunity Commission: <www.humanrights.gov.au/human_rights/briefs/brief_4.html>

Human Rights Watch (1988) *Behind Bars in Brazil*, Human Rights Watch: <www.hrw.org/reports98/brazil/>

Human Rights Watch (1997) *Punishment Before Trial – Prison Conditions in Venezuela*, Human Rights Watch: <www.hrw.org/advocacy/prisons/venez-sm.htm>

Human Rights Watch (1998) *Losing the Vote: The Impact of Felony Disenfranchisement Laws in the United States*, Human Rights Watch – The Sentencing Project: <www.hrw.org/reports98/vote/usvot98o.htm>

Ignatieff, M (1978) *A Just Measure of Pain: The Penitentiary in the Industrial Revolution 1750-1850*, Macmillan.

Inciardi, JA (1996) 'HIV risk reduction and service delivery strategies in criminal justice settings' 13 *Jnl of Substance Abuse Treatment* 421.

Independent Commission Against Corruption (1998) *Investigation into the Department of Corrective Services – Second Report: Inappropriate Relationships with Inmates in the Delivery of Health Services*, Independent Commission Against Corruption.

Intl Review of Victimology (1994) 3(1 & 2) 17-165.

Isin, EF & PK Wood (1999) *Citizenship and Identity*, Sage.

Jacobs, J (1983) 'Macrosociology and Imprisonment' in J Jacobs (ed) *New Perspectives on Prisons and Imprisonment*, Cornell Univ Press.

James, JS (1969) *The Vagabond Papers*, Melbourne Univ Press.

Jenkinson Inquiry, (1973) Board of Inquiry into Allegations of Brutality and Ill-Treatment at HM Prison Pentridge, *Report*, Victorian Government Printer.

Johnson, D & G Zdenkowski (1999) *Mandatory Injustice: Compulsory Imprisonment in the Northern Territory*, Centre for Independent Journalism.

Johnson, P (1995) 'The Victims Charter and the Release of Long-Term Prisoners' 42(1) *Probation Jnl* 8.

Joint Select Committee on Electoral Reform (1986) *Report No 2*, Commonwealth Parliament Canberra, PP No 198/84.

Joint Standing Committee on Electoral Matters (1994) *Report: the 1993 Federal Election*, Commonwealth Parliament, Canberra, PP No 416-94

Joint Standing Committee on Electoral Matters (1997) *Report: the 1996 Federal Election*, Commonwealth Parliament, Canberra, PP No 93/1997.

Joint Standing Committee on Electoral Matters (2000) *Report: the 1998 Federal Election*, Commonwealth Parliament Canberra, PP No 128/2000.

Jones, P (1991) 'HIV transmission by stabbing despite zidovudine prophylaxis' 338 *Lancet* 884.

Kaiser, GE (1971) 'The inmate as citizen' 7 *Queen's Law Jnl* 208.

Karabec, Z (1995) 'The problems of a prison system during a period of transition towards democracy' (98) *Prison Service Jnl* 18.

Karmen, A (1996) *Crime Victims – An Introduction to Victimology*, 3rd edn, Wadsworth.

Kelso, P (2000) 'Failings at Feltham that ended in racist murder', *The Guardian*, 11 November.

Kercher, B (1995) *An Unruly Child: A history of law in Australia*, Allen & Unwin.

Kerr, JS (1988) *Out of Sight, Out of Mind – Australia's Places of Confinement, 1788-1988*, SH Ervin Gallery, National Trust of Australia (NSW).

Kilroy, D (1999) 'White Wall Syndrome', paper at *Best Practice Interventions for Indigenous People*, 13-15 October, Adelaide, Australian Institute of Criminology.

Kilroy, D (2000) 'When Will They See the Real Us: Women in Prison', paper at *Women in Corrections: Staff and Clients*, 31 October–1 November, Adelaide, Australian Institute of Criminology.

King, RD (1994) 'Russian Prisons after Perestroika' in *Prisons in Context*, Clarendon Press.

Kirby Inquiry, (2000) Private Prisons Investigation Panel (VIC) (2000) *Report of the Investigation into the Management and Operations of Victoria's Private Prisons*, Private Prisons Investigation Panel.

Koch, T, (2000) 'Women Locked in with Men, *Courier-Mail*, 9 September, p 1.

Laclau, E & C Mouffe (1985) *Hegemony and Socialist Strategy: Toward a Radical Democracy*, Verso.

Lamborn, L (1987) 'Victim Participation in the Criminal Justice Process: The Proposals for a Constitutional Amendment' 34 *Wayne Law Jnl* 125.

Latour, B (1993) *We Have Never Been Modern*, Harvard Univ Press.

Legal, Constitutional and Administrative Review Committee (1998) *Queenslanders' Basic Rights, Report No 12*, Queensland Legislative Assembly.

Lessenger, JE (1982) 'Health care in jails: a unique challenge in medical practice' 72 *Postgraduate Medicine* 131.

Levine, IS (1984) 'Service programs for the homeless mentally ill' in HR Lamb (ed) *The Homeless Mentally Ill*, American Psychiatric Assn.

Livingstone, S & T Owen (1999) *Prison Law*, 2nd edn, Oxford Univ Press.

Lui, L & L Blanchard (2001) 'Citizenship and Social Justice: Learning from Aboriginal Night Patrols in NSW' 5(5) *Indigenous Law Bulletin* 16.

Lyall, I, AJ Holland & S Collins (1995) 'Incidence of persons with a learning disability detained in police custody: a needs assessment for service development' 35 *Medicine, Science and the Law* 61.

Lynn, P & G Armstrong (1996) *From Pentonville to Pentridge: A History of Prisons in Victoria*, State Library of Victoria.

McCarthy, T (1994) 'Victim Impact Statements — A Problematic Remedy' 3 *Australian Feminist Law Jnl* 175.

McCulloch, J (1998) 'Human Rights: *Craig Minogue v Human Rights and Equal Opportunity Commission*' 23(5) *Alternative Law Jnl* 244.

McDonald, AM et al (1999) 'HIV prevalence at reception into Australian prisons, 1991-1997' 171 *Medical Jnl of Australia* 18.

MacDonald, J (1997) 'Australia rejects ruling on asylum-seeker', *The Age*, 18 December, p 9

MacFarlane, IA (1996) 'The development of healthcare services for diabetic prisoners' 72 *Postgraduate Medicine* 214.

McKean, W (1983) *Equality and Discrimination Under International Law*, Clarendon Press.

Marshall, TH (1992) 'Citizenship and Social Class' in TH Marshall & T Bottomore *Citizenship and Social Class*, Pluto Press.

Martin, SL et al (1997) 'Is incarceration during pregnancy associated with infant birthweight?' 87 *American Jnl of Public Health* 1526.

Mathiesen, T (1974) *The Politics of Abolition*, Martin Robertson.

Merritt, A (1980) 'The Nature and Function of Law: A Critique of EP Thompson's *Whigs and Hunters*' 7(2) *British Jnl of Law and Society* 194.

Mickelburough P & P Anderson, (2000) 'Government moves on prison strife. Private jail grab', *Herald Sun* 4 October, p 3.

Miers, D (2000) 'Taking the Law into their Own Hands: Victims as Offenders', in A Crawford & J Goodey (eds) *Integrating a Victim Perspective within Criminal Justice: International debates*, Ashgate Publishing.

Millett, K (1995) *The Politics of Cruelty – An Essay on the Literature of Political Imprisonment*, Penguin.

Ministre de la Justice (2000) *Amélioration du Contrôle Extérieur des Etablissements Pénitentiaires*, Rapport de la Commission á Madame le Garde des Sceaux, Ministre de la Justice.

Ministry of Justice (WA) (1998) *Request for Proposal Wooroloo Prison South Project*, Wooroloo Prison South Project.

Monogue, C (2000) 'Human Rights and excursions from the flat lands', 25(3) *Alternative Law Journal* 145.

Mottram, M (2001) 'Does the watchdog have enough bite?' *The Age*, 6 January, News Extra, p 3.

Moyle, P (1994) *Private Prisons*, Pluto Press.

Moyle, P (1999) 'Separating the allocation of punishment from its administration: Theoretical and empirical observations' 11(2) *Current Issues in Criminal Justice* 153.

Moyle, P (2000) *Profiting from Punishment: private prisons in Australia: Reform or regression?*, Pluto Press.

Nagle, JF (1978) *Report of the Royal Commission into NSW Prisons*, New South Wales Government Printer.

Narey, M (2000) 'Achieving Results', speech to the Prison Service Conference at Harrogate, 1 February 2000 quoted in *Prison Service News – Magazine of the HM Prison Service*, February 2000, p 4.

National Centre for HIV Epidemiology and Clinical Research (2000) *HIV/AIDS, hepatitis C and sexually transmissible infections in Australia: Annual surveillance report*, National Centre for HIV Epidemiology and Clinical Research.

Neal, D (1991) *The Rule of Law in a Penal Colony: Law and power in early New South Wales*, Cambridge Univ Press.

Neitenstein, FW (1897) 'Crime and its treatment in New South Wales', *New South Wales Parliamentary Papers*, Vol 3.

Nelles, J et al (1998) 'Provision of syringes: The cutting edge of harm reduction in prison?' 317 *British Medical Jnl* 270.

New South Wales Bureau of Crime Statistics and Research (1974) *A Thousand Prisoners*, Statistical Report 16, NSW Government Printer.

New South Wales Department of Corrective Services (1998) *Annual Report 1997-98*, NSW Government.

New South Wales Department of Corrective Services (2000) *Annual Report 1999-2000*, NSW Government.

New South Wales Law Reform Commission (1996a) *People with an Intellectual Disability and the Criminal Justice System*, Report No 80, NSW Law Reform Commission.

New South Wales Law Reform Commission (1996b) *Sentencing*, Discussion Paper 33, NSW Law Reform Commission.

New South Wales Law Reform Commission (1996c) *Sentencing*, Report No 79, NSW Law Reform Commission.

New South Wales Parliamentary Papers (1861) Select Committee on Public Prisons in Sydney and Cumberland, NSW Parliament.

Nowak, M (1993) *UN Covenant on Civil and Political Rights: CCPR Commentary*, NP Engel.

O'Connell, M (1999) 'The Law on Victim Impact Statements in Australia' 2(1) *Jnl of the Australasian Society of Victimology* 88.

O'Neill, J (1990) 'The Punishment Salesman', *Independent Monthly*, October.

O'Neill, N & R Handley (1994) *Retreat from Injustice: Human Rights in Australian Law*, Federation Press.

Orr, G (1998) 'Ballotless and behind bars: the denial of the franchise to prisoners' 26(1) *Federal Law Review* 55.

Palley, C (1992) *The Possible Utility, Scope and Structure of a Special Study on the Issue of Privatization of Prisons*, UN Doc E/CN.4/Sub.2/1993/21, United Nations Commission on Human Rights.

Patapan, H (2000) *Judging Democracy: The New Politics of the High Court of Australia*, Cambridge University Press.

Pateman, C (1989) *The Disorder of Women*, Polity Press.

Paterson, A (1996) 'Preventing Re-Victimisation: The South Australian Experience' in C Sumner et al (eds) *International Victimology: selected papers from the 8th International Symposium of the World Society of Victimology*, Australian Institute of Criminology Conference Proceedings No 27, Australian Institute of Criminology.

Patton, P (1979) 'Of Power and Prisons' in P Patton & M Morris (eds) *Michel Foucault: Power, Truth, Strategy*, Feral Publications.

Penal Reform International (1999) *Juvenile Justice in Malawi – Time for Reform?*, Penal Reform International.

Perkins, R (1991) 'Transsexuals in Prison' in 4 *Jnl for Social Justice Studies* 97 Special Issue: Politics, Prisons and Punishment.

Peterson, N & W Sanders (eds) (1998) *Citizenship and Indigenous Australians – Changing Conceptions and Possibilities*, Cambridge Univ Press.

Portuguese Prison Service (1999) *Prisões em revista*, September.

Post, J et al (2001) 'Acute hepatitis C virus infection in an Australian prison inmate: Tattooing as a possible transmission route' 174 *Medical Jnl of Australia* 183.

Pratt, J (2000) 'Emotive and Ostentatious Punishment' 2(4) *Punishment and Society* 417.

Prisons Ombudsman (2000) *Prisons Ombudsman Annual Report 1999-2000*, HMSO.

Prison Privatization Report International (1999) No 32, November: <www.pen lex.org.uk/pages/prtprep.html>

Prison Reform Trust (2000) *A Hard Act to Follow: Prisons and the Human Rights Act*, Penal Reform International.

Prison Reform International Newsletter (1996) No 25 (June).

Pritchard, S (1998) *A Guide to the Optional Protocol to the International Covenant on Civil and Political Rights: Communicating with the Human Rights Committee*, Australian Human Rights Centre: <www.austlii.edu.au/au/other/ahric/booklet/index.html.>

Queensland Corrective Services Review (1999) *Corrections in the Balance: A Review of Corrective Services in Queensland*, Queensland Corrective Services Review.

Queensland Legislative Assembly, *(Hansard)* 3 October 2000.

Queensland Legislative Assembly, *(Hansard)* 29 October 1997.

Queensland Parliament, Parliamentary Debates 1923 (23 October).

Queensland Parliament, Parliamentary Debates 1942 (12 November).

Ramsland, J (1996) *With just but relentless discipline: A social history of corrective services in New South Wales*, Kangaroo Press.

Reeves, H & K Mulley (2000) 'The New Status of Victims in the UK: Opportunities and Threats' in A Crawford & J Goodey (eds) *Integrating a Victim Perspective within Criminal Justice: International debates*, Ashgate Publishing.

Rice, P (1988a) 'Inmates allegations unfounded says MP', *Advertiser*, 29 November, p 5.

Rice, P (1988b) 'Prison officers face inquiry', *News*, 1 December, p 43.

Rice, P (1988c) 'Prison officers march over "power abuse"', *Advertiser*, 17 November, p 5.

Rice, P (1988d) 'Putting the screws on the "screws"', *Advertiser*, 19 November, p 19.

Rice, P (1988e) 'Task force to probe prison assaults', *Advertiser*, 15 October, p 5.

Richards, C (1992) 'Victim impact statements: Victims' rights wronged' 17(33) *Alternative Law Jnl* 131.

Robertson, G (1981) 'The extent and pattern of crime amongst mentally handicapped offenders' 9 *Apex: Jnl of British Institute of Mentally Handicapped* 100.

Robertson, R (1998) 'Prison to the community in one, totally unprepared step' 317 *British Medical Jnl* 757.

Robins, LN (1993) 'Childhood conduct problems, adult psychotherapy and crime', in S Hodgins (ed) *Mental Disorder and Crime*, Sage, Newbury Park CA, 173.

Roche, D (1999) 'Mandatory Sentencing', *Trends and Issues in Crime and Criminal Justice No 138*, Australian Institute of Criminology.

Rodley, N (1999) *The Treatment of Prisoners Under International Law*, 2nd edn, Clarendon Press.

Rosa, S (2000) *Prisoners Rights Handbook*, Redfern Legal Centre Publishing.

Rose Scott Papers, Mitchell Library Mss 38/56, item 2/15, State Library of New South Wales.

Royal Commission into Aboriginal Deaths in Custody (1988) *Interim Report* (JH Muirhead), Australian Government Publishing Service.

Royal Commission into Aboriginal Deaths in Custody (1989) *Report of the Inquiry into the Death of John Clarence Highfold* (JH Muirhead), Australian Government Publishing Service.

Royal Commission into Aboriginal Deaths in Custody (1991) *National Report, Volumes 1-5*, Australian Government Publishing Service.

Rubenstein, K (1995) 'Citizenship in Australia: Unscrambling its meaning' 20 *Melbourne Univ Law Review* 503.

Ruby, CC (1994) *Sentencing*, 4th edn, Butterworths.

Ryan, M (1999) 'Penal Policy Making Towards the Millennium: Elites and populists; New Labour and the new criminology' 27(1) *Intl Jnl of the Sociology of Law* 1.

Saporta, JA & BA Van der Kolk (1992) 'Psychobiological Consequences of Trauma' in M Basoglu (ed) *Torture and its Consequences: Current Treatment Approaches*, Cambridge Univ Press.

Schneiderman, LJ & NS Jecker (1996) 'Should a criminal receive a heart transplant? Medical justice vs. societal justice' 17 *Theoretical Medicine* 33.

Seaman, SR, RP Brettle & SM Gore (1998) 'Mortality from overdose among injecting drug users recently released from prison: database linkage study' 316 *British Medical Jnl* 426.

Sebba, L (1996) *Third Parties: Victims and the Criminal Justice System*, Ohio State Univ Press.

Select Committee on the Increase in Prisoner Population (2000) *Interim Report: Issues Relating to Women*, New South Wales Parliament.

Seligman, MEP & SF Maeier (1967) 'Failure to Escape Traumatic Shock' 74 *Jnl of Experimental Psychology* 1.

Shapland, J, J Willmore & P Duff (1985) *Victims in the criminal justice system*, Gower.

Simpson, J, M Martin & J Green (2001) *The Framework Report*, New South Wales Council for Intellectual Disability.

Smith, R (1999) 'Prisoners: An end to second class health care? Eventually the NHS must take over' 318 *British Medical Jnl* 954.

Smith, L, D Indermaur & S Boddis (1999) *Report of the Inquiry into the Incident at Casuarina Prison on 25 December 1998*, Ministry of Justice (WA).

South African Human Rights Commission (1998) *Report on the National Prisons Project of the South African Human Rights Commission*, South African Human Rights Commission.

South Australia Legislative Assembly, Parliamentary Debates, *Hansard*, second reading debate, 28 May 1998.

Solzhenitsyn, A (1974) *The Gulag Archipelago*, Collins Harvill Press.

Spierenburg, PC (1991) *The Prison Experience: Disciplinary institutions and their inmates in early modern Europe*, Rutgers Univ Press.

Standing Committee on Law and Justice of the NSW Legislative Council (1999) *First Report of the Inquiry into Crime Prevention through Social Support*, NSW Parliament, Sydney.

Staples, JF (1981) 'Courts, Convicts and Labor Governments in New South Wales — From Cable to Dugan and Beyond', Eleventh Annual John Curtin Memorial Lecture, Australian National University, (roneoed lecture notes).

Steering Committee for the Review of Commonwealth/State Service Provision (2000) *Report on Government Services 2000*, Ausinfo.

Steering Committee for the Review of Commonwealth/State Service Provision (2001) *Report on Government Services 2001*, Ausinfo: <www.pc. gov.au/gsp/2001/index.html>

Stern, V (1998) *A Sin Against the Future: Imprisonment in the World*, Penguin.

Thompson, D (1999) 'Towards Restoration: Victim Awareness Programmes for Adult Offenders in South Australia', paper at *Restoration for Victims of Crime: Contemporary Challenges*, 9-10 September, Melbourne, Australian Institute of Criminology.

Thompson, EP (1975) *Whigs and Hunters*, Allen Lane.

Thornton, M (1990) *The Liberal Promise: Anti-Discrimination Legislation in Australia*, Oxford Univ Press.

Tie, W (1999) *Legal Pluralism: Towards a Multicultural Conception of Law*, Ashgate Publishing.

Tomasevski, K (1992) *Prison Health: International Standards and Practices in Europe*, Helsinki Institute of Crime Prevention.

Travis, A (1999) 'Scrubs prison officers "beyond control"', *The Guardian*, 16 June.

Trezise, P (1994) 'A response to the Royal Commission into Aboriginal Deaths in Custody 1993 implementation report', in Sansbury Association & P Trezise, *Voices Behind the Razor Wire*.

Trute, P & R Morris (1999) 'Where Now: Lewthwaite quits Waterloo for a suburb near you', *The Daily Telegraph*, 24 June, p 1.

US Department of Justice (1998) *New Directions From the Field: Victims' Rights and Services for the 21st Century*, Office of Victims of Crime, US Government Printing Office.

Vasseur, V (2000) *Médecin-Chef a la Prison de la Santé*, Le Cherche Midi Editeur.

Vaughan, B (2000) 'Punishment and conditional citizenship' 2(1) *Punishment and Society* 23.

Victoria Legislative Assembly, Parliamentary Debates (*Hansard*) 26 May 2000; 14 December 1999.

Victoria Parliament, Parliamentary Debates 1903 (4 February).

Victoria Parliament, Parliamentary Debates 1939 (4 July).

Victoria Parliament, Parliamentary Debates 1942 (23 December).

Vinson, T (1982) *Wilful Obstruction,* Methuen.

Walker, J (1994),'Trends in Crime and Criminal Justice' in D Chappell & P Wilson (eds) *The Australian Criminal Justice System: The Mid 1990s*, Butterworths.

Walker, K (1970) *My People*, Jacaranda Press.

Warner, K (1994) 'Family Group Conferences and the Rights of the Offender' in C Alder & J Wundersitz (eds) *Family conferencing and juvenile justice: The way forward or misplaced optimism?*, Australian Institute of Criminology.

Warren, N et al (1994) 'Human immunodeficiency virus infection care is unavailable to inmates on release from jail' 3 *Archives of Family Medicine* 894.

Wartofsky, M (1981) 'The prisoners' dilemma: Drug testing in prisons and the violation of human rights' 76 *Progress in Clinical and Biological Research* 57.

Webster, P (2000) 'VIP prisoners speak out against prison conditions', *The Guardian*, 21 January.

Western Australian Deaths in Custody Watch Committee (2000) *Report to the Committee Against Torture, For Consideration Together with Australia's Reports to the Committee, Pursuant to Article 19 of the Convention Against Torture,* WA Deaths in Custody Watch Committee.

Western Australian Inspector of Custodial Services (2001) *Report of an Unannounced Inspection of the Induction and Orientation Unit and the Special Handling Unit at Casuarina Prison,* WA Inspector of Custodial Services.

Western Australia Ministry of Justice (nd) *Regimen for Prisoners Placed in Separate Confinement Pursuant to Section 43 of the Prisons Act 1981,* WA Ministry of Justice.

Western Australia Parliament (1884) *Report of a Commission … to inquire into the treatment of Aboriginal Native Prisoners of the Crown in the Colony,* Western Australia Parliamentary Papers.

Western Australia Parliament (1899) *Report of a Commission appointed to inquire into the Penal System in the Colony,* Western Australia Parliamentary Papers.

Williams, P (2001) 'Deaths in Custody: 10 Years on from the Royal Commission', *Trends and Issues in Crime and Criminal Justice No 203,* Australian Institute of Criminology.

Wilmott, Y (1997) 'Prison nursing: the tension between custody and care' 6 *British Jnl of Nursing* 333.

Winter, N, AJ Holland & S Collins (1997) 'Factors predisposing to suspected offending by adults with self-reported learning disabilities' 27 *Psychological Medicine* 595.

Wolfgang, ME (1998) 'The medical model versus the just deserts model' 16 *Bulletin of the American Academy of Psychiatry and Law* 111.

Rt Hon Lord Justice Woolf & His Honour Judge S Tumim (1991) *Woolf Report: Prison Disturbances April 1990 – Report of an Inquiry,* HMSO.

Zdenkowski, G (1981) 'NSW Prisoners and Access to Courts: Disappointing Legislation' 6(3) *Legal Services Bulletin* 148.

Zdenkowski, G (2000) 'Sentencing Trends: Past, Present and Prospective' in D Chappell & P Wilson (eds) *Crime and the Criminal Justice System in Australia: 2000 and Beyond,* Butterworths.

Zdenkowski, G & D Brown (1982) *The prison struggle: Changing Australia's penal system,* Penguin.

Zelinka, S (1995) 'Racism & one response' in C Guerra & R White (eds), *Ethnic Minority Youth in Australia,* National Clearinghouse for Youth Studies. Hobart, 213-221.

Committee Against Torture (CAT) Observations

Identified in text as CAT re [country], these can be accessed at:
<www.unhchr.ch/tbs/doc.nsf/Documentsfrset?OpenFrameSet>

CAT re Turkey 1993: Activities of the Committee Against Torture pursuant to article 20 of the CAT: Turkey: UN Doc A/48/44/Add.1, 15/11/93.

CAT re: Kyrgyzstan 1999: Conclusions and Observations of the Committee against Torture: Kyrgyzstan: UN Doc A/55/44, para 70-75, 18/11/99.

CAT re Australia 2000: Conclusions and Recommendations of the Committee Against Torture: Australia: UN Doc CAT/C/XXV/Concl.3, 21/11/00.

European Committee for the Prevention of Torture (CPT) Reports

All available at: <www.cpt.coe.int/en/states.htm>

CPT 1991: Report to the United Kingdom Government on the visit to the United Kingdom carried out by the European Committee for the Prevention of Torture and Inhuman or Degrading Treatment or Punishment (CPT) from 29 July 1990 to 10 August 1990, Council of Europe.

CPT 1992: Partie I: Rapport au Conseil fédéral de la Suisse relatif á la visite effectuée par le Comité européan pour la prévention de la torture et des peines ou traitements inhumains ou dégredants (CPT) effectuée en Suisse du 21 au 29 juillet 1991, Council of Europe.

CPT 1993: Rapport au gouvernement de la République française relatif á la visite effectuée par le Comité européan pour la prévention de la torture et des peines ou traitements inhumains ou dégredants (CPT) en France du 27 octobre au 8 novembre 1991 et réponse du governement de la République française, Council of Europe.

CPT 1994: Report to the Portuguese Government on the visit to Portugal carried out by the European Committee for the Prevention of Torture and Inhuman or Degrading Treatment or Punishment (CPT) from 19 to 27 January 1992, Council of Europe.

CPT 1995a: Rapport au gouvernement de l'Italie relatif á la visite effectuée par le Comité européan pour la prévention de la torture et des peines ou traitements inhumains ou dégredants (CPT) effectuée en Italie de 15 au 27 mars 1992, Council of Europe.

CPT 1995b: Report to the Swedish Government on the visit to Sweden carried out by the European Committee for the Prevention of Torture and Inhuman or Degrading Treatment or Punishment (CPT) from 23 to 26 August 1994, Council of Europe.

CPT 1997: Report on the visit to Italy in 1995 by the European Committee for the Prevention of Torture, Council of Europe.

CPT 1998a: Report to the Netherlands Government on the visit to the Netherlands, Council of Europe.

CPT 1998b: Report to the Polish Government on the visit to Poland, Council of Europe.

CPT 1999a: Report to the Swedish Government on the visit to Sweden carried out by the European Committee for the Prevention of Torture and Inhuman or Degrading Treatment or Punishment (CPT) from 15 to 25 February 1998, Council of Europe.

CPT 1999b: 'Substantive' sections of the CPT's General Report, Council of Europe.

CPT 2000a: 10th General Report on the European Committee for the Prevention of Torture and Inhuman and Degrading Treatment of Punishments' activities covering the period 1 January to 31 December 1999, Council of Europe.

CPT 2000b: Report to the United Kingdom Government on the visit to the United Kingdom and the Isle of Man, Council of Europe.

Human Rights Committee General Comments

The following documents interpreting the ICCPR can be obtained at:
<www1.umn.edu/humanrts/gencomm/hrcomms.htm>

General Comment No 6 (1982) re article 6 — Right to Life
General Comment No 8 (1982) re article 9 — Right to Liberty and Security
General Comment No 18 (1989) re non-discrimination
General Comment No 20 (1992) re article 7 — Freedom from Torture etc
General Comment No 21 (1992) re article 10 — Humane Detention
General Comment No 25 (1996) re article 25 — right to take part in the conduct of public affairs, to vote and to be elected and to have access to public service in his country

Human Rights Committee (HRC) Communications

All Communications can be accessed at:
<www1.umn.edu/humanrts/undocs/undocs.htm>

A v Australia, Communication No 560/1993, UN Doc CCPR/C/ 59/D/560/1993 (30/4/97).
Abdool Saleem Yasseen & Noel Thomas v Republic of Guyana, Communication No 676/1996, UN Doc CCPR/C/62/D/676/1996 (31/3/98).
Albert Womah Mukong v. Cameroon, Communication No 458/1991, UN Doc CCPR/C/51/D/458/1991.

Allan Henry v Trinidad and Tobago, Communication No 752/1997, UN Doc CCPR/C/64/D/752/1997 (10/2/99).

Anthony Finn v Jamaica, Communication No 617/1995, UN Doc CCPR/C/63/D/617/1995 (4/8/98).

Ms Carolina Teillier Arredondo (on behalf of Maria Sybila Arredondo) v Peru, Communication No 688/1996, UN Doc CCPR/C/69/D/688/1996 (14/8/00).

Conroy Levy v Jamaica, Communication No 719/1996, UN Doc CCPR/C/ 64/D/719/1996 (25/11/98).

Debreczeny v Netherlands, Communication No 500/1992, UN Doc CCPR/C/ 53/D/500/1992 (1995).

Deon McTaggart v Jamaica, Communication No 749/1997, UN Doc CCPR/C/ 62/D/749/1997 (3/6/98).

Desmond Taylor v Jamaica, Communication No 705/1996, UN Doc CCPR/C/ 62/D/705/1996 (4/6/98).

Guillermo Ignacio Dermit Barbato & Hugo Haroldo Dermit Barbato v Uruguay, Communication No 84/1981, UN Doc Supp No 40 A/38/40 (1983) (27/2/81).

Herbert Thomas Potter v New Zealand, Communication No 632/1995, UN Doc CCPR/C/60/D/632/1995 (18/9/97).

Irvine Reynolds v Jamaica, Communication No 587/1994, UN Doc CCPR/C/ 59/D/587/1994 (24/4/97).

Larrosa v Uruguay, Communication No 88/1981, UN Doc A/38/40 (1983).

Leroy Morgan & Samuel Williams v Jamaica, Communication No 720/1996, UN Doc CCPR/C/64/D/720/1996 (25/11/98).

Luciano Weinberger Weisz v Uruguay, Communication No 28/1978, UN Doc CCPR/C/OP/1 (1984).

Marais v Madagascar, Communication No 49/1979, UN Doc A/38/40 (1983).

Marshall v Canada, Communication No 205/1986, UN Doc CCPR/C/ 43/D/205/1986 (1991).

Moriana Hernandez Valentini de Bazzano on behalf of herself and Luis Maria Bazzano Ambrosini, Martha Valentini de Massera and Jose Luis Massera v Uruguay, Communication No. 5/1977, UN Doc. CCPR/C/7/D/5/1977 (15/8/79).

Nicholas Henry v Jamaica. Communication No 610/1995, UN Doc CCPR/C/ 64/D/610/1995 (21/10/98).

Nqalula Mpandanjila et al v Democratic Republic of the Congo, Communication No 138/1983, UN Doc CCPR/C/27/D/138/1983 (26/3/86).

St Catherine Prison Cases (Jamaica): Communications Nos. 720/1996 (1998), 719/1996 (1998), 707/1996 (1997), 705/1996 (1998), 704/1996 (1998) and 617/1995 (1998).

Steve Shaw v Jamaica, Communication No 704/1996, UN Doc CCPR/C/ 62/D/704/1996 (4/6/98).

William Torres Ramirez v Uruguay, Communication No 4/1977, UN Doc CCPR/C/10/D/4/1977 (8/4/80).

Human Rights Committee Observations

Identified in text as HRC re [country], these can all be accessed at:
<www.unhchr.ch/tbs/doc.nsf/Documentsfrset?OpenFrameSet>

Armenia	CCPR/C/79/Add.100 (19/11/98)
Australia	A/55/40 (28/7/00)
Cameroon	CCPR/C/79/Add.116 (4/11/99)
Costa Rica	CCPR/C/79/Add.31 (18/4/94)
Gabon	CCPR/C/79/Add.71 (18/11/96)
India	CCPR/C/79/Add.81 (4/8/97)
Jamaica	CCPR/C/79/Add.83 (19/11/97)
Latvia	A/50/40 (3/10/95)
Lebanon	CCPR/C/79/Add.78 (1/4/97)
Lithuania	CCPR/C/79/Add.87 (19/11/97)
Luxembourg	CCPR/C/79/Add.11 (28/12/92)
Morocco	CCPR/C/79/Add.44 (23/11/94)
Nigeria	A/51/40 (24/7/96)
Poland	CCPR/C/79/Add.110 (29/7/99)
Russian Fed.	A/50/40 (3/10/95)
Sudan	CCPR/C/79/Add.85 (19/11/97)
Togo	CCPR/C/79/Add.36 (21/9/94)
Ukraine	A/50/40 (3/10/95)
USA	A/50/40 (3/10/95)
Yemen	A/50/40 (3/10/95)
Zambia	CCPR/C/79/Add.62 (3/4/96)

Australia's Third Periodic Report — due 1991 — is at CCPR/C/AUS/98/3 (22/7/99).

International human rights instruments

Treaties

Convention Against Torture and Other Cruel, Inhuman or Degrading Treatment or Punishment (UNCAT), GA res 39/46, [annex, 39 UN GAOR Supp (No 51) at 197, UN Doc A/39/51 (1984)]: opened for signature in 1984; entered into force in 1987; ratified by Australia in 1989: <www1.umn.edu/humanrts/instree/h2catoc.htm>

Convention on the Elimination of all Forms of Discrimination Against Women (CEDAW), GA res 34/180, 34 UN GAOR Supp (No 46) at 193, UN Doc A/34/46: opened for signature in 1979; entered into force in 1981; ratified by Australia in 1983: <www1.umn.edu/humanrts/instree/e1cedaw.htm>

[European] Convention for the Protection of Human Rights and Fundamental Freedoms (ECHR): opened for signature in 1950; entered into force in 1953: item 005 at http://conventions.coe.int/Treaty/EN/CadreListeTraites.htm

European Convention for the Prevention of Torture and Inhuman or Degrading Treatment or Punishment: opened for signature in 1987; entered into force in 1989: item 126 at <http://conventions.coe.int/Treaty/EN/CadreListe Traites.htm>

[First] Protocol to the Convention for the Protection of Human Rights and Fundamental Freedoms: opened for signature in 1952; entered into force in 1954: item 009 at <http://conventions.coe.int/Treaty/EN/CadreListe Traites.htm>

International Covenant on Economic, Social and Cultural Rights (ICESCR): opened for signature in 1966; entered into force in 1976; ratified by Australia in 1975: <www1.umn.edu/humanrts/instree/b2esc.htm>

International Convention on the Elimination of All Forms of Racial Discrimination (ICERD), 660 UNTS 195: opened for signature in 1966; entered into force in 1969; ratified by Australia in 1975: <www1.umn.edu/humanrts/instree/d1cerd.htm>

Convention on the Rights of the Child (CROC), GA res 44/25, annex, 44 UN GAOR Supp (No 49) at 167, UN Doc A/44/49 (1989): opened for signature in 1989; entered into force in 1990; ratified by Australia in 1990: <www1.umn.edu/humanrts/instree/k2crc.htm>

Australia's reservation to ICCPR article 10 (2) and (3): <www.unhchr. ch/tbs/doc.nsf/Statusfrset?OpenFrameSet>
"Article 10 In relation to paragraph 2 (a) the principle of segregation is accepted as an objective to be achieved progressively. In relation to paragraph 2 (b) and 3 (second sentence) the obligation to segregate is accepted only to the extent that such segregation is considered by the responsible authorities to be beneficial to the juveniles or adults concerned."

International Covenant on Civil and Political Rights (ICCPR), GA res 2200A (XXI), 21 UN GAOR Supp (No 16) at 52, UN Doc A/6316 (1966), 999 UNTS 171: opened for signature in 1966; entered into force in 1976; ratified by Australia in 1980: <www1.umn.edu/humanrts/instree/b3ccpr.htm>

Declarations

Declaration of Basic Principles of Justice for Victims of Crime and Abuse of Power, GA res 40/34, annex, 40 UN GAOR Supp (No 53) at 214, UN Doc A/40/53 (1985), adopted in 1985: <www1.umn.edu/humanrts/instree/i9dbpjv.htm>

Declaration on the Rights of Persons Belonging to National or Ethnic, Religious or Linguistic Minorities, GA res 47/135, annex, 47 UN GAOR Supp (No 49) at 210, UN Doc A/47/49 (1993), adopted in 1993: <www1.umn.edu/humanrts /instree/d5drm.htm>

Universal Declaration of Human Rights: adopted in 1948: <www1.umn.edu/ humanrts/instree/b1udhr.htm>

Standards, Principles and Rules

Body of Principles for the Protection of All Persons Under any Form of Detention or Imprisonment, GA res 43/173, annex, 43 UN GAOR Supp (No 49) at 298, UN Doc A/43/49 (1988): adopted in 1988: <www1.umn.edu/humanrts/instree/g3bpppdi.htm>

Basic Principles for the Treatment of Prisoners, GA res 45/111, annex, 45 UN GAOR Supp (No 49A) at 200, UN Doc A/45/49 (1990), adopted in 1990: <www1.umn.edu/humanrts/instree/g2bpt.htm>

Basic Principles on the Use of Force and Firearms by Law Enforcement Officials: adopted by the Eighth United Nations Congress on the Prevention of Crime and the Treatment of Offenders in 1990: <www1.umn.edu/humanrts/instree/i2bpuff.htm>

Principles of Medical Ethics relevant to the Role of Health Personnel, particularly Physicians, in the Protection of Prisoners and Detainees against Torture and Other Cruel, Inhuman or Degrading Treatment or Punishment, GA res 37/194, adopted in 1982: <www.unhchr.ch/html/menu3/b/h_comp40.htm>

UN Code of Conduct for Law Enforcement Officials: adopted in 1979: <www1.umn.edu/humanrts/instree/i1ccleo.htm>

UN Rules for the Protection of Juveniles Deprived of their Liberty, GA res. 45/113, annex, 45 UN GAOR Supp (No 49A) at 205, UN Doc A/45/49 (1990), adopted in 1990: <www1.umn.edu/humanrts/instree/j1unrjdl.htm>

UN Standard Minimum Rules for the Administration of Juvenile Justice ('Beijing Rules'), GA res 40/33, annex, 40 UN GAOR Supp (No 53) at 207, UN Doc A/40/53 (1985), adopted in 1985: <www1.umn.edu/humanrts/instree/j3unsmr.htm>

UN Standard Minimum Rules for the Treatment of Prisoners (SMRs), UN Doc A/CONF/611, annex I, ESC res 663C, 24 UN ESCOR Supp (No 1) at 11, UN Doc E/3048 (1957), amended ESC res 2076, 62 UN ESCOR Supp (No 1) at 35, UN Doc E/5988 (1977), adopted by the First UN Congress on the Prevention of Crime and the Treatment of Offenders in 1955; approved by the Economic and Social Council in 1957: <www1.umn.edu/humanrts/instree/g1smr.htm>

Table of Cases

Table of Statutes

Index